The Spiritual Revolution

RELIGION AND SPIRITUALITY IN THE MODERN WORLD

Series Editors: Paul Heelas, Linda Woodhead, *Lancaster University*

Editorial Advisor: David Martin, *Emeritus Professor, London School of Economics*

Founding Editors: John Clayton, *formerly University of Boston*, and Ninian Smart, *formerly University of California – Santa Barbara*

The **Religion and Spirituality in the Modern World** series makes accessible to a wide audience some of the most important work in the study of religion today. The series invites leading scholars to present clear and non-technical contributions to contemporary thinking about religion and spirituality in the modern world. Although the series is geared primarily to the needs of university and college students, the volumes in **Religion and Spirituality in the Modern World** will prove invaluable to readers with some background in Religious Studies who wish to keep up with contemporary thinking in religion, theology and spirituality in the modern world as well as to the general reader who is seeking to learn more about the transformations of religion and spirituality in our time.

Published:

Don Cupitt – *Mysticism After Modernity*
Paul Heelas, with the assistance of David Martin and Paul Morris –
 Religion, Modernity and Postmodernity
Linda Woodhead and Paul Heelas – *Religion in Modern Times*
David Martin – *Pentecostalism: The World Their Parish*
Steve Bruce – *God is Dead*
David Smith – *Hinduism and Modernity*
Peter Berger – *Questions of Faith*
Paul Heelas and Linda Woodhead, with Benjamin Seel, Bronislaw
 Szerszynski and Karin Tusting – *The Spiritual Revolution*

Forthcoming:

Bronislaw Szerszynski – *Nature, Technology and the Sacred*
Simon Coleman – *The Gospel of Health and Wealth*

The Spiritual Revolution

Why Religion is Giving Way
to Spirituality

Paul Heelas and Linda Woodhead
with Benjamin Seel, Bronislaw Szerszynski and Karin Tusting

Blackwell
Publishing

BLACKWELL PUBLISHING
350 Main Street, Malden, MA 02148-5020, USA
9600 Garsington Road, Oxford OX4 2DQ, UK
550 Swanston Street, Carlton, Victoria 3053, Australia

First published 2005 by Blackwell Publishing Ltd

2   2005

Library of Congress Cataloging-in-Publication Data

The spiritual revolution : why religion is giving way to spirituality / Paul Heelas ... [et al].
        p. cm. — (Religion in the modern world)
    Includes bibliographical references and index.
    ISBN 1-4051-1958-6 (alk. paper) — ISBN 1-4051-1959-4 (pbk. : alk. paper)
    1. Spirituality. I. Heelas, Paul. II. Series.

BV4501 .3.S663 2005
200'9'0511–dc22

                                                                                2004007692

ISBN-13: 978-1-4051-1958-0 (alk. paper) — ISBN-13: 978-1-4051-1959-7 (pbk. : alk. paper)

A catalogue record for this title is available from the British Library.

Set in 10 on 13 pt Galliard
by Kolam Information Services, Pvt. Ltd, Pondicherry, India
Printed and bound in the United Kingdom
by TJ International, Padstow, Cornwall

The publisher's policy is to use permanent paper from mills that operate a sustainable
forestry policy, and which has been manufactured from pulp processed using acid-free and
elementary chlorine-free practices. Furthermore, the publisher ensures that the text paper
and cover board used have met acceptable environmental accreditation standards.

For further information on
Blackwell Publishing, visit our website:
www.blackwellpublishing.com

For
Sebastian, Elissa and Mia
and
Sandy

Contents

List of Plates   viii
Preface   x

Introduction   1
1 Distinguishing Religion and Spirituality: Findings from Kendal   12
2 Testing the Spiritual Revolution Claim in Kendal   33
3 Evidence for a Spiritual Revolution: Britain and USA   49
4 Bringing the Sacred to Life: Explaining Sacralization
  and Secularization   77
5 Looking to the Future   129

Appendices   151
Notes   159
References   176
Index   190
Plates fall between pp. 99 and 100

Plates

Plates fall between pp. 99 and 100

Plate 1 The main street of Kendal. Private collection

Plate 2 The Kendal Project team: Benjamin Seel, Bronislaw Szerszynski, Linda Woodhead, Karin Tusting and Paul Heelas (with Abby Day, second to left). This photograph, taken in Dent (near Kendal), also illustrates the spiritual revolution in action: the team stand in front of a building that was once a chapel and is now part of a meditation centre. Private collection.

Plate 3 Imposing authority: the medieval parish church in Kendal – a congregation of humanity (Anglican). Private collection.

Plate 4 Informal relationality: inside Willow Creek Community Church, a 'seeker church' on the outskirts of Chicago – a flourishing congregation of experiential difference. Private collection.

Plate 5 Rainbow Cottage, a holistic centre on the outskirts of Kendal. Private collection.

Plate 6 Church attenders at the parish church in Kendal. Private collection.

Plate 7 Holistic contact: practitioner Linda McGarvey of Rainbow Cottage with researcher Benjamin Seel. © *The Westmoreland Gazette*

Plate 8 Life-as religion, clearly stated by an advert in the USA. Private collection.

Plate 9 'Psychological and Biblical truth': the discourse of a congregation of experiential difference. © Willow Creek Association.

Plate 10 The unique, the holistic, and wellbeing: craniosacral therapy, Kendal. © Adam Rubinstein R.C.S.T., Kendal.

Plate 11 Yoga in the mainstream of life. © Kendal Leisure Centre.

Plate 12 Soft capitalism at work ©The Guardian, image ©Getty Images. Reprinted with permission

Plate 13 Sanctified capitalism: the Congregational church opposite the main entrance to what was once the world's largest textile mill, Saltaire, near Bradford. Private collection.

Plate 14 A holistic shop overlooking the mill at Saltaire – a mill which has evolved into an upmarket wellbeing zone. Private collection.

Plate 15 Objective wellbeing culture in action.

Plate 16 Subjective wellbeing culture in action.

Plate 17 The two worlds meet: spiritual wellbeing enters the congregational domain in a parish in the south of England. © Tim Higgins.

Preface

This book explores the spiritual revolution *claim*: that traditional forms of religion, particularly Christianity, are giving way to holistic spirituality, sometimes still called 'New Age'.

In order to make headway in testing this claim, we have found it necessary not only to draw on the work of many colleagues in the sociology of religion, but to undertake research of our own. This research took the form of a locality study in the north-west of England, close to the Lake District. It was named after the town in which it took place: the Kendal Project. Although the book draws on findings from the Project, much of the volume looks at the spiritual revolution claim in connection with evidence from Britain and the USA.

The volume has been written by Paul Heelas and Linda Woodhead, who take full responsibility for its arguments, not to mention any mistakes of fact, interpretation or theory. We have been assisted throughout by Benjamin Seel, Bronislaw Szerszynski and Karin Tusting, who have commented on drafts of every chapter and whose advice has helped shape the final product. The five of us were also the team who carried out the research in Kendal, with Heelas, Szerszynski and Woodhead directing the Project and Seel and Tusting as full-time researchers.

Other individuals who have provided substantive input to the volume, and to whom we are extremely grateful, include Kajsa Ahlstrand, Andrea Cheshire, Abby Day, Eliza Forder, Gordon Heald, Sandy Miller, Rosemary Mingins, Gordon Neal, Liz Puttick, Desmond Ryan, Margaret Stelfox, and David Voas.

Funding for the Kendal Project was provided by a generous grant from the Leverhulme Trust. We thank the Trust, its Director at the time, Barry Supple, and the anonymous referees of the application. A feasibility study paving the way for the Project was funded by a seedcorn grant from the Faculty of Social Sciences, Lancaster University.

Lancaster University, its Department of Religious Studies and the Institute for the Environment, Philosophy and Public Policy (IEPPP) supported the Kendal Project in material ways, not least by providing office space and equipment. Kate Lamb of IEPPP assisted with data input, and Wendy Francis of Religious Studies helped with budgetary matters, mailings and other queries. We also received excellent support from Clare Hindle of the Lancaster University Research Support Office.

Students from the Department of Religious Studies assisted us in a number of ways: by helping us test and strengthen our ideas in our teaching, by supplying good ideas and quotes, and by assisting us in the head-count we made of the churches and chapels in Kendal.

We would like to acknowledge the helpful feedback we received from colleagues and students at other universities where we delivered papers on findings from the Kendal Project, and tried out ideas and arguments for the book. Thanks are also due to the colleagues from other universities who contributed to research meetings held during the Project. Before we began the research in Kendal, we held a weekend workshop at which specialists in research on contemporary religion and spirituality generously shared their experience and advice on how we should proceed. We would like to thank the participants: Sylvie Collins, Grace Davie, Douglas Davies, Mathew Guest, Mike Hornsby-Smith, Penny Long Marler, Bernice Martin, David Martin and Martin Stringer.

There was one person present at that workshop to whom we owe a special debt of gratitude. Steve Bruce's interest and advice have been unwavering over the whole six years it has taken to complete this project. His challenging questions, clear thought, and supportive friendship have been a spur and encouragement throughout.

Finally, we would like to thank the people of Kendal and environs who took part in our research. They granted access to their churches, chapels, meeting houses, centres, groups, practice rooms, shops, and homes. They gave generously of their time, and spoke frankly and openly about matters of personal significance. People were enthusiastic about our research, and willing to go to considerable lengths to help us achieve our objectives.

Listen! You hear the grating roar
Of pebbles which the waves draw back, and fling,
At their return, up the high strand
Begin, and cease, and then again begin,
With tremulous cadence slow, and bring
The eternal note of sadness in. . . .

The Sea of Faith
Was once, too, at the full, and round earth's shore
Lay like the folds of a bright girdle furl'd.
But now I only hear
Its melancholy, long, withdrawing roar,
Retreating, to the breath
Of the night-wind, down the vast edges drear
And naked shingles of the world.

Matthew Arnold (from 'Dover Beach')

Though the great song return no more
There's keen delight in what we have:
The rattle of pebbles on the shore
Under the receding wave.

W. B. Yeats ('The Nineteenth Century and After')

Introduction

...those contemporary aspirations towards a religion which would consist entirely in internal and subjective states, and which would be constructed freely by each of us. (Durkheim, [1915] 1971, p. 47)

...the passage from traditional forms of religion to more personal and individual expressions of what is called 'spirituality'. (The Catholic Communications Office, 2003, p. 1)

Whether we believe in God or not, I think most of us have a sense of the spiritual, that recognition of a deeper meaning and purpose in our lives, and I believe that this sense flourishes despite the pressures of our world. (Queen Elizabeth II, Christmas Day Broadcast, 2000)

The declining influence of religion – particularly Christianity – in western societies has been the chief topic of the study of religion for over a century, but in recent years the emergence of something called 'spirituality' has – increasingly – demanded attention. Survey after survey shows that increasing numbers of people now prefer to call themselves 'spiritual' rather than 'religious'. Terms like spirituality, holism, New Age, mind–body–spirit, yoga, feng shui, chi and chakra have become more common in the general culture than traditional Christian vocabulary. Even a cursory glance around the local bookshop or a stroll around the shopping centre leaves little doubt that Christianity has a new competitor in 'the spiritual marketplace'. 'The times', it seems, 'they are a-changing'.

Though it is still important to attend to the decline of traditional religion in western societies, we can no longer evade the challenge of assessing and explaining the growth of such 'spirituality'. What exactly is it? How significant is its growth? Is it altering the whole shape of the sacred landscape in the West? Are we living through a 'spiritual revolution'? These are the questions this book attempts to answer. They translate into three fairly distinct tasks that will be introduced here, and tackled in the chapters that follow.

The first is to bring some clarity to the notion of 'spirituality'. As Meredith McGuire (1997) notes, 'we do not yet have the language or conceptual apparatus for refining our understanding of spirituality' (p. 8). Only by developing such apparatus can we hope to shed light on changes in the contemporary landscape. If we are not clear what is meant by the term 'spirituality' in contrast with 'religion', then it will be impossible to make much progress.

Having clarified the meaning of 'spirituality', our next – and main – task is to assess its significance. Some understand it as the last gasp and whimper of concern with the sacred in the West, an inconsequential dabbling that is doomed to disappear almost as quickly as it appeared (Bruce, 2002; Finke and Stark, 1992). Others view it as vastly more important than that, and argue that we are witnessing a tectonic shift in the sacred landscape that will prove even more significant that the Protestant Reformation of the sixteenth century. What we are living through, they argue, is nothing less than radical change in which religion – namely Christianity – has been eclipsed by spirituality (Luckmann, 1967, 1990; Campbell, 1999). Since this 'spiritual revolution claim' is the most striking and provocative claim being made about the contemporary sacred scene, much of this book is devoted to testing it by way of research devised expressly for the purpose.

The final task is to pursue what is surely the 'holy grail' of the contemporary study of religion, namely a theory which can at one and the same time explain the decline of some forms of the sacred and the rise of others. What we offer is the 'subjectivization thesis', a thesis that attempts to make sense of both decline and growth by relating them to a single process – to what Charles Taylor (1991) calls 'the massive subjective turn of modern culture' (p. 26).[1]

The Subjective Turn

Since it underlies much of the argument of this book, we will begin with this 'massive subjective turn of modern culture', and go on to explain how it informs our approach to religion, spirituality and change.

'The turn' is shorthand for a major cultural shift of which we all have some experience. It is a turn away from life lived in terms of external or 'objective' roles, duties and obligations, and a turn towards life lived by reference to one's own subjective experiences (relational as much as individualistic). If, for example, I have slotted myself into the role of a dutiful daughter and a loving and caring wife and mother, and tend to disregard my own feelings of exhaustion, unhappiness and periodic disgruntlement because that is not what I (in the role I occupy) ought to be feeling, then I am living according to external expectations. But if I decide to heed those subjective states, to listen to what they are telling me, and to act on their prompting by altering my life in ways that better suit my own unique needs, desires, capabilities and 'relationalities', then I am turning away from life lived according to external expectations, to life lived according to my own inner experience. The subjective turn is thus a turn away from 'life-as' (life lived as a dutiful wife, father, husband, strong leader, self-made man etc.) to 'subjective-life' (life lived in deep connection with the unique experiences of my self-in-relation).

Exploring the idea a little further, the turn is away from worlds in which people think of themselves first and foremost as belonging to established and 'given' orders of things which are transmitted from the past but flow forwards into the future. Being 'higher' and 'greater' than the individual self such transcendent, collective, supra-self orders serve as people's primary 'sources of significance' (to use Taylor's 1989 useful expression). Accordingly, what matters is living one's life-as a member of a community or tradition – whether it takes the form of a kinship system, a feudal system, a nation-state, a class system or a particular religion. What matters is obeying, heeding, pursuing ways of life which stand over and above the individual self and bestow meaning upon life. These higher authorities serve to direct one's life and accord real value to it when one performs one's duties or fulfils one's obligations. In some cases the roles of life-as may appear 'natural' and be pursued unreflectively; in others there may be pressure to monitor one's life self-consciously in order to conform. Virtue and 'the good life' are characterized in terms of sacrificing, disciplining or masking those aspects of oneself that pull one away from the 'oughts' of the embedded life. The most extreme examples of life-as can be found in military contexts (where, to quote Tennyson in 'The Charge of the Light Brigade', it is 'Theirs not to make reply/Theirs not to reason why/Theirs but to do and die'), or in the religious life (where, to quote the Constitutions of the Society of Jesus, the Jesuit should become 'a corpse which suffers itself to be borne and handled in any way whatsoever').

If the 'massive turn' in modern culture is thus a turn away from life-as, it is correspondingly a turn towards subjective-life. The latter has to do with states of consciousness, states of mind, memories, emotions, passions, sensations, bodily experiences, dreams, feelings, inner conscience, and sentiments – including moral sentiments like compassion. The subjectivities of each individual become a, if not the, unique source of significance, meaning and authority. Here 'the good life' consists in living one's life in full awareness of one's states of being; in enriching one's experiences; in finding ways of handling negative emotions; in becoming sensitive enough to find out where and how the quality of one's life – alone or in relation – may be improved. The goal is not to defer to higher authority, but to have the courage to become one's own authority. Not to follow established paths, but to forge one's own inner-directed, as subjective, life. Not to become what others want one to be, but to 'become who I truly am'. Not to rely on the knowledge and wisdom of others ('To the other be true'), but to live out the Delphic 'know thyself' and the Shakespearian 'To thine own self be true'.

Thus the key value for the mode of life-as is conformity to external authority, whilst the key value for the mode of subjective-life is authentic connection with the inner depths of one's unique life-in-relation. Each mode has its own satisfactions, but each finds only danger in the other, and there is deep incompatibility between them. Subjectivities threaten the life-as mode – emotions, for example, may easily disrupt the course of the life one ought to be living, and 'indulgence' of personal feelings makes the proper discharge of duty impossible. Conversely, life-as demands attack the integrity of subjective-life. This is because the latter is necessarily unique. Given that only 'I' can be that particular individual with the particular and irreplaceable experiences and life history that make me who I am, the 'oughts' of life-as threaten not only my values but my very existence. Differing attitudes towards an institution like marriage illustrate the incompatibility very clearly. To those who believe that marriage is a sacred institution, it is obvious that one should sacrifice one's personal happiness for the sake of one's marital duty. Life-as a responsible father or a faithful wife will always trump the 'selfish' demands of subjective-life. Yet for those who cherish subjective-life, the sacrifice of desires for the sake of an 'external' institution like traditional marriage will be experienced as disruptive, undermining and damaging – for to do this is to deny, override and take away the inner realities that play such an important role in constituting individual lives and making people who they are.[2]

As to how the shift from life-as to subjective-life operates with regard to general cultural change, it is important to stress that we are not for one minute suggesting that subjective-life was absent in times past, nor that life-as has disappeared today. Far from it. Subjective-life, it is reasonable to suppose, is universal. Equally, it is reasonable to suppose that life-as formations are always required for the organization and regulation of social life.

Nevertheless, we believe that Eric Hobsbawm (1995), Ronald Inglehart (1997), Charles Taylor (1989, 1991, 2002), Joseph Veroff et al. (1981) and others are right in supposing that the subjective turn has become the defining cultural development of modern western culture. The evidence, which is extensive, will be explored throughout this volume. What we will see is that both self-understanding and socio-cultural arrangements have been developing in a 'person-centred' or 'subjectivity-centred' direction. In education culture, we see a turn towards the 'child-centred' or 'learner-centred'; in purchasing culture, towards the 'consumer-centred'; in health culture, towards the 'patient-centred'; in work culture, towards the personal development of employees. Each of these shifts involves a turn away from a more hierarchical, deferential, life-as order of things in which the teacher, the shop-keeper, the doctor, the manager was 'god'. Thus those institutions that cater for the unique subjective-lives of the 'centred' are on the increase, whilst those that continue to operate in life-as mode find themselves out of step with the times.

Distinguishing Religion and Spirituality

One of the great virtues of the language of 'life-as' and 'subjective-life' is that it enables us to sharpen up the distinction between 'religion' and 'spirituality' by distinguishing between life-as religion and subjective-life spirituality. The former is bound up with the mode of life-as – indeed it sacralizes life-as. By contrast, the latter is bound up with subjective-life – indeed it sacralizes subjective-life. Thus the former involves subordinating subjective-life to the 'higher' authority of transcendent meaning, goodness and truth, whilst the latter invokes the sacred in the cultivation of unique subjective-life.

It is important to stress that the distinction we use in this volume between 'subjective-life spirituality' and 'life-as religion' is not always identical with the ways in which the terms 'spirituality' and 'religion' are used in the culture. For example, 'spirituality' is often used in Christian circles to express devotion to God or Christ – as when spirituality is thought of as 'obedience to the will of God' with the believer entering into an intense relationship (involving self-surrender) with the divine. Such spirituality is subjective in the sense that it involves often intense experiences (of joy, awe, sorrow, gratitude etc.), but objective in the sense that it is focused on something which is and remains external to and higher than the self. This is experience of the sacred as transcendent, higher life – whether directly by way of the inspiration of the Holy Spirit, or indirectly by way of scripture and tradition. It is not an experience of the sacred as integral to, inseparable from and flowing through one's own subjective-life. As such, it might be called 'life-as spirituality' – and is clearly not the same as what we mean by subjective-life spirituality. (This is not to deny that there may be forms of Christian spirituality that are centrally concerned with the cultivation of unique subjective-life, particularly in the mystical tradition.)

But there are many common usages of 'spirituality' and 'religion' which overlap much more closely with our categories of 'subjective-life spirituality' and 'life-as religion'. Most notably the term 'spirituality' is often used to express commitment to a deep truth that is to be found within what belongs to this world. And the term 'religion' is used to express commitment to a higher truth that is 'out there', lying beyond what this world has to offer, and exclusively related to specific externals (scriptures, dogmas, rituals, and so on).[3]

The Spiritual Revolution Claim

Given the cultural significance of the subjective turn, we would expect the sacred landscape to be affected by it. If 'secular' institutions that continue to operate in life-as mode increasingly find themselves out of step with the times, whilst those that cater for unique subjective-lives are flourishing, then it is certainly worth exploring the possibility that the same thing is happening within the sphere of the sacred. What we would expect is that forms of the sacred that are experienced as compatible with the turn to subjective-life will be faring better than those that serve to reinforce life-as modes of existence.

In order to explore this possibility, we work with a simple formulation of the spiritual revolution claim:

1 Life-as forms of the sacred, which emphasize a transcendent source of significance and authority to which individuals must conform at the expense of the cultivation of their unique subjective-lives, are most likely to be in decline;
2 Subjective-life forms of the sacred, which emphasize inner sources of significance and authority and the cultivation or sacralization of unique subjective-lives, are most likely to be growing.

To put this more concretely, the expectation would be that in the West those forms of religion that tell their followers to live their lives in conformity with external principles to the neglect of the cultivation of their unique subjective-lives will be in decline. Many churches and chapels are likely to fall into this category. By contrast, those forms of spirituality in the West that help people to live in accordance with the deepest, sacred dimension of their own unique lives can be expected to be growing. These will include the multifarious forms of sacred activity which are often grouped together under collective terms like 'body, mind and spirit', 'New Age', 'alternative' or 'holistic' spirituality, and which include (spiritual) yoga, reiki, meditation, tai chi, aromatherapy, much paganism, rebirthing, reflexology, much wicca and many more (a fuller survey of such activities is offered in the pages that follow).

As for the spiritual revolution, this can be said to come about when subjective-life spirituality overtakes life-as religion. More specifically, given the primary empirical focus of this book (see below), the spiritual revolution can be said to take place when 'holistic' activities having to do with subjective-life spirituality attract more people than do 'congregational' activities having to do with life-as religion.

Testing the Spiritual Revolution Claim

This clarification of the spiritual revolution claim renders it rigorous enough to be tested empirically. The most straightforward way of doing so would be by way of existing studies and surveys of religion and spirituality in the West. Those of a more qualitative, ethnographic variety might enable us to see how much now has to do with subjective-life activities rather than those of a life-as form, whilst those of a more quantitative, longitudinal nature would help us compare the relative fortunes of these two varieties to see whether the former is overtaking the latter.

Whilst there are many excellent studies of Christianity on which we can draw in this task, there are, however, only a few that are directly focused on the issues which concern us most. And whilst there are a number of equally good ethnographic studies of 'alternative spiritualities', and there is accumulating evidence from both sides of the northern Atlantic that interest in 'expressive', 'holistic' (mind–body–spirit), or New Age spiritualities is growing, there is as yet little or no hard evidence that bears on the critical question of just how many people have become active in this sphere.

Our only option, therefore, was to carry out additional empirical research. We did so by way of a locality study of 'Patterns of the Sacred' in the relatively self-contained market town and regional centre of Kendal, Cumbria, in the north-west of England, just to the south-east of the Lake District. By taking a single relatively small locality – population 27,610 in 1999 – we could be fairly confident of systematically exploring what was going on by way of face-to-face, *associational* religious and spiritual activity. We would also be able to look at such activity in some detail through in-depth qualitative research. We would, in other words, be able to treat the town as a testing ground for the spiritual revolution claim – as a sort of 'spiritual laboratory', as one inhabitant of Kendal put it. After an initial feasibility study, the Kendal Project began in October 2000, and research continued until the end of June 2002, with some follow-up work extending into 2003. (A summary of the research strategies of the Project can be found in Appendix 1; the question of the representativeness of Kendal is addressed in later chapters, in particular Chapter Three.)

The primary concern of the Kendal Project was to study what we came to think of as the *heartlands* of religious and spiritual life. These are the places where religious and spiritual activities are most clearly visible and most richly in evidence, for it is here that women and men come together to engage in face-to-face, associational activities whose primary purpose is engagement with the sacred. One was obvious: the very public activities of church and chapel, a heartland we came to call the *congregational domain* (other than Christians, there are very few adherents of world religions in Kendal). The other was less obvious: the more 'invisible' activities of what is often called alternative or New Age spirituality – a heartland we came to refer to as the *holistic milieu*. Though there will certainly be other forms of religious and spiritual activity in Kendal (carried out in solitude by individuals, incorporated into the activities of institutions like schools or businesses), for the sake of the clarity of comparison we needed in order to test the spiritual revolution claim effectively, we decided to concentrate only on the heartlands.

We set ourselves two main empirical tasks in Kendal. The first was qualitative: to see *what* was going on. The second was quantitative: to see *how much* (of the different forms of engagement with the sacred) was going on. By investigating the *what* we were able to distinguish between those associational forms of the sacred whose primary concern was with life-as, and those whose primary concern was with subjective-life and the care of the self. We did not assume *a priori* that all of the congregational activities would fall into the former category, nor that all of the 'alternative' variety would fall into the latter. We simply wanted to find out what was the case. Chapter One provides our findings, showing how different forms of religion and spirituality in Kendal do or do not channel the sacred towards the enhancement of unique subjective-lives.

Our findings about 'how much' of the heartland activities (past and present) were concerned with life-as, and how much with subjective-life, are presented in Chapter Two. They allow us to give a clear answer to the question whether or not a spiritual revolution has taken place in Kendal. In Chapter Three we consider the wider relevance of these findings, asking whether a spiritual revolution has taken place in Britain more widely, and in the USA. In the same chapter we also consider what is happening within the wider culture: how life-as religion and subjective-life spirituality are faring in the media, schools, hospitals, purchasing-culture and other important cultural sites – and in connection with popular beliefs.

The Subjectivization Thesis: Explaining Growth and Decline

Without giving everything away by revealing at the outset whether or not we have found that the spiritual revolution has taken place in Kendal, Britain or the USA, we can say that we have found robust evidence of a pattern: a correlation between subjective-life spirituality and growth on the one hand, and between life-as religion and decline on the other. This means that our findings have a bearing on the issue that has long dominated the study of religion – the study of secularization – as well as the increasingly important issue of whether there is growth in the territory of the sacred – the study of sacralization.

Those who defend theories of secularization and those who oppose them with accounts of sacralization are divided over fact, interpretation and explanation. Controversy rages between those who claim that the sphere of the sacred is largely if not entirely undergoing relentless decline and develop theories to explain this, and those who claim that certain forms are growing and develop explanations accordingly. The title of Steve Bruce's recent book, *God is Dead* (2002), signals his role as a forceful proponent of the first view. Luckmann (1967, 1990) and Campbell (1999) articulate the second position.

Rather than viewing decline and growth as mutually exclusive, the evidence we present suggests that the West is currently experiencing *both* secularization (with regard to life-as forms of religion) *and* sacralization (with regard to subjective-life forms of spirituality). And this leads to an extremely interesting question: could it be the case that there is a single explanation of both processes? Answering this question in the affirmative, we offer neither a theory of secularization *per se*, nor of sacralization *per se*, but of coexistence. Without for a moment ruling out other explanations of change, we offer in Chapter Four what we call *the subjectivization thesis* as the key to explaining both growth and decline. The thesis invokes the 'massive subjective turn' of modern culture to explain why there are ever more people who – if they are concerned about, or become concerned with, the sacred – are much more likely to be, or become involved with, those forms which help them cultivate the unique 'irreplaceabilities' of their subjective-lives than those which emphasize the importance of conforming to higher authority.

By taking seriously the significance of the subjective turn we therefore believe that it is possible to understand more about the winners and losers in the contemporary spiritual marketplace. We show that the former are most likely to be those that appeal to the increasing numbers of people for whom subjective-life is the key source of significance. They succeed because they 'bring the sacred to life', enabling participants to remain true to themselves and their most significant relationships, and making little or no distinction between personal and spiritual growth. Conversely, the subjective turn helps explain why the losers are most likely to be those life-as forms of the sacred which cater for the decreasing numbers of people orientated to life-as sources of significance, for there are fewer and fewer who are looking for, or who remain committed to, forms of the sacred which demand the living of life according to external expectations.[4]

Summary

We are interested in the idea that the great historical bond between western cultures and a Christianity whose characteristic mode is to make appeal to transcendent authority is rapidly dissolving, and that in its place we are seeing the growth of a less regulated situation in which the sacred is experienced in intimate relationship with subjective-lives. The purpose of this volume is to shed light on the contemporary sacred landscape by considering the extent, significance and causes of this revolutionary possibility.

The unique

'I know my own heart and understand my fellow man. But I am unlike any one I have ever met; I will even venture to say that I am like no one in the whole world. I may be no better, but at least I am different' (Rousseau, 1971, p. 1). In what follows we consider the central importance in modern culture of the Rousseauian belief that 'I am unique', and what this has to do with the sacred landscape. This does not mean that we offer some sort of paean of praise for the self-centred self. 'Subjectivization' should not be confused with 'individualization'. Whilst it is true that the subjective turn sees individuals emphasizing their personal experiences as their source of meaning, significance and authority, this need not imply that they will be atomistic, discrete or selfish. For as we will see, above all else subjective-life spirituality is 'holistic', involving self-in-relation rather than a self-in-isolation. Hence it is common for the subjective turn to involve what Carson McCullers (1973) refers to as the 'we of me' (p. 39) being understood as the true, subjective, 'me'.

Chapter One

Distinguishing Religion and Spirituality: Findings from Kendal

You call us to leave our self behind . . . Son of God . . . grow in us, so that Your ways may become ours. (Intercessions, Anglican Parish Church, Kendal)

Religion asks you to learn from the experience of others. Spirituality urges you to seek your own. (From an interview with a Kendal Unitarian Christian who is also involved in holistic activities)

The aim is to build on people's own resources, spiritual resources. I never give my own ideas, but see what comes from the client. (Meg McCalden, hypnotherapy and relaxation therapy, CancerCare, Kendal)

According to the spiritual revolution claim, subjective-life spirituality is growing and life-as religion declining – to the extent that the former may be eclipsing the latter. An effective way of testing this is by comparing two distinctive associational territories, one having to do chiefly with subjective-life spirituality, the other chiefly with life-as religion. We now show that we found such distinctive but comparable associational territories on the ground in Kendal. And in the process of doing this, we put empirical flesh on the stark analytical bones of our language of subjective-life and life-as, thereby clarifying what we mean by 'the spiritual revolution'.

The Kendal Project began life with a feasibility study. Attention was paid to the designated places of worship in the town, where we hoped to find life-as religion, and to what is loosely referred to as 'alternative' or 'New Age' activities, where we hoped to find subjective-life spirituality. In particular, we wanted to know whether there were enough alternative activities taking place to justify taking things further. Having established that this was the case, the Project got underway. However, we were taking something of a gamble. We might have had a fair hunch, but we were far from certain that the congregational domain (as we came to call it) was predominantly of a life-as nature, or that the holistic milieu (as we came to call it) was chiefly focused on the cultivation of subjective-life.

We now enter into the heartlands of religion and spirituality in Kendal to show that conformity to life-as *is* in fact the dominant emphasis in the congregational domain – and, conversely, that the resourcing of unique subjective-lives *is* in fact the primary focus of the holistic milieu. We find, in other words, that the congregational domain basically has to do with people being guided by higher authority to find fulfilment in a common good, whilst the sacred of the holistic milieu basically serves to help people live out their own interior lives in their own unique ways. Accordingly, the comparison of the two associational territories undertaken in the next chapter will constitute a fair test of the spiritual revolution claim. (It would be misleading to test the spiritual revolution claim by way of this comparison were it to be the case, for example, that the congregational domain contains a considerable amount of subjective-life spirituality.)

Life in the Congregational Domain: The 'Religion' of the Spiritual Revolution Claim

When we began our research in Kendal in the year 2000 there were 25 congregations. All are rooted in the Christian tradition. (For a full list see Appendix 2.) Since all have as their main activity a weekly public congregational service that includes theistic worship, is nearly always held on a Sunday, and generally takes place in a designated building, we had little difficulty in identifying and locating them. Initial access to their corporate life proved relatively unproblematic, and further access for research purposes was kindly granted by all the congregations in Kendal.

Unity-in-variety in the congregational domain

As we pushed open the doors of the churches, chapels and meeting houses on consecutive Sunday mornings, we became aware of a similarity that overrode all other differences. To step into a worship service is to find one's attention being directed away from oneself towards something higher. By contrast, as will become clear in the second section of this chapter, to enter into the holistic milieu is to find attention directed towards oneself and one's inner life.

Thus we found all the congregations of Kendal to be united by the conviction that truth and goodness lie not in the cultivation of unique individuality so much as in curbing such individuality by way of conformity to a higher, common, authoritative good. This good may be envisioned and expressed in different ways: in rules, in ideals, in art and music, in visions of a family-based society, in concepts of God. But it is always transcendent: it is higher than those who subserve it and, as such, it binds them into something more than they would be on their own, for the whole is considered to be greater than the sum of its parts. Authority in the congregational domain lies outside rather than within, and with 'the same' rather than 'the unique'. As a consequence, life-as roles are privileged over subjective-life uniquenesses, and 'what I should be' over 'what I am'. Yet it is important to emphasize at the very outset that this does *not* mean that we found subjective-life to be wholly neglected within the congregational domain. Rather, as we shall see, we found that instead of being 'authorized' (treated as the primary authority in life) it is often 'normativized' (channelled into conformity with supra-individual norms).

The common good, the higher authority, the focus of united hope and striving in the congregational domain, is represented in somewhat different terms in different congregations. In some it takes the form of an encompassing social vision: of a united and harmonious society in which even strangers become neighbours. In others it is more closely tied to the congregation itself, to its growth in faithfulness and its success in evangelism. It can vary in scope, and it can vary in degree of other-worldliness. But in every case, we found that belonging to a congregation had more to do with being caught up into a vision of the higher good than in going inwards to discover truth and goodness by trusting and exploring one's own feelings, intuitions and experiences. Thus 83.5 per cent of respondents to our questionnaire survey of a cross-section of congregations indicated that the statement 'the important thing is to do your duty' came closer to their belief than the statement 'the important thing is to fulfil yourself' (15 per cent). (Appendix 1 provides further information about the questionnaire.) This was consonant with the way in which many congregations placed strong emphasis upon the importance of self-sacrifice, and the way in which liturgy and hymns were saturated with the language of obedience, surrender and self-giving.

The same dynamics explain the pervasive stress on deference that we found to be characteristic of congregational life. Whilst different congregations differed slightly in the degree of deference they showed their priest or minister, nearly all were characterized by a hierarchical form of organization in which the most important decisions and activities were the responsibility of a small number of authorized personnel, who were nearly always male. Such deference was but a reflection of the much greater deference that was expected to be shown to 'Almighty God'. In all but a couple of congregations God was approached by way of male pronouns and imagery, particularly fatherhood, and was portrayed as a personal being of unlimited power who created and controls all things. His will is made known in the external, mediating authorities of text, tradition and community, and is to be willingly obeyed. The underlying belief is that God – and the Bible or the church – knows what is best for us better than we know ourselves, and better than our subjectivities might tell us. As one evangelical put it, 'We're told in scripture not to go on about how we feel'; and as a member of the Roman Catholic congregation put it (having just criticized the idea that one should only go to church on a Sunday if one *feels* like it): 'Why does the church give us an obligation to go to mass? Because if left to ourselves we won't because our basic human nature, our fallen nature, is pulling us away from God'.

We found that for many in the congregational domain it was Jesus Christ who functioned as the immediate focus of devotion, reverence and deference, and as the inspiring model of perfect obedience and self-sacrifice. He was interpreted not as an example of self-realization to be imitated by 'going one's own way', but as an example of deference who must be deferred to – by 'following in his footsteps', 'obeying the Lord', 'becoming a disciple', and 'giving my life to Christ', to pick a variety of expressions we heard many times in interviews and worship services. As one evangelical Christian put it: 'All I want to do is to obey the Lord. I want to stand there on that [judgement] day and hear him say, "Well done, good and faithful servant"'.

The congregational life of Kendal is also characterized throughout by a strong ethical and metaphysical dualism – a stress on the *difference* between Creator and created, the supernatural and the natural, the overarching moral order of things and the everyday (dis)order of things, my 'life I should be living' and my actual subjective-life, the spirit and the body. Not that the body is explicitly repudiated, nor that its appetites are disciplined by way of systematic asceticism. Rather, they are handled by being channelled into acceptable forms of expression rather than being allowed to 'do their own thing'. Thus sexual activity, for example, is viewed as acceptable only when expressed in the context of faithful, loving, heterosexual marriage and family and for the sake of a higher good (love, children etc.), not for the sake of pleasurable sensation itself. That which is revealingly referred to as 'disordered' sexuality is often presented in congregational teaching as a key symptom of a disordered out-of-control society. We found the general view of such matters to be well summed up in one sermon in which the minister told the congregation that 'wholeness' (of body, mind and spirit) should be of less significance to Christians than 'holiness'.

The last example points to a final essential element in the logic of sacralized life-as in Kendal: a strong moralism. Not only is there widespread belief in overarching moral authority, there is also general acceptance that the authorities of church and chapel are there to instruct people in how to live their lives. We found the idea that there are standards, norms, ideals and expectations to which subjective-life must be conformed to be pervasive. Moral judgement and the language of 'should' and 'ought' are a central part of the currency of the congregational domain, and many interviewees spoke about how they appreciated the clear moral guidance offered by their church or chapel. It had helped them move from chaos to orderly living, from meaninglessness to meaningfulness, and from fearfulness to security. Such moralism is deeply embedded institutionally: in the very practice of preaching, the very medium of the sermon, the very office of the priest or pastor. Individuals are told what to do by higher authority, rather than being encouraged to look to their own inner resources to decide for themselves. Moral guidance is often offered in clear and concrete terms. As an OHP slide at an evangelical church, which draws on New Testament teaching to lay down the ideal characteristics of a church elder, puts it:

A person is disqualified if he is self-indulgent or self-seeking. His qualifications are that he should be an integrated/controlled personality, and that he shows concern for moral standards. At home he should always have only one wife, his home should be hospitable and his children disciplined. At work, he should be organized and focused. In the world, he should have a good reputation.

The effect of such moral preaching is to discipline subjectivities by selectively nurturing some sentiments and dispositions whilst rendering others invisible. Since anger, hatred, sexual desire and ambition (for example) find little space for expression in the congregational domain, they either have to be renounced or expressed under the cover of more acceptable sentiments. Thus it is much more common to hear members of congregations say, 'I was saddened to learn' than 'I was furious', or 'It was a humbling experience' than 'I felt proud'. It is rare to hear people speak openly in this setting about the full range of their emotions. Generally speaking, that which one should be tends to be given more prominence in the congregational domain than that which one is.

Variety-in-unity in the congregational domain

As well as this commonality, we also found variety in the congregational domain. Though we found emphasis on life-as roles to be predominant throughout, we found that this emphasis varied, and that subjectivities were handled in different ways in different types of congregation. We discovered that congregations fell into one of four main types in this regard. Making use of the typology first developed in Woodhead and Heelas (2000), we classified these as 'congregations of difference', 'congregations of humanity', 'congregations of experiential difference', and 'congregations of experiential humanity'. Congregations of difference are those which stress the distance between God and humanity, creator and creation, and the necessary subordination of the latter to the former. Congregations of humanity narrow this distance by singling out 'humanity' as something that God and human beings have in common; they tend to emphasize the importance of worshipping God by serving humanity. Both types can also take more experiential forms, placing more emphasis on the authority of subjective experience in the religious life. Thus congregations of experiential difference continue to stress the gap between the divine and the human, but believe that God can enter directly into subjective experience as the Holy Spirit. And congregations of experiential humanity, whose humanitarian stress has already diminished the gap between the divine and the human, close it still further by teaching that the divine is more likely to be found in inner experience than in the externals of religion like scripture and sacraments. (For details on which congregations in Kendal belong to which type, see Appendix 2.)

For congregations of humanity (chiefly churches of mainline-liberal denominations, both Catholic and Protestant), the authoritative common good and 'higher authority' is God-in-humanity and humanity-in-God. These churches emphasize ethics over dogma, love over the law, this world over the next, and unity over division. Since what matters, above all, is benevolence towards fellow human beings, these congregations are relatively 'liberal', offering a degree of freedom and tolerance with regard to other matters of belief and practice. The effect of their strongly moralistic emphasis on caring for others, and putting God and neighbour before self is, however, to render these the *least* subjectivized of all the congregational types. Instead of focusing on individual experiences, needs, desires, moods, bodily and emotional sensations, they direct their members' attention not inwards to themselves, but outwards towards God and fellow humans in need of care.

Within congregations of humanity the acceptable self is one that does not dwell on its own subjectivities, but expresses appropriate moral sentiments such as 'care', 'love', 'compassion' and 'gentleness'. 'God first, neighbour second, self last,' as one interviewee explained. So powerful is this message that individuals are likely to experience guilt if they pay too much attention to their own subjective-lives. We found it telling that many people within these congregations were uncomfortable talking about anything too personal – anything to do with their inner lives, including matters of faith. As one Anglican gentleman put it: 'it's something one doesn't talk a lot about...we are much better at the weather...such a deep and private thing...to leap straight into that is very difficult'. Through repetition of set liturgies, responses, hymns, and ritual actions, and by the shaping of personal time in conformity with the church's calendar, congregations of humanity conform subjectivities to common life and Christ's life. Attention falls so definitively on the higher authority of the common good that the unique remains always in the shadows of 'service' – both the worship service and service to others.

By contrast, congregations of difference and, to an even greater extent, congregations of experiential difference, give more explicit attention to individual selves and their feelings, fears, desires and hopes. (In Kendal congregations of difference are largely evangelical, whilst congregations of experiential difference are charismatic-evangelical.) Though both types of congregation are united by the stress they place on the absolute difference between God and the world, they promise that those who submit to God will be rewarded by nothing less than reconstructed inner lives – 'born again' to 'new life'. The 'trick' which such congregations play is to offer subjective enhancement and cultivation in terms that can make sense to a subjectivized culture, but to insist that this comes not through reliance on one's inner resources but through submission to the higher authority of God, Christ, the Bible and congregational instruction. As one charismatic minister in Kendal put it, quoting Bob Dylan, 'You gotta serve somebody'.

Both congregations of difference and experiential difference make a powerful appeal to people who feel their lives are not working by offering to heal their brokenness and restore joy, contentment, calm, hope and security in the Lord. They teach that each and every one of us is uniquely loved by God and called to make a free, personal decision to give our life to him, that the means of salvation is placed in our own hands in the form of the Bible, and that fulfilment will be found in surrender to Jesus and on-going, affective, relationship with him. Many such congregations pay serious attention to life problems and to the healing of minds and even bodies, and they devote considerable energy to affecting and enhancing memories, moods and feelings (for example, by extensive singing of emotive choruses). The promise is that lives that are offered up to God will be healed, enhanced, reordered and redeemed. Congregations of humanity offer to make individuals into (morally) better people; congregations of difference and experiential difference also offer to make people *feel* better.

Yet although we found individual subjective-lives to be attended to, catered for, nurtured and developed in such congregations, we did not find them to be fully authorized. Individuals are not encouraged to pursue their own spiritual paths on the basis of their own deepest experiences, but are guided by way of clearly defined, extensively articulated and tightly regulated roles and duties. Thus the climax of evangelical life is the point at which the individual surrenders his or her uniqueness and autonomy to God – the point of conversion. This becomes very clear in the 'testimony' narrative that we found to play such an important part in evangelical life in Kendal. Although testimonies as to how one was 'saved' begin with detailed attention to unique subjectivities including sexual urges, anger, drug-fuelled states of mind and so on, their climax is the point at which these 'negativities' are given over to God and destroyed in the fires of his cleansing. The language used to describe this process is that of unique life being 'broken', 'poured out', 'surrendered', 'sacrificed' and 'given over to God', as the full array of personal subjectivities is sacrificed in favour of a far smaller authorized repertoire that conforms to the laid-down lineaments of the faithful disciple. Thus the new life that begins for the born-again Christian is highly normativized: life lived according to models, rules and expectations that are detailed and often rigorously enforced by way of a 'discipling' that quickly shades into 'disciplining'.

Though these general remarks apply both to congregations of experiential difference and to congregations of difference, we also found a significant distinction between them. In the latter, authority – God and scripture – lie outside one, and the good life is the life that is lived in strict conformity to this authority. In the more charismatic congregations, however, we found some disdain for such an 'externalized' and 'rigid' understanding of Christian discipleship. As a congregational leader in Kendal put it when he explained why he left an evangelical congregation to found a charismatic one, 'For us evangelism became a living thing, an experience, people were sharing reality rather than concepts', and as another charismatic explained, 'You know, when God speaks to us, he speaks, like, into our hearts'. In congregations of experiential difference, in other words, as well as remaining external and over-against the believer, God 'comes within'. The 'Word' must be not merely followed but internalized – 'eaten' and 'swallowed'. It must go all the way down. In such congregations the real point of conversion is understood to be the point at which God, as Holy Spirit, enters directly into an individual's experience. Far from overruling unique subjective-life, the Holy Spirit becomes the inner core of subjective-life, guiding and directing it from within. The believer's life is 'possessed' by the Spirit, so that 'it is no longer I who live but [the Spirit of] Christ who lives within me' (Galatians 2:20).

Because of this inspiration from within, the worship in congregations of experiential difference is characteristically emotive and expressive, and much less externally regulated than in other types of congregation. There is little by way of set liturgy, and hierarchies of leadership are more fluid and informal. Nevertheless, there are still clear limits on what can be said, done, felt, and expressed. Subjective-life is authorized only insofar as it conforms to external expectations and guidelines – above all, biblical teaching. Individuals are encouraged not in self-expression but in Spirit-expression, and the limits of what counts as spiritual inspiration are clearly laid down. We found that only a relatively narrow range of emotions and dispositions were able to be expressed in collective worship (even in small group contexts), above all gratitude, joy, love and celebration. The purpose must always be the glorification of God, not self. As a member of a charismatic service in Kendal declared in the middle of a service: 'The Lord wants you to fix your eyes on him. Take them off yourself. Irrespective, take them off yourself, and fix your eyes on him. He'll sort out what's going on and what needs sorting out." ' And as the service leader replied in response,

> Yeah, we must keep our eyes fixed on him, on the one and only, Jesus, the Lord God. He is the only one who can lift us out of our own selves, our own introspectiveness, so to speak....Let's just start again to look at Jesus as the one who has all the answers, all the answers. He's got all authority.

Of all the congregations in Kendal, we found that it was the congregations of experiential humanity (including the Unitarian chapel and Society of Friends) that went *furthest* in authorizing subjective-life. Rather than preaching a higher truth which believers were expected to hear, follow and obey, such congregations actively encouraged individuals to forge their own unique life paths and spiritual paths in their own unique ways. 'Sermons' took the form of a personal reflection on 'what I have found to be helpful', with the preacher sometimes suggesting that those who were listening might disagree. In worship services as well as small groups, the assumption was not that authorized teachers should be instructing the rest, but that each individual had the ability and responsibility to develop a personally meaningful spiritual path. As the Unitarian minister said proudly of his congregation, they are 'people of all strands, searching for truth . . . all on their own path'. And as a member of the same congregation who was experimenting with different types of spirituality told us, what was helpful in the spiritual life was to follow 'whatever seems heart-centred to you'. In keeping with this emphasis, we found that these were the congregations which went furthest in presenting and picturing God not in terms of an external authority set over against the individual, but as the deepest, 'spiritual' dimension of all life and all human lives. Instead of there being an external check on what counts as spiritual, it is only within the depths of personal experience that the Spirit can be encountered – indeed the Spirit *is* these depths, depths in which individual life is found to connect with all other life.

Despite strong tendencies in the direction of subjective-life spirituality, however, we also found some countervailing tendencies in congregations of experiential humanity. For one thing, we found that older members of these congregations tended to be more comfortable with more structured and patterned ways of proceeding, and that moves towards a deeper emphasis on subjective-life were often being made by younger people outside the context of the main worship service (e.g. by setting up small spiritual groups). In addition, we found that these congregations share with congregations of humanity a strong stress on the overriding duty of humanitarian care. Instead of merely encouraging individuals to discover the sacred in their own way, whatever that might be, these congregations often identify the sacred task with the duty of care for fellow human beings and the whole planet (justice, peace and ecology). As a consequence, the encouragement to probe one's own spiritual depths may be checked or even contradicted by appeal to the higher good of a loving community.

Overall then, we found the congregational domain of Kendal to be a realm in which life-as roles take precedence. Rather then being encouraged to 'become themselves', those who participate in this domain are exhorted to conform their lives to higher authority. They are 'hearers', 'followers', 'disciples', 'servants', 'children' and 'sheep'. Salvation comes by hearing and heeding the voice of 'the shepherd', 'the Lord', 'Our Father', rather than by relying on one's own inner voice. The truth is 'out there' rather than within; the divine is transcendent rather than immanent. This is not to say that subjective-life is ignored or neglected in the congregational domain of Kendal, merely that it is expected to be conformed to acceptable norms rather than being regarded as a source of authority in its own right. Nevertheless, we found some interesting variations between different types of congregations in the characteristic ways in which they handle subjective-life and bring it in touch with the sacred. To sum up:

1 Congregations of humanity expect subjective-lives to be wholly dedicated to the service of God and fellow human beings. God is to be found outside oneself, in one's neighbour in need, rather than inside oneself in the depths of one's own experience. Since the imperative of self-sacrifice overrides any impetus towards self-cultivation, these congregations tend to offer *least* in terms of the cultivation and enhancement of unique subjective-life.

2 Congregations of difference render God wholly external to human beings and teach that he is known only through Jesus Christ and the

Word of scripture. Individual lives come into saving contact with the sacred only by obeying these higher authorities. Such congregations make an explicit offer of subjective reconstruction and satisfaction, but insist that this comes about not by heeding one's unique subjectivities but by putting them under the control of higher authority.

3 As their name suggests, both congregations of experiential difference and experiential humanity are the most willing to accept that God is not only external, but can also enter into individuals' unique experience. As such, they travel furthest in the direction of a subjective-life spirituality. However, congregations of experiential difference qualify this by insisting that subjective experience of God or the Holy Spirit must always be checked against the higher authority of the word of scripture. And congregations of experiential humanity step back from the full authorization of subjectively guided spirituality by steering subjective-life in a humanitarian direction.

Since none of these variations qualifies our overall observation that the congregational domain is predominantly a realm of life-as religion and life-as spirituality rather than subjective-life spirituality, they do not affect our test of the spiritual revolution claim in the following chapter. Their significance will become apparent later in the volume when we broaden our horizons to consider whether some of the more highly experiential forms of congregation found elsewhere may be developing in such a way that they have tipped over, or will at some point tip over, into the category of subjective-life spirituality, and so add momentum to a spiritual revolution. In addition, we also look at another possibility – that more subjectivized forms of life-as religion and life-as spirituality are doing relatively well, serving to slow down the decline of the congregational domain as a whole and thereby slowing down the momentum which favours the spiritual revolution claim.

Life in the Holistic Milieu: The 'Spirituality' of the Spiritual Revolution Claim

Having arrived at this 'life-as' conclusion concerning the congregational domain, we now pave the way for testing the spiritual revolution claim by showing that the activities of the holistic milieu are predominantly orientated around the cultivation of subjective-life.

Nuts and bolts

Two main forms of associational activity are found in the holistic milieu of Kendal and environs (the area within a five-mile radius of the town):[1] groups and one-to-one practices. During the autumn of 2001, there were approaching one hundred practitioners catering for the members of these groups and the clients of these one-to-one practices, all providing what they understand to be spiritually significant activities. Although the number of groups is the same as the number of one-to-one provisions, groups are more popular: around two thirds of those active in the milieu belong to them. Regarding the activities themselves, they range from aromatherapy to Buddhism, circle dancing to the Alexander Technique, naturopathy to reiki. The most popular is yoga, followed by various versions of massage, aromatherapy, homeopathy, reflexology, the Alexander Technique, tai chi, osteopathy, reiki and flower essences therapy. Activities take place in a variety of settings, including people's homes, the Town Hall and the Quaker Meeting House. Many take place at four main specialized centres, the Fellside Centre (an Alexander Technique training school), the Lakeland College of Homeopathy, Loop Cottage (largely groups and workshops) and Rainbow Cottage (largely one-to-one activities). In addition, holistic activities are catered for by relatively self-contained enclaves within institutional settings (settings which provide a wider range of provisions for the public): Kendal College (with its Holistic Therapy Diploma and various evening classes), Kendal Cancer Care (with its complementary health practices) and Kendal Leisure Centre (with its six yoga and tai chi groups). Finally, our introductory portrayal of the milieu would be incomplete without mention of one-off events – the gatherings, fairs, festivals, workshops and talks that take place as occasion demands. (Appendix 3 provides a list of holistic milieu activities in Kendal and environs taking place on a weekly basis during the autumn of 2001; Chapter Two provides an account of how we arrived at the list.)

As we enter into the holistic milieu, we turn to the nub of the matter. What evidence is there that subjective-life spirituality and the nurturing of unique subjectivities is characteristic of this territory, rather than life-as religion and life-as spirituality?

Statistics

Let us set the scene with some statistics from the questionnaire we distributed within the holistic milieu. (See Appendix 1 for more information regarding the questionnaire.) In answer to the question 'Do you believe in any of the following?' the greatest number of respondents (82.4 per cent) agree that 'some sort of spirit or life force pervades all that lives', with 73 per cent expressing belief in 'subtle energy (or energy channels) in the body'. Presented with a range of options and asked to select the statement which best describes their 'core beliefs about spirituality', 40 per cent of respondents equate spirituality with 'love' or being 'a caring and decent person', 34 per cent with 'being in touch with subtle energies', 'healing oneself and others' or 'living life to the full'. Spirituality, it appears, belongs to life-itself ('subtle energy in the body' which serves to keep us alive) and subjective-life ('love', 'caring'). It seems that spirit/energy/spirituality is understood to dwell within the lives of participants, an interpretation that is supported by the finding that very few associate spirituality with a transcendental, over-and-above-the-self, external source of significance. Just 7 per cent of respondents agreed that spirituality is 'obeying God's will'. It appears, then, that rather than spirituality serving to dictate the course and nature of life from beyond the self, it is experienced as being integral to life: 'pervading' or flowing through life, bringing life alive. (By contrast, the congregational domain questionnaire shows that almost 60 per cent believe that 'spirituality is obeying God's will', with almost 70 per cent agreeing with the statement that 'I obey God's commands'.)

Holistic activities

From the statistical evidence, then, it appears that the cultivation of unique subjectivities may indeed be central to the holistic milieu. But statistics only take us so far, especially in a setting where what matters has much more to do with activity-cum-experience than belief systems. So let us turn to our more in-depth research on whether the spiritually informed activities of the milieu serve to cultivate unique subjectivities.[2]

On entering the milieu, one is immediately struck by the pervasive use of 'holistic' language: 'harmony', 'balance', 'flow', 'integration', 'interaction', 'being at one', and 'being centred'. The great refrain, we might say, is 'only connect'. To provide three examples from the many which could be drawn upon from our interviews, yoga practitioner Gill Green says that 'what I'm aiming for really is a union between body, mind and spirit; to make people feel more integrated', kinesiologist Jan Ford Batey talks of 'dealing with emotional, mental, physical and spiritual aspects of the whole being', and astrologer Helen Williams told us that 'If you've got a sense of all the bits of you and how they can be integrated together, you can actually move through and grow'.

Above all, the activities of the milieu provide the opportunity for participants to 'grow': to move beyond those 'barriers', 'blocks', 'patterns' or 'habits' associated with 'dis-ease' by making new connections. So whether dis-ease has to do with the bad habits of the body (manifested as back aches, for example), emotional blockages or dysfunction (involving stress or anger, for example), or problems in relationships at home or at work (such as an inability to assert one's needs or a sense of low self-esteem), the important thing is to move on or 'grow' by linking up more holistically with other aspects of life – in particular with the spiritual dimension.

Reiki practitioner Fay Bailey makes the general point, 'You cannot heal one bit without the other'. And for the practitioners of the holistic milieu, the 'other' which is of greatest significance is the spiritual aspect of life. For whatever progress might be made by addressing bodily complaints (for example) by linking them up with and exploring underlying emotional factors (for example), the ultimate goal is to facilitate contact with the aspect of life which best serves the dynamics of the whole. For the spirit is that in which all things come together, and in which each life reconnects with its deepest dimension. To illustrate, yoga practitioner Celia Hunter-Wetenhall affirms the importance of 'weaving in the spiritual element, the relationship between the mind and the body and the spirit'. And Julie Wise describes her Infinite Tai Chi group as providing a 'very integrative approach' that serves 'to aid spiritual awakening and growth'. Participants, she says, are provided with the opportunity to 'undo those patterns and habits' which keep them locked into impoverished modes of being. They are enabled to get in touch with their 'true nature' – the 'energy' which, once experienced, serves to suffuse their life: 'The more you get in touch with your true nature, the more peace and love you have,' she says. Or as one-to-one aromatherapist practitioner Linda McGarvey puts it, 'because we are part of the spiritual path, the journey is towards wholeness'. What matters is 'helping people to connect with who they are and the potential of who they are', thereby 'helping each person, whatever they are, in their own personal healing process'.

Typically, then, activities enable participants to go deeper to bring spirituality (or functional equivalents such as 'energy', 'chi', 'qi', 'prana', or 'true nature') to bear on the particularities of their experiences (low self-esteem, aches and pains, stress, and so on). Holistic milieu activities facilitate the convergence of the spiritual path and the *personal* path. What lies within is often envisaged as being person-specific. Fay Bailey, for instance, spoke of that which lies 'within us and makes us a person', and Linda McGarvey of the importance she attaches to the 'deep inner self and deep inner knowing'. Numerous group facilitators and one-to-one practitioners spoke of enabling people to get in touch with and explore the 'true' self; of 'dealing with issues of all the content in life from that aspect, the core of the person, the essence of the person' as Jan Ford Batey put it; of releasing people's own spiritual resources, as others said.

Flowing from one's 'true nature', the 'inner-directed solutions' provided by the spiritual aspect of one's being serve to cultivate one's personal life accordingly. Personal life thus remains as unique or distinctive as the spirituality or 'deep inner self' which suffuses it. Participants are enabled 'to live their own truth', 'heal themselves' or, as we might say, are provided with the opportunity to *be-come* themselves. 'Live in harmony with your life', as a flyer for Raja yoga meditation puts it – 'bringing out yourself', as we might put it.

Relationships

Additional evidence that the spiritually informed activities of the holistic milieu are serving to nurture unique subjectivities is provided by the nature of the relationship between practitioners and participants. Time and time again, we hear practitioners rejecting the idea that their relationships with their group members or clients have anything to do with pre-packaged, or what we are calling in this volume 'life-as', ways of transmitting the sacred. Statements like that of homeopath Beth Tyers, 'I certainly don't have a fixed faith or dogma I adhere to' were typical. So were words to the effect of shiatsu practitioner Jenny Warne's affirmation, 'We don't want to be something that we impose on somebody else'. Jaquetta Gomes, of the

Theravada Buddhist group, explained that 'People don't want a package, they want to think for themselves'.

Far from telling their group members or clients what to think, do, believe or feel, in the manner of life-as religion, practitioners continually emphasize the importance of 'serving' their participants. Their language is of 'helping', 'guiding', 'supporting', 'working with', 'encouraging', 'enabling', 'nurturing', 'facilitating' and 'steering'. The focus is on the unique participant rather than on some higher authority or common good. Especially in one-to-one activities, but also in groups (in particular smaller ones), practitioners explore what kinesiologist Jan Ford-Batey calls 'presenting details', namely the 'issues', the hopes and fears, of their participants. Practitioners say that they are then more than happy to tailor their activities to engage with the particularities they have encountered. Clients and participants are not introduced to the central, spiritual dimension of the dynamic 'whole' until they become 'open' or 'ready to hear' about it (if at all). In short, to draw on the words of acupuncturist Janet Conway, 'Because everybody is so different, everybody is treated completely differently'.

With widely used expressions like 'child-centred education' in mind, holistic milieu practitioners are thus highly 'participant-centred'. Fully recognizing that participants, alone, can truly experience their own lives, the job of the practitioner is to enable participants to become themselves by 'trusting their own life experience', to use Julie Wise's words, by 'listening' to what their bodies, feelings, intuitions, 'inner knowledge' or personally authenticated meanings have to tell them, and by sensing what is 'out of balance' so they can 'work through their blocks' appropriately. If participants should discover that a particular activity is not working for them, then it is right for them to look elsewhere: 'They've got to find out what works for them, basically', as massage practitioner Chloe Crossley emphasizes.

Psychosynthesis practitioner Caroline Cattermole provides a good formulation of the kind of relationship – between practitioners and participants – which is widely encountered within the milieu. What she does, she says, involves 'the client having a conversation with themselves, and you are simply making sure that that conversation is an honest one'. To elaborate on this, participants are provided with the freedom to exercise their own authority whilst seeking to heal themselves, grow, develop their life-paths, live out their lives, express themselves. Practitioners certainly see themselves as able to serve their participants, but generally speaking this is done by way of egalitarian, sharing, reciprocal relationships which greatly favour the cultivation of unique lives rather than the application of the authoritative

(Freudian) 'I know better than you . . .' imposition of correct or standardized ways of life. Indeed, we encountered a number of practitioners who also participated in the activities of other practitioners. And to introduce a theme mentioned in the introduction and developed in Chapter Four, it is not an exaggeration to say that many of those active in the milieu understand themselves to be developing the 'me' of their lives by way of the 'we' of group and one-to-one encounters.

Experiences

It remains to emphasize the extent to which the holistic activities of the milieu serve to address, nourish, cultivate and enrich the experiences of subjective-life. Publicity material such as the leaflets and brochures spell out what is on offer in the holistic milieu. Yoga at Kendal Leisure Centre offers 'to take the stress out of life'; Jane Deeks's reiki offers 'a sense of wellbeing, good health, fulfilling relationships and enthusiasm for life'; Neil McKay's nutritional consultancy offers 'emotional balance' as well as 'good health'; Jenny Warne's leaflet on shiatsu explains that 'When our energy or Qi is moving freely, we experience overall wellbeing and vitality'; Bernadette Riley's brochure states that 'Rebirthing sessions develop awareness, sensitivity and self-confidence . . . a developing sense of physical safety, of trust in relationships'; and craniosacral therapist Adam Rubinstein writes of 'deep relaxation . . . calmness and wellbeing . . . vitality'.

In virtually every case, the publicity material which we have collected, which covers the great majority of the holistic activities of Kendal and environs, refers to the theme of enhancing the quality of subjective-life experiences. Hardly surprisingly, many participants refer to the same theme. To illustrate, Jeff Waters (client of kinesiologist Fiona Adams at Rainbow Cottage) talks of 'life having felt lighter and better on an emotional level', Marilyn Solsbury (yoga group member) of 'getting to a calmer side to life', and Erica Donnison (yoga group member) of yoga being 'pretty high for overall wellbeing'. Likewise, having said that 'spirituality is often about feelings', Infinite Tai Chi practitioner Julie Wise spoke of 'embracing things like our anger – love it, and by doing so to gradually transform it'.

Another way of making the point that the spirituality of the milieu is very much to do with the enhancement of the quality of personal experience is by showing that other goals are not to the fore. Consider, first, the quest for enlightenment. Questionnaire returns show that just 7 per cent consider spirituality to be 'overcoming the ego', and under 10 per cent of participants in the holistic milieu are involved with activities, in particular groups, which focus on this quest. Or consider the opposite possibility that significant numbers are deploying spirituality to advance their progress with regard to the 'externals' of life: empowering themselves by way of spirituality to make more money; or drawing on spirituality to enhance their performance of life-as roles. Without denying that some in the holistic milieu attend to the 'externals' of life, we did not meet many who were using spirituality in an instrumentalized way, as a means to achieve prosperity. Neither did we find much evidence of the application of spirituality to serve life-as duties, obligations and responsibilities. The focus is very much on making life work by enhancing the quality of personal – belonging-to-the-person – experiences rather than on improving the quality of experiences by conforming to life-as roles.[3]

To pull out the main points of our discussion of the holistic milieu: rather than imposing pre-packaged life-as values, beliefs or injunctions, the great majority of the holistic practitioners of Kendal and environs are intent on enabling their participants to *be-come* themselves. Participants are not called upon to be anything other than what they are at heart. Practitioners work with their participants to enable them to be true to their deepest experiences of themselves, to know themselves, to build upon themselves. And by virtue of being holistic, practitioners enable their participants to experience spirituality as integral to the 'wholeness' of their being. Spirituality, however directive it might itself be, is thereby experienced as flowing through subjectivities, without violating or harming the unique as the sum of personal life-experience.

Finally, although the spirituality of the activities of the milieu in Kendal and environs has a great deal to do with the nurturing of unique subjectivities, this is *not* to say that holistic spirituality is to be found everywhere in the milieu. Numbers of participants draw on activities for this-worldly, personally orientated purposes. Some practise yoga as the means to the end of alleviating stress, for example, with little holistic, let alone spiritual, significance being attached to their engagement. However, this does nothing to detract from the fact that virtually all practitioners and a great many of their participants are holistically orientated, attaching importance to subjective-life spirituality, with life-as religion scarcely in evidence.[4]

Conclusion: Two Worlds

Our research in Kendal (and environs) has revealed that the 'massive sub-jective turn of modern culture' is indeed far more evident in the holistic milieu than in the congregational domain. For we have found that whilst the former is predominantly to do with holistic spirituality which acts with and through the particularities of subjective-lives, the latter is very largely to do with theistic authority structures which direct life to be lived in accordance with 'higher' values.

Thus the congregational domain and holistic milieu of Kendal are largely separate and distinct worlds. The one emphasizes life-as and the normativiz-ation of subjectivities, the other subjective-life and the sacralization of unique subjectivities. In the former, self-understanding, change, the true life, is sought by heeding and conforming to a source of significance which ultimately transcends the life of this world; in the latter, self-understanding, change, the true life, is sought by seeking out, experiencing and expressing a source of significance which lies within the process of life itself. The one has to do with deferential relationship to higher authority, the other with holistic relationship to the spirit-of-life. Concretely, a chasm lies between what we have heard in the congregational domain ('God . . . knows what is best for us better than we know ourselves', 'Fix your eyes on him. Take them off yourself', 'Lift us out of our own selves') and the holistic milieu where 'the aim is to build on people's own resources, spiritual resources'.[5]

This is not to deny that we found something of a spectrum from congre-gations of difference and congregations of humanity at one end (placing more emphasis on truth without than truth within) to spiritualities of sub-jective-life at the other (with the importance they attach to what belongs to 'this-life'). Somewhere between the two we find congregations of experien-tial difference and, even more so, experiential humanity, whose relative openness to the entry of the sacred into personal experience brings them closer to holistic spiritualities of this-life. Revealingly, we found that most of the very few individuals who are active within both the congregational domain *and* the holistic milieu are associated with the Unitarian chapel (however, the total numbers participating in experiential religions of hu-manity are small, around 6 per cent of the congregational domain as a whole). Overall then, we found very little overlap between the 'two worlds' of the congregational domain and holistic spirituality, with only around 4 per cent of congregational members having participated in the previous week in holistic activities that they regarded as having spiritual or religious significance, and only 6.4 per cent agreeing with the statement that 'alternative or complementary non-church forms of spirituality have things to teach Christianity'.

Post-modernists write about the disintegration of boundaries, the fusion or 'hybridization' of previously distinct beliefs and activities, and of people drawing on provisions which used to be kept apart. Journalists speak of a new 'pick 'n' mix' attitude to religion and spirituality. In Kendal at least, such a post-modern condition is scarcely in evidence. Instead, the congregational domain and holistic milieu constitute two largely separate and distinct worlds. So far as the spiritual revolution claim is concerned, this means that they can readily be used to see how life-as religion and subjective-life spirituality are faring – and thereby test the validity of the claim that the latter is overtaking the former.

Chapter Two

Testing the Spiritual Revolution Claim in Kendal

Scholars have talked about the decline of the sacred, seeing it being replaced by secularity, but have failed to see fully how understandings of the sacred were changing. (Robert Wuthnow, 1998, p. 3)

The emergence of Life, rather than God, as the site of worship. (Jackie Stacey, 2000, p. 124)

We have supposed that what has been happening has been the *secularization of religion*, and we have failed to see the much greater extent of the *sacralization of life*, even though it has already deeply affected us all. (Don Cupitt, 1999, p. 2)

The previous chapter has established that we can use the two associational heartlands of Kendal to determine whether those forms of the sacred which respect, relate to, resource or serve peoples' unique subjective-lives are faring well whilst those which do not are faring badly. In this chapter we therefore see whether a revolution is underway – or has taken place – in the way in which the sacred is embodied, experienced and understood in face-to-face settings.

Our initial task is to provide a snapshot of the numbers of people involved in the congregational domain and the holistic milieu. This will tell us whether the spiritual revolution has already taken place in the realm of associational activities. We can then move on to the second task: tracing change over time. This will enable us to see whether the spiritual revolution is likely to take place sometime soon, even if it has not already done so.

Counting the heartlands

The congregational domain

Locating the congregations we planned to count involved some detective work, for we were anxious not to miss any. Many were prominent in the town, for they are housed in dedicated and purpose-built historic churches and chapels which often have a powerful visible presence. Phone directories, tourist information lists and newspaper advertisements of worship service times helped us locate the harder-to-find congregations, some of them quite recently established, and some 'hidden' in a meeting hall or (in one case) a cemetery chapel. Having looked into the possibility that there might be churches outside the town boundary that were heavily used by Kendalians, and which might therefore have to be included in our count, we found that they very largely served their local communities. We therefore confined our attention to the places of worship where most of the churchgoing population of Kendal are to be found, namely those within the town itself.

Having located all the congregations, we established contact with their leaders, and gained permission to undertake our research. Initial observation of their activities helped us think through the issue of what to count. Since worship was the central activity for all these congregations, it was clear that we needed to count the numbers involved in worship. Since Sunday continues to be the main day of worship for the congregations of Kendal, we decided that it would be best to count attendance at Sunday worship. Although the 'typical Sunday attendance' figure that this would yield is one of the best-established measures of congregational vitality in the study of Christianity, there has recently been debate about its validity. After having considered the arguments in favour of alternative measures like average weekly attendance over a month, however, we were satisfied that typical Sunday attendance would be the best measure for our purpose of testing the spiritual revolution claim.[1]

Having made these decisions about what to count, we began to think about how best to undertake the task. We could have used one or more of the well-established methods for determining attendance figures: surveys (doorstep, postal or telephone) or clergy estimates. However, such methods are not necessarily reliable. Research in Britain and the USA, reviewed in Chapter Three, indicates that polling among the general population may yield exaggerated figures of attendance. Aiming to be as accurate as possible, we therefore decided to adopt the strategy of counting every single person entering a place of worship in Kendal on a typical Sunday. To the best of our knowledge, this is the first time that such a headcount has been carried out in Britain since Richard Mudie-Smith (1904) organized a similar count in London in 1903. Though a challenge to organize and administer, such a headcount would yield an accurate and reliable figure for typical Sunday attendance in Kendal.

Our plan was to station counters at every entrance to every church, chapel or meeting house in Kendal on a typical Sunday. We discussed the count with congregational leaders in advance (though we did not disclose the date it would be carried out), and we noted down all the Sunday service times, and the number of entrances to each building. Since we needed 29 'counters', we asked 24 volunteers from amongst our Religious Studies undergraduates at Lancaster University to serve as additional counters alongside the core research team. After a pilot count at one of the medium-sized churches in the town, a 'master plan' was drawn up for the co-ordination of the day. All the counters were issued in advance with clear instructions concerning their duties, and were trained in how to undertake the count.

The headcount was carried out on Sunday 26 November 2000, a day which we took to be pretty typical in that it did not fall in, or near, a holiday period or church festival day. Counters were stationed at every entrance to every church, chapel or meeting house, at least half an hour in advance of every service of the day. They were asked not only to count attenders but to record their gender and estimate their age. To this end they were supplied with count sheets on which they were asked to place a tally mark for each attender in one of the following categories: 'baby' (too young for counter to distinguish gender), 'child, M or F' (primary school age), 'adolescent, M or F' (high school age) and 'adult, M or F' (18 and above). Where churches had more than one service, in order to avoid double or treble counting individuals who had already attended a service, counters asked each person whether they had attended earlier that day. At three sites where this proved difficult, congregational leaders or greeters were asked to estimate numbers of double attendances.

Everything went according to plan. By the end of the day we were in possession of a sheaf of count sheets on the basis of which we could tally overall numbers and work out gender ratios and age profiles for each congregation. Once we had analysed the data, we sent all congregational leaders a summary of the figures we had gathered, and asked them to complete a brief questionnaire to compare our numbers with their own clergy estimates of typical Sunday attendance. It was found that in most cases the numbers were very similar (apart from the Salvation Army where we had been forewarned that owing to practical transport difficulties that week the attendance would be lower than usual).

Our key finding was that 2,207 people (adult and younger) attended the 25 churches and chapels of the congregational domain on Sunday 26 November 2000; that is 7.9 per cent of the total population of Kendal.

The holistic milieu

According to Steve Bruce (1996a), it is 'clearly impossible' to 'count the numbers involved' in the 'New Age' (p. 222). Difficult, yes; impossible, no. The task was demanding, for it was by no means easy to track down all those activities which have to do with holistic spirituality. Furthermore, it was by no means easy to count those who are involved in these activities, an obvious challenge being to find a way to avoid double (treble, etc.) counting of participants.

Preparing for the count

At the very beginning of the Kendal Project, we had to decide whether it would make sense to count holistic milieu participants on a 'typical day' – thereby retaining strict comparability with the congregational domain count. The holistic milieu, however, has no single day similar to the Christian Sunday. Nevertheless, the rhythm of activity is of a similar weekly order: the weekly group, the weekly visit to the one-to-one practitioner, or even more frequent participation. The only realistic way forward, then, was to decide to count on the basis of participation during a typical week.[2]

We also had to make a decision regarding the kind of associational activity we were to count. We had to specify those associational activities which were similar enough to the congregational domain to ensure that we could compare like with like, whilst at the same time being different enough to ensure that we could compare the relative vitality of subjective-life forms of the sacred with those of a congregational, life-as variety.

In order to retain comparability with the congregational domain, we employed the following specifications. First, given that our study of the congregational domain has not included anything which individuals might do on their own (such as praying or reading the Bible), we determined that we would only count those involved in associational, face-to-face activities (rather than people meditating alone or reading mind-body-spirit books, for example). Second, given that our study of the congregational domain has only looked at designated places of worship (not Christianity in schools, for example), we determined that we would count only those involved in activities taking place within their own self-contained contexts (rather than taking place within and with reference to such broader institutional contexts as schools or businesses). And third, just as congregational activities are taken to be of sacred significance by those who lead them, so we determined that we would only count those involved with activities which were taken to be of sacred significance by those who provide them.

In order to make sure that there was also the necessary difference with the congregational domain to make it possible to test the spiritual revolution claim, we of course decided that we would only count those activities which had to do with the cultivation of subjective-life spirituality in the understanding of the practitioners who offered them.

Having specified what to count, our next task was to locate it. As we have already explained, where the congregational domain was concerned we restricted our study to the town boundary, since church and chapel provision for Kendal's population is largely concentrated within that area. In order to be comparable, however, we found that holistic milieu research needed to take place not just in the town, but within a five-mile radius of the town. This was because two key holistic centres which lie just outside the town (Loop Cottage and Rainbow Cottage) cater for a significant number of Kendalians. If we had excluded the activities taking place within them, we would have failed to count a significant segment of Kendal's holistic scene. When we come to calculate the numbers involved in the holistic milieu, we therefore express them not as a proportion of the Kendal population (as for congregational numbers), but as a proportion of the population of 'Kendal and environs' (1999 population 37,150).

Turning to how we found the specific activities we wanted to count, we wanted to make sure that we did not miss anything relevant to do with subjective-life spirituality. Guided by our four specifications, we therefore sought to build up a list of every activity which *might* have to do with the kind of spirituality under consideration. This 'mapping' exercise was not a light task. For whereas most of the congregations of Kendal meet in clearly identifiable buildings, associational activities beyond church and chapel are often considerably more difficult to locate. Groups (for instance tai chi) or one-to-one encounters (for instance aromatherapy) often take place in rented rooms and halls, or in private houses. Accordingly the mapping involved a considerable amount of detective work. Visits were made to cafes, shops, other public places such as the Town Hall, the Library, leisure and tourist information centres and specialized centres for holistic healing and spirituality like Rainbow Cottage, to look for flyers and cards advertising anything of spiritual or spiritual-cum-religious significance. These adverts varied widely from minimal, handwritten details ('Elaine, Shiatsu and Reiki, phone...') to professionally produced posters or leaflets. Noticeboards, local newspapers (free and sold), more specialized regional publications such as the North West listings magazine *Cahoots* and the Cumbria *Green Handbook*, national New Age and holistic health magazines like *Kindred Spirit*, *Caduceus* and *Body and Soul*, as well as the Cumbria *Yellow Pages*, were all checked for leads. And at the same time visits were made to groups and centres, in order to get to know people who could direct us to other practitioners, many of whom who did not advertise.

In order to test the spiritual revolution thesis, however, we needed to take a second step. It was crucial that we whittled our initial, most inclusive, list down to *just* those activities which practitioners saw as having a 'spiritual dimension', and which, more precisely, had to do with subjective-life spirituality. Accordingly, we interviewed all the group facilitators and virtually all the one-to-one practitioners (a number by telephone). In addition, fieldwork enabled us to establish close relationships with key networkers – people with wide-ranging experience and knowledge of the kind of activities we wanted to find out about. On the basis of all this research we compiled a list of activities to be counted: a list which included practitioners who used the term 'spiritual' – or close cognates such as 'chi', 'energy' or 'vibrational qualities' – to refer to the 'flow' or inherent nature of life, and which excluded those who said that what they practised did not have a spiritual dimension. (Some osteopaths, for example, were therefore included, whilst others were not.) Overall, then, all the activities that made it onto our 'counting' list had group facilitators and one-to-one practitioners who attached at least some importance to 'inner' spirituality – to the task of enabling their participants to get in touch with inner 'energy' or 'spirit' which could holistically heal, empower and fulfil their lives. (See Appendix 3 for a summary of the activities we identified.)

The count itself

In order to ascertain the number of individuals involved in groups during a typical week, we attended all those groups run by practitioners who took their activities to be of spiritual significance as the Kendal Project ran its course. Attendance figures were noted down, and group practitioners were asked how representative they were. Figures were only revised on the basis of information given by group facilitators when there seemed to be very clear reasons why they were abnormal. Otherwise, it was assumed that divergences from norms would even out between groups overall.

In trying to gauge the numbers of clients going to the one-to-one spiritual practitioners of Kendal and environs during a typical week, we were faced with a far more challenging task. Many one-to-one practitioners could not say what a typical week was because numbers could vary so much from one week to another. The estimates that they were willing to give were often based on different time scales. One person might say, 'up to five people a day, three days a week'; another might say, 'about 20 or 30 at any one time'; another, 'about 20 a month'; still others, 'it's too difficult to estimate' or, 'about 200-300 on my books'. Using such information was tricky. Some answers, such as the overall number of clients on a practitioner's books, could not be used, in this case because different clients' patterns of attendance vary widely from two or three visits a week to a one-off visit for a particular ailment – so knowing how many clients practitioners have on their books gives little clue as to how many they will see in an average week. But where practitioners gave figures for different lengths of time, such as daily, weekly or monthly figures, these could be standardized using simple, but conservative, maths. Where practitioners did not give a number of clients, it was sometimes possible to assign conservative estimates based on some knowledge of their practice, such as how many days a week they worked. Working carefully through our list of one-to-one practitioners, it was thus possible to come up with a conservative overall weekly estimate of the number of clients attending one-to-one practitioners with a spiritual dimension to their practice at a location in or within five miles of Kendal.

A picture of the numbers involved in a typical week was beginning to build up. However, fieldwork had made it increasingly apparent that although there were around 840 'acts of participation' each week, a fair number of those 'acts' were by the same individuals engaging in more than one activity. To retain comparability with our headcount of the congregational domain, we had to find a way of avoiding double (treble, etc.) counting. Furthermore, fieldwork was making it increasingly clear that not all participants found their activities to be of spiritual significance (some, for example, told us that they were practising yoga to 'de-stress'). In order to address such issues, and gather other information, we used the holistic milieu questionnaire (see Appendix 1). By providing respondents with a list of all the activities (taken to be spiritual by their practitioners) that we had found in Kendal and environs, and by asking them to tick the activity or activities they had been involved in during the preceding week, we were able to measure the extent of multi-participation and reduce our weekly participation figures accordingly. We were also able to establish the numbers who regard their activities as having 'a spiritual dimension' (see below).

So what were our key findings? During the autumn of 2001, 95 spiritual practitioners were providing the activities of the holistic milieu of Kendal and environs. Of these, 41 were group practitioners serving 63 different groups, while 63 were one-to-one practitioners serving individual clients and having an estimated average of four clients per practitioner per week. (Thus nine practitioners serve both groups and individual clients.) Having established during the first year of the Kendal Project that some 840 associational encounters were taking place weekly, we then carried out questionnaire research which enabled us to assess the number of people who were taking part in more than one associational encounter per week. This provided us with our final figure: during a typical week, 600 people were involved in the 126 separate activities provided by the holistic practitioners of Kendal and environs: 1.6 per cent of the population. Two thirds of the 600 people, it can be added, were participating in groups, and one third in one-to-one activities, with significant numbers engaging in more than one activity – whether group, one-to-one or both.[3]

These figures had been determined by the end of 2001. At the close of the Kendal Project (at the end of June 2002), and thus with an additional six months of research completed, we were finally in a position to scrutinize all the information we had gathered – questionnaire findings, field notes, interviews, the primary literature we had collected – to assure ourselves that we had *only* counted those involved with spiritually informed activities which can be drawn upon to cater for unique subjective-life. Only then were we in a position to assure ourselves that the spirituality of the holistic milieu of Kendal and environs is predominantly of subjective-life significance. In short, only at the end of the Project did we definitively conclude that the milieu – and the number of people involved – provided what was required to test the spiritual revolution claim. (See Chapter One for the detailed evidence.)[4]

Counting the Heartlands Over Time

The decline of the congregational domain

Reliable longitudinal data is hard to come by for the congregational domain in Kendal. Some churches and chapels have no records at all.

Others have only partial and/or patchy records. Openings, closings and mergers of various churches and chapels add a further complication. What is more, there is a frequent lack of comparability between and within the data that *is* available. Some congregations record attendance numbers, others record numbers of communicants, still others record membership figures (with membership itself being defined in different ways), and some congregations have changed the way they count at some point in their record-keeping. Prior to the Kendal Project, there had been no systematic study of the congregational domain in Kendal, and subsequent to Horace Mann's (1854) census of churchgoing in 1851, there appears to have been no serious attempt to arrive at a reliable figure for church attendance in the town.

In order to build up a picture of the changing numbers in the congregational domain in Kendal over time we have therefore relied on two methods. The first was to gather what figures we could for the main types of congregation in Kendal that were discussed in the last chapter. We tried to select as representative a sample of congregations as possible, though our final selection was constrained by availability of records (most notably, the lack of reliable longitudinal figures for a congregation of difference). The congregations selected were Holy Trinity Anglican Church (congregation of humanity), St Thomas's Anglican Church (congregation of experiential difference), New Life Community Church (congregation of experiential difference), and the Society of Friends (congregation of experiential humanity). The second method was to draw on trend data for Great Britain as a whole, particularly that gathered in the three clergy-estimate censuses for typical Sunday church attendance carried out by Peter Brierley in 1979, 1989 and 1999. Since our longitudinal data for particular types of congregation largely corresponds with national findings, and since our head count figure of 7.9 per cent is identical with Peter Brierley's (2001) figure for Great Britain (p. 2.23), the picture in Kendal is unlikely to deviate significantly from the national picture.

Both the local and the national data suggest severe and relentless decline in overall church attendance in Kendal since the 1960s (for the picture prior to that time, see Chapter Five). To begin with the national longitudinal figures, according to Brierley (2001, p. 2.23) 11.8 per cent of the population of Great Britain attended church in 1980, 11 per cent in 1985, 10.3 per cent in 1990, 8.8 per cent in 1995, and (as we have just seen) 7.9 per cent in 2000: a decline of almost exactly one third over just 20 years.

Clearly these figures conceal differing rates of change experienced by different types of congregation. But if we turn next to the figures we gathered from the four Kendal churches, the picture – though more differentiated – is still one of decline (relative to the population). The raw, non-adjusted, attendance figures at Holy Trinity and St Thomas's show congregational numbers to have been fairly static since the 1960s; New Life (founded in 1981) experienced growth until the late 1990s followed by decline; and the Society of Friends has been in decline since the 1960s. If population growth over the same period is taken into account, we find that none of these congregations has managed to keep pace – and that all but New Life have declined by around a half since the 1960s, for the population of Kendal grew from 18,599 in 1961 to 27,610 in 1999 – that is, by 48.4 per cent. Indeed, at the time of our research we did not find any hard evidence to suggest that *any* of the congregations of Kendal, of whatever type, had managed to keep pace with population growth (other than for a short period, probably no more than a decade, as in the case of New Life).[5]

Thus, taking population growth into account, the overall picture is of the steady decline of the congregational domain in Kendal. In terms of absolute numbers most congregations have been static or declining since the 1960s, and relative to the growth of the town the congregational domain appears to have followed the national trend and declined by around a half since that time.

The growth of the holistic milieu

Academics rarely claim that holistic ('alternative', 'New Age' or 'expressive') spiritualities are in decline. Even secularization theorist Steve Bruce (1996a) writes of 'the flowering of alternative ideas and therapies' and the 'enduring demand for such practices' (pp. 233-4). Such claims have been supported by various forms of evidence, including mind-body-spirit book sales and population surveys. To the best of our knowledge, however, no one has ever addressed the matter by way of a locality study, charting face-to-face holistic activities over time.[6]

One way of building up a picture is by way of memories. To this end, we interviewed some 25 long-standing participants in the holistic milieu. Naturally, their oral histories cannot be taken as the gospel truth. However, by comparing the interviews it was possible to arrive at what appeared to be a reasonably reliable delineation of the broad contours of change. In addition, we collected old brochures and flyers advertising holistic activities – material which helped confirm the picture provided by the oral histories.

We also delved into the past by way of the *Yellow Pages*, the trade listing phone directory in the UK. Using the British Telecom Archives' records of the *Cumbria and North Lancashire Yellow Pages*, which ran back to 1969, we were able to chart the number of one-to-one Kendal-based 'complementary therapists' advertising their services. The picture which emerges is of growth, from virtually nothing to almost 40 services in 1999. Given that not all complementary therapists (say homeopaths) see their practices as having a spiritual dimension, this research strategy does not in itself provide an exact measure of change with regard to the number of holistic activities taken to be spiritual by their providers. But our mapping at the beginning of the Kendal Project of all those activities in Kendal and environs which *could* have been of spiritual significance (thus including all homeopaths, for example) shows that roughly two thirds of one-to-one or 'complementary' practitioners (as of 2001) see their practice as having a spiritual dimension: a ratio which can be used to shed light on the past in that when we find ten adverts for Kendal complementary therapists in 1990, it is likely that six or so will have been providing spiritually significant provisions.

So what has emerged from our study of the past? The Kendal of the 1960s and 1970s, say interviewees, was 'a well-heeled market town', 'conservative with a small "c"', a traditional place 'with only four types of vegetable available in local greengrocers'. So it hardly comes as any surprise to find yoga teacher Celia Hunter Wetenhall reporting that 'Kendal was not touched by the sixties'. As the 1970s progress, however, we find the first clear signs of the emergence of holistic activities: the odd yoga group, regular Transcendental Meditation meetings in someone's home, around three complementary therapists advertising their wares.

More groups appeared during the earlier 1980s, for example Kendal's first Buddhist group (formed 1982) and first astrology classes (1985). An Alexander technique school, running a three-year teacher training programme, was established in 1985 in a building which became known as the Fellside Centre. This also provided an important venue for new groups and one-off workshops with activities like Universal Peace Dancing, psychodrama, tai chi, and energy and auric work. There was a sense, interviewees report, of the coalescence of a new spiritual network in Kendal as the 1980s wore on. Overall, though, by say 1987 there were still relatively few spiritual groups. And neither were there many one-to-one practitioners: Ian Watson (today co-director of the Lakeland College of Homeopathy) told us, for example, that only one homeopath (practising for just one day a week) was active in Kendal around 1985. Another homeopath, Sally Holligan, reported that, 'If you said to someone that you were studying homeopathy, they would often say "What's that then?"'

During the later 1980s, however, the development of the holistic milieu entered a new phase. A real turning point was reflected in the founding of the New Age high street shop 'Turning Point' in 1988. Suzanna Michaelis, hands-on healer and facilitator of Findhorn-inspired workshops, reports that between 1989 and 1991 cards began to appear in cafes and the like for homeopathy, acupuncture and massage bearing names she had never heard of before (prior to this, she knew all the practitioners in the area). In 1992 CHOICE (Complementary Health Options In a Caring Environment) was initiated, and in 1993 Ian Watson founded the Lakeland College of Homeopathy and Personal Development. From an initial intake of 18, by 2001 the college had over 140 students enrolled on three-year and post-graduate courses. Kendal College started running a Holistic Therapy Diploma in 1994 (Celia Hunter Wetenhall, having estimated an intake of 16, was shocked to find 40 had enrolled), and also started running evening courses on crystal healing, the Alexander technique, and astrology. Rainbow Cottage, providing outlets for one-to-one practitioners and a room for spiritual groups, was established by Linda McGarvey in 1999; and Loop Cottage – a somewhat more casual centre for groups and workshops – developed during 1997.

Just as the growth of centres and courses took off during the later 1980s, so did the number of spiritual groups – Buddhist and yoga groups, for example. One-to-one activities have also grown since the later 1980s. Thus the number of complementary therapists advertising in the *Yellow Pages* started to rise quite sharply as the 1980s drew to a close. Indeed, their numbers have roughly tripled since 1990 (from 10 in that year to 36 in 1999) – an increase which of course includes non-spiritual forms of complementary activities, but which also includes the approximately two thirds of one-to-one practitioners who consider their activities to be spiritually significant.

Given that our research indicates that the number of groups also approximately tripled during the last 10 or so years of the twentieth century, we can work backwards from the 126 separate activities on offer in 2001 to conclude that about 40 activities would have been available in 1990 (our evidence also indicating that there were around 30 in 1987, when the growth of the groups and one-to-one activities of holistic spiritualities began to take off). Overall, the evidence unequivocally demonstrates growth: from the virtually non-existent in 1970 to all that is available today – or, to put it somewhat differently, from virtually nobody involved with groups or one-to-one practices in 1970 to the 600 of a typical week of 2001. Furthermore, although the fact that the population of Kendal has grown by 48.5 per cent between 1961 and 1999 means that the congregational domain has declined considerably more than is suggested by how congregations themselves have been faring (and perceive themselves to have been faring), the population increase does very little to undermine the picture of holistic milieu growth. For to all intents and purposes the holistic milieu has grown from scratch, and it grew by around 300 per cent during the 1990s, when population growth was just 11.4 per cent.

Comparing the Two Associational Domains of Kendal: A Spiritual Revolution?

Recalling the numbers involved in the two associational heartlands, at the time of our study 2,207 people (or 7.9 per cent) were active in the congregational domain of Kendal, and 600 people (or 1.6 per cent) in the holistic milieu of Kendal and environs. So we can say with some confidence that during a typical week in 2001 there were *five times* as many people involved in the congregational domain as there were in the holistic milieu.

Regarding the two associational heartlands, it is thus perfectly clear that a spiritual revolution has not taken place. However, it is equally clear that the holistic milieu is growing whilst the congregational domain is declining. So *if* the holistic milieu continues to grow at the same (linear) rate as it has done since 1970, and *if* the congregational domain continues to decline at the same (linear) rate as it has done during the same period, a spiritual revolution would take place during the third decade of the third millennium.

This speculative scenario is critically assessed later in the volume. What is immediately apparent, however, is that although claims of a spiritual revolution are exaggerated, a major shift has occurred in the sacred landscape. The 1851 Religious Census showed that up to 47.7 per cent of the population of 11,829 in Kendal took part in religious worship on census day (Mann, 1854, pp. 39-55). Even though this number is swollen by double and triple attendances, it points to a society in which churchgoing was normal rather than exceptional, and in which the congregational domain occupied an unchallenged position as the monopolistic supplier of the sacred in Kendal. By the time we undertook our research in Kendal, however, the congregational domain was facing serious sacred competition for the first time in its history.

Even though the spiritual revolution has not taken place, a number of 'mini-revolutions' clearly have. One mini-revolution concerns the relative size of the holistic milieu and the major denominations within the congregational domain – for the holistic milieu now outnumbers every single major denomination besides the Anglicans. Thus our count shows that in comparison with the 600 people active in the holistic milieu, on a typical Sunday there are 531 Roman Catholics, 285 Methodists, and 160 Jehovah's Witnesses – and 674 Anglicans. And if what is happening elsewhere in Great Britain, where Anglicanism is one of the most swiftly declining denominations, is anything to go by, it is virtually certain that there will soon be more people active in the holistic milieu in Kendal than in Anglican churches. Other mini-revolutions concern the relative vitality of particular types of holistic activity and various denominations. Take yoga, for example, the most popular form of holistic group activity in Kendal and environs: around 250 people are active during a typical week. This means there are more people involved in a yoga group in Kendal than in any denomination besides the Anglican, Roman Catholic or Methodist.

Before drawing the discussion to a close, three important considerations remain to be addressed. The first derives from the fact that according to the holistic milieu questionnaire 55 per cent of the respondents to the multiple choice question 'Does this activity [practised during the last seven days] have a spiritual dimension for you?' answered in the affirmative. This means that during a typical week not 1.6 per cent but 0.9 per cent of the population of Kendal and environs were involved in what *they* (together with the practitioner) took to be spiritually significant associational activities. What is to be made of this finding? Should we use the 0.9 per cent figure, rather than the 1.6 per cent finding, to compare with the 7.9 per cent figure for the congregational domain?[7]

The validity of testing the spiritual revolution thesis by comparing the 1.6 per cent figure for the holistic milieu with the 7.9 per cent figure for the congregational domain lies with the fact that it compares like with like: namely the numbers involved in associational activities which are taken to be of spiritual or religious significance by those who organize them. If we had tried instead to use the 0.9 per cent figure for comparative purposes we would have faced the difficulty of arriving at a comparable figure for the congregational domain – namely the percentage attending Sunday worship who consider their activity to be of religious or spiritual significance. We know from fieldwork in Kendal that people attend churches and chapels for a wide variety of reasons, not all of which might be thought of as religious (or spiritual): for moral reasons (e.g. to uphold civic values), for social reasons (one interviewee described his church as 'the best club in town'), in order to have their children experience the benefits of church involvement, to 'get in touch' with a departed relative, to meet new people (especially in the case of newcomers), to find a space to relax and reflect – and so on. Since we have not been able to quantify such matters, and given the difficulty in doing so, we do not think that it is useful to use the 0.9 per cent figure for comparative purposes. (Interestingly, however, even if we were to compare like with unlike by using the 0.9 per cent figure for the holistic milieu and 7.9 per cent for the congregational domain, if the latter continues to decline at same rate as in recent decades, and the former to continue to grow as it has done, then the spiritual revolution can still be predicted to take place just a few years later than if the 1.6 per cent figure is used.)[8]

The second consideration derives from the fact that we have compared typical Sunday attendance (for the congregational domain) with typical weekly attendance (for the holistic milieu). But what of longer time spans? If research elsewhere in Britain is anything to go by, monthly church attendance figures tend to exceed weekly figures by a multiplier of about 1.5 (Benson and Roberts, 2002), and yearly attendance figures (not including attendance at a baptism, wedding or funeral) by a multiplier of around 2.2 (Brierley, 2000, p. 78). And we know from our research in Kendal that people are often involved in holistic activities for a relatively short period of time, their place then being taken by others – which suggests that the longer the time span we take, the greater the number of individuals that will be found to have been involved in the milieu. However, since formidable research difficulties – to do with tracking participation and avoiding counting people more than once – mean that monthly or yearly figures cannot readily (if ever) be established for the holistic milieu, we feel confident that the comparison we have carried out provides the most reliable measure of the relative strength of the two heartlands.[9]

The final consideration is that talk of a 'spiritual revolution' can easily give the misleading impression that sacred activities are growing overall. To the contrary, our findings show that even if a spiritual revolution is underway, it is taking place within a realm of associational activities which is in decline. For the growth of the (relatively small) holistic milieu is not compensating for the decline of the (considerably larger) congregational domain.[10]

Summary

Kendal has not experienced a fully fledged spiritual revolution, even though the sacred landscape has altered quite dramatically since the 1960s, with mini-revolutions graphically illustrating the degree of change. The decline of life-as forms of religion is clearly in evidence, as is the turn to spiritualities of subjective-life – albeit within an overall framework of secularization. And to set the tone for the last chapter of this volume, if the trends we have charted continue into the future, a spiritual revolution will take place within the next 30 or so years.

Chapter Three

Evidence for a Spiritual Revolution: Britain and USA

Two extraordinary facets of contemporary spirituality immediately leap out to confront a sociologist of religion. The first is the sheer – and exponentially exploding – panoply of various regimes, spiritual therapies and groups available in any large or middle-sized American city... (John A. Coleman, 1997, p. 9)

...the culture of Christianity has gone in the Britain of the new millennium. Britain is showing the world how religion as we have known it can die. (Callum Brown, 2001, p. 198)

Eight out of ten Americans, not just 'religious' people, express desire for spiritual growth. (George Gallup Jr. and Timothy Jones, 2000, p. 45)

In this chapter we move further afield in our quest to test the spiritual revolution claim. As we do so we become increasingly reliant on research carried out by others. Though we draw on work of the highest quality, it has rarely been designed with our questions in mind. That is one reason why the conclusions of this chapter must be less determinate than those that have preceded it. Another has to do with the chapter's scope. It is one thing to ask whether the spiritual revolution has taken place in a town with some 28,000 inhabitants (Kendal), but quite another to ask whether it has taken place on a national or international scale. Towards the end of this chapter we also move away from the relatively clear-cut business of measuring associational religious and spiritual activity to the more tricky business of assessing whether a spiritual revolution has taken place in the culture at large and in the realm of personal belief.

We turn first to Britain and the USA to compare the numbers involved in congregational and holistic milieu activities. Do we find much the same picture as in Kendal? The USA is particularly intriguing in this regard, since it is now widely claimed to be 'exceptional' (Finke and Stark, 1992; Warner, 1993; Berger, 1999; Davie, 2002). The most common claim is that there is simply 'more' religion in the USA. Our interest lies in another possible form of exceptionalism: could it be the case that there is more evidence for the spiritual revolution claim in the USA than in Britain?

Remaining with associational activities, we then consider another interesting possibility. In Kendal we have seen that the congregational domain is characterized predominantly by life-as religion rather than subjective-life spirituality. Now we consider evidence that congregational activities elsewhere may be serving to authorize and cultivate unique subjective-lives. To the extent that this is true, we would have further evidence to support the spiritual revolution claim – evidence provided by what is taking place within rather than outside the congregational domain. We enter Christian territory on both sides of the Atlantic to consider this possibility.

Finally, we broaden the picture by moving beyond the realms of congregational and holistic milieu associational activities altogether. We consider whether the spiritual revolution is underway, or has taken place, with regard to widespread cultural provisions, including products on sale in shops, media content, and activities in educational and health care contexts. We also consider another possibility: that subjective-life spirituality may be flourishing in the realm of beliefs. Could it be the case that cultural provisions and popular beliefs indicate that the spiritual revolution has made more headway outside the realm of 'heartland' associational activity than within it?

These are big issues and big questions. We cannot hope to settle them definitively in a single chapter. We can, however, marshal available evidence to provide provisional answers.

Spiritual Revolution in Britain and the USA?

Britain

According to our measure of activity during a typical week, the spiritual revolution has not taken place in the associational heartlands of Kendal, but can the same be said for Britain as a whole?

Until now the problem with determining the current level of weekly church attendance in Britain has been not a lack of data, but discrepancy between different sources of data. According to national sample polls, attendance has been at the level of around 12 per cent or more for several decades. For example, the British Social Attitudes survey of 1997 reported that 12 per cent of the population of Britain attended weekly (Brierley, 2000, p. 72), and the Soul of Britain survey of 2000 provided a figure of 15 per cent (Heald, 2000). According to the polls the proportion claiming to have gone to church on the Sunday prior to interview has been relatively steady since the 1950s at 10 to 15 per cent (Field, 2001, p. 10).

Since 1979, however, polls have been supplemented by another source: Peter Brierley's surveys of church attendance in Great Britain, which are based on individual clergy reporting levels of typical Sunday attendance in their own churches and chapels. These surveys report a lower level of Sunday church attendance in Great Britain than the polls: 10.3 per cent in 1990 and 7.9 per cent in 2000 (2001, p. 2.23). Brierley concludes that people say they go to church more often that they really do, and that the 'reporting factor' is about double the true level of churchgoing – a ratio that has not varied in the 20 years since his surveys began (p. 5.15).

For the first time, our headcount of congregational members in Kendal allows us to adjudicate between these discrepant findings. Our results support Brierley's findings over the polls, for Brierley finds that 7.9 per cent of the population (4,604,500 people) attended church on a typical Sunday in the year 2000, and our head count revealed that 7.9 per cent of the population of Kendal (2,207 people) attended church on a typical Sunday in 2000. This finding would not be decisive if there were good grounds for thinking that Kendal was not representative of the UK as a whole, but we will see below that in socio-demographic terms Kendal does not seem to deviate from the national picture in any striking way (other than its 'whiteness'). Nor do we know of any reason for thinking that the congregational domain in Kendal is particularly unusual.

In any case, the Kendal Project yielded additional evidence to support the accuracy of data yielded by clergy-reporting over that based on self-reporting. In 1998, before we carried out our headcount in Kendal, and before clergy and congregational leaders had been told such a count would take place, we asked them to estimate the numbers in their congregations on a typical Sunday. The total clergy-estimate figure came to 2,466. Since this is only slightly higher than the figure yielded by the headcount carried out two years later, it helps confirm the accuracy of individual clergy-reporting as a source of information about attendance.

Thanks to these findings we are now able to rely on Brierley's research with confidence, including his findings about the decline of the congregational domain in Great Britain over time. It will be recalled from Chapter Two (p. 41) that Brierley's surveys reveal the severe and ongoing decline of regular attendance in the congregational domain in Great Britain over the last couple of decades: by almost exactly a third since 1980 (2001, p. 2.23). Evidence presented in Chapter Five (p. 139) shows that Sunday attendance has probably declined by around a half since 1950.

When we shift attention from the congregational domain to the holistic milieu, we find that it is far harder to arrive at a figure for national involvement. Given the amount of research that would be required to establish the number of people practising holistic, mind-body-spirituality activities, on a weekly basis, in various kinds of localities (inner city, rural, etc.) and regions (north, south west, etc.), it is hardly surprising that a considerable amount of work remains to be done. So how are we to proceed?

Our strategy is to extrapolate from Kendal findings to arrive at a figure for Great Britain. To do this, though, we obviously have to show that Kendal findings are representative of the national picture. But how can we do this when we do not know the numbers involved in holistic milieu activities, on a weekly basis, in the nation as a whole?

To tackle this problem, we draw on the few relevant figures which are available for the nation. These derive from research which has been carried out into complementary and alternative medicine (or CAM). CAM figures are not perfect for our task. Many of those providing CAM activities do not consider their practices to be of spiritual significance, and many of the activities we found in Kendal and environs (such as yoga or tai chi) are not discussed in much of the CAM literature. However, if we can show that the numbers involved with CAM activities which belong to the holistic milieu of Kendal and environs are in line with national figures, we can support the case for using Kendal Project findings to provide a national figure for holistic milieu participation during a typical week.

Simon Mills and Sarah Budd (2000) estimate that there are 6,943 aromatherapy practitioners in the UK (p. 17). The predicted number for Kendal and environs is thus four or five; we found six. Regarding reflexology, the Mills and Budd national figure is 12,648 (p. 37). The prediction for Kendal and environs is eight; we found eight. Given that we have only found one anomaly (homeopaths, the prediction being that we would find one whereas we actually found nine), we can thus be confident that the CAM activities of the holistic milieu of Kendal and environs are representative of Britain as a whole. In addition, Mills and Budd estimate that there are 60,000 practitioners of CAM in the UK (p. 55). This indicates that we ought to find 38 practitioners based in an area with the population of Kendal and environs; we found 42.

CAM activities are generally taken to involve one-to-one participation. So we have to ask: what of the group activities of the holistic milieu of Kendal and environs? Pulling together evidence from a variety of sources, we estimate that between 400,000 and 500,000 people are participating in yoga groups in the nation, and around 100,000 in tai chi groups. The former figures predict between 253 and 316 participants in Kendal and environs (we found 250), the latter 63 (we found 63). So it looks as though these two group activities are also in line with Britain as a whole. Furthermore, if CAM activities of Kendal and environs are representative, there is no reason to suppose that the same does not apply to group activities.

What makes us even more confident of being able to extrapolate from our 1.6 per cent weekly participation figure for the holistic milieu of Kendal and environs to provide a figure for the nation is that data concerning the town of Kendal itself corresponds very closely with that for England and Wales. Adding together the 2001 Census figures for the 14 Kendal wards, and comparing them with the overall statistics for England and Wales, we find that Kendal's age and gender structure is typical, so is occupational grouping (albeit being slightly skewed towards lower income occupations), and so is social gradation and educational attainment (the fact that Kendal College is not a college of Higher Education explaining the fact that there are somewhat fewer full-time students than the national figure).

Overall then, it is safe to extrapolate from the fact that 1.6 per cent of the population of Kendal and environs are involved on a weekly basis in associational activities regarded as spiritually significant by practitioners. This means that slightly over 900,000 inhabitants of Great Britain (57,103,927 according to the 2001 Census) are active on a weekly basis in the holistic milieu of the nation (913,663 to be exact) – of whom 146,000 are spiritual practitioners. (It is interesting to compare this with the 1994 figure provided for GPs by The Royal College of General Practitioners, namely 37,352; or the widely cited figure of 25,000 therapists in Britain, with an equal number of clergy.) We can also assume that just as 55 per cent of the holistic milieu of Kendal and environs take their current holistic practice to be of spiritual significance, so will around 55 per cent of the milieu of the nation – that is, about half a million people. (The number would obviously rise if one included those engaged with spiritually significant practices during any time in the past but who are no longer currently practising on a group or one-to-one basis). In addition, and thinking of the mini-revolutions we discussed in the last chapter, the fact that 250 of the 600 individuals (42 per cent) of the holistic milieu of Kendal and environs practise yoga during a typical week in Kendal and environs suggests that approaching 400,000 individuals in the holistic milieu of Great Britain practise this activity during a typical week – a larger number than are attending many of the main Christian denominations (Methodists totalling 372,600 in 2000, Pentecostals 216,400, according to Brierley (2001, p. 2.23)).

To close our discussion of the holistic milieu in Britain, we must consider how it has been faring over time. In Kendal and environs, it will be recalled from the last chapter, we found virtually no evidence of associational holistic activities prior to 1970. We are pretty confident that much the same applies to the nation overall. Even where the counter-culture was most in evidence, namely university towns and rural areas like the Welsh Borders, there were very few groups and one-to-one activities of the kind we find today. This is not to deny that the 'sixties' (running from the mid-1960s to the mid-1970s) saw plenty of subjective-life spiritual activity – whether exploring 'inner space' by way of LSD, music, nature or the journey to the East. Indeed, it is highly likely that in Britain, especially in university towns and some rural areas, there were as many if not more individuals pursuing subjective-life spirituality in (say) 1970 than in (say) 1985. However, the incontestable fact is that the subjective-life spiritual groups and one-to-one activities by which we measure growth have grown nationally since the 1960s – just as they have grown in Kendal. They must have done so in order to have attained their current numerical significance relative to the situation in 1970.[1]

We conclude that just as the spiritual revolution, as we have defined it by reference to the relative weight of congregational and holistic milieu activities, has not taken place in Kendal, so it has not taken place in Britain. True, there might well be some hot spots around the nation where it has taken place (places like Totnes and the Dart valley, perhaps, or specific localities of north London). Equally, there might well be some 'cold spots' where there is little sign of a spiritual revolution taking place. But considered overall the sacred landscape in the country remains dominated by the congregational: the same ratio that applies to Kendal, namely 1:5 in favour of the congregational domain, applies also to Great Britain.

The implications for the scholarly literature are clear. Insofar as associational involvement is concerned, the figure we have arrived at for the holistic milieu (900,000 plus) shows that Bruce (1996b) is wrong when he claims that 'the number of people [in Britain] who have shown any interest in alternative religions is minute' (p. 273). Certainly the 900,000 plus figure is no more 'minute' that the 2001 Census finding that there are 558,810 people of Hindu affiliation in the UK, some of whom will not be participating in temple associational activities. (For comparative purposes it is worth noting that the census yielded a figure of 1,591,126 for Muslim affiliation.) Where associational involvement is concerned, those like Campbell (1999) and Luckmann (1990) who suggest that a spiritual revolution (or something very close to it) has already taken place in countries like Britain are also wrong – or perhaps premature. And, we can add, our findings support those – most noticeably Bruce (2002) – who see secularization continuing in Britain. For whether it be Kendal or the nation, the holistic milieu has not become large enough to compensate for the decline of the considerably larger congregational domain.

USA

In the USA, unlike Great Britain, there is widespread confidence that the congregational domain is in robust good health. In a typical week, many books and magazines tell us, 40 per cent of the population will be in church – making the USA an 'exceptionally' Christian nation when compared with Britain and the rest of Europe. The most important source for this commonly cited 40 per cent figure is the Gallup polls of congregational attendance. The finding is based on responses to the question: 'Did you, yourself, happen to attend church or synagogue in the last seven days, or not?' Other sources, however, arrive at different figures for weekly congregational attendance. For example, the General Social Surveys that, like Gallup, ask questions of a representative sample of the US population, report a figure of 30 per cent attending 'nearly every week' in 2000 (Wuthnow, 2003, p. 3).[2]

An even lower figure has been arrived at by researchers who set out to test the accuracy of the polls' self-reported attendance figures by counting attendance in different ways. Using three different forms of data collection (clergy-reporting, headcounting and counts of cars in church parking lots) a 1992 study of church attendance in an Ohio county, and of Catholic churches in 18 dioceses, found that actual weekly attendance was slightly over half the rate indicated by national polls (Hadaway, Marler and Chaves, 1993). Additional research by this team of scholars, using a variety of methods including headcounts, has consistently arrived at a figure of typical weekly attendance of 'probably between 22 and 24 per cent' (Marler and Hadaway, 2000, p. 42; see also Chaves and Cavendish, 1994; Hadaway, Marler and Chaves, 1998; Marler and Hadaway, 1999; Hadaway and Marler, 2003). Though the higher self-reported figure yielded by the polls has been vigorously defended (Hout and Greeley, 1998), the accumulating evidence convinces us that the lower figure is more likely to represent the true picture (and the methods used to arrive at it are more readily comparable with those which yielded the figures of 7.9 per cent for Kendal and Great Britain). We conclude that the proportion of the population regularly involved in the congregational domain is probably about three times higher in the USA than Great Britain, not five times higher.

How do the two domains compare over time? We have noted that attendance in Great Britain has declined by a half since 1950 – has the same thing happened in the USA? It is even harder to answer this question than to find out about current attendance levels in the USA, since data derives either from polls or from ecclesiastical-reporting (data collected by denominations/national church bodies concerning their own levels of adherence). We have already noted the tendency of self-reporting to exaggerate attendance levels, and ecclesiastical-reporting seems beset by other difficulties, not least that church bodies tend to report 'adherence' rather than 'attendance' and to define it in very different ways – many adherents may have stopped attending long ago.

Most of the national sample polls suggest that churchgoing reached a peak in the USA in the 1950s in the immediate aftermath of World War II, and then fell quite sharply in the 1960s and/or early 1970s before levelling out. According to the Gallup polls, for example, 49 per cent of the US population attended church in 1958 and the level had fallen to 40 per cent in 1975, since when it has been fairly steady; the General Social Surveys agree but suggest very slight decline in the 1990s (Gallup and Lindsay, 1999, p.15; Wuthnow, 2003, p. 3). A similar picture emerges from ecclesiastical-reporting, with the *Yearbook of American and Canadian Churches* recording a drop in adherence of 12 percentage points between 1970 and 2001 (Lindner, 2003), and data collected by the Glenmary Institute showing a drop in adherence of 4 percentage points between 1971 and 1990 (Johnson, Picard and Quinn, 1974; Quinn, Anderson, Bradley, Goetting and Shriver 1982; Bradley, Green, Jones, Lynn and McNeil, 1992).[3]

It can be argued in favour of such data that even if individuals and denominations exaggerate their levels of attendance and adherence, such exaggeration is likely to be stable over time. Against this, Hadaway, Marler and Chaves (1993) have suggested that whilst individuals' perceptions of their behaviour may have remained constant since the 1950s, their actual behaviour appears to have changed considerably. They suggest that whilst church attendance is still perceived as socially desirable in the USA, fewer people now attend, and that the gap between what people do and what they say they do may have widened steadily. Hadaway, Marler and Chaves (1998) offer evidence to support this hypothesis from Catholic (clergy-reported) attendance rolls in San Francisco, which show attendance declining by a half, whilst self-reported levels remain steady. The implication is that churchgoing in the USA may have fallen from a 'real' level of 40 per cent in the early 1960s to the 22-4 per cent level today, thus mirroring the decline of around 50 per cent which has been experienced over the same period in Great Britain. Independent supporting evidence for a decline of this sort of magnitude comes from time-use studies conducted in the USA since the 1960s which reveal a fall in attendance from around 40 per cent to around 25 per cent (Presser and Stinson, 1998).

Although there are counter-arguments in favour of the accuracy of the more optimistic trend-data yielded by the polls, we believe the weight of evidence points to some significant decline of the congregational domain in the USA since the 1960s. In the absence of conclusive data on the rate of this decline, however, we can safely say only that it lies somewhere in the range between about 5 and 50 per cent. We conclude that even though the United States may not be quite as 'exceptionally' religious as some like to claim, its congregational domain is significantly more robust than in Great Britain: involving three times more of the population, and declining less quickly.

Turning from the congregational domain to the holistic milieu of the USA, establishing the weekly numbers of those involved in associational subjective-life activities provided by spiritual practitioners is no easy task. So far as we are aware, research focusing on this topic has not been carried out in the USA.

A way forward is to draw on self-reported poll data. According to Wade Clark Roof (1999), 14 per cent of baby boomers (namely those born between 1946 and 1962) are 'metaphysical believers and seekers' (p. 204). Since baby boomers constitute one third of the USA population, around 5 per cent of the general population belong to what Roof describes as the 'subculture' (p. 203) of those who emphasize 'immanent' spirituality and 'self-expansiveness' (p. 211) – what we are calling subjective-life spirituality. But how many are also involved with relevant associational activities during a typical week? Roof states that a third of his metaphysical believers and seekers report that they are 'in support groups where they can share experiences and receive spiritual support from others like themselves' (p. 205). Expressed as a proportion of the national population, this means that around 1.65 per cent are involved with spiritually significant associational groups.[4]

Since this figure only refers to baby boom metaphysical believers and seekers involved in spiritually significant support groups, it does not take into account the numbers involved with one-to-one holistic activities (such as spiritual aromatherapy) or those group activities (such as yoga) which do not appear to qualify as 'support groups'. We also have to bear in mind that the 1.65 per cent figure does not include those who are more concerned with drawing on holistic spirituality to address dis-ease (etc.) than with spiritual seekership-cum-metaphysics, nor those who draw on mind-body-spirituality resources in secular ways, without any 'spirituality'. And, of course, the 1.65 per cent figure does not take into account people who might be involved with the holistic milieu but who belong to the two thirds of the population who are not baby boomers.

The number of those involved in the holistic milieu of the USA is clearly higher than that indicated by the 1.65 per cent figure. But how much higher? One argument derives from the fact that it is highly unlikely that 'metaphysical believers and seekers' who are also involved in groups amount to more than 20 per cent of those active in Kendal's holistic milieu. Given that it is reasonable to suppose that the holistic milieu of the USA is unlikely to be so very different from its equivalent in Kendal (or Britain), we can infer that it is five times as big as the percentage of people who are 'metaphysical believers and seekers' – so if 20 per cent of the milieu in the USA are seekers, the total percentage involved in the holistic milieu would be around 8.[5]

Another argument involves CAM usage. Figures provided by Eisenberg, Davis, Ettner et al. (1998) indicate that 19.5 per cent of the USA population saw an alternative, one-to-one therapist in 1997. Thomas, Nicholl and Coleman (2001) arrive at a broadly comparable figure for England of 13.6 per cent (p. 2). Assuming that spiritually inclined practitioners make up at least as large a proportion of CAM practitioners overall in the USA as in England, that means that the number of clients seen by spiritual CAM practitioners in the USA in a given year is about 50 per cent higher than in England. And given that there is no obvious reason why temporal patterns of use in the USA should be radically different from England, we can conclude with some confidence that in a given week approaching 50 per cent more people in the USA consult a spiritually orientated CAM healer than in England. Furthermore, if there are proportionately more spiritually orientated CAM healers than in England, it is reasonable to assume that there are also more spiritually orientated group practitioners – which means that the USA milieu as a whole could well be approaching 50 per cent larger than the 1.6 per cent figure for England (or Britain).[6]

There is little doubting the fact that the holistic milieu of the USA is larger than the 1.65 per cent figure of 'metaphysical believers and seekers'. Our first argument indicates that it could go up to 8 per cent; our second that it could go up to close to 2.5 per cent. But has the holistic milieu grown? It is true that holistic milieu activities were present in places like the San Francisco Bay area by the earlier 1970s – Wuthnow (1976) reports that 8 per cent of inhabitants of the Bay area had had first-hand experience of yoga during this period. However, it is surely the case that Coleman's description of the contemporary situation 'in any large or middle-sized American city', provided at the start of this chapter, would not have applied in 1970. Summarizing evidence drawn from a range of sources – including primary material (in particular adverts for events in hard copy 'listings' and on websites), articles which have appeared in the press and magazines like *Time*, and academic publications – the picture is of growth. If the Web had existed in 1970, we very much doubt that around 15,000 different sites would have been advertising yoga in New York – as they do today.[7]

Pulling things together, can we conclude a spiritual revolution is under-way in the USA, and is possibly more advanced than in Great Britain? With around 22 to 24 per cent of the population probably attending on a typical Sunday, the congregational domain is clearly larger than in Great Britain where the equivalent figure is 7.9 per cent. The holistic milieu of the USA is also larger than the 1.6 per cent of Britain – but on any reckoning, it is by no means large enough for a spiritual revolution to have taken place. As for that critical test of the development of what could turn out to be a spiritual revolution – namely the ratio between congregational and holistic numbers in a given week – we have seen that in Great Britain it is 5:1 in favour of congregational numbers. If the congregational domain of the USA involves 24 per cent of the population and the holistic milieu 8 per cent, the ratio is 3:1; but if the (approaching) 2.5 per cent holistic milieu figure is used, the ratio is around 10:1. Until further research has been carried out, it would be foolhardy to suggest a precise ratio.[8]

Looking at the longitudinal evidence, although we are pretty certain that the decline of the congregational domain in the USA is taking place at a faster rate than is often thought, sound evidence to say how fast it is declining is simply not available. There is certainly no reliable evidence to show that it is declining as fast (or faster) than the congregational domain in Great Britain – evidence that would be required to help support the case that the trends that there is greater momentum behind a spiritual revolution in the USA than in Great Britain. As for the holistic milieu, since it is now almost certainly bigger in the USA than in Great Britain, and was probably much the same size in 1970, it has almost certainly grown at a faster rate since the 1960s. That said, however, we do not know enough about its current size to be able to assess the scale or momentum of its growth. As things stand at the moment, then, the only safe conclusion is that the congregational domain is declining in the USA and the holistic milieu is growing – trends which certainly have to be present if a revolution is to take place in the future.

A Spiritual Revolution in Christianity?

Up to this point we have tested the spiritual revolution claim – that subjective-life spirituality has become, or is set to become, more important than life-as religion – by treating the congregational domain and the holistic milieu as separate 'blocs'. In the case of Kendal, we have shown that this was justified by the fact that there was very little evidence of subjective-life spirituality in the congregational domain, or of life-as religion in the holistic milieu. But could it be the case that in Britain more widely, and in the USA, subjective-life spirituality is becoming increasingly influential *within* Christianity? If this were true it would mean that our simple comparison of holistic and congregational vitality has under-estimated the vitality of subjective-life spirituality in the sacred landscape as a whole. We must therefore look within the congregational domain on both sides of the Atlantic to see whether a life-as emphasis in Christianity is being supplanted by developments of a more subjectivized nature. Given the internal variety of the congregational domain, the best way of doing this is by considering in turn each of the four main varieties of Christianity which we outlined in Chapter One. As well as exploring the nature and degree of subjectivization within each variety, we will consider their fate in recent decades.

Congregations of difference

Given that congregations of difference are defined by their orientation towards the higher, external authority of a God to which human beings must conform their lives in order to be saved, it might seem unlikely that the influence of subjective-life spirituality could creep into this sector of Christianity. In-depth qualitative research like Ammerman's (1987) study of a conservative Baptist congregation in the USA confirms the picture of strongly 'differentiated' communities in which individuals defer to God, women to men and children to parents, and in which life is lived according to very clearly defined roles authorized by the infallible word of scripture.

In his studies of evangelicals and evangelicalism in the early 1980s, however, Hunter (1987) discovered evidence of a growing liberalization and subjectivization in evangelical ranks. He found 'self-sacrifice and moral asceticism' giving way to a 'fascination with the self and with human subjectivity' (pp. 65-71). But a recent study which replicated Hunter's research design discovers that the 'coming generation' of evangelicals has not subjectivized as uniformly as Hunter predicted (Penning and Smidt, 2002). To the contrary, American evangelicals appear to have become somewhat more conservative with regard to theology, morality (particularly with regard to the family) and politics. Only where self-identity is concerned is there is evidence of a growing subjective turn, with 94 per cent of evangelicals in 1996 agreeing that 'self-improvement is important to me' compared with 87 per cent in 1982, and 75 per cent feeling 'a strong need for new experiences' compared with 68 per cent in 1982 (p. 89).

What we seem to be finding in Christian congregations of difference is a growing recognition of the importance of (the quality of) subjective-life, and a concern with its cultivation, but only insofar as it is contained and constrained by a strict theological and moral framework.[9] What we do not find is any clear evidence of an authorization of subjective-life in moral and religious matters. Even when the language of 'spirituality' and 'spiritual growth' is adopted, it is used to speak of a life in which the individual listens and conforms to God-given rules and roles rather than to his or her inner feelings, convictions, instincts and judgements. Indeed many congregations of difference have begun to draw a sharp and critical contrast between fully subjectivized forms of spirituality (often categorized unfavourably as 'New Age') and the true Christian way. The same critique is offered by conservative Catholics as by conservative Protestants: that

New Age spirituality is a new form of 'gnosticism' which turns the proper order of things upside down by putting human beings in the place of God.

As for the fortunes of congregations of difference, in Britain (including Kendal) some of the smaller denominations of hard difference have declined very fast since the 1960s, even to the point of near extinction (the Christadelphians in Kendal, for example). Yet attendance in the single largest conservative evangelical denomination in England, the Baptists, has almost managed to keep pace with population growth since the late 1970s, which in the rapidly secularizing British context represents remarkable success (Brierley, 2000, p. 37). This success is echoed in the USA, where the (more conservative) Southern Baptist Convention (SBC) has been one of the most successful of all large US denominations over the same period, as Kelley (1995) pointed out (pp. xi-xii, 20-5). However, although the SBC as a whole is still growing, its rate of growth in the 1990s slowed to around 0.6 per cent (Wuthnow, 2003, p. 10; Shibley, 1996, p. 58; Roozen and Hadaway, 1993, pp. 52-3).

Congregations of experiential difference

Though they share important characteristics with congregations of difference, congregations of experiential difference place greater stress on the importance of inner experience of the divine by way of the Holy Spirit. In Kendal we found such Christian experientialism to be firmly constrained by a framework of life-as roles (see Chapter One), but there is growing evidence to suggest that elsewhere, particularly in the USA, it may be breaking free of such constraints to take a more fully subjectivized form. Thus Donald Miller (1997) argues that the most successful congregations of experiential difference in the USA represent a 'new paradigm' within Christianity. Could it be that the new paradigm is beginning to embrace subjective-life spirituality, and is thus the vanguard of the spiritual revolution in the congregational domain?

In support of this conclusion, one can cite evidence presented by Miller in his study of new paradigm megachurches. Here the needs, desires, experiences, skills, hurts, traumas, dilemmas and 'uniquenesses' of the individual are taken far more seriously than is common elsewhere in the congregational domain. Not only are there many small groups in which 'individualities' can be expressed and 'healed' (see below), but these churches organize their lives, worship and teaching in such a way that the impression of external dogma and authority bearing down on the individual is minimized. The importance of correct dogmatic belief is downplayed in favour of direct personal experience of God-as-Spirit (Miller, 1997, pp. 120-33). 'External', 'institutional' features of congregational life including an ordained and robed priesthood, set liturgies and formal church music, are rejected in favour of relaxed and informal worship and lay participation in every aspect of congregational life (though there is always a chief pastor with full-time assistants). The message is that God is to be known not only by way of external conformity, but in deep inner experience and transformation of a highly holistic nature – in which body, mind, emotions and spirit are all involved.

Thus in many ways the 'spirituality' of the new paradigm churches seems designed to fit around the subjective-life of the unique individual, rather than vice versa. Yet there is a good deal of counter-evidence which suggests that although these congregations may be more subjectivized than other parts of the congregational domain, they are still nowhere near as subjectivized as the holistic milieu, or even the general culture. For although they recognize, appeal to, cater for and even help cultivate individuals' subjective-lives, they do not go so far as to authorize them. They embrace 'seekers' with warmth, tolerance and openness, but their intention is not to encourage them to continue in their own way, nor to suggest that they give more heed to their subjectivities than to the Word of God. The intention is to 'convert' individuals – to bring them to the point at which they (voluntarily) surrender to the authority of the God of Jesus Christ and are 'reborn' as children of God by the action of the Holy Spirit (Sargeant, 2000). The aim, in other words, is that life-as (a discipline of Christ etc.) should possess and control subjective-life.

Nowhere is this resistance to the full authorization of subjective-lives clearer than in such congregations' strong support for a very particular cluster of 'family values', centred around 'traditional' gender roles. For example, individuals 'struggling' with same-sex relationships may be encouraged to join small groups designed to 'help' them. The aim, however, is not to listen to them and honour their sexual orientation (as it would be in subjective-life spiritualities), but to reorient inner and outer life in a more 'Godly' and 'biblical' direction. This is life-as spirituality rather than subjective-life spirituality.

Though Miller does not supply numbers, he thinks that the new paradigm megachurches are growing rapidly, and their sheer size is certainly impressive (they normally have a membership of well over 2,000). The most informative numerical data comes from the Faith Communities Today study which estimates the membership of US megachurches as lying in the region of 1.2-2 million, with 'nearly all of the growth of the megas' having taken place 'since the 1970s' (Lindner, 2003, pp. 16-19; see also Bradley et al. 1992, p. 453 and Roozen and Hadaway, 1993, pp. 25-8). However, not all megachurches are new paradigm churches, and not all congregations of experiential difference are new paradigm churches. Just as in Kendal, experiential congregations of difference may also take the form of individual congregations within broader denominations which have been strongly influenced by the charismatic renewal movement which got underway in the 1970s (most towns in Britain and the USA will have at least one such congregation; most cities many more). Whilst there has been no systematic attempt to assess the growth of such congregations, studies like Francis, Lankshear and Jones (2000) in Britain and Shibley (1996) and Tamney (2002) in the USA suggest that since the 1980s they have been more successful than any other type of congregation. Such success seems to have been largely at the expense of other varieties of Christianity, with research by Perrin, Kennedy and Miller (1997) revealing that the majority of affiliates to the 'new paradigm' megachurches were raised in congregations of humanity.

Congregations of humanity

Because congregations of humanity are often referred to as 'liberal', it might be assumed that they are the most likely to be open to the influence of the subjective turn in the religious life – since they appear to provide the necessary basis of freedom and tolerance. As we saw in Kendal, however, worship in such congregations is very much focused on praise of God, and preaching tends to take a humanitarian rather than a libertarian direction, with more emphasis being placed on duty and self-sacrifice than on freedom, self-realization and the cultivation of unique subjective-life. This emphasis on life-as duties is often reinforced by the survival of hierarchical, directive and dominating ecclesiastical and organizational structures, residual clericalism, and formalized liturgical worship.

What we found in Kendal appears to be typical of congregations of humanity in Britain more generally. Thus we have found no significant evidence of a systematic and officially sponsored turn towards subjective-life spirituality in congregations of humanity. This is not to deny an apparent growth of interest on the part of some individual members of such congregations in some more subjectivized forms of Christian spirituality – in 'mysticism', 'Celtic spirituality', meditation and so on. Nor is it to deny that individual congregations – such as St James, Piccadilly – and retreat centres may cater for such spirituality (see p. 69). The point, however, is that such activities remain peripheral to the official life of the average congregation of humanity. Though mainline Christianity in the USA may show some greater tendencies towards subjectivization (Tamney, 2002), here too institutional and humanistic checks appear to hold in the majority of congregations, as recent studies by Balmer (1996) and Ammerman (1997a, 1997b) indicate. Again, this is not to underestimate the significant revival of interest in 'spirituality' on the part of some individuals and pioneering congregations (such as Grace Cathedral in San Francisco). It is simply to note that such interest has not been sufficient to shift the emphasis of the worshipping life of the average congregation of humanity away from duties and obligations to God and neighbour towards the cultivation of unique subjectivity. Even the conservative critics of liberal Christianity tend, rightly, to accuse it of humanizing rather than subjectivizing (Reeves, 1996; Norman, 2002). (see Chapter Five for further reflection on this topic.)

As for the fortunes of congregations of humanity, there is broad consensus about their steep decline over the last three decades. In England typical Sunday attendance in the (Anglican) Church of England declined by 47 per cent between 1979 and 1998, in the Methodist Church by 44 per cent, and in the United Reformed Church by 39 per cent (Brierley, 2000, pp. 33-8). In the USA adherence levels in mainline Protestant congregations declined by 8.5 per cent between 1971 and 1990, at the same time that the national population increased by 19.9 per cent (Shibley, 1996, p. 27). Attendance in the Roman Catholic Church in England declined by 42 per cent between 1979 and 1998 in the UK (Brierley, 2000, p. 34), and it is likely that significant Roman Catholic decline has also occurred in the USA.[10] There is as yet no evidence of bottoming out in these rates of decline.

Congregations of experiential humanity

Finally we come to congregations of experiential humanity, many of which are associated with the Unitarians and the Society of Friends (Quakers). Given their heritage and their traditional tendency to stress the authority of the voice of God speaking in the heart of the individual, it is no surprise to find that congregations of experiential difference are more likely to embrace a spirituality orientated around subjective-life than are other varieties of Christianity. Though there is a dearth of research in this area, what we found to be true in Kendal appears to hold good in Britain and the USA more generally. As Pilgrim (2003) finds in Britain, many such congregations appear to be divided between those (usually older members) who tend to stress authoritative humanistic values, and (usually younger) members who give greater authority to personal experience in the spiritual life. In some cases, those who move furthest towards the latter position may find themselves moving outside congregational life altogether – following a path set by Emerson well over a century before when he abandoned Unitarianism in favour of spiritual 'self-reliance'.

In England average Sunday attendance levels in the Society of Friends rose 110 per cent between 1989 and 1998 (Brierley, 2000, p. 45), whilst in the United States data collected by the Glenmary Institute indicates that the number of adherents fell by 17 per cent between 1980 and 2000 (Quinn et al. 1982; Jones et al., 2000). (The contrast may be accounted for by the fact that attendance at some Quaker congregations seems to be growing, whilst numbers of committed 'members' has been falling.) The Glenmary data shows Unitarian-Universalist adherence in the USA growing by 17 per between 1980 and 2000. Yet despite this fairly healthy picture, overall numbers involved in congregations of experiential humanity remain tiny and represent only a small fraction of congregational activity – Quakers represented just 0.2 per cent of English attenders in 1998, whilst Quakers and Unitarian-Universalists combined represented 0.2 per cent of adherents in the USA in 2000 (Brierley, 2000; Jones et al., 2000).

Small groups

In this volume our main concern is to test the spiritual revolution claim by reference to weekly involvement in the associational activities of the congregational domain and the holistic network. For the sake of simplicity, 'countability' and comparability, we have deliberately excluded 'para' organizations and affiliations from our considerations of the congregational domain. As we broaden our focus, however, it is important simply to note the explosion of small groups in the USA, many of them attached to congregations. Wuthnow (1996) estimates that around 40 per cent of the adult population of the USA (75 million people) claim to be involved in 'a small group that meets regularly' (p. 45), that 57 per cent of the groups in question are 'part of the regular activities of a church or synagogue' (p. 92), and that a majority of all small groups are estimated to have a religious or spiritual focus (p. 76). Wuthnow also suggests that small groups lend themselves to the cultivation of a less 'transcendent' form of spirituality because they allow the expression and 'sharing' of personal, intimate, experiences, problems, hopes and desires on the part of every member of the group. It is possible, then, that the spirituality of the spiritual revolution may be more in evidence in such groups than within congregational worship (though our own research in small groups attached to evangelical congregations in Kendal – and elsewhere – finds even small group subjective-life sharing in the congregational domain to be constrained by a framework of life-as roles).

Conclusion

We find no reason to argue with the growing number of studies which find evidence of subjectivization within many parts of the congregational domain (Tipton, 1982; Hunter, 1987; Hammond, 1992; Miller, 1997; Shibley, 1996; Smith, 2002; Tamney, 2002). Our conclusion is simply that such subjectivization does not go deep enough to add weight to the spiritual revolution claim. It is a question of perspective: whether one sees the subjectivization glass as half full or half empty. Relative to much pre-existing Christianity, there has certainly been a significant subjective turn, especially in congregations of experiential difference, which promise a good deal by way of the enhancement of subjective-life. But from the perspective of the holistic milieu, or much of the general culture, even congregations of experiential difference seem 'half empty' where the full expression of the authority of each unique subjective-life is concerned.

Our only qualification is that much of the evidence which leads us to this conclusion concerns the 'supply-side' of religion, and it may be that there are many individuals within congregations who ignore the 'official' emphasis on life-as and use the resources provided to cultivate their subjective spiritual lives in their own unique ways. This is even more likely to be true of individuals involved in small groups linked to congregations. It may be that their numbers are growing, and these numbers would certainly count towards the spiritual revolution claim. However, we cannot, add them to our estimation of a spiritual revolution, since the task of arriving at a sensible estimate of their significance is impossible on the basis of existing evidence.

A Spiritual Revolution in the Culture?

Broadening our approach still further, we move beyond congregational and holistic associational activities to see whether there is more subjective-life spirituality than life-as religion in the culture at large. For could it be the case that what we might call the 'cultural transformation' variant of the spiritual revolution claim is better supported than the 'associational heartlands' rendering?

This is a huge topic, and a definitive answer to the question would require thorough investigation of the presence or absence, growth or decline, of life-as religion and subjective-life spirituality in the educational system, in health provision, in the workplace – and in all the other main spheres of modern society. It would involve an exploration of wellbeing culture to see which sorts of religion and spirituality are faring best in fitness centres, spas, hotels and shops. And it would necessitate a detailed content survey of books, magazines, newspapers, websites, television and radio programmes, adverts, songs and films and other media of communication and entertainment. Given the scale of these tasks, and given the fact that a great deal of research remains to be done, the following discussion is necessarily provisional. We offer no more than a quick review of key evidence. We believe this is enough, however, to allow us to draw at least a tentative conclusion about the validity of the cultural transformation claim with regard to Britain. (Our evidence concerning the USA is here confined to endnotes.)

To begin with purchasing-culture, research by one of our students, Andrea Cheshire, shows that in January 2001 56 of the 187 high street shops of Kendal were selling products like books, crystals and CDs which signalled, encouraged or facilitated holistic spirituality.[11] When the research was replicated in April 2003 it was found that the proportion of shops supplying such goods had risen from 30 per cent to 45 per cent. By contrast goods related to life-as religion like Bibles, cards and crucifixes were stocked by just 7 per cent of Kendal's high street shops in 2003. Looking at the situation more generally, many major national chains like Boots, Sainsbury's, the Body Shop, Lush, Dr & Herbs and W. H. Smith now contain products which can be drawn upon for holistic mind-body-spirituality purposes.[12] Virtually all urban centres of any size also have specialist shops. By contrast, Christian provisions are extremely rare in national high street chains, and the only shops dedicated to them tend to be Christian bookshops (often church-supported), or clergy outfitters and suppliers. In Kendal there is one small evangelical bookshop and one Christian cafe/drop-in centre, both of which are subsidized by Kendal congregations.

Taking our discussion of purchasing-culture a little further, many providers and provisions cater for cultivation of subjective wellbeing. High street goods – from magazines to perfumes – promise to make people 'feel better about themselves'. So do provisions which involve more by way of face-to-face contact: fitness, health, beauty and leisure centres, spas and massage centres (including provisions at airports), courses, workshops, personal development or life coaching programmes, adult education classes, retreats, outlets in up-market hotels, many sports centres and gyms, and so on. In all these 'quality of life' contexts, it is far more common to find practitioners engaged with subjective-life spirituality than Christian instruction. Every leisure or fitness centre that we have visited in Britain runs yoga or tai chi classes. By contrast, life-as religion and spirituality is noticeable by its absence. The only significant exception concerns spiritual retreats, normally held in designated Christian retreat centres, which are often historic buildings owned by major Christian denominations. Our enquiries suggest that the market for such retreat activity is growing, with particular demand for retreats that involve one-to-one spiritual direction aimed at personal spiritual growth (tellingly, we also found the term 'spiritual accompaniment' beginning to be offered as a substitute for 'spiritual direction', and 'spiritual guide' for 'spiritual director'). What is more, this is the one area of Christian activity in Britain where we found evidence of the sacred being unambiguously associated with the cultivation of subjective wellbeing: most strikingly in Christian 'massage retreats', but also in explicit advertising of the benefits to be had by way of 'relaxation', 'inner calm', 'focus' and so on.[13]

Discussion of purchasing-culture must also dwell on another highly significant fact: the veritable explosion of interest in books to do with holistic spiritualities of life. Located most obviously in those sections of major bookstore chains labelled 'Mind Body and Spirit' or words to that effect, the topic also makes its appearance in many publications shelved under headings like 'Health and Beauty' or 'Self Help'. According to Liz Puttick (2003), mind-body-spirit literature's 0.9 per cent share of the total market for books in Britain in 1998 jumped to 3.8 per cent in 1999 and then to 5.8 per cent in 2002 – to become a bigger sector of publishing than cookery, history, sports or business.[14] According to the *Bookseller* (2002, p. 13), 'the self-help genre and the broader mind, body and spirit category accounts for between 7 per cent and 12 per cent of sales in bookshops around the world, and continues to grow', whilst 'James Redfield's *The Celestine Prophecy* [was] the biggest selling book in the world during the 1990s'. And as the Mind Body Spirit section of major bookshops expands, so the sections formerly devoted to 'Religion', 'Christianity' and 'Theology' shrink. In Ottakers, the major bookshop in Kendal, for example, the Mind Body Spirit section has grown to become one of the largest sections in the shop in recent years, whilst Christianity is represented by nothing more than a few Bibles and prayer books. In the UK as a whole, 6.8 per cent of books published in 1928 were classified as 'religious'; by 2000 that had fallen to 4.2 per cent (Brierley, 2001, p. 6.3).

As for newspapers, we have recently conducted several content surveys (each taking place for a month of publications). We found that the two middle-class, middle-brow English newspapers, the *Daily Express*, with its 'mindbodyspirit. Life on Wednesday' and 'Express Woman. Alternative Health' sections, and the *Daily Mail* (with relevant articles), have far more content on holistic spirituality than theistic religion. And whereas holistic spirituality is generally presented in a favourable light, articles on Christianity often dwell on the bad news (declining attendance, internal wrangles, sex abuse scandals). Even the broadsheets *The Times* and *The Observer*, the former with its Saturday 'Body & Soul' supplement and the latter with its regular 'Barefoot Doctor' feature, have considerably more of the holistic than the theistic (though the editorials of *The Times* are more likely to represent a broadly 'Christian' viewpoint than a holistic one).[15]

Regarding magazines, our visits to W. H. Smith show that it stocks few (if any) which mention Christianity, let alone dwell on it. But their health, beauty, glamour, celebrity and lifestyle magazines are full of a concern with wellbeing of body and mind, which by no means infrequently involves discussion of spiritual health and growth as well. W. H. Smith is about to stock the most explicitly spiritual magazine they have ever taken – *Spiritual Lifestyles*.[16] (An exception concerns the more 'life-as' women's magazines with telling titles like *Woman*, *Woman's Own*, *Good Housekeeping*, which tend to focus only on family, home and bodily health matters – but have no explicitly religious or spiritual content.) Film, television and the Internet also appear to be giving increasing space to new forms of spirituality.[17]

Partly, but by no means only, through the influence of the media, key terms of subjective-life spirituality – such as feng shui, chakra, chi, yin and yang, tao, meditation and a whole host of 'life' idioms – have now entered into everyday language – see Cupitt (1999) on 'the new religion of life in everyday speech'; see also Partridge (2004). By contrast, theistic language has lost its vitality in ordinary language, with expressions like 'goodbye' (God be with you), 'bless (you)' losing their original theistic reference, and new theistic idioms failing to emerge.

What about production-culture? Robert Peel, the father of the nineteenth-century Tory Prime Minister, would employ only Methodists in his Lancashire cotton mills and calico printing factories because of their sobriety, honesty and responsibility. To all intents and purposes, the harnessing of theistic religion to the ends of production-culture in Britain had ceased by the end of the nineteenth century – and there have been no serious signs of revival. By contrast holistic, 'New Age' spiritualities of life (and productivity) are clearly a growing force in 'softer', 'person-centred' forms of capitalism.[18]

In the cultural sites looked at thus far, subjective-life spirituality clearly has a much greater presence than theistic religion. Furthermore, there is ample evidence that the holistic presence has grown. Prior to around 1970, 'New Age' management trainings simply did not exist. High street stores did not stock 'spiritual' products until quite recently. The expression 'Mind-Body-Spirit' did not become popular within the book-selling trade until the 1990s. Newspapers did not contain sections or articles extolling the holistic during the 1960s. These changes are telling, but before drawing a conclusion about cultural transformation, we must consider other cultural sites in which holistic spirituality is also growing, but where there is less clear-cut evidence of it having overtaken life-as religion.

Looking first at mainstream education-culture, the influence of 'religion' has been waning since the 1950s, whilst that of 'spirituality' has been waxing. Up to the later 1960s, the emphasis in the British public educational system was very much on 'Religious Instruction', which assumed the truth of Christianity. Today, however, 'All schools are legally required to attend to the spiritual developments of their pupils and the quality of provision for spiritual education is regularly assessed by OFSTED [the inspection service for schools in England and Wales]' (Wright, 2000, p. i). OFSTED defines 'spiritual development' as relating 'to that aspect of inner life through which pupils acquire insights into their personal existence which are of enduring worth . . . a non-material dimension to life', and explicitly states that ' "spiritual" is not synonymous with religious'. Yet the contemporary picture remains mixed due in part to the fact that central government regulation and inspection tends to be more relaxed in relation to religion than most other areas of the curriculum, leaving greater scope for individual education authorities, schools and teachers to set their own policies. In many primary and secondary schools, the emphasis given to spiritual-cum-personal growth is certainly greater than that which is given to any form of 'religious instruction'. In others (including church schools) Christianity is still privileged, and daily collective worship 'of a broadly Christian character' is still compulsory in state schools (though the law seems to be ignored by a majority). Sunday Schools, however, are in very serious decline. In a 1957 Gallup survey 73 per cent of Britons said they had attended Sunday School regularly. By the year 2000 the number of Sunday School attendees in Britain had fallen to 4 per cent of the popula-tion (Bruce, 2002, pp. 68, 104).[19]

Looking next at mainstream health-culture, it is clear that there have been many recent moves within the British National Health Service, both official and unofficial, to introduce more by way of spirituality and spiritual care. Many trainee nurses learn about spiritual care; hospital and ward mission statements often use the language of spirituality (or care for the 'whole' person); GPs increasingly refer patients to body-mind-spirituality practitioners (House of Lords, 2000); and some doctors seek qualifications in CAM themselves. Even though they often have Christian foundations, many hospices are also drawing increasingly on themes from holistic spir-ituality (see, for example, Tony Walter (1996) on spirituality in connection with 'living with dying' (p. 353), and Walter, 2002.) In hospitals the role of the hospital chaplain, traditionally an ordained Christian minister, is also in transition, with new understandings of hospital chaplaincy being couched in terms of a duty of care for the spiritual health of all patients and staff regardless of their religious commitments (see, for example, Woodward, 1995). As in education-culture, however, the picture in health-culture at the turn of the millennium today remains mixed, with institu-tional and financial factors lagging and inhibiting cultural shift towards a more holistic understanding of health care. In the meantime, CAM provi-sions (often with a spiritual dimension) continue to proliferate.[20]

To conclude this brief investigation of cultural transformation with regard to the sacred: although the spiritual revolution has not taken place with regard to weekly associational activities, it looks very much as though it has occurred, or is occurring, in significant sectors of the general culture – that is, the culture to which the majority of people have access and on which they exert influence, particularly by way of market demand. In this regard at least, we believe that Luckmann, Campbell and other proponents of the spiritual revolution claim – or something close to it – have got it right.[21]

A Spiritual Revolution in Personal Belief?

Given cultural transformation with regard to the sacred, we might expect a related revolution in the realm of personal belief. Is there evidence that the growing presence of subjective-life spirituality in the general culture is associated with a shift in beliefs about the sacred?

Just as more detailed and comprehensive study of religion and spirituality in the culture remains a research challenge, so does the in-depth study of personal beliefs.[22] Until further research has been carried out, we must rely on the findings of general surveys. According to Robin Gill, C. Kirk Hadaway and Penny Long Marler's (1998) extensive review of almost one hundred surveys, during the 1940s and 1950s 43 per cent of the population of Britain believed in 'God as Personal' compared with 38 per cent who believed in 'God as Spirit or Life Force'. During the 1990s, however, the respective figures became 31 per cent and 40 per cent. The apparent conclusion – that more obviously Christian theistic belief has been overtaken by belief having more to do with spirit/uality-cum-life – is supported by the 'Soul of Britain' survey carried out in 2000 which finds that only 26 per cent now believe in 'a personal God', with 44 per cent either reporting belief in 'some sort of spirit or life force' or 'there is something there' (Heald, 2000). The same poll also finds that 31 per cent consider themselves to be 'a spiritual person', and 27 per cent say that they are 'a religious person'.[23]

In the USA, it is true that belief in a personal God remains much higher than in Britain and Europe – 72 per cent of the population say they believe in God described as the 'all-powerful, all-knowing, perfect creator of the universe who rules the world today' (Barna, 2001). But 10 per cent now believe that God 'represents a state of higher consciousness', whilst an additional 7 per cent believe that God is 'the total realization of personal human potential' (Barna, 2001). And Phillip Hammond's (1992) survey shows that 29 per cent agree with the statement 'People have God within them, so the church isn't really necessary' (p. 80). What is more, according to Gallup and Lindsay (1999), 'In 1984, just over half of the nation (56%) felt the need to

experience spiritual growth and development. By 1998 ... eighty-two percent of adults now feel the need to grow and mature spiritually' (p. 66). In
addition, almost a third of respondents in a recent Gallup poll 'defined
spirituality with no reference to God or a higher authority', and when asked
'Do you think of spirituality more in a personal or individual sense, or more
in terms of organized religion and church doctrine?' 72 per cent opted for
the 'personal or individual sense' (Gallup and Jones, 2000, pp. 49-50).[24]

Findings like these would appear to show that beliefs more obviously akin
to inner-life-spirituality have become of considerable importance. Indeed,
some of the longitudinal data we have cited would appear to indicate that
inner-life beliefs have overtaken, or are overtaking, beliefs more obviously
belonging to a traditional theistic frame of reference. However, in the final
analysis we are not sure that survey findings can really shed all that much
light on how subjective-life spirituality and life-as religion beliefs are faring
among the population. Much survey data seems too open to interpretation
for determinate conclusions to be drawn. To illustrate by reference to that
key word, 'spirituality': 57 per cent of those responding to our questionnaire
study of the congregational domain of Kendal said that spirituality is
'obeying God's will', with the proportion rising to 92 per cent for Parr
Street (a congregation of difference) and 100 per cent of New Life (a congregation of experiential difference). In the USA, Wuthnow (2003) reports
that 50 per cent of those who 'value spiritual growth' agree with the statement that 'Everything in the Bible should be taken literally, word for word'
(pp. 40-1). 'Spirituality', it is clear, need not signify subjective-life spirituality. To provide another illustration, the 40 per cent of the British population
who report belief in 'God as Spirit or Life Force' could be referring to that
which informs from 'within' – or they could be referring to a source of
agency which operates much like the traditional Christian God; and the 31
per cent who report belief in 'God as Personal' could be referring to the God
of theism or to the god within or 'as' the person.

Therefore, even though the longitudinal survey data we have presented for
Britain could very well indicate that a shift is underway from beliefs to do
with life-as religion to beliefs to do with subjective-life spirituality, and although similar evidence from the USA could very well indicate that spiritual
and personal growth now mean much the same thing for many people, we are
reluctant to draw the conclusion that such evidence offers straightforward
support for the spiritual revolution claim. There is clearly a pressing need for
survey questions to be reformulated in order to discriminate more effectively
between life-as religion, life-as spirituality and subjective-life spirituality.

Conclusion

The first conclusion of this wide-ranging chapter is that associational sub-jective-life spirituality has not eclipsed associational life-as religion either in Britain or the USA, even though the congregational domain is declining in both countries and the holistic milieu is growing. The relative success of congregations of experiential difference helps explain why the congrega-tional domain has not declined more rapidly. It is undoubtedly the case, however, that the developments which might lead to a spiritual revolution in the future are considerably more advanced than they were 40 years ago – especially in Britain.

The second conclusion is that even though a spiritual revolution has not taken place in associational activities relating to the sacred, it has taken place in key sectors of the culture. It may also have taken place in the realm of personal belief – though additional research is required to establish the point.

Our explorations of the associational heartlands of Britain and the USA lead to a final conclusion concerning what we call the *subjectivization pat-tern* or *claim*. This is more encompassing than the spiritual revolution claim, for whereas the former only involves a comparison of associational life-as religion with associational subjective-life spirituality, the latter in-volves comparison of different forms of associational life-as religion and spirituality *with each other* and with associational subjective-life spirituality (according to their relative degrees of subjectivization). Taken as a whole, the following pattern emerges from the evidence we have gathered in this chapter. In terms of numbers:

1 Holistic milieu, subjective-life spirituality – which pays *most* attention to the cultivation of unique subjectivities – tends to be faring *best*.
2 Religions of experiential humanity and experiential difference – which address unique subjectivities whilst placing them within a life-as frame of reference – tend to be faring *relatively well*.
3 Religions of difference – which pay some attention to unique subjectivities whilst emphasizing life-as 'oughts' – tend to be faring *relatively badly*.
4 Religions of humanity – which pay *least* attention to unique subjectivities – tend to be faring *worst*.

Clearly we are speaking here only of fortunes *within* the realm of sacred associational activity. Equally clearly, we are assessing the fortunes of the four main types of activity relative to one another. We say that (2) is faring 'relatively well' and (3) 'relatively badly', because we are comparing them with the greater growth of (1). If we were to compare (2) or even (3) with (4), we would of course have to say that it is faring relatively well. In other words, compared to that which is relatively 'empty' of attention to unique subjectivities (religions of humanity), experiential religions of difference can be said to be 'half full' – and so do (relatively) better. But compared to that which is 'full' of such attention (subjective-life spirituality), religions of experiential difference seem 'half empty' – and so do (relatively) badly.

In the next chapter our primary aim is to explain the fortunes of the two 'extremes', on which the spiritual revolution claim focuses. Thus we attempt to explain why holistic activities which enable individuals to live out their own unique lives in their own unique ways are generally faring well, and why associational activities which neglect, regulate, over-rule, dominate or possess subjectivities in the name of a higher, life-as authority are generally faring much less well. In rather less detail, we will also briefly consider why different forms of life-as religion and spirituality fare may be faring better, or worse, than others.

Chapter Four

Bringing the Sacred to Life: Explaining Sacralization and Secularization

Become what you are! (Friedrich Nietzsche, 1981, p. 252)

I am a part of all that I have met. (Alfred Lord Tennyson, 'Ulysses')

'Personal experience' constitutes 'personality'. (Max Weber, in Gerth and Mills, 1997, p. 137)

For many people today, to set aside their own path in order to conform to some external authority just doesn't seem comprehensible as a form of spiritual life. (Charles Taylor, 2002, p. 101)

Contemporary quests for spirituality are really yearnings for a reconstructed interior life. (Wade Clark Roof, 1999, p. 35)

We have seen that there is a connection between the associational activities of subjective-life spirituality and growth on the one hand, and the associational activities of life-as religion and overall decline on the other. But why should the numbers involved in the holistic milieu be growing whilst the total number involved in the congregational domain is declining? In this chapter we offer the 'subjectivization thesis' as an explanation of the co-existence of secularization and sacralization in the contemporary sacred landscape. After a brief introduction to the thesis, we use it first to explain the growth of the holistic milieu, then the decline of the congregational domain. Our aim is not only to illuminate the evidence by way of the theory, but to test the theory by way of the evidence. As we do so we refine the thesis in order to take account of some of the most striking features of the contemporary sacred landscape, including the crucial role played by gender. Above all, we argue that by way of this single theory it is possible to make sense of apparently contradictory trends – towards growth in some forms of associational activity oriented towards the sacred, and decline in others.

The Subjectivization Thesis

In a nutshell, the subjectivization thesis states that 'the massive subjective turn of modern culture' favours and reinforces those (subjective-life) forms of spirituality which resource unique subjectivities and treat them as a primary source of significance, and undermines those (life-as) forms of religion which do not. In other words, the thesis explains the varied fortunes of different forms of religion and spirituality today by reference to a single process – the widespread cultural shift in emphasis from the value ascribed to life-as to the value ascribed to subjective-life. This does not, however, imply that the subjective turn will necessarily encourage people to stay (or become) involved in associational forms of religion or spirituality – merely that *if* they are (or do), their involvement is more likely to be with those which cultivate subjective-life than those which prioritize life-as beliefs and values.

Underlying the subjectivization thesis is the Durkheimian principle that people are more likely to be involved with forms of the sacred which are 'consistent with their ongoing values and beliefs' – as Joseph Tamney (2002, p. 227) puts it – than with those which are not. In a society in which life-as roles are central, one can therefore expect to find forms of life-as religion which reinforce and legitimate those roles, and support and resource people in living life in terms of them, to be doing better than those forms of spirituality which undermine or ignore such roles. (For example, in highly stratified, hierarchical societies charismatic forms of spirituality with egalitarian tendencies are unlikely to become mainstream.) Conversely, when the cultivation of unique subjective-lives has greater cultural priority in society, then those forms of spirituality which cater for subjective-life tasks – offering individuals a sense of harmony and serenity, for example – are likely to fare much better. This is not to imply that religion is merely an epiphenomenon of culture, nor to deny that there can be 'prophetic' forms of religion and spirituality which challenge prevailing cultural values. It is merely to suggest that the latter will be marginal rather than dominant in the sacred landscape of their time.

When we apply the general Durkheimian principle to a society characterized by the subjective turn, we can see that it is reasonable to expect that the greater the number of those who prioritize subjective-life as their source of significance, the greater the likelihood that forms of the sacred which work for them will grow. Conversely, the smaller the pool of people who prioritize life-as as their primary source of significance, the greater the likelihood that forms of the sacred which work for them will decline.[1]

The evidence which undergirds the claim that there has been a massive turn to subjective-life in contemporary Western societies is weighty. Ronald Inglehart's analysis of successive rounds of value surveys shows that the number of 'post-materialists' has been growing steadily, both in absolute terms and relative to the number of 'materialists'. The latter are those whose prime concern is with obtaining the material necessities and securities of life, whilst the former are those who value self-expression and are intent on 'maximizing subjective well-being' (1997, p. 36). 'In 1970-71', writes Inglehart,

> Materialists held an overwhelming numerical preponderance over postmaterialists, outnumbering them by nearly four to one. By 1990, the balance had shifted dramatically, to a point where materialists outnumbered postmaterialists by only four to three. Projections...suggest that by the year 2000 materialists and postmaterialists will be about equally numerous in many Western countries' (1997, p. 35).

A growing body of literature exploring various aspects of the subjective turn supports Inglehart's findings. Charles Taylor's work has already been mentioned. Other influential studies include Robert Bellah et al's *Habits of the Heart* (1985), Anthony Giddens's *The Transformation of Intimacy* (1993), Martin Gross's *The Psychological Society* (1979), Philip Rieff's *The Triumph of the Therapeutic* (1987), Richard Sennett's *The Fall of Public Man* (1977), Joseph Veroff et al's *The Inner American* (1981), and Daniel Yankelovich's *New Rules* (1981). None of this literature suggests that the subjective turn has affected the whole of Western culture, nor that all Westerners now subscribe to subjective-life values. The suggestion is rather that the turn is becoming increasingly influential and thereby placing life-as values increasingly on the defensive.

As we have suggested previously in the volume, the subjective turn is bound up with the development of a wide array of provisions and activities. To give just a few examples, the 'disciplined' family of traditional values has increasingly been replaced by the expressive family of emotional bonds. The hierarchical command structure of the old-style business, where everyone has their place, now has to compete with flatter, more fluid and individual-worker-centred systems, and with business cultures which promise to 'bring life back to work' and encourage people to 'grow' in their 'learning environments' by way of a self-work ethic (work which enables one to 'work' on oneself). Similarly, educational provisions have shifted in emphasis from authoritative teaching of the facts of the matter to 'bringing out' the abilities of the child. Personal, relational life now has less to do with belonging to a specific, ordered community, and more to do with developing an array of interactions which serve to cater for different aspects of subjective-life concern. Voluntary associations, which have grown since the 1950s in Britain, show a distinct shift from those run along life-as lines (traditional women's organizations and trade unions are in decline) to those of a more 'quality of subjective-life' variety (support groups and pre-school play groups are growing). Nursing and caring staff are encouraged to pay as much attention as possible to the quality of life of their patients (in rehabilitation wards for the elderly, for example). Complementary and alternative medicine, which includes emphasis on the importance of the healing of feelings, grows in significance annually, as do hospices in which the subjective lives of the terminally ill and their family become the focus of attention and care. Similarly, the number of counsellors, therapists and (most recently) 'life trainers' has expanded significantly since the 1960s.[2]

One can also cite the growing cultural prominence of provisions which enable people to reflect on private or subjective-life. For example, daytime TV shows probe life-issues; *Big Brother* and other reality TV shows display people's lives; biographies and autobiographies increasingly take the form of what Virginia Woolf called 'life-writing' or 'the writing of the self'; books and articles devoted to matters of psychology and self-help proliferate; even the weather forecast ceases to be an authoritatively intoned summary of meteorological 'facts' and becomes the weather-with-feeling. In the realm of advertising, the trend is also towards the personalized: the presentation of variety to cater for individual tastes, and the appeal to the life-enhancing. And last, but by no means least, there is the role played by what might be called 'the ethic of subjectivity', which is evident in the value attached to self-expression and fulfilment; to doing 'what feels right', 'following your heart', 'being true to yourself', cultivating 'emotional intelligence' and respecting other people's feelings. Very telling in this regard is the value which has come to be attributed to 'feeling', and being 'comfortable' (as in 'how do you feel about that?' and 'are you comfortable with this decision?').

Though many more examples could be given of how cultural provisions and activities have become more person-centred and subjectivity-centred, this should suffice to give an indication of the cultural significance of the subjective turn. It is not our intention to evaluate this turn, nor to decide whether it is really as liberating as many feel it to be. No doubt many institutions that embrace the turn have developed sophisticated new methods of control and regulation, including accountability systems, in-spections, mentoring, job descriptions and performance-related pay. No doubt the subjective turn flourishes, in part, because it proves compatible with the demands of late capitalism (for flexibility of labour, individual entrepreneurship, 'expressive' consumption and so on) (Rose, 1999). But important though they may be, none of these considerations alters the fact that very significant cultural value has come to be ascribed to being treated as a uniquely valuable person, finding out about oneself, expressing oneself, discovering one's own way of becoming all that one can (reasonably) be – themes, we shall shortly see, which are central to the most widespread cultural expression of the turn to date, namely subjective wellbeing culture. Meanwhile, the idea of denying or sacrificing oneself for the sake of a supra-self order of things, or even of living by reference to such an order, becomes culturally marginal. Deference to 'higher authority' could hardly be said to be at the forefront of recent cultural change.

It can safely be concluded that the subjective turn, from life as 'expected', 'given' and 'laid down' to the interior experiences of subject-ive-life, is of considerable significance. Given the Durkheimian principle, we would expect the realm of associational activities focused on the sacred to be affected accordingly, with the subjective-life activities of the holistic milieu growing *because* they cater for the subjective turn of the culture, and the life-as activities of the congregational domain declining *because* they do not cater for the turn to subjective-life. As we have seen in previous chapters, this expectation seems to be fulfilled insofar as we have detected a pattern whereby those forms of the sacred which cater for the cultivation of unique subjective-life are faring better than those which do not. What we hope to demonstrate in this chapter is that this pattern is not a mere coincidence, but that it is their ability or inability to cater for the subjective turn which is a key *cause* of the growth or decline of those different forms of associational activity orientated towards the sacred.

It could, of course, be objected that the subjectivization pattern is a mere coincidence, and that secularization and sacralization in the contem-porary sacred landscape should therefore be explained by other factors. For example, it might be argued that people are leaving the churches because they have lost their faith rather than because their subjective-lives are not being catered for. In order to strengthen the case for the subjectivization thesis we must therefore appeal to independent evidence that the subjective turn is indeed operative. We must show that an important reason for the growth of the holistic milieu is that it *in fact* caters for people who identify with the cultural turn, and that an important reason for the decline of the congregational domain is that selves valuing subjective-life as a source of significance have *in fact* stopped attending.

Not that we wish to suggest that the subjectivization thesis could ever bear the burden of explaining sacralization and secularization *in toto*. It would be unrealistic to imagine that there could be any single cause of such massive and complex phenomena. We are proposing the subjectivization factor only as one explanation amongst others in relation to religious and spiritual decline or growth, and we would expect to bolt on other, complementary, factors as and when the evidence suggested that was appropriate. However, since we find a good deal of evidence to support the subjectivization thesis, and little that counts against it, we have considerable confidence in its value. If not the only key to explaining change, it certainly invokes a dynamic that should not be ignored.

The Growth of the Holistic Milieu

The argument in general

It will be clear by now that our general argument is that the growth of associational, holistic spiritualities of life owes a very great deal to their ability to cater for the values and expectations, potentialities and vulnerabilities of those who attach importance to subjective-life as a primary source of significance. To attach value to subjectivities is to attach value to the unique (for one's subjective-life is the sum of a particular life-history), to the authority of the person (for only the person has first hand, experiential knowledge of the unique), and to freedom (for liberation from life-as formations is required if one is to have the freedom to be unique and to cultivate and express life accordingly).

In the realm of associational activity orientated to the sacred, these values are catered for when the sacred is experienced as dwelling within the unique. Because the inner 'You' knows you, it is experienced as truthful, real, reliable, effective. When the sacred flows from within subjective-life, it offers 'inner solutions' which are uniquely appropriate to the challenge and opportunity of becoming fully alive in the here-and-now. Subjectively orientated selves seek forms of the sacred which enable them to monitor their progress in life by reference to the quality or authenticity of personal, experientially informed knowledge and authority, rather than by reference to the standards of an overarching order which, since it is not of one's own making, is therefore alien. Such an 'inner' sacred offers people the freedom to find their own path rather than telling them the path which they ought to follow, and it enables them to test activities to find what works best for their experiences of life. Conversely, they do not look for forms of the sacred which transcend the particularities of their lives. They greatly prefer personal exploration and discovery to the authority or 'straightjacket' of established orders which, by virtue of being overarching, cannot take account of individual uniqueness. The sacred 'without' can only too readily serve to disrupt life understood as the sum of distinctive and irreplaceable life-experiences 'within'.

The 'practice of experience' rather than the practice of belief systems; the cultivation rather than the repression of the unique; the freedom to explore and express the truth of one's being rather than adhering to the truth of tradition – subjective-life spirituality works for those who draw on the sacred to seek sources of significance within their subjective-lives.

The development of 'the new age of wellbeing'

As its influence has extended during the last few decades, the subjective turn has increasingly taken shape in subjective wellbeing culture. This culture has become the most widespread expression of the subjective turn to date. By making reference to this significant development, we can substantiate our general argument that the success of holistic spiritualities is linked to their ability to cater for the subjective turn. That is to say, the growth of subjective-life spiritualities owes a great deal to the fact that they attract people who are already involved with the culture of subjective wellbeing. More specifically, we argue that holistic spiritualities of life provide a relatively specialized or distinctive variant of the much more widespread culture of subjective wellbeing. This means that these spiritualities can attract those involved with the more widespread culture who are looking for activities which are in tune with what they are already familiar with *whilst* taking them further or 'deeper'. The success of the subjective turn, institutionally embedded in subjective wellbeing culture, thus contributes directly – and increasingly – to the success of the holistic milieu.

Subjective wellbeing culture in general

In a branch of the newsagents and bookseller W. H. Smith, centrally located in a large city of northern England, there is a large array of wellbeing publications. Around the perimeter of the area devoted to the topic there are sections labelled 'cookery', 'nature', 'gardening', 'travel', 'self-help', 'self-development' and 'beauty'. 'Health' and 'mind, body, spirit' are to be found around the central area. The Dalai Lama's *The Art of Living* is displayed at the very centre. What all these sections have in common is a concern with experience: the experience of good food, travel, health, oneself. Even though many of these books may make reference to the outside world, their prime objective is to help enhance readers' inner worlds – to improve the quality of their subjective-lives.

We use the term 'subjective wellbeing culture' to refer to all those cultural provisions or activities which explicitly dwell on enhancing the quality of subjective-life. In contrast to those provisions or activities which dwell on the 'facts' or 'necessities' of life (the travel book which concentrates on the price of getting from A to B, the training which concentrates on the technicalities of being an effective manager), subjective wellbeing culture is considerably more psychologized. For example, health care in subjectivized settings in hospitals is not simply a matter of hygiene or providing medical treatment – it is also being aware of the value of making sure that the patient feels as comfortable as possible. The seminars, trainings, courses and workshops of soft capitalism are more concerned with the personal qualities of participants than with abstract or functional procedures. Child-centred teachers concentrate on the development of the 'whole' child, not teaching the same to the same. Many advertisements emphasize the experiential rather than the utility value of products (for example those car adverts which internalize the car as experience – 'the journey of your life' – rather than mentioning technical specifications, or the sticker on the back of a Wilton Broadloom carpet sample which announces its 'Emotional Benefits'). A great many health clubs, detox centres, gyms, sports centres, fitness centres, spas or beauty salons go beyond (or within) the task of simply keeping fit or looking good. Supermarkets subjectivize food and other provisions (Sainsbury's, with its 'Making life taste better' slogan, for example, or Marks & Spencers' Café Revive chain – not just a place to eat, for this is where to go to 'relax ... refresh ... rewind ... revive'). Or we can think of all those publications – not least articles in the press and popular magazines – which cater for those who want to attend to feeling good about themselves.[3]

Given that the subjective-life of any one person is bound up with a distinctive life-history, subjective wellbeing culture focuses on the value of that uniqueness. Provisions and activities have to acknowledge the authority of personal experience. (To exercise superior, external authority to tell people what their subjective-lives ought to be like is to diminish or take away their uniqueness – thereby undermining what subjective wellbeing culture is all about.) In accord with the authority of personal experience, the ethic of unique subjectivity pervades subjective wellbeing culture as a whole. The health club chain Fitness First's slogan, 'Be yourself only better' says a very great deal; Sainsbury's in effect rewrites the Shakespearian 'To thine own self be true' as 'Be good to yourself'. Cultural provisions or activities cater for the value attached to having the freedom to be in touch with, or true to, subjective-life as a source of significance. Hence the evocative nature of subjective-life advertising, promising feelings but not what to feel (a photo of a car combined with just one word, 'desire'); hence the Timberland slogan, 'Follow your own path. Begin your journey at www.timberland.com'; hence the emphasis on the unique – or personalized – to cater for the unique. And, thinking of other regions of wellbeing culture, hence the importance attached by hospices to encouraging personal relationships to help enable the terminally ill to enrich their lives, to 'live with death'; hence the care taken to respond to the personal needs of the elderly in subjectivized rehabilitation wards; and hence the importance attached to 'learning from experience' in many educational circles.

Subjective wellbeing culture, we may conclude, has to do with the cultivation of 'good' feelings, and is ultimately focused on feeling good about oneself. But that is not to deny another major characteristic, namely the importance attached to relationships, albeit subjectively based rather than role-based relationships. To transform one's bathroom into a personalized spa or to experience one's garden as a tranquil haven or one's car as a vehicle of desire involves the cultivation of a relationship with those 'objects'. The activities and provisions of subjective wellbeing culture typically promise to work 'through' the person, offering to enable people to 'feel good about themselves' by way of a better relationship with their own inner life and subjective experiences. For Sainsbury's, food does not just serve to make you feel better by satisfying your appetite – it has to do with 'Making life taste better'. For the Body Shop, scent does not simply make you smell nice – it serves as 'the scent of your soul'. For La Source, a holiday is not just about having a good time – it enables you to experience the 'amazing things which happen when you introduce your body to your mind'. Holistic themes are in evidence. And by no means infrequently, the 'whole' includes a spiritual dimension. At least in Britain, the expression 'mind-body-spirit' (or something akin to it) has become widely adopted – by book shops, newspapers and magazines, for example. It is difficult to find a fitness centre or spa which does not cater for the spiritual dimension of wellbeing for those who seek it. Products – such as those found in the wellbeing zones of major stores in Britain – link health, relaxation or beauty with 'inner' dimensions ('the truth of who you are', 'your natural self', your 'energy' or 'spirit'). And spirituality also enters into the holistic discourses and practices found in mainstream professions – including teaching and nursing.[4]

In recent decades, subjectivized wellbeing culture has developed into a major sphere of provision and activity. Comparing the situation in the USA between 1957 and 1976, Joseph Veroff et al. (1981) concluded that 'there has been a shift from a *socially* integrated paradigm for structuring well-being to a more personal or *individuated* paradigm for structuring well-being'. They write of 'the diminution of role standards as the basis for adjustment', 'increased focus on self-expressiveness and self-direction in social life' and of 'a shift of concern from social organizational integration to interpersonal intimacy' (p. 529). More recently, Inglehart (1997) concludes that 'Increasingly, the publics of advanced industrial societies have come to emphasize quality of life concerns' (p. 36). Suffice it to say, for present purposes, that everything under discussion has grown, or has been developed, since the 1950s, with the most rapid growth occuring most recently.[5]

Subjective wellbeing culture in particular: the 'new age of wellbeing'

The next step of our argument is to show that the holistic milieu has its home within the more general culture of subjective wellbeing whilst *also* being a relatively distinctive or specialized variant of the more widespread culture. For if this is true, growth could well owe a considerable amount to the more specialized variant appealing to those who are already involved with the more general.

Looking first at what the holistic milieu has in common with the more widespread culture of subjective wellbeing, the key lies with the value which both ascribe to the cultivation or nurturing of subjectivities. Both thus share the 'logic of the unique' – they pay attention to and respect the unique, and provide the opportunity for participants to exercise their authority to 'be' or 'turn into' themselves by finding their own paths on the basis of their own experience; they enable people to remain true to their unique subjectivities whilst developing the quality of subjective-life.

As we have seen in Chapter One, the holistic milieu of Kendal has a great deal to do with the cultivation of subjective-life. It thus comes as no surprise to find that 'wellbeing' is often referred to – and in ways which are very similar to (if not identical with) usage within the more general culture. To illustrate by reference to advertising brochures, homeopathist Maggie Dudley offers 'restoration of health and well being'; reiki master Lucy Trufkruyer indicates that her practice 'energises, relaxes, and promotes a feeling of wellbeing'; kinesiologist Fiona Adam writes of 'Higher energy levels, Improved fitness, Greater flexibility, Clearer thinking, Better sleep, Less stress'; Ruth Francis advertises 'Therapeutic Massage for tension, stress, and increased well-being'; and rebirther Bernadette Riley notes the 'direct connection between mental and physical well-being and the openness of the breathing'. Further afield (elsewhere in Britain, the Netherlands, Scandinavia and the USA, for example), primary material (brochures, websites, books, articles, magazines, 'listings'), scholarly publications and our own interviews paint much the same picture. It is also noteworthy that best-selling 'wellbeing' books, listed by www.amazon.co.uk or www.amazon.com, frequently have titles which link spiritual practices and the quest for quality of life (Anton Simmha's *Ashtanga Yoga. Exercises and Inspirations for Well-Being*, for example). And perhaps the best-known person in the world of subjective-life spirituality – Deepak Chopra – has established 'The Chopra Centre for Well Being'.[6]

Another way of emphasizing the fact that much of the holistic milieu and the more general culture of subjective wellbeing have a great deal in common is to bear in mind the point made earlier that subjective-life spirituality is by no means absent in the more general world of wellbeing. However, the holistic milieu does not simply replicate provisions that are on offer more generally. One of the most important distinguishing characteristics of the activities on offer in the milieu is that they are of an 'intensive', face-to-face relational nature – something that is not in evidence, for example, when people read in private about spirituality and wellbeing. Second, these relational activities are of a more specialized kind than those found elsewhere in subjective wellbeing culture. When holistic spiritualities of life are drawn upon by schools or businesses, for example, it is within the context of achieving broader institutional aims ('the spiritual, moral, cultural, mental and physical development of pupils at the school and of society', according to the 1988 Education Reform Act; becoming a more effective manager, according to New Age business consultants or trainers). In the holistic milieu, however, the focus is on nurturing the quality of personal subjective-life *per se*. And third, spirituality is considerably more prominent in the holistic milieu than in much of the more general culture of subjective wellbeing. In many quarters of the more widespread culture, of course, spirituality is not to be found at all (the self-help literature which adopts the psychological frame of reference, for example). And in other quarters, spirituality is only mentioned in passing – or just hinted at (as with the 'Ohm by Olay' advert, 'Holistic beauty from head to soul. Feel beautiful inside and out. Experience Ohm'). In the holistic milieu, by contrast, practitioners all consider their activities to be of spiritual significance, and all participants are at least offered the opportunity of 'going deeper' to explore and experience the spiritual dimension of the holistic mind-body-spirit dynamic. 'The deeper the better' captures the general sentiment.

The path from general subjective wellbeing culture to the holistic milieu

Above all, then, the holistic milieu offers a 'new age of wellbeing', and represents a relatively distinctive manifestation of the more widespread culture with which it is so closely connected. So we now explore what this has to do with the growth of holistic activities, the argument being that the growth of the holistic milieu owes a great deal to the fact that it caters for those who want to go *further* along the path towards subjective wellbeing. Although subjective wellbeing culture in general might have much to offer, the holistic milieu in particular provides a way of deepening the quest. The fact that the latter has much in common with the former means that it is relatively easy for people to step into the more specialized. More specifically, the fact that holistic themes (including holistic spirituality) are found within the broader culture means that the culture can serve to 'prime' people for the activities of the holistic milieu. At the same time, however, the relatively specialized nature of the holistic milieu contributes to its appeal and allows it to capture a niche market by offering more than is available elsewhere in the culture. In sum, the appeal and the growth of the holistic milieu owes a great deal to its success in attracting people who want to pursue the quest for subjective wellbeing by way of activities which are neither just more of the same as those on offer more generally, nor too different or strange.

An excellent illustration of the priming process is provided by the fact that the most popular activities of the holistic milieu in Kendal and environs, and no doubt elsewhere, include yoga, massage (including Indian head massage), aromatherapy, homeopathy and reflexology. For these activities are also among the most popular in subjective wellbeing culture in general: the books, the articles, the high street products, the references on TV chat shows, the literature for teachers and parents on spirituality and children, the literature on spirituality and nursing or counselling, a taste of first-hand involvement whilst at a spa, and so on. Those seeking ways of improving the quality of their subjective lives (or the lives of others) are thus likely to encounter these provisions or activities (and others), become familiar with them, perhaps learn a considerable amount about them. And it is then but a relatively short step to move into the more specialized realm of the holistic milieu: the step from seeing yoga on TV to trying out beginners' yoga at a leisure centre; from reading about reflexology in the *Daily Mail* or in Boots' *Health and Beauty* magazine to trying it out for oneself; from selecting aromatherapy products for use in the bathroom to having an aromatherapy massage; from having an Indian head massage at a beauty salon to going to an Indian head massage specialist; from reading that massage works by way of 'energy' to rejuvenating the body by going along to a one-to-one practitioner; from reading about what celebrities are doing to seeing if it works for oneself. (See Heelas and Seel, 2003, for more on the priming process.)

Especially for the considerable number of people who believe in a 'spirit or life force' (40 per cent, according to a finding reported in the last chapter, p. 73), it is by no means difficult to move along the path from the wider culture of subjective wellbeing into the holistic milieu itself. Addressing much the same wellbeing and 'ill-being' issues as those addressed by wellbeing culture at large (see below for further discussion), the milieu is in tune with the broader culture. Those conversant with the broader culture are thus unlikely to dismiss the milieu as counter-cultural, strange or deviant. Furthermore, those who might be considering becoming actively involved need not be put off by the spirituality of the milieu. The fact that practitioners do not impose spirituality on those who are not inclined to see if it works for them means that it is perfectly possible to be active in the milieu without having to 'go deeper' into the spiritual dimension.[7] The fear of 'indoctrination', in particular with regard to emotions, is also lessened by virtue of the fact that those who might be inclined to enter the holistic milieu do not have to face the hurdle of encountering doctrinal belief systems; do not have to make commitments to life-as teachings, telling them what they ought to believe, what they ought to do, what they must sacrifice; do not have to face the prospect of being preached at or judged. Unlike 'religion', we were told on a number of occasions, 'spirituality is without the baggage'. As in subjective wellbeing culture more generally, the *pragmatic individualism* of holistic milieu activities means that what matters is finding out 'what works' by way of the truth of one's experience, not obeying what others take to be *the* truth whatever the particularities of one's life experiences might have to say.[8]

It might be a short step from the more general subjective wellbeing culture to the holistic milieu, but a step it is. To read about reflexology is not the same as practising it with a reflexologist. But the fact that there *is* a step surely contributes to the appeal – and thus growth – of the holistic milieu. For by virtue of providing something 'more' than can be found elsewhere in subjective wellbeing culture, the milieu stands out from the crowd. What is on offer are 'inner solutions' for going further along the path to subjective wellbeing: activities which are specifically focused on the holistic nurturing of unique subjectivities; activities which provide the opportunity for sustained, intensive or focused practice; activities which enable participants to establish close relationships with practitioners who are experienced with the ways of spirituality. In short, the holistic milieu caters for those who want to go deeper in their exploration of what works in experience.

Evidence

Charting what would appear to be the obvious path for people to follow to enter the holistic milieu is one thing. Demonstrating that significant numbers have actually followed the path from the more general subjective wellbeing culture is another. We concentrate first on the evidence that many of those attracted to the milieu are looking for subjective wellbeing, whether or not they have been involved with subjective wellbeing culture. We then consider whether there is any evidence to show that prior contact with subjective wellbeing culture in particular has had a role to play.

Questionnaire research amongst those active in the holistic milieu in Kendal and environs shows the importance for these participants of the quest to improve the quality of subjective-life. Provided with a list of reasons for originally trying the activity in which they had been involved during the past seven days (or the most significant of these activities if they had participated in more than one), respondents were asked to rank them in order of importance. The percentages of those selecting our various options as their first choice are shown in Figure 4.1. (See www.kendalproject.org.uk for more detailed results regarding Question 3 of the holistic milieu questionnaire.)

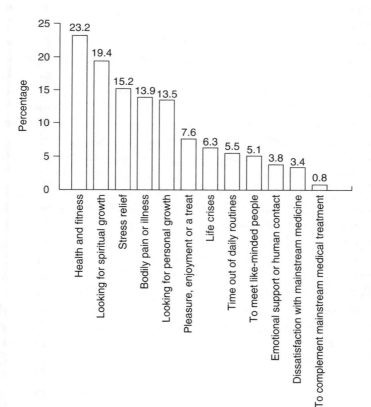

Figure 4.1   Reasons for involvement

Concentrating on the first five of the options, where we find most of the replies, 'health and fitness' and 'stress relief' are pretty clearly to do with subjective wellbeing culture. For in answer to another of the questions we asked, namely 'how would you describe your state of health these days?', approaching three quarters reply 'very good' or 'good', which suggests that large numbers are intent on further enhancing the quality of experienced health and fitness rather than curing or even preventing illness (cf. Fuller, 2001, p. 102). Regarding 'bodily pain or illness', few are seriously ill – in response to our question, 'How would you describe your state of health these days?', only 3 per cent answer 'poor', none reporting 'very poor'. (Respective figures for the general population are 6 and 2 per cent (Heald, 2000).) For many, what matters is dealing with relatively minor complaints (backaches being one of the most common) to obtain a sense of wellbeing, rather than the instrumental, raw necessity of staying alive. As for 'looking for spiritual growth' and 'looking for personal growth', spiritual growth could have more to do with the quest for 'truth' (for example) than with wellbeing *per se*; and personal growth could have more to do with, say, developing one's skills for the job market than with enhancing the quality of experience. However, the fact that so many of the activities of the milieu emphasize wellbeing (an emphasis communicated to those who might be interested in participating by way of advertising material and word of mouth) means that it is highly likely that most of those who prioritize spiritual or personal growth as their reason for having become involved know that 'growth' concerns subjective-life. Furthermore, as we saw in Chapter One, under 10 per cent say that spirituality is 'overcoming the ego', which is a strong indication that only a few are intent on liberating themselves from 'ego-attachments', including wellbeing desires.

Many of those attracted to the holistic milieu, it is apparent, are motivated by the search for subjective wellbeing: an interpretation of questionnaire evidence which is buttressed by the argument that it is very difficult to see why many should be attracted *unless* they were interested in improving the quality of their subjective-lives. Quite simply, given the importance of subjective wellbeing within the holistic milieu, it quite naturally tends to attract people with appropriate interests or concerns.

Thus far we have provided evidence that the holistic milieu has grown because it has attracted people who are looking for ways of improving the quality of their subjectivities.[9] We now have to consider the question: is there any evidence that prior contact with subjective wellbeing culture has played an important role? Although it is possible that some people who subscribe to subjective beliefs and values but have little or no acquaintance with the culture have been attracted, it is highly and increasingly likely that many people enter the milieu by way of prior participation in some of its widespread provisions and activities. For as the latter proliferate, it becomes increasingly difficult to avoid contact with subjective wellbeing culture, and unlikely that people with a subjectivized orientation would want to avoid contact. So those looking to improve their quality of subjective-life are likely to turn to subjective wellbeing culture, and in doing so they are more likely to become primed for involvement with the holistic milieu than those who are not engaged with the more general culture of wellbeing.

Looking at the socio-cultural characteristics of those who have become active within the milieu, interviews carried out during the Kendal Project show that the great majority of those who referred to their employment had been, or currently were, involved with professions having to do with wellbeing culture, and in which one could expect to find subjective-well-being values in evidence. Job descriptions include: 'special needs teacher', 'art teacher', 'college lecturer', 'psychiatric nurse', 'social worker in child abuse', 'adult education', 'primary school teacher', 'head teacher', 'nurse', 'care worker', 'working with abused children', 'educational therapist', 'lecturer in art and design', 'ecologist', 'environment agency officer', and 'religious education advisor'.[10] Many are (or have been) active in person-centred or expressive careers of this variety, it is reasonable to infer, because of the value they attach to improving the quality of life. Furthermore, interview material also provides evidence of downsizing. Although we cannot provide an exact figure, the picture which has emerged from the ethnography is of significant numbers within the milieu who have moved from reasonably well paid careers, which left them little time for themselves, to work, often of a part-time nature, which provides greater opportunities for the development of subjective-life (see below).

As for educational background, returns from the questionnaire distributed to the holistic milieu show that 57 per cent have a university or college degree, a percentage which is way above the national average of 20 per cent at the time (20 or 30 years ago) when most obtained their qualifications. And as Inglehart's (1997) survey research shows, the higher the level of educational attainment the greater the likelihood of a shift of emphasis from seeking value by way of achievement in the material world to seeking value by way of what subjective-life has to offer – and, we can add, thereby being likely to be involved with aspects of subjective wellbeing culture including the holistic milieu.[11]

Together with the key consideration that a significant number of those attracted to the holistic milieu have been, or are, active in wellbeing careers where they will have acquired considerable experience of what is involved in nurturing subjective-life, subjective wellbeing culture is predominantly populated by women. This suggests that women are more likely than men to encounter the messages, provisions and activities which serve to prime them for what the holistic milieu has to offer. The fact that the holistic milieu is predominantly populated by women also serves to indicate that subjective wellbeing culture has had a role to play in stimulating interest. (The role played by gender is explored in considerably greater depth in the next section.)

Thus the evidence to date strongly suggests that the subjective turn, as manifest in subjective wellbeing culture, explains much of the growth of the holistic milieu. And it is surely not a coincidence that the milieu has grown during exactly those decades which have also witnessed the development, indeed the fully-fledged establishment, of the subjective wellbeing cultural 'industry'. Holistic spirituality engages with this culture, and provides the opportunity for people to see if they can go deeper into what it is to *be* themselves, thus enhancing the quality of their lives.[12]

Revisiting the Subjectivization Thesis: The Growth of the Holistic Milieu and the Significance of Gender and Age

The gender puzzle

According to our questionnaire survey, 80 per cent of those active in the holistic milieu of Kendal and environs are female; 78 per cent of groups are led or facilitated by women; 80 per cent of one-to-one practitioners are women.[13] The conclusion is obvious: much of the growth of associational, holistic spiritualities of life is due to the fact that women have decided to participate. Why should this be the case?

We are immediately faced with a puzzle. We have been arguing that the subjective turn plays a key role in explaining the growth of the holistic milieu. Most generally, the subjective turn involves the turn to what Dick Houtman and Peter Mascini (2002) call 'moral individualism' – namely 'the granting of a moral primacy to individual liberty' (p. 459). The person serves as the locus of moral authority, with value being attached to staying true to oneself rather than succumbing to outside agency. However, as Houtman and Mascini also say, 'We know of no research demonstrating gender differences with respect to [moral] individualism' (p. 464).[14] Hence our puzzle – if indeed the gender ratio is 50:50 among subjectivized selves as gauged by moral autonomy, how are we to explain the fact that the ratio of the holistic milieu is 80:20 in favour of women?

Revisiting the subjectivization thesis

The answer must lie with the fact that the subjective turn involves not one but two modes of moral individualism or autonomous selfhood. One is more characteristic of men, which means they are not likely to be attracted to the associational activities of subjective wellbeing culture in general or the holistic milieu in particular. The other largely involves women, which means they are much more likely to be attracted to these spheres. Though the subjective turn is so often discussed as a single and undifferentiated process, we must therefore revisit and refine it in the light of our empirial findings.

Most comprehensively, and by definition, the subjective turn is the turn to the autonomous self. It is a turn away from being told what or how to be yourself to *having the freedom to be yourself*. To be, or become, oneself obviously entails that one assumes – by way of culture and/or experience – that one *has* a self to be and become; you cannot be autonomous without having what Lionel Trilling (1974) refers to as the 'internal space' from which to act (p. 24). Since the autonomous self cannot be a life-as self, it must be based not on external obligation but on what one 'is' – one's own unique subjective-life. So one acts on the basis of an intuition that all is not well with a situation, or on the inner promptings of one's conscience, or the realization that a relationship is having a negative effect on one's sense of wellbeing, the sense one gets that another person is in distress, and so on.

But the direction that subjective-life may take as it extends out beyond its autonomous basis can vary. Our findings suggest that this variation can be thought of in terms of a spectrum between two poles. At one extreme lies what we will call *individuated subjectivism* and at the other *relational subjectivism*, with many intermediate positions in between. Every person who tries to live by the authority of subjective-life rather than, or together with, external guidance or dictation can be located somewhere along this spectrum.

The position of the individuated subjectivist is well described by Clifford Geertz (1984) when he writes of 'The Western conception of the person as a bounded, unique, more or less integrated motivational and cognitive universe, a dynamic center of awareness, emotion, judgement, and action organized into a distinctive whole and set contrastively both against other such wholes and against its social and natural background' (p. 126). At this end of the spectrum of the subjective turn, the 'voice of the unique' lies with the experience of the self operating as a (relatively) self-contained entity. Typically, subjective-life is catered for by going outside oneself to find external solutions, rather than by going deeper into one's inner life. The quality of subjective-life is enhanced by addressing the problem of not feeling successful enough, of not having enough pleasurable experiences, of not having achieved all one might achieve, and so on. Subjectivities are catered for by going out into the world to procure the commodities (a new house) or success (promotion) which serve desire, happiness or content-ment. (Bellah et al. (1985), in the footsteps of Durkheim, refer to this position as 'utilitarian individualism'.) The emphasis is on subjective-life developed by way of atomized (self-reliant, self-sufficient) agency, on the self as unique and distinct. Competition is likely to be a more important theme than the connections of personal relationships, and there are obvious links between this mode of selfhood, possessive individualism, and entre-preneurial capitalism.

At the other end of the spectrum the subjective turn takes a relational mode. The commitment to autonomous subjective-life and the cultivation of the unique remains, but with an emphasis on the relational and going deeper. Steven Lukes (1973) writes that 'The very idea of *self*-development logically implies that the development is autonomously pursued – though clearly its course can be *substantially assisted* by providing the appropriate conditions and encouragements' (p. 136; our emphasis). Although the point is often neglected in the literature on the subjective turn, as is indi-cated by the fact that the term 'expressive *individualism*' is often used in this connection (see, for example, Bellah et al., 1985), Lukes reminds us that other people can have an important role to play. One can, of course, seek to cultivate one's subjective-life by oneself. Hermits aside, though, it is surely the case that the cultivation of subjective-life best takes place in the context of personal encounters: 'talking things through' with a friend; visiting a therapist, counsellor or human resource specialist; reading biographies or autobiographies; viewing close relationships on TV; reflecting on one's relationship with one's children or parents; discussing bad or good personality qualities with pupils at primary school, and so on. And unlike individuated (let alone life-as) modes of subjective-life, relational subjectivism is associated with the tendency to *go deeper*: one finds out more about oneself by discussing one's anger with a close friend or by dealing with jealousy with a lover, for example. Finally, it must be emphasized that the relational mode of subjective-life selfhood need *not* imply a diminution of the unique, autonomy or moral individualism. Since no one person has the same relationships as another, the more variegated the relational life the more unique the 'me' becomes – with the 'voice of the unique' speaking accordingly. Recalling the words of Carson McCullers, cited at the end of the Introduction to this volume, relational subjectivity is all about 'the we of me' – developing one's own subjective-life, be/coming oneself, relating to one's life, *through* one's relationships. In this context interdependence goes together with independence.[15]

Previously in this volume we have tended to refer to what Charles Taylor (1991) calls 'the massive subjective turn of modern culture' (p. 26) in its most general sense, as having to do with the turn to autonomy and the subjective-life which is thereby entailed. Prompted by our research findings and the gender puzzle, we must now nuance this usage more precisely. Taylor completes the sentence above by speaking of the subjective turn as being towards 'a new form of inwardness, in which we come to think of ourselves as beings with inner depths' (p. 26). Without disagreeing, we note that the subjective turn *can* go all the way to such 'depths' (typically involving, we would argue, relational subjectivism), *or* remain at the level of a more individuated and externally orientated form of subjectivism (often dismissive of the deeper subjective turn). By broadening out our understanding of the turn in this way, we have therefore distinguished between two modes or aspects of autonomous personhood: individuated subjectivism, where the strong tendency is to be externally orientated, seeking indirect solutions (material, etc.) to cater for subjective-life, and relational subjectivism, where the tendency is towards concentrating more directly on the exploration of the intricacies of the inner life. And as we shall now see, this distinction enables us to tackle the gender puzzle.

Relationality

Given that both women and men are equally subjectivized in the general autonomous/moral individualism sense, we have to explain why women are more likely than men to be attracted to the holistic milieu and subjective wellbeing culture. So let us apply our distinction – between relational and individuated forms of subjective-life – to the puzzle of explaining why more women than men are attracted to subjective wellbeing culture and the holistic milieu. The key to solving the puzzle is that more women than men tend to emphasize relational subjective-life, and conversely that more men than women tend to emphasize the individuated or distinct variant. Accordingly, since subjective wellbeing culture and the holistic milieu is so relational, their provisions or activities attract subjectively orientated women (in particular) who seek to develop their subjective-lives through associational encounters. And since much of subjective wellbeing culture and the holistic milieu *in toto* emphasize 'inner' relationality, their provisions or activities are considerably less likely to appeal to those men (in particular) who seek to develop their subjective-lives by going out into the world to achieve and compete whilst retaining their own boundaries and sense of being in control. Hence the high percentage of women in the milieu.

In order to substantiate these points in greater detail, the first thing to re-emphasize is the strongly relational nature of the holistic milieu. In answer to the (single response) question 'Which of the following is the best description of your core beliefs about spirituality?', 21 per cent of respondents to the holistic milieu questionnaire used in the Kendal Project answered 'Spirituality is being a decent and caring person'; 20 per cent 'Spirituality is love'; and 10 per cent 'Spirituality is healing oneself and others'. In other words, over half associate spirituality with relationality. What is more, in response to another question ('Do you believe in any of the following?'), 82 per cent expressed belief in 'some sort of spirit or life force that pervades all that lives'. Recalling Chapter One, it is also clear that practitioners in the holistic milieu of Kendal and environs – and no doubt elsewhere – are very much concerned with developing close, *reciprocal*, egalitarian, trusting, holistic relationships with their participants. What matters is intimate disclosure, the encounters of what Giddens (1992) calls the 'pure relationship'. What matters is growing oneself through the experiences of associational activities. Whether it be practitioners, one-to-one or group participants, the important thing is to share, express, care and to go beyond the 'the distinct' as that is marked out by life-as roles, rules and conventions. The spiritual dimension is (basically) understood as the dimension at which all life connects, and where the individual realizes her or his true nature in relationship with the 'whole'.[16]

Granted that the milieu is strongly relational, what is the evidence to support our argument that this is a key factor in explaining the predominance of women? More exactly, what is the evidence that more women than men seek to develop their subjective-lives through relationships – and so are more likely to turn to relational, holistic milieu activities? An important source of evidence is provided by subjective wellbeing culture. Many more women than men are active in this culture, with many encountering provisions, or participating in activities, of a relational kind. Of particular note, significantly more women than men are active in person-centred occupations where subjective wellbeing values are important – nursing, caring, primary school teaching and human resource development, for example. Research carried out by Thomas, Nicholl and Coleman (2001) on associational CAM activities shows that the female–male ratio is 60:40 in favour of women (with over 70 per cent of 'over the counter' sales being to women). (See also Wootton and Sparber, 2001.) Jackie Stacey (2000) reports that 67 per cent of those purchasing 'healing and self-improvement/awareness' literature are women (p. 117). Debra Gimlin, in her *Body Work. Beauty and Self-Image in American Culture* (2002) finds women to be preponderant, with (for instance) 90 per cent of both students and instructors of aerobics being female (p. 51). In their study of the beauty salon, Ursula Sharma and Paula Black (1999) find women – for there are virtually no men – to be adopting an increasingly 'therapeutic' dimension, encounters within the salon providing the opportunity for discussing personal issues, especially relationships. Our own relatively informal research indicates that women outnumber men in fitness and health centres, and that very few men indeed are to be found in holistic spas. Likewise, content analysis indicates that there are vastly more articles in magazines and newspapers dwelling on subjective wellbeing for women than on subjective wellbeing for men. More generally, Paul Ray and Sherry Anderson (2000) report that there are twice as many women as men amongst the 24 million 'core cultural creatives' (people greatly concerned with quality of life issues) in the USA, with 91 per cent of core cultural creatives affirming that 'helping other people' is 'very or extremely important' and 89 per cent believing that 'every person has a unique gift to offer' (p. 15).

Plate 1   The main street of Kendal. Private collection.

Plate 2   The Kendal Project team: Benjamin Seel, Bronislaw Szerszynski, Linda Woodhead, Karin Tusting and Paul Heelas (with Abby Day, second to left). This photograph, taken in Dent (near Kendal), also illustrates the spiritual revolution in action: the team stand in front of a building that was once a chapel and is now part of a meditation centre. Private collection.

Plate 3   Imposing authority: the medieval parish church in Kendal – a congregation of humanity (Anglican). Private collection.

Plate 4   Informal relationality: inside Willow Creek Community Church, a 'seeker church' on the outskirts of Chicago – a flourishing congregation of experiential difference. Private collection.

Plate 5   Rainbow Cottage, a holistic centre on the outskirts of Kendal. Private collection.

Plate 6   Church attenders at the parish church in Kendal. Private collection.

The Westmorland Gazette, September 28, 2001

Alternative
spirituality
is growing
fast in
a South
Lakes
town...

SOOTHING:
Linda McGarvey
giving a client
an aromatherapy
massage at
Rainbow
Cottage,
Endmoor.
(C1H21026)

Plate 7   Holistic contact: practitioner Linda McGarvey of Rainbow Cottage with researcher Benjamin Seel. © *The Westmoreland Gazette*.

Plate 8   Life-as religion, clearly stated by an advert in the USA. Private collection.

A *Safe Place* is an informative on-going support group to help men and women grow and heal through the pain of sexual, emotional and relational struggles.

Book study along with periodic presentations by licensed Christian therapists provide an integrative teaching of psychological and Biblical truth pertaining to same sex issues, emphasizing growth in healthy relating patterns with oneself, others and God.

Small group interaction will also facilitate
healing and growth through gracious, supportive relationships.

Plate 9   'Psychological and Biblical truth': the discourse of a congregation of experiential difference. © Willow Creek Association.

WHAT ARE HOLISTIC THERAPIES ?

The holistic approach of natural therapies recognises that all our experiences, past and present, contribute to our current state of health.

This may include physical traumas, illnesses and accidents, and environmental factors as well as stress and unresolved emotional issues.

Such experiences sometimes get 'locked up' into the body's tissues.

These patterns of stored traumas and stresses can restrict the body's normal easy functioning and may give rise to problems over the years.

The effect may be physical, such as pain, migraine or digestive disorders, or emotional such as anxiety and depression.

The right holistic therapy for you can help restore your well-being.

Plate 10   The unique, the holistic, and wellbeing: craniosacral therapy, Kendal. © Adam Rubinstein R.C.S.T., Kendal.

Plate 12 Soft capitalism at work ©The Guardian, image ©Getty Images. Reprinted with permission.

Plate 11 Yoga in the mainstream of life. © Kendal Leisure Centre.

Plate 13   Sanctified capitalism: the Congregational church opposite the main entrance to what was once the world's largest textile mill, Saltaire, near Bradford. Private collection.

Plate 14   A holistic shop overlooking the mill at Saltaire – a mill which has evolved into an upmarket wellbeing zone. Private collection.

Plate 15 Objective wellbeing culture in action. © Spar (UK) Ltd.

Plate 16 Subjective wellbeing culture in action: an advert from Tetley which appeared in *The Guardian Weekend*, 17 October 2002. © Tetley (GB) Ltd.

With Adrian Moorhouse – world champion swimmer

St Mary's Aylesbury
for Church and Community

Body & Soul

Touching the Spirit of Well being

Saturday, 22 May 2004
11am – 3pm

at St Mary's Church, Aylesbury

An opportunity to experience energy for
Well being and health
Demonstrations of Tai Chi, and Circle Dance
Sign up: enrolling for new classes

Experience meditation relaxation, head and shoulders
massage and aromatherapy

Exhibitions and display of the life of St Mary's
Fairly traded coffee, tea and snacks.

Further details: phone Tim Higgins 424276 or 437641

Plate 17 The two worlds meet: spiritual wellbeing enters the congregational domain in a parish in the south of England. © Tim Higgins.

Cutting a long story short, what we find is that whether we look at person-centred occupations, CAM, those health and fitness activities which involve self-expression (as provided by Fitness First, for example), or the literature which encourages self-development through 'relational' activities like gardening, cooking or interior design, those active in subjective well-being culture are by no means unfamiliar with 'the we of me'. And since those attaching importance to the relational path to experiential wellbeing are predominantly women, it makes perfect sense that those who turn to the associational activities of the holistic milieu are also predominantly women. Conversely, it makes equal sense to conclude that an important reason why significantly fewer men are active in the milieu is that fewer are accustomed to, or value, the intimate, expressive, relational path to subjective wellbeing – indeed, that many are threatened by what an interconnected 'we' might do to the 'me' as a (relatively) protected, guarded, bounded, private entity. In the words of Calvin Mercer and Thomas Durham (1999), 'people with a masculine orientation are too agentic, self-differentiating, and analytical to become engulfed in the mystical experience' (p. 180).[17]

Having established that more women than men are involved with subjective wellbeing culture, and so are more likely to come across, and be attracted by, holistic milieu activities, we might leave it at that. But that still leaves open the fascinating question of *why* this should be: why women should be more likely to fall at the relational end of the spectrum of subjectivism than the individuated end, and hence be more attracted to subjective wellbeing culture, and the holistic milieu, in greater numbers than men (thus contributing substantially to the growth of the milieu). Without attempting to give anything like a full response to this question, we can identify some key considerations.

Most have to do with deeply entrenched cultural values and divisions of labour. On the basis of what must surely be the most comprehensive review of relevant large-scale surveys to date, Geert Hofstede (2001) concludes that 'almost universally women attach more importance to social goals such as relationships, helping others, and the physical environment, and men attach more importance to ego goals such as career and money' (p. 279). On the basis of their survey carried out in the USA, Joseph Veroff et al. (1981) find that 'women orient their behavior and self-definition toward other people more than men do' (p. 128), and note that 'more men than women give positive differentiations of the self from other people' (p. 125) and that women 'hold more internal aspirations for identity' (p. 127); and Francesca Cancian (1987) writes of the 'opposition of masculine freedom to develop oneself vs. feminine attachment to others' (p. 6), continuing, 'women are expected to be responsible for close relationships, and men to be independent and preoccupied with work' (pp. 10-11). Citing Carol Gilligan's (1982) research on the psychological development of men and women, she agrees that from the male cultural perspective, 'development itself comes to be identified with separation, and attachments appear to be developmental impediments', and that 'Women emphasize attachment in their personal development' (p. 5).[18]

Subjective wellbeing culture aside, women continue to have prime responsibility for the subjective wellbeing of others, whether close family and friends or those with whom they interact in voluntary or paid work. As noted above, they still outnumber men in the 'caring' professions. Even when care for subjective wellbeing is not part of the 'job description', women may still find themselves taking responsibility for this, as Rosemary Pringle (1989) finds in the case of secretaries, Lisa Adkins (1995) for women in the tourist industry, Arlie Hochschild (1983) for air hostesses, and Margaretha Järvinen (1993) for women in the sex industry. In the home women continue to have more responsibility for childcare than men, whether they are full-time mothers or working mothers. Julia Brannen and Peter Moss's (1991) study of 250 dual-earner households after the birth of a first child finds that it is women rather than men who become the 'managers' of the new lifestyle and take prime responsibility for childcare. Similarly, Hochschild's (1989) study of dual-earner parents in the USA found that domestic work was shared in only 18 per cent of households, and that 'most women still did most of the work' (p. 20). Women also take more responsibility for the subjective wellbeing of their spouse and other close kin. Husbands aside, Christine Delphy and Diana Leonard (1992) find that more than 1 in 10 adult women in Britain have someone other than a child who 'depends on them for some sort of care', and that the number rises for women over 40 (pp. 228-36). Micaela di Leonardo (1987) explores how women also take responsibility for maintaining kin relationships between households by way of 'the conception, maintenance and ritual celebration of ties, including visits, letters, telephone calls, presents and cards to kin; the organisation of holiday gatherings; the creation of quasi-kin relationships... the mental reflection on all these activities' (pp. 442-3). Robert Putnam (2000) supplies quantitative evidence to support these observations, adding that 'Although American boys and girls in the 1990s used computers almost equally, boys were more likely to use them to play games; girls more to email friends' (p. 95).

It is not simply that women find themselves with primary responsibility for the wellbeing of those close to them, but that they tend to take responsibility for care of the *whole* person – body, mind and sometimes spirit. In some workplaces, this is becoming more formalized and recognized, as in schools and hospitals (see Chapter Three pp. 71–2), but in general women's primary responsibility of care for mind and body is culturally expected, even though it is given little cultural validation (Hochschild, 2003). As Dorothy Smith (1974) puts it in her famous essay on why male academics are more able than women to cultivate 'disembodied reason', men characteristically spend far less time caring for 'the particularities of persons in their full organic imme-diacy' (p. 66). Women are more likely to spend time looking after the bodies of children and other dependents, cooking in order to nourish bodies, and cleaning, purchasing and sprucing in order to turn 'houses into homes' (Delphy and Leonard, 1992). Where mind and spirit are concerned, women also undertake a majority of what Hochschild (1983) calls the 'emotional labour' required to maintain subjective wellbeing, whether in comforting children, supporting and chatting with friends, or flattering men and making them feel (sexually) good about themselves. Sally Cline and Dale Spender (1988) find that even in conversation women spend more time 'feeding' the interchange, especially when they are talking to men.

Given that more women than men are concerned with the *personal* sub-jective wellbeing of others in their everyday lives, it is not surprising to find that they are more likely to enter subjective wellbeing culture and/or the holistic milieu. Quite simply, subjective wellbeing culture caters for those who already value being caring and expressive, being a person through reciprocal relationships, who appreciate the value of improving the quality of subjective-life – rather than concentrating on improving the quality of life by way of autonomous, individuated and competitive agency in the world.

Going deeper

Thus far our exploration of the 'gender puzzle' has worked from the most specific (the holistic milieu), through subjective wellbeing culture, to the most general (the culture at large). It is time to reverse the order, to trace paths from the most general into the milieu.

Consider a young woman leaving school to start a career in a person-centred job like nursing. Even if she is no longer motivated by Christian teachings about women's 'calling' to care for others (as many nurses once were), she is likely to be already embedded in personal relationships as a key source of significance – at home (perhaps helping her mother care for other members of the family), at school (Collins, 1997) and during leisure time, with all that that entails with regard to the value of going 'deeper' into friendships. Being primed in this way to value the care of others, she may view nursing as an attractive option because of the opportunities it offers for 'whole person care'. But as the years roll by, disillusionment may set in. The mission statement of the ward might be about 'wellbeing', but the reality of the ward is that there is simply not enough time to talk with patients about their subjective wellbeing concerns. The 'iron cage' of bureaucracy and targets dominates life. So what can be done to 'go deeper and become more authentic'? Looking for more opportunity to improve quality of life, looking for greater recognition of what she has to contribute, looking for a more congenial space to care for her own subjective wellbeing as well as that of others, the nurse begins to engage with holistic milieu activities on a one-evening-a week basis. Her intention may be to explore ways of enhancing her contribution to the workplace and alleviate the more life-as, iron cage, aspects of her working environment. Our nurse might not go any further. Or she might join the ranks of those seeking to become a holistic milieu practitioner. (We estimate that about a sixth of those active in the holistic milieu of Kendal and environs aim to join the sixth who are already practitioners.) After some time as a 'learning' participant, she decides to go part-time in nursing, or perhaps give it up altogether, in order to escape from the restrictive life by setting up an outlet offering some form of body-mind-spirituality provision in the holistic milieu.

Evidence from the Kendal Project, particularly interviews which provided life-histories, suggest that our nurse is far from unusual. A related pathway into the holistic milieu may be from other forms of work, in other professions besides the caring professions, which have been found to ride rough-shod over wellbeing issues (care of self and others). Alternatively, given the responsibility for holistic care that women often assume in the home setting, they may enter the holistic milieu by a domestic route. Whatever route they take, it is likely that those who enter subjective wellbeing culture and the holistic milieu will be seeking not only to continue or deepen a responsibility of care for others, but also to devote more attention to their own wellbeing. Women who have been devoted to 'giving out' for many years (caring for the family, caring for the home) may feel that their own subjective wellbeing is restricted, by duties or obligations, or neglected, perhaps by an individuated husband or by thoughtless teenagers. (Interestingly, the first usage recorded by the *Oxford English Dictionary* runs, 'Man did but from the well-being of this life from woman take', dated 1613.) They may feel that the time has come to balance care for others with care for self, and to seek greater 'harmony' in their lives. They have forgotten, or not been able, to care for their own wellbeing. The time comes when giving out needs to be complemented by 'taking in'. Women – most especially those who are not dominated by life-as roles and who thus appreciate what subjective-life relationality can offer – accordingly turn to where support can be found.

According to this account, many of the women who turn to holistic milieu activities are primarily concerned with caring for their own subjective wellbeing (of body, mind and spirit). The value of caring for others is by no means absent in the milieu, practitioners in particular attaching great importance to this. But a considerable amount of evidence from Kendal and elsewhere suggests that care for the self is at least as important. What matters, in this regard, is engaging with activities which enable one to address the problem of the 'drained-out' self – by being cared for, touched and listened to; by exploring ways of cultivating a sense of being recognized, valued, affirmed or esteemed; by cultivating a sense of being what one has to offer as a unique person.[19]

As for the evidence, the reader will recall from Chapter One that the characteristic language of the milieu of Kendal and environs makes frequent reference to the attention paid to 'your true nature', 'the essence of the person' and the 'deep inner self'. The theme of 'integration' and 'centring' is also encountered, the implication being that lives dispersed by way of looking after a diverse array of concerns can achieve a better 'balance' and 'harmony' of responsibilities and be re-integrated. Likewise, there is a strong emphasis on what is offered by way of easing stress, fatigue, low energy levels and 'blocked' energies. As we saw earlier in this chapter, 'health and fitness' is the single most important reason given for current participation in the activities of the holistic milieu, with 'stress relief' being third. The significance of bodily issues as a reason for being active in the holistic milieu should not be underestimated (see the 'Age' subsection, below, for further discussion), though it is also important to note that in a holistic context it is not apt to completely separate bodily concerns from other dimensions of health and wellbeing. In her research amongst those active in holistic wellbeing in Lancaster (20 miles to the south of Kendal), Eeva Sointu (2004) argues that what women experience above all in the holistic milieu is 'recognition', with body, mind and spirit concerns being taken more seriously than in other spheres of their life. These are issues of personal concern that may not be taken seriously by a husband, that can perhaps not be voiced to colleagues, which might be dismissed as trivial or untreatable by a GP, but which can be heard and recognized by a (normally female) practitioner or fellow-participant. In the process one's sense of oneself grows, as does one's self-esteem and ability to face, deal with, understand and 'manage' one's subjectivities.

Whether the emphasis lies with relationships, as with patients in a hospital, one's spouse or one's friends, or issues more specifically focused on one's personal subjective wellbeing, as with feeling in tune with oneself, or both in tandem, the paths to the holistic milieu which we have been dwelling on have one thing in common: relationality. In answer to the (open-ended) question of the holistic milieu questionnaire, 'What would you say are the three most important problems facing you, personally, these days?', by far the most recurrent topic concerns relationships. It is not just that self issues are being dealt with in a relational context, they are also being placed in a framework that seeks to restore healthy relation between body, mind and spirit, and between self and others. Help is offered in dealing with relationships which are currently hindering the experiencing of oneself as complete and integrated – relationships that are too restrictive or demanding to allow one to creatively develop one's unique gifts and the full range of what one has to offer by way of oneself. Linda McGarvey speaks for many in the holistic milieu of Kendal and environs when she refers to people seeking 'the journey towards wholeness'; 'people are finding out who they really are, and not who they've been taught to be or what their life experiences have taught them'; participants are finding out 'fully who we can be'; people want 'to connect with who they are and the potential of who they are'. In short, the mode of *relational autonomous subjectivism* cultivated in the holistic milieu enable many participants to explore more deeply what they already know to be the case – that they have more to offer, both with regard to themselves and to others – than is allowed expression in everyday, relational and other, spheres of life.[20]

Drawing our exploration of the role played by gender to a close, there are two remaining topics to address. First, although the holistic milieu attracts women seeking greater depth in their lives and relationships, Kendal Project findings do not support the view that those attracted are especially unhappy with their everyday lives nor suffering from significant forms of 'deprivation'. Questionnaire results show that almost 80 per cent rate their satisfaction with their home life between 8 and 10, where 10 is most satisfied, the mean of 8.1 comparing with the national mean of 7.9 (Heald, 2000); that 71 per cent say their health is 'very good' or 'good' compared with the national figure of 70 per cent (Heald, 2000); that around 80 per cent of those in employment rate their level of work satisfaction at 6 to 10 on the scale of work satisfaction (10 being most satisfied); and that 51 per cent are married – very close to Heald's (2000) figure of 54 per cent for Britain. (See also note 9, p. 167.) The conclusion to be drawn is that the holistic milieu appeals to those who are sufficiently satisfied with their lives to believe that they are worth improving, but sufficiently dissatisfied to believe such improvement is desirable. It takes both humility ('my life is not as good as it could be') and confidence ('I have the potential to be a better person/I deserve a better life') to enter.

The second topic involves looking at the other side of the coin, namely why men only comprise some 20 per cent of the milieu in Kendal and environs, and around the same percentage elsewhere. As we have already suggested, men with a subjective-life bent are more likely to be individuated than women, and thus might well be dismissive of the intimate, self-disclosing relationality of the majority of holistic milieu activities. The ideals of masculinity to which many men aspire involve maintaining relatively clear boundaries between self and others, and going out in the world to exercise their autonomy and competitive spirit to achieve subjective wellbeing. As one holistic practitioner told us with a smile, 'Men do like to be in charge, and this is something they can't be in charge of!' As one of our male postgraduates commented, 'Why should men enter the milieu when there's nothing tangible to achieve?'. It is not that men do not desire subjective wellbeing, but they may find it difficult to acknowledge their need and desire, and even more difficult to explicitly ask for or offer help in the cultivation of subjective wellbeing (just as men are somewhat more reluctant to visit the doctor than are women). As holistic milieu practitioner Tessa Logan put it, 'I'm sorry to say it, but women are more open than men. They talk about intimate things more. Men are more guarded and protective of their views. They tend to talk more about things like sport'. Furthermore, the masculine ideal of autonomy and self-sufficiency may explain why it is relatively common to hear men (and sometimes women) dismissing subjective wellbeing culture and the holistic milieu as 'narcissistic', 'pampering', and 'touchy-feely'. Equally, the attachment of many men to the ideal of 'rational' autonomy may be the cause of another common cluster of negative comments about the 'irrational', 'unscientific', 'unprofessional', 'not qualified', 'flaky', 'mumbo-jumbo', 'intangible' nature of the holistic milieu.

Age

Not only is the gender profile of the holistic milieu of Kendal and environs significantly different from the general population, so too is the age profile. Seventy three per cent of all those active in the holistic milieu of Kendal and environs are aged 45 and over, with 55 per cent of all participants aged between 40 and 59 – in Kendal as a whole, only 12 per cent fall into the latter age range. Forty five per cent of all those active in the milieu are women aged between 40 and 60, with the equivalent figure for males being just 10 per cent.[21] Furthermore, the majority of participants have not been involved prior to mid-life. This is indicated by the fact that under 15 per cent of respondents to the holistic milieu questionnaire are in their twenties and thirties; it is even more strongly indicated by the fact that around 40 per cent of practitioners (who are much more likely to have been involved in the milieu for longer periods than most participants) have only been practising for up to four years. In addition, given the growth of the milieu during the 1990s (when it tripled in size), and given the age profile, it stands to reason that many must have entered during mid-life. So how are we to explain the 'mid-life factor' – why the majority of participants only enter the holistic milieu in mid-life?

Although we do not have as much systematic evidence as we would like, it is clear that a considerable numbers of those active in the milieu – most obviously practitioners (around one sixth of participants) and those clients and group members who are most involved (around another sixth) in that many of them are intending to become practitioners in the future – have downsized or downshifted.[22] Accordingly, let us see if the literature on downshifting can shed light on the mid-life issue.

According to Clive Hamilton's (2003) research, '25 per cent of British adults aged 30-59 have downshifted over the last ten years', the average reduction in income being 40 per cent (pp. vii, viii). ('Downshifters' are defined as those who agree with the question, 'In the last ten years have you voluntarily made a long-term change in your lifestyle, other than planned retirement, which has resulted in you earning less money?' (p. vii)).

Figures are much the same for the USA. What is significant with regard to our age puzzle is that the primary reason given for downshifting by people in their thirties and forties is that they want to spend 'more time with family' – 37.5 per cent of this age range give this answer, compared with just 19 per cent of those in their fifties (p. 20). What people in their fifties are much more likely to say (25 per cent, this making this the second most important reason for downshifting overall) is that they are seeking a 'healthier lifestyle'. Only 9 per cent of those in their thirties and forties give this response (p. 20)

The picture which emerges is of younger adults prioritizing relationality and the fulfilment of family life (and perhaps friendship networks as well), and of older adults prioritizing health. This is not so surprising, given that the younger are much more likely to be raising families, whilst the children of older people have very probably left home (in Kendal and environs, for example, only 19 per cent of respondents to the holistic milieu question-naire report they have children aged under 18 living in their household, compared with the national figure of 35 per cent (Heald, 2000)). And of course, the older one becomes, the more health concerns are likely to loom large.

Applying this to explain the 'mid-life factor', the likelihood is that younger parents (whether single or married) will be too involved with the relationalities of family life, and/or friendship networks that may have per-sisted from their student days, to feel that they would benefit from explor-ing their subjective-lives further by entering the holistic milieu. In addition, and bearing in mind the numbers of women in their twenties, thirties and forties who now also go out to work, it is also highly likely that few women feel that they have the time to add another sphere of activities to their constant round of work and home. (See Hochschild, 1997, on the 'time bind'; and Hochschild, 2003, p. 2 on the point that in the USA in 2000 close to 70 per cent of married women worked for pay, compared to 40 per cent in 1950 and less than a fifth in 1900.) However, as the family dimin-ishes in size, with teenagers going off to college or university or leaving home to get a job elsewhere, relational life at home diminishes as a source of significance. And for many parents who, these days, are tending to have children later in life than in the past, this may coincide with entering their later forties and fifties. All of which conspires to make the motivation to look beyond the home to find ways of improving the quality of relational subjective-life much stronger. For women sympathetic to relational subject-ive-life values, the holistic milieu beckons. With more time and freedom to look beyond the home, and accumulated experiences on which to draw and reflect, they may enter into holistic activities in order to improve the quality of their lives and relationships. More specifically, some might well be seeking to reactivate the relationality which they nostalgically recall from the times at college or university, before they got swamped by family and work.

As we saw earlier in this chapter, Kendalians involved with the holistic milieu refer to 'health and fitness' concerns as their primary reason for originally embarking on the activities with which they are currently involved. A separate (open-ended) question enquiring about the main problems facing them also shows that health and fitness are important concerns. This very much matches Hamilton's (2003) finding that health is prioritized by those who downsize and who are aged between 50 and 60. Responses to our open question make it very clear that 'health' rather than 'illness' is the operative word in this context. (As noted above, most report 'very good' or 'good' health.) Given their age, it is not surprising that these 'later mid-lifers' should be more aware of 'ageing' than younger people, and more concerned to do something about it. Whilst specific ailments like fatigue, a bad back, headaches and so on may prompt people to enter the milieu, care for the 'whole person' is likely to become a more pressing concern – not least because the 'spirit' of the milieu encourages participants to think and act in a more holistic way. And the cultivation of the whole person, with the energy flowing through the self, should mean that they are in the best possible shape to stay 'young' longer – to weather the storms which inevitably lie ahead.

Further research is required in order to probe deeper into the 'mid-life factor'. Interviews carried out during the Kendal Project suggest further hypotheses that could be tested. It could be argued, for example, that it takes time to accumulate the life-experiences which may take one to the holistic milieu (the divorce, the sense of fragmentation which can arise from running a home and going out to work, the 'unresolved' issues about relationships, the emerging sense of 'who I am') which come to the fore as one gets older and has more time (with the teenagers having left home, etc.) to reflect on how to 'work things out'. Or that it is largely in the second half of life that people become aware of the limits of life, of 'time running out', of the importance of making the most of what is left ('life is not a dress rehearsal'). As an informant from nearby Lancaster says, 'People who find themselves in holistic activities – they've probably had a journey to get to that point... and they've probably developed some self-awareness'. For women in particular, it may take until mid-life to rid themselves of the widespread cultural belief that their happiness comes from 'outside' (by way of the 'knight in shining armour', the romance, the perfect family, the beautiful house) and to realize that they need to take responsibility for their own happiness (Langford, 1999). It could also be argued that it takes time to become disillusioned by what various forms of 'life-as' have to offer, including mainstream professions (not least caring wellbeing professions), and to reach the point where one is no longer willing to put up with bureaucratic restrictions ('I finally realized that I couldn't influence the system'). Then again it could be argued that for many women who juggle the demands of work and family it is not until mid-life that they have the opportunity (the money, and the time, particularly if they have taken early retirement,[23] to explore aspects of their personal lives which have not been catered for by work and home life – perhaps self-esteem, perhaps a desire to reactivate the relationality of their youth, perhaps simply a desire to live a 'richer' life.[24]

Finally, what of people who have yet to reach 30 years of age? As Inglehart's (1997) survey findings indicate, younger people are more likely to value subjective-life than older people (and see Houtman and Mascini, 2002, p. 465). Research from a more ethnographic point of view supports the judgement that many younger people are deeply involved in relational subjective-life and value it highly (see, for example, Collins, 1997 on schools, Lynch, 2002 on clubbing). Given this orientation, one might expect young people to find the basic values of the holistic milieu congenial, and to be more involved with activities than we found to be the case in Kendal and environs (where only just over 1 per cent of participants are aged between 20 and 30). This is another issue which requires further research. What we can hypothesize is that a great many pre-30s (not just in Kendal, of course, but more generally) have ample relationality by way of the mobile phone, the love affairs, the extensive friendship networks, the clubs and bars, the personalized work groups. Subjective-life is rich and full in such regards, which means there is little if any need for the holistic milieu to serve as a source of relational significance. Health is likely to be as good as it is ever going to be. In addition, very long working hours (typical, for example, of work in finance, media or advertising industries), and the desire to keep up with all the friends and forge intimate relationships, leaves very little time to become involved with holistic activities. And finally, the limits of 'life' have not yet made themselves felt. (See Heelas and Seel, 2003 for further discussion.)

The Decline of Congregational Activities

The argument in general

Turning now to the congregational domain, our task is to show that the same dynamic of subjectivization that can help explain the growth of the holistic milieu can also shed light on the decline of congregational activities.

As we have seen in Chapter One, when we move from the holistic milieu to the congregational domain we move into a very different world: a world of life-as religion rather than subjective-life spirituality; of praising God rather than delving into the self; of 'doing your duty' rather than 'doing your own thing'. Such religion is likely to hold far more appeal for those who resist the subjective turn than for those who go along with it. It speaks their language, meets their expectations, and reinforces their values. It offers shape, order and meaning to life by way of clear and highly direct-ive teachings. It helps people go beyond what they would otherwise be by way of clearly defined, externally laid-down roles and duties that are not only socially approved but divinely sanctioned. By way of preaching, teach-ing and ritual, life-as religion offers assistance in fulfilling roles more effect-ively and indwelling them more completely – becoming, for example, a better mother, a more devoted disciple, a more Godly father, a more obedient child, a Christian more closely conformed to Christ, or more selflessly devoted to the task of serving humankind.

Life-as religion also appeals in terms of what it can deliver in terms of the wider contexts of life. At the level of the family, for example, it offers stability and security through conformity to externally laid down rules and roles, sometimes of a hierarchical nature (as when biblical teaching insists that wives should obey their husbands, and children their parents). Within congregational life it can sanctify hierarchies of leadership and control, as well as supporting the roles of those responsible for more 'mundane' ser-vices of care and maintenance (running the Sunday School, cleaning the church). And within civil and national life, life-as religion promises to re-inforce or reintroduce clearer roles, responsibilities and regulations (keep-ing Sunday special, supporting the nuclear family, upholding respect for those in authority, sanctifying 'the American way of life' and so on).

So long as these tasks are widely approved of, life-as religion is likely to flourish. In the 1950s, for example, following the trauma of world war and faced by the fear of cold war, a conservative mood took hold in the West which sought security in the roles and values of the traditional home, community, bureaucracy and workplace. Church attendance grew. Within a single generation, however, the mood changed again, as significant numbers of the baby boom generation reacted against the values of their parents. As subjective values moved from the counter-culture to mainstream culture in the decades that followed the 'revolution' of the sixties, so approval of life-as values and the institutions that upheld them also waned. In the process, hierarchically structured forms of voluntary association that had been popular until the 1960s suffered a massive decline in active membership (Hall, 1999). Political parties, working men's clubs, traditional women's organizations like the Women's Institute or the Mothers' Union and so on simply lost their appeal for generations that wished to live their lives in their own unique ways rather than slotting into pre-existing roles and offices (the most important of which were often reserved for men).

Why should the churches be immune? Since there is no good reason to think they have been, our argument in what follows is that the very same process that helps explain these other social changes also helps explain the decline of Christian congregations. In a nutshell, our argument is that churches and chapels have suffered because many people are simply no longer willing to submit to the roles, duties, rituals, traditions, offices and expectations which these institutions impose. In support of this argument, we begin by marshalling evidence which indicates that the congregational domain continues to be populated by those who favour life-as, and has failed to widen its appeal to those more influenced by the subjective turn. We go on to show that it is no coincidence that the decline of the congregational domain has coincided exactly with the period during which the subjective turn has been gathering cultural momentum – and in which other forms of life-as voluntary association have also been declining. And we look in some detail at the explanations for leaving which are offered by those who have turned their backs on the congregational domain.

Without dismissing the importance of other causes of congregational decline, our argument is thus that subjectivization is a, if not *the*, major cause of such secularization in the post-war period. We show that the subjectivization thesis can help explain secularization as well as sacralization, and we conclude by indicating how it can also help explain the varying fortunes of different types of congregation.

The picture today

We have shown that the growth of the holistic milieu can be explained in terms of its success in attracting subjectivized selves. To show that the opposite is true for the congregational domain, we need to show that it has failed to attract this growing constituency. Above all, we need to show this by demonstrating that those who remain active within the domain are predominantly of a life-as disposition, far more likely to display support for higher authority than the authority of the unique inner life.

In Chapter One we established that the cultural expressions of the congregational domain of Kendal (preaching, worship and so on) display a characteristic commitment to the higher authority of a common good. Now we need to ask whether this commitment is shared by the majority of congregational members. Our interviews suggest that it is. With the exception of some members of congregations of experiential humanity, most congregational members speak of the good life in terms of faithfulness, following, fitting in, being respectful, doing one's duty, serving others, and remaining obedient to God, scripture and the church. The following comments from Kendal are typical of many others we might cite: 'I think what we wanted [for our children] was a basic grounding in the principles of right and wrong, for starters, but that linked to a Christian sense of right and wrong. The idea being that it would give them a reference point . . . ' (a couple from the Roman Catholic church). 'Bending your heart and your mind totally to God, giving him your free will and bending your will to his, is the only true offering that you can give' (another couple from the same church). 'If this is what we believe that God says, we can't compromise that . . . we're not going to adapt things to suit what we think . . . You're not making God in your image. We live in a world that doesn't have absolutes, you know. Generation X it is, you know' (an elder from Parr Street Evangelical Church). 'I am constantly trying to make Jesus Lord of my life, which means doing what he wants rather than what I want!' (female member of New Life Community Church). 'I think I would say that I go to church because I've been brought up to it, and I'm used to it . . . the sad thing is that people now feel so like a fish out of water coming to church . . . Now [turning to the interviewer], what about your religion . . . ?' (female member of Holy Trinity Anglican church).

Questionnaire research in the congregational domain confirmed this picture. When asked, for example, 'What is the highest authority in your life?' 91 per cent of respondents replied 'God', 'the church' or 'scripture', whilst just 7 per cent replied 'Your own reason or judgement' and 2 per cent 'Your intuition or feelings'. Similarly, when asked 'What is most important to you?' 70 per cent replied 'Serving God' or 'Deepening my relationship with Christ', 15 per cent 'Loving fellow humans', with just 9 per cent saying 'Spiritual growth' and 6 per cent 'Finding happiness in my life'. (Such responses contrast starkly with the more 'subjectivized' responses given by those within the holistic milieu – see Chapter One.)

What we discovered in Kendal by way of in-depth and largely qualitative research is confirmed at the opposite end of the methodological and geographical scale by national and international surveys of religion and values. In his extensive surveys of value commitments, for example, Shalom Schwartz finds evidence of a strong correlation between life-as values and life-as religion. Schwartz and Huismans' (1995) study of religious believers and attenders from five different countries uncovers their consistently strong orientation to values of 'traditionalism' (submission of self to transcendent authorities and past ideas) and 'conformity' (subordination toward persons with whom one is in current interaction). The authors conclude that 'the overall pattern of consistent religiosity-value correlations suggests that valuing certainty, self-restraint, and submission to superior external verities inclines people to become more religious' (p. 105). (See also Farias, forthcoming, on the life-as profile of his sample of Catholics in England (p. 11)).

Schwartz's discovery of a strong correlation between 'conformist' values and religion is confirmed by Ronald Inglehart's analyses of successive rounds of the World Values and European Values Surveys. Inglehart finds that materialists are significantly more likely to attend church and adhere to (life-as) religious norms than post-materialists. For example, a survey of six European nations in 1970 showed that 38 per cent of materialists 'attend at least weekly', compared to 11 per cent of post-materialists (Inglehart, 1977, p. 89). Analysis of a larger range of surveys of both European and World values administered between 1980 and 1986 leads Inglehart (1990) to the conclusion that 'in every country studied, Materialists are substantially more likely than Postmaterialists to adhere to traditional Judaeo-Christian norms' (p. 185).[25]

Such findings are further supported by studies of the congregational domain in the USA which probe the nature of affiliation and disaffiliation. Extensive research by Dean Hoge (1974, 1979), David Roozen (1977 research cited in Hoge and Roozen, 1979, pp. 59-61), and Hoge and Roozen (1979) uncovers a strong and continuing correlation between conservative, life-as value commitments and church affiliation during the 1950s, 1960s and 1970s. See also Hoge, Johnson and Luidens (1994) on 'a generalized lack of interest' in mainstream religion by 'boomers' (p. 176). Jackson Carroll and Wade Clark Roof's (2002) study of generational diversity in contemporary congregational cultures finds that 'the churched population is more conventional and traditional-minded than the unchurched across all three generations [i.e. pre-boomers, boomers and post-boomers]' (p. 81). Phillip Hammond (1992) discovers that those low on his 'personal autonomy index' are much more likely to be involved with congregational religion than those who are high (pp. 68-9). In addition, research amongst returnees to the congregational domain finds that the reasons they give for returning have far more to do with the attraction of life-as than of more subjectivized values. Thus Hoge, McGuire and Stratman (1981) find that only 18 per cent of Catholic returnees in the USA come back 'in search of an answer to spiritual needs', whilst 55 per cent return because they have children they want to be reared as Catholics, 8 per cent because they were influenced by a spouse or relative, and 14 per cent out of a feeling of guilt (p. 139).[26]

If the congregational domain is largely populated by those who are committed to living by way of conformity to higher authority rather than forging their own unique, experientially grounded life paths, the opposite side of the coin is of course that a strong commitment to subjective-life values is likely to correlate negatively with congregational involvement. Schwartz and Huismans (1995) note a negative correlation between religiosity and the cluster of 'Stimulation and Self-Direction values' that 'emphasize change and following one's independent judgements wherever they lead' (p. 92), also writing that 'valuing openness to change and free self-expression inclines people to become less religious' (p. 105). Summarizing data from 43 countries, Inglehart et al. (1998) find fewer post-materialists than materialists attending services (V147). Hammond (1992) finds that a high score on his 'Personal Autonomy Index' is 'strongly and negatively related to parish involvement' (p. 66). Drawing on survey data from the Netherlands, Dick Houtman and Peter Mascini (2002) find that there is a strong correlation between 'individualization' ('the granting of a moral primacy to individual liberty') and non-participation within the congregational domain. Since they also find that individualization may correlate not only with non-religiosity, but alternatively with involvement in subjective-life spirituality, they conclude that, 'a process of individualization has seriously undermined the moral basis of the Christian tradition... [and] caused the decline of the Christian churches since the 1960s and the rise of the New Age and nonreligiosity during the same period' (p. 468).

There is therefore considerable evidence to suggest that the congregational domain continues to be populated largely by those who are sympathetic to the values of life-as, and that it has failed to attract or retain those more sympathetic to the subjective turn. Since the numbers of subjectively orientated selves has been growing for several generations now, this failure of appeal is almost certainly a significant cause of decline. In order to test this hypothesis further, we need to widen our historical perspective in order to see whether there is evidence of correlation between the gathering pace of subjectivization since the 1950s and the increasing rate of congregational decline over the same period.

The picture over time

When we asked older members of Kendal congregations what had changed most in their lifetimes, they often commented: 'Women don't wear hats anymore'. Further questioning revealed the abandonment of hat-wearing – especially but not exclusively in church – to be a symbol of more far-reaching change. Change from a time when society was organized in a more orderly and role-governed fashion to a time when 'anything goes'. Change from a time when people 'knew their place' in the social hierarchy and expended considerable effort in defending and marking out that place, not least by way of dress and religious affiliation. Change from a time in which gender roles were more carefully distinguished and demarcated, and the deference of women to men in home, church and society was more widely accepted. Change from a time when churches and clergy had a central role in society and were able to legitimate and reinforce social distinctions. Change, in short, from the agricultural-industrial society of the 1950s that prized stability and security to the advanced industrial, late capitalist society of today that values personal flexibility and change.

Earlier in this chapter we imagined the life-path of a nurse who enters the holistic milieu during mid-life. If she had been born in the 1930s rather than the 1950s (or later), her story might have been rather different. She would likely have been socialized into Christian values at home, in school, and in the church and/or Sunday School to which her parents took her. Her faith, idealism and desire for a career of her own led her into nursing, since she found the caring, self-sacrificial and other-regarding role of the nurse to be strongly endorsed in Christian circles and literature (by contrast, other careers for women tended to be frowned on, and the importance of their taking up domestic roles and not 'stealing' jobs from male breadwinners received new emphasis in the immediate post-war years). When she met the man of her dreams she gave up work in order to raise her children, taking them to church as her parents had taken her, so that they might find comfort and inspiration in religion as she herself had done. By mid-life she had become a respected and popular member of her local community, spending her spare time running the Mothers' Union and leading a Girl Guide pack. Hats have always loomed large in her life: the hat she still wears to church, the beret she wore as a schoolgirl, the nursing cap she wore after gaining her qualifications, the veil she wore to get married, the hat she wears when 'Guiding'. Her daughter, however, absolutely refuses to wear a hat, and has given up churchgoing as well. Not that she is a 'rebel': she shares her mother's belief in the importance of relationships and is affectionate and caring. But she lives her life in a way that was unimaginable for her mother, and she has no desire to inhabit many of the roles that have given meaning and dignity to her mother's life. For although they are united by their relational orientation, the daughter's relationality had its basis in subjective-life values, whilst her mother's is grounded in the guidance of life-as roles.

According to the social historian Callum Brown (2001), Christianity in the 1950s – and for a century before – became so closely bound up with the defence of 'traditional', 'feminine' roles for women that the sexual revolution of the 1960s proved the single most important cause of 'the death of Christian Britain'. Women of the baby boom generation and after threw out the baby of churchgoing together with the bathwater of traditional gender roles. The keys to understanding secularization in Britain, Brown argues, are consequently 'the simultaneous de-pietisation of femininity and the de-feminisation of piety from the 1960s' (p. 192). One does not have to accept Brown's exclusive focus on disillusionment with traditional gender roles to accept his wider point: that the rejection of life-as, and particularly of roles of defence and subordination, has been a major cause of disaffiliation from the congregational Christianity that supported these roles.

If one looks to the biographies and autobiographies of the generation that lived through the upheavals of the sixties, one can see just how far-reaching the rejection of 'straight', 'square', 'established' society really was

– and why all the institutions and roles bound up with it suffered, not least the churches. The 'revolution' affected men as much as women, and has changed their attitudes to church as well. To cite just one example, Alan Watts's tellingly titled autobiography *In My Own Way* (1973), recalls how the young Alan 'felt physically sick' at the sight of upper-class ladies in fur coats and hats seated at the front of church and how, despite his later ordination as an Anglican priest, he gradually came to find Christianity's entire 'life-denying' and role-reinforcing stance intolerable. His solution was to abandon Christianity altogether in favour of 'atheism in the name of God; that is the realization that ordinary everyday life and consciousness is what the Hindus call *sat-chit-ananda*, and which I translate as "the which than which there is no whicher"' (p. 116).

Survey evidence supports the impression that the counter-cultural turn of the 1960s has led directly to congregational decline. Since young people, rather than already socialized adults, tend to be most exposed to and most influenced by new cultural currents, we would expect to find that levels of congregational disaffiliation amongst those who were coming of age in the 1960s – and thus coming under the influence of subjective-life values – were unusually high. Robert Wuthnow's research in the 1970s confirms these expectations at every point. By using surveys to compare the behaviours and attitudes of the generation unit exposed to counter-cultural values with those of previous generations, he finds not only that between 1959 and 1971 the proportion of those aged 21 to 34 attending church weekly declined 27 points, compared to 14 points for persons aged over 35, but that this difference between generations is greater than the differences found prior to the 1960s, thus suggesting 'a cohort difference attributable to events having taken place during the 1960s' (Wuthnow, 1976, pp. 856-8). What is more, he finds that even rather crude measurements of counter-cultural involvement indicate that such involvement accounts for most of the differences in religiosity between the generations in question. (For more on the impact of the sixties, see Hammond, 1992, for example pp. 7-8.)

Wuthnow's (1976) discovery that 'the relatively sharp reversal of trends in organized religious commitment seems explicable only as a consequence, in part, of the more general countercultural unrest that preceded and accompanied it' (p. 854) is confirmed by Roof's (1993) later study of the religious attitudes and behaviours of the baby boom generation. Using a large range of items to test counter-cultural subjective involvement, including reliance on inner authority, Roof finds such involvement to be the single best predictor of congregational disaffiliation (see Figure 4.2 below). He also finds that a large set of indicators of traditional theistic belief diminish with exposure to the counter-culture, including picture of God, belief in the devil, and (negative) attitude to meditation (pp. 123-5). This research demonstrates that young people's detachment from the congregational domain has not only continued since the sixties but has intensified, with their religious commitment declining steadily over time. What is more, young people have been leaving the churches at an earlier and earlier age, the average age for defection falling from 21 for older baby boomers to 18 for younger baby boomers (p. 155).

The alienation of young people from the congregational domain might not be so serious for the churches if it were not for the fact that churches survive and grow chiefly by recruiting the children of churchgoers (Hirst, 2003). Research in the USA confirms that the chief cause of congregational decline since the sixties has been not adult defection, but the failure to retain the children of existing churchgoers (Hadaway and Marler, 1993). The hope that baby boomers who left when they were young might boost numbers by returning when they get older has not been fulfilled, with a smaller proportion of each generation of 'dropouts' becoming a 'returnee' in later life (Marler and Roozen, 1993). The widening and deepening subjectivization

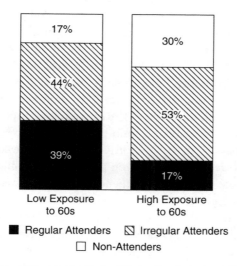

Figure 4.2   Exposure to sixties and level of religious attendance in early 20s. From *A Generation of Seekers* by Wade Clark Roof, p. 170. (c) 1993 by Wade Clark Roof. Reprinted by permission of HarperCollins Publishers Inc.

of each successive cohort of young people since the 1960s (Inglehart, 1997) appears to be a key cause of congregational decline.

Reasons for leaving

Another way of testing the influence of subjectivization on congregational decline is by considering the reasons people give for ceasing to attend church or chapel. Hoge and Roozen's (1979) survey-based study of church decline finds that commitment to values that are perceived to be incompatible with those of the congregational domain is a much more important factor in disaffiliation than is loss of belief. Their finding is confirmed by the fact that 'Belief in God or a universal spirit' in the USA (currently at 96 per cent, as reported by Gallup and Jones (2000, p. 177) has been high for many decades, despite falls in attendance. But which values are important in this regard, and does in-depth research amongst 'dropouts' suggest that subjective-life values have a particularly important role to play?

In 1978 the Princeton Religion Research Center's survey of the *Unchurched American* reported that, 'The unchurched are the most likely to say, "when I grew up and started making decisions on my own, I stopped going to church"' (p. 14). Twenty years later Philip Richter and Leslie Francis's (1998) study of UK church leavers found that 37 per cent of their sample agreed with the statement, 'I was tired of being told how to behave by the church' (p. 51). What both studies suggest is that commitment to personal autonomy, independence, and freedom play an important role in disaffiliation from the congregational domain. As a male Roman Catholic explains in Hoge et al.'s (1981) study of dropouts, '[one day] I just said to myself, "these people aren't going to tell me what to do anymore"... I had had it' (p. 108). Individuals who like making up their own minds are likely to react badly to being preached at. Young people who are determined to forge their own, independent identities may be as hostile as older people to being told what to think, feel and do, and just as committed to 'living my own life in my own way'. Some just want to be able to decide for themselves, others cease to believe that there is any truth besides personal truth. As a female dropout in Hoge, Johnson and Luidens's (1994) study of mainline and ex-mainline boomers puts it, 'The church is wrong when it says "This is absolutely the truth"...although you might know it within yourself, it's not something provable' (p. 157).

Some of those who leave the congregational domain seem to be rational, individuated subjectivists who want to make their own minds in their own way; their motto might be Thomas Paine's 'my mind is my church'. But there are probably as many, if not more, who leave because they do not like the way church makes them *feel*. In some cases, it is simply that they feel nothing very much at all, except perhaps 'bored'. People may describe their experience of church as 'dull', 'cold', 'formal', 'unexciting', 'dead', with attendance 'having nothing to offer me'. 'What's the point in going?', some of our students respond when we ask why they don't attend church, 'you don't get anything out of it, it simply does not touch my life, it's meaningless'. It is clear that few church services offer the strongly affective, intense experiences which young people can find elsewhere, whether by way of relationships, music, movies, clubs and so on. Studies from the UK suggest that young people today are more likely to find meaning, orientation and value in such experiences than in life-as orientated institutions, whether ecclesiastical or otherwise (Collins, 1997; Lynch, 2002). In other cases, church dropouts report that church makes them feel positively bad, contributing to subjective 'ill-being' rather than wellbeing. This is particularly common when people feel judged and found wanting by congregational standards. Thus a gay man comments that, 'whenever I went into a church...I had this feeling that I was hiding a part of myself (Hoge et al., 1981, pp. 41-2).[27] A middle-aged defector from a congregation of humanity in Kendal recalls, 'As I walked out of the church door I said to myself: that's the last time I'm going in there to be made to feel guilty'. And a female dropout we interviewed explained that she left church because of 'bitchy' comments made about her private life and her desire to wear white on her wedding day despite 'living in sin' with her boyfriend: 'I just wanted to do my own thing: I wasn't having anyone telling me what to do'.

It is not simply that some people find that congregational involvement does not improve their wellbeing and quality of life – though 75 per cent of those questioned by the Princeton Religion Research Center say they would welcome 'more emphasis on self expression' in churches and synagogues (1988, p. 13) and 51 per cent of Richter and Francis' respondents agree that 'The church failed to connect with the rest of my life' (1998, p. 51). People also complain about congregational life failing to meet spiritual needs. To cite the Princeton Religion Research Center's findings again, six in ten of the unchurched agree that 'most churches and synagogues have lost the real spiritual part of religion', and one in five 'want deeper spiritual meaning than I found in the church or synagogue' (1978, pp. 8, 15). Similarly, Richter and Francis (1998) find that 45 per cent agree that 'People have God within them so churches aren't really necessary', and 41 per cent that 'I wanted to follow my own spiritual quest, without religious institutions' (p. 51).

Interviews tell the same story. To cite a couple of examples from Kendal and nearby, we spoke to one woman in her forties who contrasted the lack of personal and spiritual support she found in church with the life-changing experience of joining a support group: 'A one hour service on Sunday? I mean it's not really enough time to address your self-esteem issues is it!...I didn't find any help in the churches...I found it in a Twelve Step Programme...*that* was the start of my personal journey.' Another woman of the same age talked about her formation in an Anglican boarding school, and remarked, 'I didn't see my Christian upbringing as being spiritual. It was all about dogma, beliefs. Something outside me. There was nothing that ever touched me'. Her confirmation service proved to be her 'unconfirmation', for she felt nothing and experienced nothing throughout the course of this supposedly life-changing ritual. 'It was only when I began Transcendental Meditation many years later', she explained, 'that I found the spirituality I wanted...the spirituality within each individual.' A middle-aged female Anglican lay official quoted by Richter and Francis's (1998) study tells of 'a gradual process of getting angry' with the church before leaving, 'getting in touch with a much more feminine sort of spirituality' and learning to live 'most deeply in yourself' (pp. 18, 31, 47). She contrasts her own rebellion with the loyalty of her mother: 'I don't think *she* would [ever] presume to say, "And what about *me* in all of this"' (p. 42). Another female dropout comments, 'Following my heart and following God is really what the whole reason for my leaving was about' (p. 43).

Of course, these are not the only reasons for leaving the congregational domain. Studies of disaffiliation often uncover other areas of dissatisfaction, many having to do with 'local' factors such as a falling out with a clergyman or a lack of rapport with other congregational members. Other factors probably include increased choice of options for the use of leisure time, and increased pressure on time, especially for women coping with the demands of both career and a growing family. Disillusionment with religion due to its perceived tendency to give rise to violent conflict, and disillusionment with a God who allows 'bad things to happen to good people' may also play a role. It is highly likely that several reasons combine together to lead an individual finally to decide to cease attending church or chapel. More research is needed to build up a fuller picture. But the sorts of comments we have cited above stand out as having a central importance, and confirm that commitment to subjective-life values – whether individuated or relational, rational or affective – is often a key element in an individual's decision to cease attending church.

Counter-evidence and argument

As well as amassing evidence that supports the subjectivization thesis, it is important to consider what might count against it. Most important in this regard is the body of literature that suggests that 'strict' and 'conservative' churches are growing rather than declining, and that it is their life-as strictness and conservatism that causes them to grow. This case is made most powerfully in Dean Kelley's *Why Conservative Churches are Growing* ([1972] 1995), and has been restated by Laurence Iannaccone (1994), Roger Finke and Rodney Stark (1992) and Stark and Finke (2000). Insofar as the category of what Kelley calls 'strict religion' might be thought to be close to what we are calling 'life-as religion', this seems to contradict the subjectivization thesis. The latter leads us to expect that life-as religion will decline as the subjective turn takes hold, whereas Kelley can be read to be claiming that life-as religion has been doing well since the seventies.

The contradiction may not be as great as it seems. For one thing, we have never suggested that the subjective turn characterizes the whole of Western culture, nor that individuals are powerless to resist it. It is highly likely that pockets of life-as culture will persist, that certain varieties of Christianity will form such pockets, that Christianity can and will be effectively mobilized in Durtheimian fashion to support threatened forms of life-as (for example, traditional gender roles), and that under such circumstances Christianity may do well, becoming a 'haven' or Counter-culture for those who wish to resist the subjective turn of the wider culture. This outcome is particularly likely in a country as large as the United States, where congregations of difference are able to shelter from the subjective turn within a sub-culture of their own making (with home schooling, Christian universities, Christian television channels and so on). In all these respects we can agree with Kelley, Stark and others regarding the relative success of 'conservative' religion since the seventies, especially in the USA. The point at which we part company with them, however, is the point at which they suggest that conservative religion may come to occupy more than a minority position in the society and culture of subjectivized societies. As Christian Smith's (1998) recent study of American evangelicalism indicates, the 'protesting' counter-cultural status of such congregations is likely to energize and sustain them, whilst also ensuring that they will not expand greatly if at all beyond their current size nor shed their 'beleaguered' status.

We also believe that the Kelley thesis fails to differentiate sufficiently between what we have been calling religions of difference and religions of experiential difference. As we have seen in the previous chapter, the latter have demonstrated greater vitality than the former since the seventies. As we have also seen, the latter are significantly more subjectivized than the former, albeit not as subjectivized as holistic spirituality. As a growing number of studies suggest, the success of congregations of experiential difference appears to lie not so much in their strictness, as in their ability to combine normative strictness with attention to and reconstruction of inner lives (Tipton, 1982; Shibley, 1996; Miller, 1997; Griffith,1997; Tamney, 2002). As Mark Shibley (1996) puts it in his study of Southern Baptist congregations, those that fare best do so 'precisely because they attend to the therapeutic needs of individuals' (p. 137); as one of our students puts it, such congregations are attractive to subjectivized selves because 'the self becomes important to God'; as a convert from Roman Catholicism to a charismatic congregation explained, 'I was looking for *life*. That life flow...' (Hoge et al., 1981, p. 121). Since we have been arguing that the relative success of 'strict' congregations is actually the success of congregations in which an overarching framework of theistic authority is combined with concern for the healing, cultivation and enrichment of subjective-life, the fortunes of this variety of congregation confirm rather than disconfirm the subjectivization claim and thesis (though not the spiritual revolution claim).[28]

The subjectivization thesis: explaining the general and varied fortunes of the congregational domain

To sum up this discussion of congregational decline, our argument in general has been that the congregational domain's failure to retain or attract subjective-life orientated selves has been a significant cause of its decline. This stands in stark contrast to the success of holistic forms of spirituality, which have proliferated because they have been able to capitalize on the wider – and growing – cultural demand for subjective wellbeing.

Further support for the subjectivization thesis arises from the fact that it makes perfect sense of the varied fortunes within the congregational domain which were uncovered in the previous chapter. Given the increasing momentum of the subjective turn and the quest for personal wellbeing, the subjectivization thesis would predict that congregations of humanity will be faring worst, since they offer least by way of subjective wellbeing. It would predict that congregations of difference will be faring better insofar as they offer to enhance subjective wellbeing by reconstructing inner lives through conformity to God's laws. And it would predict that congregations of experiential difference and experiential humanity will be faring best, due to their ability to bring the sacred within the realm of personal experience, where it may have a direct impact on subjective-life and wellbeing.[29] As we have seen in Chapter Three (pp. 60-7) all these predictions are borne out by the facts.

Conclusion

Madeleine Bunting (1996) writes, 'People are turning inside themselves for answers rather than looking to external religions which people have to fit into rather than finding something which fits them. People are taking more control over all aspects of their life, spiritual and health, rather than letting other people tell them what to do or believe' (p. 3). Not many people these days would say 'yes' to Thomas Carlyle's question in his 1840 lectures *On Heroes, Hero-Worship and the Heroic in History*: '…does not every true man feel that he is himself made higher by doing reverence to what is really above him?'. For the pressing values of the culture in which we live are along the lines of 'Life is not made for you; you have to make it' or 'Take responsibility for finding your own ways of being and fulfilling yourself'. In the words of Zygmunt Bauman (2000), 'Needing to *become* what one *is* is the feature of modern living' (p. 32). And in the words of Gordon Allport (1962), what matters is 'the *right* of every individual to work out his own philosophy of life to find his personal niche in creation, as best he can. His freedom to do so will be greater if he sees clearly the forces of culture and conformity that invite him to be content with a merely *second-hand* and therefore for him, with an immature religion' (pp. vii-viii; our emphases).

The basic premise of the subjectivization thesis is perfectly simple. With ever-increasing numbers of people having come to value what subjective-life has to offer, the tendency is for forms of associational activity that locate the sacred within to be doing well. For when the sacred, or spirituality, is experienced as lying at the heart of who you are, as coming from 'You' (not least by way of relationships) it can hardly dictate or constrain who you are. How can spirituality impose a life on you when it is experienced to be your true life? By contrast, with ever-declining numbers of people having faith in life-as values, the trend is for forms of associational activity, where the sacred operates from without, to be in overall decline. For religion which tells you what to believe and how to behave is out of tune with a culture which believes that it is up to us to seek out appropriate answers for ourselves. How can any other source tell me how to live my life, when only I can know from inside who I really am and what I may become? In short, subjective-life spirituality serves and reflects contemporary core values, in particular those associated with going deeper into Trilling's 'internal space' in order to 'live *out*' of one's life. The thrust of life-as religion, on the other hand, is to rein in the potentially anarchic and 'selfish' possibilities of 'being yourself only better'.

This is not to deny that life-as religion can change and that some important changes in a subjectivized direction can be observed. Queen Victoria's first Prime Minister, Lord Melbourne, is reported to have complained, after hearing an evangelical sermon, that 'Things have come to a pretty pass when religion is allowed to invade the sphere of private life'. Times have certainly moved on. We have seen that those forms of congregational religion which have done most to cater for the enhancement of 'private life' are faring significantly better than others, thereby lending further support to the subjectivization thesis – but not going so far as to support the spiritual revolution claim.

Although we have been concentrating on the holistic milieu and the congregational domain in this chapter, the subjectivization thesis can also be used to help explain changes that are underway beyond these two associational heartlands. There is a clear link, for example, between the trend towards more subjectivized (child-centred) teaching in primary schools, and (patient-centred) caring in the NHS, and the growth of subjective-life spirituality in these spheres. (This is not to deny that other factors have a role to play, most obviously that inclusive spirituality works in multicultural settings, whereas more exclusivistic life-as religion runs into the difficulty of not being able to cater for a diverse spread of faith.) There are also pretty clear links between the increasing popularity of subjective-life values, the shift to mind-body-spirit provisions in the general culture, and the increasing popularity of beliefs of a non-theistic, inner variety among the population.

In this chapter we have concentrated on providing evidence to support the subjectivization thesis as it applies to Britain (and in some measure to the USA). Clearly, the thesis is only of explanatory value when and where the subjective turn is in evidence. We are not for one moment suggesting that it is relevant to the situation in sub-Saharan Africa, for example, where the subjective turn is scarcely in evidence, where life-as religion is flourishing, and where there are much more pressing needs than the cultivation of unique subjectivities – most especially sustaining life-itself.

One thing we have not concentrated on in this chapter is the fact that the subjective turn has gathered pace at a time – during and since the sixties – when overall associational involvement with the sacred has been in decline. At least in Britain, and almost certainly in the USA, the growth of the holistic milieu has not compensated for the decline of the congregational domain. The 'massive subjective turn of modern culture', it thus appears, has resulted in the secularization of the associational territory as a whole. In a volume devoted to exploring the decline of life-as religion and the growth of subjective-life spirituality, we cannot enter into the complicated matter of establishing whether there is a causal link between the subjective turn and overall secularization – and thereby establishing the significance, or lack of significance, of other developments (such as increasing pressures on the time available to women who go out to work and run the home). (For ingenious and pioneering theoretical and empirical work on such matters, see Houtman and Mascini, 2002 – research which does much to confirm the subjectivization thesis, and which has the added advantage of testing a rival theory of change, namely rationalization; see also Yves Lambert, 1999 for a programmatic statement.)[30] Here we limit ourselves to just one point: that the main reason for overall secularization is probably that the holistic milieu has – to date – attracted a relatively small constituency. We have noted that the intimate and personally relational concerns of the milieu are likely to alienate those – especially many men – who seek to develop the quality of their subjective-lives by acting as individuated selves in the world; that during the last few decades the milieu does not seem to have attracted many younger people; and, we can add, that it has not appealed to elderly people who continue to support the life-as values in which they were raised. The simple fact that the holistic milieu has not exercised a wider appeal can thus greatly help explain why its growth has not been able to compensate for congregational domain decline.[31]

We draw this chapter to a close with an argument which we think sets a research agenda for the future. Although the subjective turn is unquestionably a major feature of the cultural landscape in which we dwell, a great deal supports the contention that another major feature has emerged in the form of 'new' versions of life-as regulation and control with forceful life-as capacities. One can think of the technologies of surveillance (which force one to drive *as* a good motorist, for example) or the auditing, monitoring, inspecting, the performance-related pay and the public performance tables, which impose themselves within the modern workplace, and require one to work as the institution demands if one is to be successful. Without going into any more details, it is perfectly clear that we spend a great deal of time in a world of 'meet them or else . . . ' targets, the process of targeting meaning that we have to channel our efforts in highly regulated ways – thereby serving to instil a very effective, because apparently self-chosen, life-as dimension to significant parts of many peoples' lives.

Our culture is experiencing a fundamental clash of values: on the one hand those associated with the cultivation of unique subjectivities, on the other those associated with the iron cage of having to live *the targeted-life*. In some spheres, like public-sector teaching or nursing, the clash may be acute. In others it may be better 'managed'. But given the prevalence of this clash, and given the preference on the part of increasing numbers of people for finding the freedom, the opportunity to be and become themselves, it is likely that many will use their 'free' time to seek liberation from their standard/ized, in effect *regimented*, work lives. If they engage with associational forms of the sacred, they are therefore much more likely to be involved with freedom-loving spiritualities of life than with role-enforcing life-as religion. Seeking to escape from externally imposed targets elsewhere in their lives, they will not want more of the same in the sphere of the sacred.

Chapter Five

Looking to the Future

...it will be those people who can keep alive and cultivate into a fuller perfection the art of life itself, who will be able to enjoy the abundance when it comes. (John Maynard Keynes, 'Economic Possibilities for our Grandchildren', 1931, p. 368)

[England] is littered with people who used to go to church but no longer do. We could well bleed to death. The tide is running out. At the present rate of change we are one generation from extinction. (Peter Brierley, 2000, p. 236)

Does the future belong to the holistic milieu? And is there any reason why the congregational domain should not decline to the 3 or 4 per cent regular attendance level it has reached in, for example, Sweden? In this chapter we consider whether the trajectories of growth and decline we have found in Britain will be sustained in the future. Or whether it is likely that the growth of the holistic milieu will 'top off' and even turn into decline, whilst the decline of the congregational domain will 'bottom out', and perhaps turn into growth.

We argue that the future of associational forms of the sacred in Britain depends on the future of 'the massive subjective turn of modern culture', and the ways in which religions and spiritualities relate to it. Since we have explained developments to date by reference to this cultural turn, it makes sense to treat it as the key to unlocking the future. So we begin by looking at some of the reasons we think that the long-standing, deeply embedded subjective turn is going to persist, if not intensify – thereby providing a basis for prediction. We then go on to look in greater detail at what could well happen to the holistic milieu and the congregational domain in the future. Finally, we pull things together to reflect on whether the holistic milieu will become larger than the congregational domain – thereby bringing about a spiritual revolution.

The Cultural Momentum Factor

From an empirical point of view, the force of the subjective turn is clearly seen in the fact that institution after institution has shifted from emphasizing life-as formations as the primary source of significance to catering for subjective-life. Examples have already been provided: the development of child-centred education, managerial-centred soft capitalism, patient-centred health care – of subjective wellbeing culture in all its many forms. Indeed, it is difficult to think of institutions which have not moved some way towards paying more attention to how people experience their own personal lives, and it is virtually impossible to think of an institution which has gone against the grain to become more focused on life-as – the institutional shift to subjective-life being clearly linked with a shift in self-understanding.

From a more explanatory point of view, the momentum of this cultural current is bound up with that of other major developments which, like subjectivization itself, have had a central role in shaping the world in which we now live. We might think of the process of pluralization. With more and more forms of life coming to co-exist, any particular form loses the credibility it had when it existed alone. The authority which a religion has when it is presented as 'the truth', for example, is undermined when other religious 'truths' enter the picture; and so people turn to their subjective-lives for a 'deeper truth'. Or we might think of the 'democratic revolution' and the closely allied development of the ethic of humanity. By emphasizing the value of equality, and the importance of respecting the freedom of others to decide how to live out their own lives, these developments generate reactions against life-as systems – or meta-narratives – which violate equality and which do not respect the unique subjective-life. Or we can recall the process of autonomization, whereby people come to think of themselves as sovereign agents, and aim to enrich the quality of their subjective-lives by going out into the world in order to feel powerful or successful (for example). Then again, we might think of the process whereby people who perceive themselves to be locked into anonymous 'iron cages' of procedures, rules and regulations turn to their private, personal lives to find meaning, satisfaction and significance.[1]

'Suppose that a hundred years hence', John Maynard Keynes (1931) wrote some 70 years ago, 'we are all of us, on average, eight times better off in the economic sense than we are today' (p. 365). 'Thus', he continues, 'for the first time since his creation man will be faced with his real, his permanent problem – how to use his freedom from pressing economic cares, how to occupy the leisure, which science and compound interest will have won him, to live wisely and agreeably and well' (p. 367). For a large proportion of the population of the West, Keynes's predictions about increased affluence and 'the art of life itself' coming into prominence have come true. Greater prosperity has provided the resources required for the cultivation of subjective wellbeing (patient-centred nursing is not cheap, neither is child-centred education). It has meant an increase in the number of people who feel that there must be more to life than wealth-creation. And it has allowed growing numbers of 'post-materialists' to devote more time and energy to concerns which go beyond material wellbeing. Thus in Kendal, a considerable number of spiritual practitioners have downsized to devote more of their lives to the pursuit of quality of life; in Britain, Hamilton (2003) reports an estimated 1.7 million downshifting in 1997, 2.6 million in 2002 (p. 11); on an international scale, Inglehart's (1997) World Values surveys provide detailed evidence of the connection between economic development and the attention paid to subjective wellbeing.[2]

This brief foray into some of the dynamics of modern times enables us to conclude that the massive subjective turn is integral to the world in which we currently live. Short of radical change – such as would be brought about by a long lasting collapse of the standard of living, for example – it is highly unlikely that the quest for 'quality of life' will not remain firmly on the agenda for the foreseeable future.

What are the implications for the future of life-as religion and subjective-life spirituality? In Chapter Four we argued that since life-as religion (necessarily) performs life-as functions and appeals to those who have life-as requirements, the subjective turn undermines the significance of what life-as religion has to offer. The situation is exacerbated by the fact that life-as religion cannot authorize the cultivation of unique, personal subjectivities. And the result is the decline of the congregational domain to date. Given that the subjective turn is not going to go away, we see absolutely no reason why this undermining process should not continue in the future. Hence the basis of our prediction that the congregational domain in Britain is likely to continue to decline, even though, as we shall argue later in this chapter, decline may 'bottom out'.

In Chapter Four we also argued that since subjective-life spirituality performs subjective-life jobs, the subjective turn means that holistic activities can benefit from the increasing number of people who are dwelling on the never-ending task of improving the quality of their own subjective-lives. Looking to the future, so long as value continues to be attached to the development, cultivation and exploration of subjective-life, and so long as subjectivized culture extols the virtues of wellbeing, there is every reason to suppose that the future of subjective-life spiritualities is secure. What has happened to date is likely to continue to happen in the future; there is no reason to suppose that activities (such as yoga) which are currently experienced as 'working' will not be experienced as 'doing the job' in the future. Hence the basis of our prediction that the holistic milieu of Britain is here to stay, even though, as we shall argue, growth is likely to slow down somewhat.

Holistic Milieu Scenarios

Having discussed what underpins our predictions, we now look in some detail at how the holistic milieu of Britain could fare in the future. We look first at two storms that appear to be brewing and which could result in the milieu going into decline.[3]

The 'last gasp of the sixties' scenario

The first possible storm concerns the age profile of those involved in the holistic milieu. Kendal Project research shows that 48 per cent of the spiritual practitioners operating at the time of our study were aged between 45 and 54, 23 per cent were older, 30 per cent younger. Of this younger cohort, 17 per cent were aged between 40 and 44, 11 per cent were in their thirties, and just 1.3 per cent were under 30. It is not as though group members and one-to-one clients are much younger, with almost three-quarters of those active in the holistic milieu being over 45 years old. Given that much the same age profile applies to the holistic milieu of the UK, it looks as though few of those currently active in the milieu will still be with us 40 to 50 years from now.

Looking more closely at this scenario, there is another consideration to take into account. It goes without saying that the existence of the milieu depends upon people serving as spiritual practitioners. Many practitioners came of age during the 'sixties', that is, during the period between the mid-1960s and the mid-1970s when subjective-life spirituality became relatively widespread among younger college or university people. Many would thus appear to owe a great deal to their first-hand experiences of 'sixties values'. (As Ken Wilber says, 'the new age is a product of the baby-boom phenomenon, the "60s" generation' (cited by Rose, 1998, p. 9).) With so much apparently depending on this particular cohort, which is moving into old age, the 'last gasp of the sixties' scenario could be pretty bleak. True, 30 per cent of spiritual practitioners in Kendal are under 45, but only 12 per cent of these are under 40. So it may be that replenishment is not taking place at a rate which will compensate for the loss of the sixties practitioners.[4]

The declining sacred capital scenario

To make matters worse, there may be another storm on the horizon. According to a questionnaire finding from our study of Kendal's holistic milieu, 58 per cent of the largely middle-aged people active in the milieu report that they have been 'brought up with a religious faith' at home, 54 per cent at school, and 57 per cent at church. (There is no reason to suppose much the same does not apply to the holistic milieu of the UK as a whole.) So it seems possible that the growth of the milieu has owed a considerable amount to the fact that it caters for many who were already in possession of 'sacred capital': people who became disillusioned with Christianity earlier in their lives, but who have retained faith that the sacred might have something to offer. (Although 57 per cent of those active in the Kendal holistic milieu report that they used to attend church regularly, 80 per cent of this number say that they had stopped attending by the age of 24.) However, younger people today have been brought up in a society where regular church attendance is much lower, where there are considerably fewer Sunday Schools, and where there is much less transmission of Christianity by way of family or school. So if the declining sacred capital scenario is correct, the holistic milieu is going to run into difficulties. Its momentum will suffer when there are fewer 'believers' around who are seeking an alternative to the Christian religion of their younger days.

The cultural transmission scenario

Can it be argued, though, that 'fair weather' is more likely to lie ahead? To take the 'last gasp' scenario first, there are good reasons for thinking that the future does not depend, at least so critically, on those who came of age during the sixties. For younger people – too young to have directly experienced the sixties – are nevertheless growing up in a world where holistic spirituality has become mainstream. So the sixties are no longer needed: younger people are quite likely to encounter holistic themes by way of all those culturally acceptable, plausible, sometimes positively engaging, provisions which we have discussed in the last two chapters of this volume. Whether it be by way of education-culture, media-culture, purchasing-culture, health-culture, production-culture, wellbeing-culture or some combination of these, younger people can readily become familiar with subjective-life mind-body-spiritualities, learn something about what is on offer and perhaps become 'primed' to become actively engaged with them when the time is right.

It is true that in Kendal and environs just 1.3 per cent of all those active in the milieu were under 30 years of age, with only 27 percent of the number of all those active being younger than 45 and 17 per cent younger than 40. But there is evidence elsewhere of younger people showing interest in holistic spiritualities of life. As suggested in Chapter Four (p. 110), it may simply be that their priorities – relationships, student life, family life, making their way in the world and so on – mean they do not have the time (or the resources) for much associational participation, and that those wellbeing or 'life-issues' which are catered for by holistic activities have yet to become of concern. So our expectation is that the holistic milieu will attract more participants, including those who will become practitioners, as they enter their mid-lives and have reason to dwell on improving the quality of their subjective-lives. And after all, 27 per cent of all those involved in the holistic milieu of Kendal and environs are younger than 45, which is not an inconsiderable figure.[5]

As for the declining religious capital scenario, although *religious* instruction and education might have become less significant (see Chapter Three), this is not to say that Britain has become a society of atheists. Far from it: the Soul of Britain survey reports that just 8 per cent identify as 'a convinced atheist' (Heald, 2000). The decline of religious capital, then, has not resulted in a world of atheists – a world which would make life very difficult for holistic spiritual practitioners. Instead, the development of cultural renderings of holistic themes has no doubt encouraged, and been encouraged by, beliefs of a 'life-force' or 'spiritual' variety, and has generated a 'spiritual capital' which will increasingly take over the role once played by having been brought up in the Christian faith.

Prediction: holistic milieu

We therefore predict that the storms will not develop, and that the holistic milieu of the UK will continue to grow. But at what rate?

'New Age' or 'alternative spiritualities', it is often claimed, are 'individualistic' or 'relativististic', with 'diffuse' beliefs. With little consensus among participants, beliefs are not sustained or reinforced by way of shared 'plausibility structures'. Beliefs are 'precarious', and transmission to others (children, friends, etc.) is 'weak' (see, for example, Bruce, 2002). Accordingly, growth is likely to slow down, if not turn into decline. In response to this argument, our short answer is that the holistic milieu of Kendal, as elsewhere, has not only persisted over the years but has grown – a point which makes it extremely difficult to claim that transmission is weak. Of course, we cannot rule out the possibility that the holistic milieu would have grown faster if transmission had somehow been more effective, or that the future would be more promising if transmission were somehow to be improved. But this is speculation. What we do know is that growth has taken place, and that the milieu is no more likely to be adversely affected by transmission factors in the future than it has been in the past.

Furthermore, a considerable amount of evidence shows that the holistic milieu is far from being as diffuse, individualistic, superficial (or shallowly 'consumerist') as is often claimed. A recurrent theme of this volume is that the holistic milieu is characterized by relationality; by the expression and cultivation of unique, and thus autonomous, subjective-lives *within* associational settings. With so much sharing going on – especially in the highly intimate, disclosing encounters of one-to-one activities, activities which also take place between practitioners – it is not surprising to find that key holistic themes like 'subtle energy' (for example) are found among the great majority of participants of Kendal and environs (see Chapter One). Indeed, although 45 per cent do not experience their current activity as being of spiritual significance, 90 per cent believe in spirituality. And far from being superficially involved, we found many of those active in the milieu, especially practitioners, to be deeply embedded in the activities of subjective-life spirituality. In Kendal and environs, 30 per cent of acts of weekly participation are by people who are currently practising more than one activity (see Chapter Two, p. 40). In addition, on average all those currently active in the milieu have been involved with six of the activities comprising the milieu today (see Appendix 3) during the past (that is, prior to the one, sometimes two or three, but rarely more, activities they had been attending during the week when the holistic milieu questionnaire was distributed).[6] What is more, many more also meditate or practise yoga (for example) at home, with the questionnaire showing that 55 per cent meditate at home, 46 per cent practise yoga, and many also read relevant literature (60 per cent reading 'spiritual or religious (not specifically Christian) books or magazines'). It comes as no surprise, then, to find that 32 per cent of the participants in the Kendal holistic milieu who have children report that their offspring share their own interest in holistic milieu activities – not an especially high figure, but high enough to indicate that parental transmission (alone) is not without importance.[7]

Even if it is still argued that there are transmission problems, the fact remains that there is no reason to think they are going to make any more difference to the future than they have to the past. It is unlikely, however, that the holistic milieu will continue to grow at the rate it did in Kendal in the later 1980s and the 1990s (a rate which is probably typical for Britain as a whole). For during this period the milieu had a golden 'market opportunity'. With the expansion of subjective wellbeing culture during the last decade or two, spiritual practitioners have been able to cater for an increase in the number of people interested in associational, holistic, quality of life provisions. Recalling Kendal findings, however, 80 per cent of those active in the milieu are women, 83 per cent of all those active are older than 40, 45 per cent of all participants are women aged between 40 and 60, over half of all participants have attended university or college, and many work (or have worked) in people-centred wellbeing professions. Those attracted, in other words, represent a relatively small sector of the population. Drawing on 2001 census data concerning occupation and educational attainment in England and Wales, there are likely to be around 1000 women in Kendal and environs in their forties and fifties with the kind of cultural capital that makes the holistic milieu an attractive option. So the 45 per cent of those active in the milieu during any given week who are women in their forties and fifties (numbering 270 individuals) represent around 30 per cent of this number. The milieu, in other words, seems to have attracted a considerable proportion of its primary 'market niche' already.[8]

We might well conclude that this means that there will be very little growth in the future, if any at all. In actual fact, we think that slowish growth will be the order of the day. For the market niche is likely to expand gradually. After all, this is *not* a counter-cultural niche, and the subjective turn will continue to support rather than threaten it. Holistic wellbeing culture is surely not going to stop developing and growing in influence. College and university educational courses are devoting ever more resources to preparing students for person-centred careers in the caring and human resource development professions, for example, which will surely continue to proliferate. It is true that unless the milieu broadens its appeal by gender, age, educational background or occupation it might not continue to expand at the same rate as it has during the recent past. But grow it will. There is too much in the culture, and too many beliefs of the 'some sort of spirit or life force' variety, for it to do otherwise.

During the last 30 years, the holistic milieu of Britain has grown to involve 1.6 per cent of the population during a given week. With growth continuing, but possibly slowing down somewhat, our prediction is that weekly participation in the milieu will double in size over the next 40 or 50 years to take in a little more than 3 per cent of the population of the nation.[9]

Another possibility

Even as we write this chapter, however, we keep coming across new evidence – from Britain and more widely – that suggests our prediction for the holistic milieu may be too cautious. Let us mention just a few examples, which suggest that the market niche is in fact already expanding.

In the USA, the circulation of the *Yoga Journal* has increased from 90,000 in 1998 to 300,000 in 2002. And it would appear that much of this increase is due to the increasing popularity of yoga among younger people: 25.2 per cent of the 15 million adults practising yoga (an increase of 28.5 per cent on the previous year) are aged between 25 and 34, only slightly less than the 26.9 per cent aged between 45 and 54 (15.7 per cent being between 35 and 44) (Harris Interactive Service Bureau 2003 survey of 4,000 respondents, statistically representative of the USA adult population). (The survey also finds that that 25.5 million are very or extremely interested in yoga, and that 35.3 million intend to take up yoga during the next 12 months – numbers which presumably include many younger people.) Then there is Franz Hollinger and Timothy Smith's (2002) cross-cultural survey, which finds that 'most students have some experiences with such practices' (including 'spiritual techniques' and 'alternative medicine and healing'): although, it should be added, 'only a relatively small proportion practises one or more methods regularly' (p. 246). (See also Houtman and Mascini, 2002, p. 464 for the picture regarding younger people and the Netherlands.)[10] In addition, there is also some evidence of yoga attracting more men – 'real men' doing 'athletic yoga' according to John Capouya (2003). Likewise, new men's magazines like *Best Life* (in the USA) suggest there is a new market amongst men for subjectivized wellbeing culture – which could mean that the 'niche' on which the holistic milieu can draw is set to expand considerably.

Evidence of this sort – and more could be provided – cannot be ignored when considering the possibility that the market niche will also expand in Britain. Aside from anecdotal evidence of yoga (tai chi, etc.) becoming popular among young adults in cities like London, we have to take into account the fact that GPs are increasingly making referrals to CAM practitioners (see Chapter Three, p. 72). There are also clear signs that in addition to more 'orthodox' activities (such as osteopathy), GPs are increasingly encouraging patients – by no means just mid-life, well-educated women – to turn to activities like yoga, tai chi or combinations of the two. Furthermore, we can note the proliferation of holistic activities within the educational system (in particular colleges with health, fitness or beauty courses, for example), where younger people predominate. Then there are the (preventative) health projects, such as government 'local health forums', that are being established in inner cities, in particular, where holistic activities are in evidence. (See al Yafai, 2003 on 'healthy living centres', where reflexology, massage and shiatsu, for example, can be found.) And in addition, there is no doubting the fact that more and more 'soft capitalism' companies are providing healthcare or wellbeing advice and provisions – many of which can readily lead into the body, mind, *spirituality* dimension (see Roberts and Kelleher, 2004). We have even come across Hindu temples/community centres/societies offering mind-body-spirituality, with the Gujarat Hindu Society and temple in Preston, one of the largest in Britain, currently offering popular courses in 'Holistic Living', including reiki (specifically aimed at youth) and aromatherapy.

The upshot is that our prediction that the growth of the holistic milieu in Britain will be slower than during the 1990s could be wrong. The developments highlighted here mean that growth may continue at a high rate – high enough to bring about a spiritual revolution. Currently, though, the milieu caters largely to the relatively small market niche we have described. Since evidence of expansion beyond this niche is not yet extensive, we remain content for now with the prediction above.

Congregational Domain Scenarios

Though the continuing momentum of the subjective turn bodes well for the holistic milieu, it bodes ill for the congregational domain. Insofar as the latter remains predominantly in the business of supporting and secularizing life-as roles, its future is precarious – but *how* precarious? There are three main scenarios to be considered.

The continuing decline scenario

Strong support for the scenario of continuing decline comes from the existing trend data for Christianity in Britain. Decline has now been sustained for over a century with no significant reversals, save a short period of growth between 1945 and 1965. According to the most reliable sources, congregational membership shrank from 33 per cent of the population in 1900 to 29 per cent in 1930 to 24 per cent in 1960, followed by swifter decline from 24 per cent in 1960 to 12 per cent in 2000. Figures for typical Sunday attendance show the same pattern: from 19 per cent of the population in 1903 to 15 per cent in 1951 to 12 per cent in 1979 to 10 per cent in 1989 and 8 per cent in 2000.[11] If we step even further back in time to 1851 when Mann carried out his famous census of *Religious Worship in England and Wales* (1854), the percentage of the population attending church on census Sunday was around 39 per cent, although this may fall to about 24 per cent if those who attended two or more times are only counted once (Gill, 1993). Overall the picture is one of gradual decline in both membership and attendance between 1851 and 1960, with a short 'blip' of growth in the 1950s, followed by accelerated decline from the 1960s to the present.

With the rate of decline of the last few decades in mind, Bruce (2003) forecasts that, 'three decades from now, Christianity in Britain will have largely disappeared . . . In 2031 . . . British Methodism will die and other denominations will be close behind' (p. 61). But there is an even worse scenario for the churches. Brierley's surveys show that the decline of the congregational domain in England speeded up in the 1990s. In the first 10-year period covered by his surveys (1979-1989) church attendance dropped 1.8 per cent. In the second nine-year period (1989-1998) it dropped 2.4 per cent, that is, 0.6 per cent more. If this rate of decline were to continue, then in the next nine-year period (to 2007) the drop could be by a further 3 per cent, and in the following nine years (to 2016) by 3.6 per cent. By that time only 0.9 per cent of the English population would still be attending church (Brierley, 2000, p. 28).

Even though it would be statistically unsound to make such a forecast on the basis of a single nine-year period, there are some good reasons for thinking that this scenario of accelerated decline – perhaps to near zero – may be likely. The most important reasons concern the demographic pro-file of the congregational domain, and transmission issues. Brierley (2000) notes that in the last two decades of the twentieth century the age profile of congregations has changed, with the average age climbing and the pro-portion of young people declining. The average age of a churchgoer is now higher than the average age in the population, and the number of young people, under age 19, attending church has halved in the last 20 years to 25 per cent of all churchgoers (p. 95). In Kendal our headcount revealed that 17 per cent of congregational attenders were under 18 (25 per cent of the UK population as a whole is under 19) (Brierley, 2001, p. 4.3). And of these, 12 per cent were babies and children and 5 per cent adolescents. This would suggest that a significant and growing proportion of the chil-dren of churchgoers cease to attend as soon as they are able to do so, and that this haemorrhage is a major and accelerating cause of congregational decline. When the current (older) generations of churchgoers die out, there will be very few people to take their place. Of course this need not be fatal if, like the holistic milieu, the congregational domain can be sustained by people joining it in later life, but there is no evidence that this is happening on anything approaching a significant scale. Nor should this be surprising, for unless the general culture can 'prime' people to enter an associational heartland – as in the case of the holistic milieu – the only real entry route is by way of socialization within that heartland (which is most likely when parents bring children to church). The fact that the numbers who are being successfully socialized in this way is shrinking so fast, and that the general culture does little to reinforce Christian beliefs, adds weight to the scenario of accelerating decline.

It can also be argued that congregational decline begets decline. Belief may seem less plausible when there are fewer who share it. A shrinking group worshipping in a building designed for many more cannot generate the 'collective effervescence' experienced in a larger assembly. The experi-ence can readily be of the 'empty crowd' (to paraphrase Gill, 2003). The quality of the worship may fall, as anyone who has tried to sing unaccompanied hymns to tape-recorded organ music will testify. The 'cost' of attending will become higher as the jobs necessary to maintain a congregation fall on fewer shoulders, and as finances become stretched. An older congregation may have less energy or enthusiasm for evangelism. And young people are unlikely to be attracted to congregations where the average age is far higher than their own.

For all these reasons, the scenario of the continued decline of the congregational domain as a whole must be taken seriously. Attendance in Great Britain continues to plummet, and in countries like Sweden where attendance has already fallen to a considerably lower level, there is no evidence of overall bottoming out.[12]

The bottoming-out scenario

Even though the congregational domain as a whole is declining, we have noted in earlier chapters that some forms of congregation have been able to buck the general trend, even in Britain. Could it be that some forms of congregation will exhibit sufficient vitality in the years ahead to hold their own, or even to grow? And if they do, will this prevent the congregational domain as a whole from declining to zero and lead instead to a bottoming out in overall attendance levels? There are three main ways in which this could happen: by retaining and attracting people who are attracted to the security of life-as religion; by attracting those with an orientation towards subjective-life or by retaining and attracting individuals who value the authoritative approach of life-as religion, but also seek some subjective enhancement.

Retaining and attracting those who value life-as

Given their predominantly life-as profile, it is most likely that contemporary congregations will be able to strengthen their attendance figures by retaining or attracting individuals who seek externally authorized frameworks of meaning and value. They will succeed if they are able to stabilize, dignify and sacralize forms of life which significant numbers find attractive, and which may be felt to be unsupported or under threat in the culture more widely. There are a number of areas in which such life-as provision may be made.

First, congregations may continue to play a role in upholding 'social' roles, duties and obligations, such as the role of 'good citizen' and 'good neighbour' at local, civic, national and international level. Churches may provide the spaces where people can gather for civic or national celebrations or after disasters, and serve as the point at which 'society' can hold up an ideal image of itself, affirm core values and reinforce its identity (thus 72 per cent of the population identified as 'Christian' in the UK census of 2001, even though few attend church regularly). Congregations may serve as the place in society where people still think of and act on behalf of the 'distant other', including those in need in developing countries. They can also serve as rallying points for the local community, perhaps as providers of welfare and 'social capital' – visiting the elderly, looking after the bereaved, caring for the socially marginal and so on.

Second, congregations may continue to support a particular vision of the ideal family, and the domestic and sexual roles which are seen as essential to its continued health and wellbeing. There may be increasing demand for this provision if a significant portion of society continues to feel that 'family values' based around the preservation of heterosexual marriage, the nuclear family and differentiated gender roles are being undermined by social and cultural developments such as a climbing divorce rate, co-habitation, growing support for homosexual unions and increased tolerance of new forms of sexual relationship and identity. Those who wish to uphold more clearly defined roles for men and women, husbands and wives, parents and children, may turn to congregations for support. Many churches, both Protestant and Catholic, currently appear to be catering for such demand by upholding traditional gender roles as God-given, condemning homosexual activity, campaigning on behalf of the nuclear family and offering a wide array of family-orientated provisions.

Third, congregations may continue to supply a range of more strictly religio-cultural goods. By way of teaching, worship, example and institutional reinforcement they may continue to support and reinforce religious roles, bring people into meaningful contact with a transcendent God, preserve connection with a 2,000 year old tradition of life and thought, and bring externally defined meaning, structure and purpose to individual lives in the process.

Which of these functions are likely to be the most important in the future, and which forms of congregation will be best equipped to meet demand for them? Given their established humanitarian emphasis, congregations of humanity are best placed to uphold social and civic functions. However, these are the very functions for which demand seems to be declining (Putnam, 2000). In any case, congregations can continue to carry out their social and civic functions without necessarily attracting any more regular attenders – as we see in the Church of Sweden, for example, or in English villages, where many want the church to remain as a focus of community, but few have the time to support it. (Similarly, even if demand for 'occasional offices' like baptism and marriage remains, this does not help raise regular attendance levels.)

By contrast, there is less evidence of a slowdown in demand for the other two areas of life-as provision, namely support for family values and provision of strictly religio-cultural goods. The congregations best placed to benefit are congregations of difference and experiential difference, which offer the most prescriptive and detailed teachings on how Christians should comport themselves in relation to one another (particularly with regard to sexuality) and in relation to God. Of course it could be argued that the subjective turn will undermine demand in these areas, but it can equally be argued that it will benefit congregations that function as safe havens and counter-cultural refuges for those who prefer to be guided by authoritative tradition rather than rely on their own subjective resources. What is more, in upholding family values and supplying religio-cultural goods, the only real competition such congregations currently face is from other forms of life-as religion such as orthodox Judaism and Islam, and there are often cultural barriers to entering such religions. Consequently, if congregations of difference and experiential difference do benefit from continuing demand for the supply of these life-as services, this could help bring about a bottoming out of overall congregational decline.

Attracting those who value unique subjective-life

Since the subjective turn has very considerable momentum, an alternative way in which attendance could be boosted would be if congregations were able to attract those who wish to cultivate their subjective-lives.

Given that they are the most likely of all types of congregation to encourage and resource unique subjectivities, and to authorize and facilitate encounter with the sacred in the depths of personal experience, congregations of experiential humanity have the greatest potential in this regard. However, there are two serious stumbling blocks in the way. First, many such congregations retain a high moral tone centred around selfless support of humanitarian values, which is likely to be off-putting for those who feel that value commitments should be freely chosen rather than externally imposed. The emphasis placed by many Unitarians and Quakers on the importance of 'community' and, even more importantly, of humanitarian ('justice and peace') causes of universal applicability, may alienate those who are seeking to explore their personal and spiritual depths in their own unique ways. Second, subjectivized Christian congregations face serious competition from the holistic milieu. Unless congregations of experiential humanity can offer something uniquely appealing to subjective-life orientated selves seeking spiritual depth, the latter are more likely to follow the more direct route from subjective wellbeing culture into the holistic milieu. Even if congregations of experiential humanity can succeed in diverting some who seek to develop inner life into their activities, they currently constitute such a small proportion of the total congregational domain (around 5 per cent in Kendal) that this would be unlikely to be able to bring about a bottoming out of attendance in the congregational domain as a whole.

Given the lack of attention they currently pay to the cultivation of unique subjective-lives, congregations of humanity seem much less likely to be able to attract those who wish to encounter the sacred 'in my own way'. However, our research in Kendal revealed that a few subjective-life orientated souls *are* 'clinging on' in such congregations. This may be indicative of the fact that these congregations have at least the *potential* to appeal to those who seek personally meaningful forms of spirituality. For one thing, the relative lack of didacticism in such congregations compared to congregations of difference and experiential difference gives participants a measure of freedom to think their own thoughts and pursue their own personal spiritual paths – even if it means 'letting the service wash over' and 'ignoring a lot of what goes on' (as one Anglican in Kendal put it). For another thing, these congregations have the strongest liturgical and ritual traditions, which can be compatible with subjective-life spirituality insofar as ritual and symbol are open-textured and non-dogmatic enough to provide a point of focus for individual meditation and spiritual growth. (It is highly likely that the rapid growth of Eastern Orthodoxy in Britain is due to its attracting 'cultured' inner-directed selves; strong attendance levels at many cathedrals seems to witness to the same phenomenon.) Finally, congregations of humanity have the potential to appeal to those who value subjective-life because they contain within their own historic traditions the traces and legacies of subjectivized forms of Christianity, most notably in ascetic and mystical traditions which hold out the ideal of union with God through the indwelling of the Holy Spirit (Woodhead, 2004). However, apart from a few limited spheres (spiritual retreats, spiritual literature, conferences and workshops on Christian meditation) there is, as yet, no evidence of congregations of humanity attracting a constituency of subjective-life orientated selves in anything like the numbers that would be necessary to halt their own decline, never mind that of the congregational domain as a whole. (A very speculative scenario about how this might change would be that current controversies in 'broad' churches like the Anglican communion might lead eventually to schism that might leave a 'liberal' wing of the church free to develop in a more subjectivized direction by reclaiming a heritage of experiential Christian spirituality for its followers, and making it central to its life and organization.)

What of congregations of difference and experiential difference? Might they be able to attract or retain those seeking to cultivate inner life? To date we have found little evidence that such congregations are able to appeal those who prefer to rely on their own subjective resources than on external guidance. Both types of congregation continue to insist that the individual is 'saved' only through surrender (of mind, body and spirit) to the transcendent God who is made known above all in Christ and in scripture, and both types of congregation are united in opposition to 'secular modernity', including subjective and humanist values (Marsden, 1991). Where congregations of experiential difference go further than congregations of difference is in teaching that the sacred can be encountered not only from 'without', but from 'within', by way of direct experience of God as Holy Spirit. This lends congregations of experiential difference much greater potential to attract those who seek subjective satisfaction and who wish to encounter the sacred in the depths of personal experience. At present, however, such congregations insist that inner experience of the sacred must be checked and validated by the 'higher' external authority of scripture and of authorized interpreters of scripture (pastors and elders). To a greater extent than congregations of humanity and experiential humanity they preach strict codes of morality and duty, based on biblical norms. Unless this changes, even congregations of experiential difference are unlikely to attract those of a subjectivized disposition, unless the latter are in the process of becoming disillusioned with subjective-life values and looking for stronger normative frameworks. A 'conversion' would be needed.[13]

Retaining and attracting those who seek subjective enhancement in a framework of life-as roles

The conclusion to which we are drawn is that whilst the congregational domain is more likely to attract those who retain a commitment to life-as than to subjective-life, congregations of experiential difference have an advantage over other forms of congregation in that they may be able to attract not only those who seek the sacred in external obligation, but those who also wish to encounter the sacred in the depths of inner experience. They seem to have secured a competitive edge by virtue of the fact that they both resist the subjective turn by offering clear normative guidance *and* cater to it by offering intense personal experience of the sacred. As such, experiential congregations of difference can appeal to those who seek a clear framework of roles, obligations and duties, but *also* want their subjective lives to be healed, stimulated, enhanced, and transformed through contact with the Holy Spirit. What this means, in more concrete terms, is that they are likely to attract 'respectable' individuals and families – from tradespeople to administrators to solicitors to businesspeople – who long for a more stable, ordered, hierarchical, respectful, family-based, 'wholesome' society, but who want their religion to make a difference to the quality of their subjective-lives. They want to 'feel' the presence of God, to 'taste and see' how good the Lord is, to experience 'his blessings' in every aspect of their lives. Given the 'joy' they have themselves experienced through being 'born again', they are likely to be active in trying to convert others so that they too may experience the richness of a life lived 'in the Lord' and in everyday, moment-to-moment, deeply subjective relationship with him.

As regards the future, the key question is whether there will be enough such people around in the future to allow congregations of experiential difference to stabilize or grow, and in doing so slow down the decline of the congregational domain as a whole. This depends, in part, on whether the children of those who currently attend will be effectively socialized into the faith of the parents. The danger is that they will be attracted by the more thoroughly subjectivized forms of life on offer in the culture than by the regulated subjective satisfactions available in congregations of experiential difference. Another danger is that charismatic enthusiasm wanes as intense experience cannot be sustained, and so leads to congregational decline. In Kendal and in England as a whole there is evidence of a slowdown in growth rates of the more 'charismatic' forms of evangelical congregation since the 1990s (Percy, 2003; Brierley, 2000, p. 54).

On the other hand, it is likely that those who seek clear moral and religious validation of traditional family values (amongst other things) will continue to be attracted to what Christianity has to offer. And given that the subjective turn is likely to prime even those who believe that the truth is 'out there' to think that it should also be experienced within, and harnessed to the healing and enhancement of subjective-life, we would predict that congregations of experiential difference are likely to grow at the expense of 'drier', less experiential and subjectively focused forms of congregation (both congregations of humanity and of difference). In support, there is clear evidence that the successful 'new paradigm churches' in the USA have grown (see Chapter 3 pp. 63-4), and they have done so by attracting people away from congregations of difference and congregations of humanity (Perrin, Kennedy and Miller, 1997). We also note that congregations of experiential difference are often extremely active in evangelical endeavour (for example the Alpha Course), and that they are often more successful than other forms of congregation in offering strong educational provision at the congregational level – which may help socialize and retain young people.

We therefore think it likely that congregations of experiential difference will be able to sustain their current levels of attendance. In support, Greater London, Berkshire and Surrey – affluent 'home counties' where many congregations of experiential difference are located – are the only counties in England that experienced static rather than declining attendance levels between 1989 and 1998 (Brierley, 2001, p. 2.15). At worst, such congregations will probably suffer only very gradual decline (in England, evangelicalism as a whole declined by 3 per cent between 1989 and 1998 (Brierley, 2000, p. 51)). In either case, the relative vitality of congregations of experiential difference means that they may well be able to prevent overall congregational 'decline to zero', and make the bottoming-out scenario more likely – for such congregations constitute a sizeable proportion of the congregational domain as a whole. (Currently, evangelicalism makes up 37 per cent of the congregational domain in England (Brierley, 2000, p. 67); in Kendal, congregations of experiential difference make up 21 per cent of the congregational domain, whilst congregations of difference make up 18 per cent.)

The revival scenario

The final scenario holds that both the continuing decline and the bottoming-out scenarios are too pessimistic about the future of congregational Christianity and that Christianity will stage a revival, just as it has in the past. This seems unlikely, since previous revivals, like that stimulated by Methodism in the eighteenth century, took place in populations where

Christian capital was still high. Some suggest that the 'secular' West will be reconverted by missionaries from overseas. However, it is hard to believe that missionaries would have any success in converting the denizens of a widely subjectivized culture which has actively rejected associational forms of Christianity. Still others argue that people will grow sick of the shallow and illusory rewards of an 'individualistic' and 'materialist' culture and return to the churches to fill the spiritual gap in their lives. The evidence (Chapter Four), however, suggests that 'post-materialists', with their quality-of-life values, are much more likely to be attracted to the holistic milieu than the congregational domain.

Prediction: congregational domain

Drawing our discussion of congregational scenarios to a close, we find no strong evidence to support the more optimistic scenarios, some evidence to support the most pessimistic scenario of a decline to (near) zero, but the greater weight of evidence supporting the bottoming-out scenario – with the domain being supported by the relative vitality of the life-as spirituality of experiential congregations of difference. More precisely, we would expect overall congregational decline to continue for the next 25 to 30 years as attendance at congregations of humanity shrinks to around 1 per cent of the population or below, but we would expect attendance at congregations of experiential difference to remain fairly steady, thus leading to a levelling out of the congregational domain at around 3 per cent of the population by 2030. This prediction is based on religions of humanity continuing to decline at the same rate (around 50 per cent) as over the last two decades, and on attendance at congregations of experiential difference remaining fairly steady, or declining very gently, over the next three decades.[14]

The Spiritual Revolution: Past, Present and Future

Some hundred years ago, Durkheim drew a distinction between 'a religion handed down by tradition' and 'a free, private, optional religion, fashioned according to one's own needs and understanding' (cited in Pickering, 1975, p. 96). Writing at much the same time, William James, Simmel, Troeltsch and others drew similar distinctions. They too thought that spiritualities of life were a growing force, so they would not be surprised by the extent to which the spiritual revolution has developed since their time, nor about our predictions. Arguing that the sacred gravitates towards ultimate value to affirm, enhance, validate and express that value, they all reflected on the significance that was coming to be placed on subjective-life. As Simmel (1997) put it so vividly, 'This emotional reality – which we can only call life – makes itself increasingly felt in its formless strength . . . claiming inalienable rights as the true meaning or value of our existence' (p. 24). And as it progresses, the turn to subjective life draws the sacred within.

Following the lead of these giants of the past, we have argued in this volume that a major cultural development – 'the massive subjective turn of modern culture' – has served to fuel the growth of subjective-life spirituality and to undermine life-as religion. To summarize our findings concerning the situation in Great Britain today, around 4,600,000 are active in the congregational domain on a typical Sunday, and around 900,000 in the holistic milieu during a typical week. This means that the claim that a spiritual revolution has taken place is exaggerated. Nevertheless, we have demonstrated that a major shift has occurred in the sacred landscape since the fifties and sixties, and is still continuing. Even though it cannot be described as a full-blown revolution, we have noted a few 'mini-revolutions' that have already occurred. When the spiritual revolution claim is taken to include what is happening within the 'cultural canopy', including the cultures of education, healthcare and wellbeing, its validity is considerably enhanced. Had it been possible to quantify the growth of subjective-life spirituality within and on the fringes of congregational activity, particularly in small groups, we might have found additional evidence to support the claim.

Looking to the future, much suggests that the cultivation of subjective-life is going to remain of central importance and attain increasing cultural significance. Having considered the most likely scenarios for associational forms of the sacred in this chapter, we have concluded that the holistic milieu will continue to grow, albeit at a slower rate than in recent years, to perhaps double its size during the next 40 or 50 years. We have also concluded that although the congregational domain will decline to around a third of its current size by 2030, decline is likely to be stemmed by the relative vitality of experiential religions of difference. Pulling these two conclusions together, we predict that in 40 or so years time the congregational domain and holistic milieu of Britain will have become much the same size. Between 3 and 4 per cent of the population will be active in each during a typical week. As to whether a spiritual revolution will take place after that – well, predicting the future has its limits.

In any case, this volume does not stand or fall with the accuracy of its prediction. Predictions are fun. More importantly, they serve to focus the mind on current trends and their longer term significance. It may be, for instance, that the spiritual revolution will take place in the next 40 or 50 years – as will happen if the holistic milieu widens its appeal, if experiential religions of difference fail to halt overall congregational decline, or if both processes operate. The main purpose of the volume has not been to foretell the future, but to study the tectonic shifts currently underway in the sacred landscape. We have demonstrated that we are living through a period of unique change, and we have tried to characterize and explain the nature of this change. As we learn more about the values, beliefs, experiences, activities and general outlook of the generation that is currently coming to maturity, we will learn more about what may happen next. So far as the fate of religion and spirituality are concerned, the future is very much in their hands.

Appendices

Appendix 1: The Kendal Project: Summary of Research Strategies (1 October 2000–30 June 2002)

Why Kendal?

Once we had decided to undertake a locality study, we had to select a town. It need not have been Kendal but, for the following reasons, it was.

Practicality. The chosen locality was within easy reach of our homes and workplace, and we had some prior knowledge of the town and useful contacts within it.

Size. With its population of just under 28,000 Kendal was the right size to research with the resources at our disposal. Our feasibility study showed it had enough churches, chapels and 'alternative' forms of spiritual practice to make it possible to test the spiritual revolution claim.

Boundedness. Kendal is a fairly self-contained town. With the nearest other towns being 10-25 miles away (Windermere, Penrith, Lancaster), the majority of people could be expected to conduct much of their religious or spiritual lives within or near the town rather than travelling elsewhere.

Homogeneity. Kendal has no significant ethnic communities. Whilst it would have been interesting in its own right to study a more multi-cultural town, it would also have made things considerably more complex. Since we were treading new ground as it was, and since we had limited time and resources, we were happy to have one less complicating factor.

Division of Labour

We knew from our feasibility study in Kendal (research carried out by Margaret Stelfox during 1998) that the main forms of associational activity oriented to the sacred fell into one of two categories: congregational or 'alternative' (which we later termed 'holistic'). We also knew that the task of studying each one was of roughly the same magnitude. We therefore divided our research and researchers roughly equally between these two 'heartlands'. Linda Woodhead and research associate Karin Tusting took responsibility for the congregational domain, Paul Heelas, Bronislaw Szerszynski and research associate Benjamin Seel for the holistic milieu. Team meetings were held on a regular, typically weekly, basis.

Sequence of Tasks

1 Mapping the associational activities
Certain tasks had an obvious priority in the Project, most obviously the identification of all examples of associational activity that could be relevant (see Chapter Two for details of how this was done). Each activity was listed and a data sheet about it was prepared, either on the basis of a visit or a telephone interview.

2 Follow-up research of the associational activities
By the time the Kendal Project had ended, all the 25 congregations in Kendal had been visited at least once. All the holistic milieu group and one-to-one practitioners had been interviewed at least once, and approximately 60 per cent of the holistic milieu groups had been studied at first hand.

3 Longitudinal research
Initial archival research into how the numbers involved in the congregational domain of Kendal had changed over time was carried out by Margaret Stelfox during the feasibility study. Detailed study of the attendance records of four congregations was carried out by Abby Day and Rosemary Mingins. The longitudinal picture of the holistic milieu was built up during the course of the Project by way of the three methods outlined in Chapter Two (pp. 42–5).

4 Identifying and researching representative case studies
Selection of representative examples of the main types of activity characteristic of each of the two heartlands took place a few months after the commencement of the Project. The three holistic case studies selected were Rainbow Cottage, Infinite Tai Chi, and Yoga at Kendal Leisure Centre. Four congregational case studies were

selected: New Life Community Church, Holy Trinity (Anglican) Church, Parr Street Evangelical Church and the Unitarian Chapel. Case study research continued until the end of the Project. The full-time researchers, Seel and Tusting, were responsible for this research, which was chiefly carried out by way of participant observation and interview. The former was recorded as fieldwork notes, the latter as full interview transcriptions. Interviews were both semi-structured and unstructured, usually took place in people's homes and lasted for between one and two hours. In total around 200 case study interviews were carried out.

5 Counting

The congregational domain was counted first, whilst the more complicated business of counting in the holistic milieu took place over a more extended period. The methods employed are outlined in Chapter Two (pp. 33–40).

6 Questionnaires

The design and distribution of questionnaires was deliberately left to the end of the Project, when we had a better idea of what we still needed to find out and confirm/disconfirm, and could see how best to frame our questions (in language appropriate to those who would complete them). The two questionnaires – for the congregational domain and the holistic milieu – were designed in tandem and had some common questions, but differed somewhat in nature and purpose. Whilst the holistic questionnaire was designed to provide information about the milieu as a whole, the main purpose of the congregational questionnaire was to provide information about the four main varieties of Christianity in Kendal. Copies of the questionnaires and results can be found at www.kendalproject.org.uk.

We distributed 516 copies of the congregational domain questionnaire to the four case study churches as well as the Roman Catholic Church; 187 were completed and returned (almost entirely by post), a response rate of 36 per cent. Administration of the holistic questionnaire was more complicated. In order to handle the fact that confidentiality/anonymity considerations meant that we could not make direct contact with clients of one-to-one practitioners (in particular), we distributed the questionnaire to all spiritual one-to-one practitioners who were happy to help, together with all spiritual group practitioners whose groups were scheduled to meet during our chosen week. Asked to fill one in themselves, practitioners were also asked to give the questionnaire to willing one-to-one clients and group participants or to those who came along during a particular week in November 2001. A pre-paid envelope was enclosed with each questionnaire, respondents being requested to reply within 10 days. Since we do not know how many questionnaires were distributed by the practitioners, we cannot provide a response rate in the normal way. Nevertheless, the 252 replies we received from 252 individuals make up 42 per cent of the 600 people who we finally determined to be active during a typical week in the life of the holistic milieu.

Strategy for Writing the Book

The task of writing this volume was divided equally between Heelas and Woodhead, with Heelas taking responsibility for producing drafts of material dealing with the holistic milieu, Woodhead those dealing with the congregational domain, and both working on general conceptual and theoretical themes. After these had been produced, the material went through four further stages. First, each author scrutinized the work of the other and made suggestions for revision. Second, the agreed draft which emerged from this process was sent to all the team members. Third, team comments and suggestions were incorporated and accommodated at the discretion of the authors. Finally, both authors read through all the material in order to ensure uniformity and make final revisions.

Appendix 2: The Congregational Domain in Kendal (November 2000)

Congregation	Total attenders by congregation	Type of congregation (variety of religion)	% of total churchgoing in Kendal by type
1 Allhallows (Church of England)	11	Religion of humanity	
2 Fellside Methodist	15	Religion of humanity	
3 Holy Trinity and St George R.C.	531	Religion of humanity	
4 Holy Trinity (Kendal Parish Church) (Church of England)	195	Religion of humanity	
5 Sandylands Methodist	94	Religion of humanity	
6 St George's (Church of England)	110	Religion of humanity	
7 Stricklandgate Methodist	176	Religion of humanity	

8 United Reformed Church	81	Religion of humanity	Religion of humanity = 55%
9 Bethel Evangelical (independent)	19	Religion of difference	
10 Church of Jesus Christ of Latter Day Saints (Mormons)	26	Religion of difference	
11 Jehovah's Witness, Highgate	98	Religion of difference	
12 Jehovah's Witness, Parkside	62	Religion of difference	
13 Kendal Christadelphians	16	Religion of difference	
14 Parr Street Evangelical Church (ex-Brethren, independent)	154	Religion of difference	
15 South Lakes Christadelphians (self-report)	10	Religion of difference	
16 Our Lady and Saint Oswald (Anglo-Catholic)	5	Religion of difference	Religion of difference = 18%
17 Heron Hill Free Church (independent)	29	Religion of experiential difference	
18 New Life Community Church (independent)	56	Religion of experiential difference	
19 Salvation Army	22	Religion of experiential difference	
20 St Thomas's (Church of England)	300	Religion of experiential difference	
21 St Thomas's, Hallgarth (Church of England church plant)	58	Religion of experiential difference	Religion of experiential difference = 21%
22 Beacon of Light Spiritualist Church	32	Religion of experiential humanity	

Continued

Appendix 2—*Continued*

Congregation	Total attenders by congregation	Type of congregation (variety of religion)	% of total churchgoing in Kendal by type
23 First Church of Christ, Scientist	33	Religion of experiential humanity	
24 Society of Friends (Quakers)	29	Religion of experiential humanity	
25 Unitarian Chapel	45	Religion of experiential humanity	Religion of experiential humanity = 6%
Total	2207		

Appendix 3: Forms of Holistic Milieu Activities in and within Five Miles of Kendal (Autumn 2001)

Activity	Number participating
Acupressure	12
Acupuncture	51
Alexander technique courses and one-to-one activities	77
Aromatherapy	97
Art therapy/groups	20
Astrology	36
Buddhist groups	43
CancerCare group	19
Chinese College of Physical Culture group	9
Chiropractice	36
Circle dancing	47
Counselling (Co-counselling/Person-centred counselling)	50
Craniosacral therapy	34
Energy management workshops	7
Flower essences therapy	54
Foot massage	48

GreenSpirit group	5
Healing/Spiritual healing groups and one-to-one activities	48
Herbalism	34
Homeopathy course and one-to-one activities	88
Hypnotherapy	24
Indian head massage course and one-to-one activities	25
Inter-faith group	38
Iona group	7
Kinaesiology	13
Massage	89
Meridian therapy	2
Metamorphic technique	9
Naturopathy	2
Nutritional therapy	7
Osteopathy	62
Pagan activities	11
Palm readings	13
Play therapy	3
Psychic consultancy	22
Psychotherapy group/Psychosynthesis group	20
Rebirthing	12
Reflexology	79
Reiki group and one- to-one activities	61
Relaxation therapy	17
Sai Baba group	5
Sea of Faith group	14
Shiatsu	35
Spinal touch therapy	3
Tai chi/Chi kung groups	63
Taizé singing group	19
Tarot card reading	30
True Vision group	3
Universal Peace dancing group	30
Vision therapy	5
Wild Women group	2
Women's spirituality group	7
Yoga groups	128

The figures in the table are from the holistic milieu questionnaire (response rate 42 per cent). They show the number of respondents who practised each kind of activity during a particular week in the autumn of 2001 and/or prior to that. Activities other than those indicated as being groups take a one-to-one form. 'One-off' events are not included.

It should be borne in mind that some respondents were involved in more than one activity. It must also be emphasized that the 42 per cent response rate means that the figures cited here do not represent the total numbers participating in each activity.

It should also be noted that when, as is normally the case, Christian-inspired associational activities such as Taizé have a life-as orientation (generally taking take place within congregational settings or being affiliated to congregations) they have not been included in the holistic milieu.

Notes

Introduction

1 The themes and arguments explored in this volume owe a great deal to the following, together with many other scholars: Bellah et al. (1985), Berger et al. (1974), Durkheim (1971), Gehlen (1980), James (1960), Luckmann (1967, 1990), Simmel (1997), Roof (1993, 1999), Taylor (1989, 1991, 2002), Tipton (1982), Troeltsch (1931) and Wuthnow (1998). For the development of our own thoughts, see for example Heelas (1996, 2002a), Woodhead (2004) and Woodhead and Heelas (2000).

2 This is also why the turn to subjective-life is bound up with an emphasis on the value of individual freedom. The latter is a facilitating rather than a primary value. What is of 'ultimate' value is the unique subjective-self. But that self can only be itself – discover itself, express itself, fulfil itself – if it is free from external, compulsion, control, regulation and intrusion. As Lukes (1973) puts it, 'The very idea of *self*-development logically implies that the development is autonomously pursued' (p. 136).

3 Our use of the terms 'life-as religion' and 'subjective-life spirituality' should not for one moment be taken to imply that we are reducing whatever is taken to be sacred or ultimate to socio-cultural formations or subjectivities. Life-as Christians believe in a God who transcends this world and our experience of it. And although we use the term 'subjective-life spirituality' because what matters is experience (which can only be subjective), this by no means rules out the fact that this form of spirituality is also taken to belong to the very act of being alive. The language is of 'spirituality is love, love is spirituality' (for example) and 'life force or energy' (for example).

4   It must be emphasized that this does not rule out the fact that life-as religion
    can flourish when life-as forms of life are present – in conservative rural areas or
    in city ethnic neighbourhoods, for example.

Chapter 1   Distinguishing Religion and Spirituality: Findings from Kendal

1   See Chapter Two (p. 37) for why activities taking place in the environs of Kendal
    are included in the holistic milieu.
2   What follows is largely based on an analysis of some 100 interviews and discus-
    sions. Fieldwork notes have also been taken into consideration.
3   Although participation has little if anything to do with dictating how life-as
    roles ought to be performed, a number of participants told us that their holistic
    activities served to improve the quality of their lives as (for example) teachers.
4   See Chapter Two for further discussion of points summarized in this paragraph.
    It should be borne in mind that although one or two of the Buddhist groups
    might be relatively tradition-informed, they belong to the holistic milieu in that
    subjective-life is catered for; and participants are typically involved in other
    holistic activities. We should also point out that we have debated long and hard
    about whether to include the Baha'i group in the holistic milieu. On the one
    hand there is an emphasis on immanent spirituality and many participants are
    active in the milieu; on the other hand, the otherness of God is also empha-
    sized. After much deliberation, we have finally decided not to discuss the Baha'i
    faith in this book. As Baha'i participants number 13 or so people, the figures
    presented in what follows are not affected in any significant regard. Obviously, if
    the faith were larger in Kendal, with many participants not active in the holistic
    milieu, we would have included Baha'is in the category of life-as religion.
5   Those thinking in terms of the legacy of the Frankfurt School (in particular
    Adorno, Fromm, and that latter-day descendant, Foucault) will object that we
    are ignoring the argument that the holistic milieu actually functions in a 'forma-
    tive' or life-as way. Whatever the truth of this argument, our characterization of
    the holistic milieu in this chapter has relied on what we know to be the case:
    namely, what participants have to say.

Chapter 2   Testing the Spiritual Revolution Claim in Kendal

1   The debate has been provoked, in part, by the fact that the Church of England
    has recently changed its policy for gathering data on its attendance levels, from
    counting typical Sunday attendance to counting average weekly attendance
    during a month. This policy has been criticized, not least because it breaks the

continuity with existing time-series data (Gill, 2002). A reason we decided to use the measure of typical Sunday attendance rather than average weekly attendance was because it would allow us to make comparisons with the existing congregational data. In addition, our purpose was simply to arrive at one reliable measure of attendance – a measure as close as possible to the 'typical weekly' way in which we planned to measure the incidence of holistic milieu participation.

2   The possibility of our using a longer time-span is discussed later in this chapter. Weekly participation within the congregational domain (see note 9 below) is almost certainly very similar to typical Sunday participation – which (alone) justifies our use of a typical weekly time span for the holistic milieu. It should also be noted that we decided not to include one-off workshops, fairs or other events in our holistic milieu count – their irregularity means that it would have been difficult to produce a weekly figure that was anything more than a rough estimate, and given that one-off events almost certainly attract many already active in the holistic milieu, it would have been extremely difficult (if not impossible) to avoid multiple counting (for that would have involved collecting the names of everybody attending events).

3   We arrived at the figure for the number of individuals involved during a typical week on the basis of our mapping exercise (which gave us the number of acts of participation in a given week) and on the basis of what respondents to the questionnaire said about the number of activities they had participated in during 'the past seven days' (Q1). We have also taken into account the fact that multi-participants were more likely to come across a questionnaire and so fill it in.

4   Some 15 respondents to the questionnaire added activities to the list provided in the questionnaire (see Appendix 3), including, for example, channelling, pilates, a Sufi group, and a gathering of Brahma Kumaris (the latter involving around 12 people, practising what is described as 'body, mind, spirit' meditation). Although we are not certain that *all* these activities are provided by practitioners who consider them to be spiritual, or that they take place within Kendal and environs, it is very likely that the additions to the list show that we had not managed to identify everything of relevance. Given the particular difficulties of tracking down activities in the rural area around Kendal, this is not surprising. (As Heelas knows from his life in the Yorkshire Dales, activities in rural areas are, for example, run from converted farmhouses, with no advertising other than word of mouth.) Our figure of 600 participants is thus on the conservative side.

5   Other than New Life (for which we have hard evidence), other congregations that appear to have experienced brief spurts of growth at some point(s) between the 1960s and early 1990s are: the Jehovah's Witnesses (religion of difference), Parr Street (religion of difference), Heron Hill Free Church (religion of experiential difference), and St Thomas's, Hallgarth (another religion of experiential difference, and a church plant).

6   Löwendahl (2002) is one of the few scholars to have found evidence (in Sweden) suggesting that the 'New Age' might be in decline.

7   The 55 per cent figure rises to 62 per cent when the activity, or activities, took place during the previous week and/or prior to that. Both these figures have been determined so as to avoid counting acts of multi-participation.

8   Hard data is extremely difficult to obtain – even if people go to church or chapel for non-religious reasons, many are unlikely to want to talk about this; and it is not at all clear how one could establish whether or not those who say they attend for religious reasons are 'actually' there for other reasons. We should add that the 0.9 per cent holistic figure was not determined until the questionnaire research was carried out towards the end of the Kendal Project- which meant that, even if it had been possible, we did not have the opportunity to try and find ways of arriving at a comparable figure for the congregational domain.

9   As for shorter time spans, it could be argued that just as we measured participation in the holistic milieu by way of the 'typical week', so should we have gauged congregational domain participation by taking attendance at mid-week services into account as well as Sunday attendance. We did not do this, partly because the 'typical weekly' measure is rarely used in other studies (which means it is of little comparative value), and partly because of the amount of resources which would have had to be devoted to meeting the challenge of avoiding double counting. In any case, our research in Kendal indicated that mid-week attendance is low, and would appear largely to involve people who also attend on Sundays. So even if we had adopted the 'typical week' approach, it is unlikely that it would have made a significant difference to the 7.9 per cent figure we have arrived at.

10   Since 16 per cent of the people active in the holistic milieu are also regular churchgoers, overall associational activity is slightly smaller than the 9.5 per cent total arrived at by simply adding together the 7.9 per cent and 1.6 per cent of the two heartland territories.

Chapter 3   Evidence for a Spiritual Revolution: Britain and USA

1   Although no one systematically counted groups and one-to-one activities in Britain during the 'sixties', primary and secondary literature shows that there were few activities of the kind found today. Being a 'child of the sixties', Heelas has monitored particular localities (for example Oxford) over the years – the picture is unquestionably one of growth. It can be noted that the Festival for Mind Body Spirit – presenting the kind of activity which we are using to gauge change – was not established until 1977. De Michelis (2004) estimates that numbers practising the two major schools of Postural Yoga have increased by

300 per cent from 1970 (to reach around 120,000 participants by 1992-3); de Michelis also reported research based on Lexis-Nexis findings regarding UK newspaper articles, namely that there were no articles on yoga in 1980, with numbers progressively increasing to 3,675 in 2001 (2004, p. 194).

2   Hadaway, Marler and Chaves (1993) survey academic and popular publications to show how frequently the 40 per cent figure is cited (pp. 741-2).

3   The higher rate of decline indicated by the *Yearbook* may be a function of the fact that not all the same church bodies report in the *Yearbook* each year, and some of them change their counting methods. The same problems beset the Glenmary data, but we have here relied on Shibley's analysis of the data which attempts to correct these problems (Shibley, 1996), to which we added Roman Catholic numbers drawn from the Glenmary data.

4   Although it is almost certainly the case that polls over-report congregational attendance, surveys could under-report those involved with 'alternative' or 'New Age' spiritualities – the argument being that in the USA the latter activities do not have the same social or cultural acceptability as the former.

5   Regarding the 20 per cent figure for Kendal, it is certainly unlikely to be higher. Among other considerations, 45 per cent of participants do not attach spiritual significance to the activity or activities which they are currently practising (see Chapter Two, p. 46). As for the point that the holistic milieu of the USA is not likely to be so very different from that found in Kendal or Britain, the primary material we have collected, together with other publications (including the academic), serve to show that a participant in Britain is readily going to feel at home in the USA (or indeed in many other countries). True, prosperity or 'how to' spiritualities (for example) are more significant in the USA – but the 'flow' of 'New Age' themes and practices is such that the holistic milieus of the two countries have much more in common than not.

6   Additional evidence concerning the greater size of CAM in the USA is provided by figures for over-the-counter sales. For the USA see Astin (1998) and Eisenberg, Davis, Ettner et al. (1998); for Britain see White and Ernst (2000) and Thomas, Nicholl and Coleman (2001). This comparison suggests that CAM could be up to 100 per cent larger in the USA.

7   For evidence regarding the growth of yoga, see the Harris Interactive Service Bureau (2003) findings provided in Chapter Five; see also Ray and Anderson (2000, pp. 328-32), including growth figures from the four million yoga participants in 1990 to the 18 million they report for 1998 (p. 329). Figures for CAM are also included (p. 330); other evidence for the growth of CAM activities is provided below, in Chapter Four, note 5.

8   Whatever the exact size might be, the milieu is surely large enough to cast doubt on the claims of those who say that it is numerically insignificant. Referring to the 'New Age' in 1992, Finke and Stark wrote of 'a blip, not an eruption' (p. 244): hardly an eruption, it is true; but even 10 or so years ago, it

was probably more than a blip. In contrast, Fuller's (2001) account of numerical significance suggests that the percentage could well be closer to 8 per cent than the lower figure we have provided. (Fuller estimates, for example, that 'a full 20 per cent of the population can be said to be sympathetic with the New Age movement' (p. 99).) This is also indicated by a key finding from a survey which discovers that 7 per cent practise yoga in the USA (Harris Interactive Service Bureau, 2003) – a percentage for the adult population, and which includes people who practise yoga alone, but which is nevertheless indicative.

9   A good ethnographic illustration is provided by Griffith's (1997) study of the Women's Aglow movement.

10   Whilst the Glenmary data indicates steady growth of Roman Catholic numbers between 1970 and 2000 in the USA, Hadaway, Marler and Chaves (1998) and Hadaway and Marler (1998) who relied on the more reliable clergy-reported attendance figures in their study of Catholic attendance in the Archdiocese of San Francisco discovered a drop in attendance of almost 50 per cent between 1961 and 1996. Church participation of Roman Catholics, once much higher than that of Protestants, has dropped over the last 30 years to near parity with that of the latter (Roozen and Hadaway, 1993, p. 252), whilst disaffiliation is high and switching to other denominational families is increasing (Roof and MacKinney, 1987; Hadaway and Marler, 1993).

11   We deliberately avoid the term 'consumer culture' because it implies (1) that what is consumed is absorbed by the consumer – and expelled as waste product, and (2) that the purchasing choice and subsequent involvement with the purchased good is relatively trivial and undemanding. Our objection is simple: that which is purchased need not be consumed in either of these senses (a copy of the Bible or Kant's *Critique of Pure Reason*, for example).

12   See Lau (2000) on 'New Age capitalism' in the USA, including strongly holistic-orientated companies like the Aveda Corporation.

13   Thus the Roman Catholic 'Jesuit Spirituality Centre' (Loyola Hall, Merseyside) offered the following retreats for 2003: 'Rest and Relaxation', 'Spirituality of Aging', 'God of the Senses', 'Changing Direction', 'What We May Be', 'Finding the Still Point', 'Celtic Spirituality', '12 Step Spirituality' and 'Sacred Touch'.

14   It is important to add the proviso that this is partly due to recategorization and consolidation by booksellers – although this in itself is indicative in that the mind-body-spirit category has served as the vehicle for reorganization. In the USA, according to Puttick (2003), 90 million mind-body-spirit books were sold during 1998.

15   The place of 'religion' in the USA media is explored by Silk (1998), who finds that 'religion' still has prominence, and that coverage is generally bland and uncritical.

16 Health and women's magazines in the USA are probably more spiritually in-
    clined than in Britain, and there are more magazines dealing primarily with
    inner-life spirituality. There seem to be more of the latter on sale in shopping
    malls and major bookstores than Christian equivalents.

17 On religion, spirituality and the Internet, see Zaleski (1997), Dawson and
    Hennebry (1999) and Hadden and Cowan (2000); on popular culture in the
    USA, see Ostwalt (2003), Moore (2003), and the review provided in *Religious
    Studies Review* (1999, 25 (1), pp. 3-11).

18 See, in particular, Salamon (2000, 2001, 2002); see also Bell and Taylor
    (forthcoming), Carrette and King (2004), Casey (2000), Hicks (2003) and
    Mitroff and Denton (1999). On soft capitalism and spirituality, see Thrift
    (1997) and Heelas (1996, 2002b). In the USA, however, Christianity does
    seem to be harnessed to 'capitalist' ends more frequently – as book titles like
    Jesus CEO, *The Management Methods of Jesus* and *God is My CEO* indicate.

19 See also Best (1996) on education and spirituality. Courses including reference
    to spirituality are now widely available in vocationally orientated colleges (in-
    cluding Kendal College), adult education centres and similar institutions. In
    the USA, there is still serious controversy surrounding prayer in public schools.
    However, there are more private schools, many of them religious. Likewise, the
    home school movement is growing rapidly, especially in conservative evangel-
    ical circles. See Smith (2003) and the review in *Religious Studies Review* (1997
    23 (1), pp. 35-9) for the overall situation in the USA.

20 The growth of CAM has been discussed earlier in this chapter. For more on
    spirituality in health care contexts, including nursing, see Gilliat-Ray (2003),
    Harrison and Burnard (1993) and Orchard (2001). Spirituality is also increas-
    ingly in evidence within the helping professions. During the later 1980s, it can
    be noted, the World Health Organization added the word 'spiritual' to its
    definition of health.

21 In the USA our strong impression is that the picture regarding a spiritual
    revolution in the culture is both similar and different: similar in that holistic
    spirituality has also grown to become far more visible within mainstream cul-
    ture in the last few decades; different in that Christianity has continued to
    maintained a high cultural profile over the same period. The USA is also able
    to sustain Christian 'sub-cultures' in a way that is impossible in Europe (Bruce,
    2002, pp. 220-8 and Chapter Four, p. 123).

22 The most pressing research challenge involves further study of the beliefs of
    the very large number of Westerners who are neither atheists/agnostics nor
    involved in associational religious or spiritual activities (Heelas, 2002a).

23 Elsewhere in Europe, Houtman and Mascini (2002) find that 27 per cent of
    their respondents to a study carried out in the Netherlands agree with the
    statement 'There is a God who personally occupies himself with every human
    being', 33 per cent agreeing that 'There has to be something like a higher

force that controls life' (p. 462). In Sweden, a third of the population believe in 'the God within' (Anders Bäckström, personal communication).

24 For further information from the 'being religious/being spiritual' literature, see for example Marler and Hadaway (2002), Scott (2001) and Zinnbauer, Pargament, Cole et al. (1997).

Chapter 4 Bringing the Sacred to Life: Explaining Sacralization and Secularization

1 Durkheim (1971) himself very much concentrated on explaining traditional life-as religion (defined as 'a unified system of beliefs and practices relative to sacred things, that is to say, things set apart and forbidden' (p. 47)) by reference to life-as socio-cultural formations. He did not apply his replication approach to explain another form of the sacred which, like so many others of his time, he was acutely aware was a growing force, namely one which consists 'entirely in internal and subjective states, and which would be constructed freely by each of us' (p. 47).

2 See Hall (1999) on voluntary associations; see also Putnam (2000, pp. 183-4) and Veroff et al (1981, p. 537). For an example of the subjectivization of politics, see Mulgan (1994) on how personal sources of significance can inform a 'new politics' of 'life values'; Chambers (1997), who defines wellbeing as 'the experience of good quality of life' rather than in terms of 'wealth' (p. 9), addresses the world of development agencies (see also Nussbaum and Glover, 1996).

3 Regarding one sector of wellbeing publications, Bunting, in a revealing article entitled 'Finding your inner cook' (2000) writes: 'Cookery books have an appeal much like *The Little Book of Calm*: it's the feel-good market with plenty of comforting advice on how to live your life'.

4 Chapter Three provides more information concerning spirituality in (subjectivized) cultural settings. More generally, Singer (1993) provides a philosophical rendering of quality-of-life ethics (see also Kleinig, 1991); and Nussbaum (2003) explores wellbeing and emotions in connection with the Aristotelian concept of *eudaimonia* ('a complete human life'). Regarding cultural analysis, Baudrillard argues that 'individuals no longer compete for the possession of goods, they actualize themselves in consumption, each on his own' (in Poster, 1988, p. 12); Campbell (2004) explores what he calls the 'emotional ontology' of 'modern consumerism'; and Gimlin (2002) argues that activities like aerobics 'release notions of selfhood from the physical' (p. 50). From the point of view of primary material, advertisements and products provide a good indication of values found in subjective wellbeing culture – for example, L'Oréal's 'Because you're worth it' and 'Because I'm worth it'; 'personalized jewellery, glassware,

rugs, paintings and a variety of other items using an individual's genetic DNA fingerprint' (Designa Gifts, offering products which could not be much more personalized); 'True to life' and 'Turn back in time' (Earth Therapeutics skin lotion); 'Live your dream – change your life' (advert for a motorhome).

5 A good index of the growth of subjective wellbeing culture is provided by studies of complementary and alternative medicine. According to Thomas, Nicholl and Coleman (2001), '8.5% of the adult population [of England] had seen a practitioner for one of the six main therapies [acupuncture, homeopathy, etc.] in the past six months in 1993, compared to 10.6% in 1998' (p. 9); regarding the USA, Eisenberg et al. (1998) report that 'Use of at least 1 of 16 alternative therapies during the previous year increased from 33.8% in 1990 to 42.1% in 1997' (p. 1569). The House of Lords Report (2000) provides a summary of various surveys, includes data concerning the large volume of over-the-counter sales (of herbal medicine, for example), and provides evidence that CAM (largely) belongs to subjective wellbeing culture (Chapter 1). Ray and Anderson (2000) provide commercial indicators of the importance of subjective wellbeing culture in the USA, an estimated $230 being spent at the end of the last century in the area of 'lifestyles of health and sustainability' (p. 329).

6 We are not suggesting that the holistic milieu *in toto* is simply a wellbeing zone. If Kendal is anything to go by, there are certainly participants within the milieu who are seeking enlightenment or 'truth' – but numbers are small, and even the activities which are most focused on spirituality as an end in itself also function holistically.

7 Recall the finding, provided in Chapter Two, that only 55 per cent of those active in Kendal's holistic milieu experience a 'spiritual dimension' in connection with the activity – or activities – they have practised during the previous week. It should also be borne in mind that holistic milieu brochures or websites often uses 'intermediary' terms like 'centredness', 'energy flow' or 'going deeper' – terms which suggest that there is more to life than it might appear, but which do not explicitly refer to spirituality.

8 It is noteworthy that if the holistic milieu of Kendal is anything to go by, ease of access is facilitated by the (virtual) absence of life-as new religious movements – those which Barker (1999) describes by reference to 'the unambiguous clarity and certainty in the belief systems', and the 'commitment' which is expected (p. 20).

9 This argument can be refined by showing that *particular* forms of wellbeing and ill-being are of little significance. As is shown by the responses to question 3 of the Kendal holistic questionnaire (p. 91 above), only 7.6 per cent of respondents prioritize 'pleasure, enjoyment or a treat' as their reason for becoming involved. And only 6.3 per cent refer to 'life crises'. Questionnaire returns, together with ethnographic research, also provide little support for the idea that people become involved with the milieu because they have lost faith in the

modern world. Berger, Berger and Kellner (1974) were surely correct in arguing that loss of faith in the mainstream played a major role in the development
of the counter-cultural 1960s. But belonging as it does to subjective wellbeing
culture, the holistic milieu is far from being counter-cultural – a point supported by questionnaire and other findings from Kendal which show that
participants are largely satisfied with their everyday lives in society. (See
www.kendalproject.org.uk for relevant questionnaire returns; and see the
following section of this chapter 'Revisiting the Subjectivization Thesis'.)

10   The largest number of those responding to the question 'What is your occupation?', amounting to 37 per cent, say they belong to a 'professional or technical occupation'; 34 per cent fall into the 'other' category of the
questionnaire, almost certainly including many of the 95 or so of the practitioners of Kendal's holistic milieu; and only 7.5 per cent describe themselves as
a 'manual worker'.

11   Findings from Kendal are very much in line with those reported from elsewhere. Roof (1993) writes of the 'highly active seekers' of his baby boomers
sample, 'Many have scaled down their expectations and work in the lower-
paying service professions such as teaching, nursing, social work, and counseling' (p. 81); see also Yankelovich (1981) and his finding that over half of those
most concerned with self-fulfillment have received some college education with
many in 'white collar' jobs (pp. 59-61). Although McGuire's (1988) study of
'alternative healing' in the USA includes a somewhat more diverse array of
activities than are to be found in the holistic milieu of Kendal, it is nevertheless
significant that McGuire reports that respondents 'are clearly middle-class . . .
well-educated, social, culturally, and residentially established' (p. 13). Bruce
(1996a) writes of 'the university educated middle classes working in the expressive professions: social workers, counsellors . . . ' (p. 218). Houtman and
Mascini (2002) provide evidence regarding levels of education (p. 464). The
Harris (2003) poll of yoga participants in the USA shows that around 90 per
cent have been to college or university, with over 30 per cent being on quite
high incomes. Jones (2003) gives data for Ramatha's School of Enlightenment, including the fact that 71 per cent are professionals (p. 261); Brown
(1997) reports that those involved with channeling 'are well educated and
often affluent' (p. 7). Frisk (2003) provides educational data for Sweden
(p. 243), Mercer and Durham (1999) data for those most likely to have 'mystical experiences' (p. 176). See Gallup and Lindsay (1999) on the link between
educational attainment and 'spiritual growth' in the USA (p. 79), and Veroff
et al. (1981, p. 101) on the link between education and the cultivation of
subjective-life. See Wootton and Sparber (2001) for a profile of those involved
with CAM, including data on education and income; Sharma (1995, chapter
1) for information concerning a range of countries; and see Kelner and Wellman (1997, p. 211) on educational attainment.

12   It is extremely important to note that we are not for one moment denying the role played by the holistic milieu – most noticeably by holistic milieu practitioners – in contributing to the development of the more general culture of subjective wellbeing. Holistic milieu practitioners publish books (at least 10, that we know of, have come out of Kendal and environs); practitioners are called upon to contribute to the business activities of soft capitalism, both in the realms of production and (more importantly) advertising and consumption (as consultants, etc.); practitioners are involved in the development of holistic spas (and indeed work within them); and so on. Then there is the role played by influential people like Leslie Kenton (one-time editor of the health and beauty section of *Harpers and Queen*) writing within the mainstream who are also deeply versed in holistic spiritualities.

13   Gender findings from Kendal are very much in line with those reported from elsewhere. See, for example, Brown (1997, p. 95); Frisk (2003, p. 243); Houtman and Mascini (2002, p. 468); Jones (2003); Lowendahl (2002); McGuire (1988, p. 12); Rose (1998, p. 6); Wootton and Sparber (2001) and Sharma (1995, e.g. p. 35) for CAM. The 'Yoga in America' questionnaire carried out by the Harris Interactive Service Bureau (2003) finds that 76.9 per cent of practitioners are women.

14   It is indicative that Inglehart, Basanez and Moreno (1998) find a very small difference between the percentages of males and females holding post-materialist values (V405). See also Mitchell (1983, p. 279).

15   Some excellent illustrations of what we mean by relational subjectivism, interfusing the relational with the autonomous, are provided by many of the great Romantics, Lukes (1973), writing that for Wilhelm von Humboldt, for example, the '"true end of man" was "the highest and most harmonious development of his powers to a consistent whole" [but] whose "highest ideal [was] the co-existence of human beings", constituted in "a union in which each strives to develop himself from his own inmost nature"' (p. 68). More recently, consider Cancian's work (1987), whose general theme is that couples increasingly combine self-development with commitment, and whose conclusion is that 'There is plenty of evidence that the interest in personal growth during the seventies was linked to close relationships; intimacy, not isolation, was a sign of the developed self' (p. 9; see also p. 39). Another good example, now regarding the contemporary situation, is provided by Richard Sennett (1977), writing that 'The reigning aspiration today is to develop individual personality through experiences of closeness and warmth with others' (p. 259). See also Giddens (1993) and, from a social constructivist point of view, Gergen (1987). Or we might think of Brother David Steindl-Rast: 'When I talk about a shift to "personal experience", I don't mean "private". "Personal" is defined in terms of your relations . . . You become a person more deeply through your relations to other persons' (cited by Cimino and Lattin, 2002, p. 16).

16   Farias (forthcoming) provides a sophisticated social psychological analysis of what he calls 'New Age', showing that what he calls a 'hybrid form of individualism' emphasizes both the subjective-life of the 'holistic' and 'personal autonomy' (p. 12). This is characterized as 'holistic individualism' (p. 13). And see Hedges and Beckford on 'Holism, Healing and the New Age' (2000) and their exploration of the theme that 'The true self is not . . . an island or an atom: it is only one part of a much larger whole' (p. 172).

17   It could be objected at this point that some holistic milieu activities are not especially holistically interpersonal or intimate. Many yoga groups, for example, involve individual practice with little verbal self-disclosure. Our response is that bodily movement is highly expressive, communicative, self-disclosing, with relationships being established with the practitioner. Furthermore, the perception of many men is that yoga groups – predominantly involving women – are contexts which belong to women and where your body is going to be revealed: perhaps in ways which are going to make men feel clumsy and awkward. How many middle-aged men want their bodies to be taken seriously in public?

18   As to why there should be a gendered division of labour, debate currently rages between earlier feminist analyses which attributed differences to an early, somewhat passive, process of socialization (e.g. De Beauvoir, 1993; Gilligan, 1982) and more 'post-modern' feminist analyses which place more emphasis on the active and discursive negotiation of sex roles throughout a lifetime (e.g. Stanley and Wise, 1983; Davies, 1989; Butter, 1990).

19   Care for the body may be an obvious place to start, particularly since women's responsibilities often leave them with less time for themselves than men, more tired than men, and reporting lower levels of health (Brannen and Moss, 1991). Having someone else take care of their bodies may be full of significance for the authorization and enhancement of subjective-life, particularly if Adkins (1995) is right in her observation that women are more likely then men to feel 'limited ownership of their bodies' (p. 159). Adkin's point is echoed by Gilligan (2002) and by Young (1990) in her aptly titled discussion of 'Throwing it like a Girl'. Both authors investigate psychological and other causes of women's limited ownership of their bodies and (in Gilligan's case) of men's limited ownership of emotional vulnerability and relationality.

20   One way of conceptualizing the holistic milieu is as an experimental social space in which women are attempting to retain commitment to relationality, but to give this commitment – which has previously been validated by now threatened institutions of life-as like the church – a new, more subjectivized basis. In other words, many activities in the holistic milieu represent an attempt to reconcile the (often) culturally divergent imperatives to 'be all I can be' and retain commitment to care and relationality. If this characterization is correct, then the milieu is undertaking what Hochschild (2003) considers to

be the most pressing need of our times, reconciliation between 'care' and 'the demands of our workplaces, the equality of the sexes, and the very structure of honour in modern life' (p. 3).

21   The age profile of Kendal is very much in line with England and Wales, the 2001 Census showing (for example) that 19.56 per cent of the population of Kendal are aged between 45 and 59, the equivalent figure for England and Wales being 18.93 per cent. The age profile of the holistic milieu is much the same elsewhere, including the USA: see Heelas and Seel (2003); McGuire (1988, p. 13); Cimino and Lattin (2002, p. 27); Wootton and Sparber (2001) for CAM. See www.kendalproject.org.uk for an age profile graph for the holistic milieu of Kendal and environs.

22   Regarding practitioners, many have given up careers which leave little or no time for milieu activities, moving to jobs which enable them to practise for two or three days a week, earning (on average) around £20 an hour.

23   21 per cent of participants in the holistic milieu of Kendal and environs are retired.

24   Although we do not have the space to explore the full implications of the fact here, it is significant that Hall (1999) reports that voluntary associations as a whole are 'For the most part . . . the preserve of those in middle age' (p. 455). Thinking back to points raised earlier in this chapter, it is also noteworthy that those involved in voluntary associations are increasingly drawn from the ranks of women (p. 437); that involvement correlates with level of education (p. 435); and that the large majority are middle-class (p. 438). It is clear that much the same socio-demographic factors are at work as with regard to holistic milieu participation. Hall himself draws particular attention to the role played by higher levels of education, especially of women (p. 437); see also Sharma (1995, chapters 1 and 3) on complementary medicine.

25   Using global data (as from Hofstede, 2001, for example), we have toyed with the idea of trying to see if there are cross-cultural correlations between the percentage of 'life-as' selves in various populations and the amount of life-as religion. Although there are some correlations, there are too many variables (such as the cultural revolution in China) to make this a very useful exercise. Comparing countries such as the USA and, however, which have shared cultural features, could be a much more useful activity – and one which we hope to pursue in the future.

26   The Princeton Religion Research Center's study of *The Unchurched American* (1988) finds that 'I wanted a child of mine to receive religious training' was a less important reason for returning (23 per cent) than the (somewhat inconclusive) 'I felt an inner need to go back to church' (40 per cent) and 'I felt an inner need to rediscover my religious faith' (27 per cent).

27   Yip (2000) records many similar remarks, supportive of the subjectivization thesis, made by disaffected gay Christians in the UK.

28 A number of studies which have tested Kelley's thesis by looking for factors that predict growth (or decline) failed to find a significant correlation with congregational strictness (see, for example, Hoge and Roozen, 1979 and Perry and Hoge, 1981). Studies of church leavers in both the UK and USA both find that dropouts are more likely to say they left because their congregation was 'too conservative' (around 33 per cent) than 'too liberal' (around 7 per cent) (Richter and Francis, 1998, p. 118; Hoge et al., 1981, p. 96 – both arrive at exactly the same figures). In a recent study, Thompson, Carroll and Hoge (1993) found that 'being theologically liberal was a plus for church growth' (p. 197).

29 Some congregations of experiential difference in Britain, and many more in the USA, go even further by offering material prosperity and/or healing of the body – perhaps by way of a 'miracle' (see, for example, McGuire, 1988; Percy, 1996; Poloma and Hoelter, 1998).

30 The research of Inglehart and associates is also highly relevant to the general argument of this chapter, Ingelhart (1997) stating that 'Despite their relative alienation from traditional religion...postmaterialists are *more* apt than the materialists to spend time thinking about the meaning and purpose of life.... Traditional beliefs and the established religious organizations may be losing their adherents, but spiritual concerns are becoming more widespread' (p. 285; see also p. 284; and Inglehart, 1990, pp. 187, 192).

31 The fact that the associational territory is in overall decline alone suffices to explain why we distance ourselves from those who adopt a homeostatic view with regard to the fortunes of different forms of the sacred – namely that as one form of the sacred declines another will grow to take its place (see, for example, Stark 1985). It can be added that *if* trends in Kendal and environs carry on as charted from the 1960s, the 2001 figure of 9.5 per cent for the congregational domain and the holistic milieu will not be matched until approaching the end of the century.

Chapter 5   Looking to the Future

1 The ways in which these (and other) processes operate is complex, including the fact that they often clash with one another. The literature on the topic is huge, with only some of the more important publications being referred to in this volume.

2 It can readily be argued that the growth of subjective wellbeing culture is a key element of the 'logic' of contemporary capitalism, which has seen the development of an 'experience economy', where 'experiences' serve as the product that encourages consumer activity. Informed by a long-standing aspect of consumer culture – the way it serves as a utopian 'castle of romantic dreams' (Campbell,

1987, p. 227) – 'inner capitalism' capitalizes on the fact that subjective well-being is a never-ending quest (for 'ill-being' can never be eradicated). Among other considerations, it can also be argued that the growth of subjective well-being culture owes a considerable amount to the widespread view that 'life is not a rehearsal' – (relative) loss of faith in the heavenly life-to-come contributing to the value attached to making the most of life in the here-and-now. A more comprehensive explanation of the development of subjective wellbeing culture would certainly have to take into account the role played by German Romanticism: its translation, during the nineteenth century, into popular activities (in particular being close to nature); and during the Third Reich (when nature was also important, as well as related activities such as homeopathy) (Harrington, 1996).

3   See Heelas and Seel (2003) for more detailed discussion of holistic milieu scenarios.

4   Evidence drawn from a wide variety of sources, too numerous to be cited here, provides support for the ageing cohort scenario in that the age of those participating in various 'new age' activities does indeed increase as one moves through the decades since the sixties.

5   See Heelas and Seel (2003) for some of the evidence of interest – and beliefs – among younger people, and the matter of (some) younger people turning to holistic milieu activities as they grow older. Evidence against the ageing cohort or 'last gasp of the sixties' scenario has also been provided in the 'Age' subsection of Chapter Four – namely that at least in Kendal, the majority of participants have not become involved prior to mid-life (p. 107).

6   The average of six activities is an underestimate in that we know that a number of participants will also have been going to activities run outside Kendal and environs – including varieties which are not on offer in the town and environs. Given that many have not been practising for a very long time, the average figure of six indicates a high level of embeddedness. It can be added that one person (the 'record holder') had previously been involved with 33 of the different activities listed in Appendix 3.

7   Regarding shared knowledge, it is significant that 90 per cent of respondents provided the correct answer to Q31 of the holistic milieu questionnaire: namely, 'What is chi?'. See Heelas (1998) for further discussion of the complicated matter of 'individualism' and shared 'beliefs'. It can be added that evidence from the Kendal Project does not provide support for the argument that diffuseness (or incoherence) means that the spiritual aspect of activities will not fare well in the future. There is no reasons to suppose that developments to date – meaning that 90 per cent of respondents currently believe in spirituality (Q9) with 71 per cent stating that spirituality is of important in their lives (Q12) – will change in the future. And regarding Bruce's (1996b) claim that 'the most popular products [of the 'New Age'] are those which are the most

secular' (p. 273), around 50 per cent of participants in the most popular activity, yoga, consider their participation to be of spiritual significance – and there is nothing to show that this figure was higher in the past. Furthermore, questionnaire responses (Q3, Q4) indicate a distinct shift – from 'looking for spiritual growth' being the fifth most frequently cited reason for originally becoming involved in the current activity of respondents to being the most frequently cited reason for being currently involved. (More generally, see Kelner and Wellman, 1997, p. 211.)

8   Since numbers of people join and leave the milieu, it is almost certainly the case that a higher proportion of the 'market niche' population than indicated by this figure have been involved.

9   If the milieu were to grow at the same (linear) rate as it has done since the beginning of the 1970s, it would double in size in around 30 years time; if it were to sustain the growth seen in Kendal (and elsewhere) during the later 1980s and during the 1990s, it would double in size in around 20 years time.

10   Bearing in mind evidence presented in the last chapter, it can readily be argued that many young adults, with their subjectivized, relational values on the one hand, and the stresses of making a career on the other, provide fertile territory for the growth of yoga and cognate activities.

11   These figures are drawn from Wraight and Brierley's (1999, pp. 12-25) collation of relevant research, including the authoritative data provided by Currie, Gilbert and Horsley (1977).

12   Figures supplied by the Church of Sweden Research Department for the period 1998-2002 show that the number attending the main 11.00 am Sunday service of the Church of Sweden is now so small that it would only be a slight exaggeration to state that the only people attending on a regular basis are those employed by the Church itself. A headcount carried out by Heelas in 2002 in the Swedish town of Smedjebacken (population approximately 10,000) provides a typical Sunday attendance figure of 100 (1 per cent).

13   Conversely, when members of such congregations orientate themselves towards subjective–life they tend to step *out* of their existing congregations, sometimes into the half-way house of a much more subjectivized 'post-evangelical' movement and/or an 'alternative worship' community (Guest, 2002).

14   As for the future of the congregational domain in the USA, the evidence suggests that the same scenario will take place, but that bottoming out will take place at a much higher level than in the UK due to the greater vitality of congregations of experiential difference (and possibly the growing subjectivization of congregations of humanity). As to why congregations of experiential difference should be faring better in the USA, we suspect the reason is that there is a much larger and more organized constituency in the USA dedicated to the maintenance of life-as values and – correspondingly – more life-as jobs

to perform. This seems evident first in relation to national and civic values and roles (membership of congregations is still widely assumed to be a part of good citizenship), and second in relation to family values and gender roles (hence the central importance given to these matters by many campaigning Christian groups, and the intensity of Christian concern over issues like abortion and homosexuality). We can also note the continuing 'culture wars' in the USA, which seem to have the effect of both reinforcing commitment to subjectivized values and opposing life-as values. But given that the USA is also a highly 'post-materialist' and subjectivized society, it is not surprising that 'dry' religions of difference do less well (even where they can maintain their own subcultures) than more subjectivized religions of experiential difference which offer enhanced subjective-life in and by way of life-as roles.

References

Adkins, Lisa 1995: *Gendered Work: Sexuality, Family and the Labour Market*. Buckingham, UK: Open University Press.

Allport, Gordon 1962: *The Individual and His Religion*. New York: Macmillan.

Ammerman, Nancy 1987: *Bible Believers: Fundamentalists in the Modern World*. New Brunswick, NJ: Rutgers University Press.

Ammerman, Nancy 1997a: *Congregation and Community*. New Brunswick, NJ: Rutgers University Press.

Ammerman, Nancy 1997b: Golden Rule Christianity: Lived Religion in the American Mainstream. In David D. Hall (ed.), *Lived Religion in America: Toward a History of Practice*. Princeton, NJ: Princeton University Press, pp. 196-216.

Astin, John A. 1998: Why Patients Use Alternative Medicine. *Journal for the American Medical Association*, 279 (19), pp. 1548-53.

Balmer Randall 1996: *Grant Us Courage. Travels Along the Mainstream of American Protestantism*. New York: Oxford University Press.

Barker, Eileen 1999: New Religious Movements: Their Incidence and Significance. In Bryan Wilson and Jamie Cresswell (eds), *New Religious Movements: Challenge and Response*. London: Routledge, pp. 15-31.

Barna Research Online 2001: Beliefs: General Religious: God. <http://www.barna. org/cgi-bin/PageCategory.asp?CategoryID = 2>.

Bauman, Zygmunt 2000: *Liquid Modernity*. Cambridge, UK: Polity.

Bell, Emma and Scott Taylor forthcoming: 'From Outward Bound to Inward Bound'. The Prophetic Voices of Discursive Practices of Spiritual Management Development. *Human Relations*.

Bellah, Robert N., Madsen, Richard, Sullivan, William M., Swidler, Ann and Tipton, Steven M. 1985: *Habits of the Heart: Individualism and Commitment in American Life*. Berkeley: University of California Press.

Benson, Paddy and Roberts, John 2002: *Counting Sheep: Attendance Patterns and Pastoral Strategy.* Cambridge, UK: Grove.

Berger, Peter (ed.) 1999: *The Desecularization of the World: Resurgent Religion and World Politics.* Washington, DC: Ethics and Public Policy Center; Grand Rapids, MI: W. B. Eerdmans.

Berger, Peter, Berger, Brigitte and Kellner, Hansfried 1974: *The Homeless Mind: Modernization and Consciousness.* Harmondsworth, UK: Penguin.

Best, Ron (ed.) 1996: *Education, Spirituality and the Whole Child.* London: Cassell.

Bookseller 2002: Mind, Body & Spirit. Special edition, 29 November.

Bradley, Martin B., Green, Jr., Norman M., Jones, Dale E., Lynn, Mac, McNeil, Lou 1992: *Churches and Church Membership in the United States 1990: An Enumeration by Region, State and County Based on Data Reported for 133 Church Groupings.* Atlanta, GA: Glenmary Research Center.

Brannen, Julia and Moss, Peter 1991: *Managing Mothers: Dual Earner Households after Maternity Leave.* London: Unwin Hyman.

Brierley, Peter 2000: *The Tide is Running Out: What the English Church Attendance Survey Reveals.* London: Christian Research.

Brierley, Peter (ed.) 2001: *UK Christian Handbook: Religious Trends 3 (2002-2003).* London: Christian Research.

Brown, Callum C. 2001: *The Death of Christian Britain: Understanding Secularisation 1800 – 2000.* London: Routledge.

Brown, Michael F. 1997: *The Channeling Zone: American Spirituality in an Anxious Age.* Cambridge, MA: Harvard University Press.

Bruce, Steve 1996a: *Religion in the Modern World: From Cathedrals to Cults.* Oxford: Oxford University Press.

Bruce, Steve 1996b: Religion in Britain at the Close of the 20th Century: A Challenge to the Silver Lining Perspective. *Journal of Contemporary Religion*, 11 (3), pp. 261-75.

Bruce, Steve 2002: *God is Dead: Secularization in the West.* Oxford: Blackwell.

Bruce, Steve 2003: The Demise of Christianity in Britain. In Grace Davie, Paul Heelas and Linda Woodhead (eds), *Predicting Religion: Christian, Secular and Alternative Futures.* Aldershot, UK: Ashgate, pp. 53-63.

Bunting, Madeleine 1996: Shopping for God. *The Guardian*, 16 December, pp. 2-3.

Bunting, Madeleine 2000: Finding Your Inner Cook. *The Guardian*, 11 December, p. 21.

Butler, Judith 1990: *Gender Trouble: Feminism and the Subversion of Identity.* New York: Routledge.

Campbell, Colin 1987: *The Romantic Ethic and the Spirit of Modern Consumerism.* Oxford: Blackwell.

Campbell, Colin 1999: The Easternisation of the West. In Bryan Wilson and Jamie Cresswell (eds), *New Religious Movements: Challenge and Response.* London: Routledge, pp. 35-48.

Campbell, Colin 2004: I Shop Therefore I Know that I Am: The Metaphysical Basis of Modern Consumerism. In Karin Ekstrom and Helen Brembeck (eds), *Elusive Consumption*. Oxford: Berg, pp. 27-44.

Cancian, Francesca M. 1987: *Love in America: Gender and Self-Development*. Cambridge, UK: Cambridge University Press.

Capouya, John 2003: Real Men do Yoga. *Newsweek*, 16 June, pp. 78–9.

Carrette, Jeremy and King, Richard 2004: *Selling Spirituality. The Silent Takeover of Religion*. London: Routledge.

Carroll, Jackson W. and Wade Clark Roof 2002: *Bridging Divided Worlds: Generational Cultures in Congregations*. San Francisco: Jossey-Bass.

Casey, Catherine 2000: Spirit at Work. Incorporating the New Age? Paper delivered at the Working Knowledge Conference, Sydney, Australia, 11-13 December.

Catholic Communications Office 2003: Jesus Christ: The Bearer of the Water of Life. A Christian Reflection on the 'New Age'. <http://www.vatican.va/roman_curia/pontifical_councils/interelg/documents/rc_pc_interelg_doc_20030203_new-age_en.html>.

Chambers, Robert 1997: *Whose Reality Counts? Putting the First Last*. London: Intermediate Technology.

Chaves, Mark and Cavendish, James C. 1994: More Evidence on U.S. Catholic Church Attendance. *Journal for the Scientific Study of Religion*, 33 (4), pp. 376-81.

Cimino, Richard and Lattin, Don 2002: *Shopping for Faith: American Religion in the New Millennium*. San Francisco: Jossey-Bass.

Cline, Sally and Spender, Dale 1988: *Reflecting Men: At Twice their Natural Size*. London: Fontana.

Coleman, John A., S.J. 1997: Exploding Spiritualities: Their Social Causes, Social Location and Social Divide. *Christian Spirituality Bulletin*, 5 (1), Spring, pp. 9-15.

Collins, Sylvia 1997: Young People's Faith in Later Modernity. Guildford, UK: University of Surrey Libary.

Cupitt, Don 1999: *The New Religion of Life in Everyday Speech*. London: SCM.

Currie, Robert, Gilbert, Alan and Horsley, Lee 1977: *Churches and Churchgoers: Patterns of Church Growth in the British Isles since 1700*. Oxford: Clarendon Press.

Davie, Grace 2002: *Europe: The Exceptional Case. Parameters of Faith in the Modern World*. London: Darton Longman and Todd.

Davies, Bronwyn 1989: *Frogs and Snails and Feminist Tales*. Sydney: Allen and Unwin.

Dawson, Lorne L. and Hennebry, Jenna 1999: New Religions and the Internet: Recruiting a New Public Space. *Journal of Contemporary Religion*, 14 (1), pp. 17-39.

De Beauvoir, Simone 1993: *The Second Sex*. London: D. Campbell.

De Michelis, Elizabeth 2004: *A History of Modern Yoga*. London: Continuum.

Delphy, Christine and Leonard, Diana 1992: *Familiar Exploitation: A New Analysis of Marriage in Contemporary American Societies*. Cambridge, UK: Polity.

Durkheim, Emile [1915]1971: *The Elementary Forms of the Religious Life*. London: George Allen & Unwin.

Eisenberg, David M., Davis, Roger B., Ettner, Susan L., et al. 1998: Trends in Alternative Medicine Use in the United States, 1990-1997. *Journal of the American Medical Association*, 280 (18), pp. 1569-76.

Farias, Miguel forthcoming: A Social-Psychological Study on the Adherence to the New Age Movement. Oxford: Department of Experimental Psychology, University of Oxford.

Field, Clive D. 2001: 'The Secularized Sabbath Revisited': Opinion Polls as Sources for Sunday Observance in Contemporary Britain. *Contemporary British History*, 15 (1), pp. 1-20.

Finke, Roger and Stark, Rodney 1992: *The Churching of America, 1776-1990*. New Brunswick, NJ: Rutgers University Press.

Francis, Leslie J., Lankshear, David W. and Jones, Susan H. 2000: The influence of the Charismatic Movement on Local Church Life: A Comparative Study among Anglican Rural, Urban and Suburban Churches. *Journal of Contemporary Religion*, 15 (1), pp. 121-30.

Frisk, Liselotte 2003: New Age Participants in Sweden. Background, Beliefs, Engagement and 'Conversion'. In Mikael Rothstein and Reender Kranenborg (eds), *New Religions in a Postmodern World*. Aarhus: Aarhus University Press, pp. 241-55.

Fuller, Robert C. 2001: *Spiritual, But Not Religious: Understanding Unchurched America*. Oxford: Oxford University Press.

Gallup, Jr., George and Jones, Timothy 2000: *The Next American Spirituality: Finding God in the Twenty-First Century*. Colorado Springs, CO: Victor.

Gallup, Jr., George and Lindsay, D. Michael 1999: *Surveying the Religious Landscape: Trends in US Beliefs*. Harrisburg, PA: Morehouse.

Geertz, Clifford 1984: 'From the Native's Point of View': On the Nature of Anthropological Understanding. In Richard A. Shweder and Robert A. LeVine (eds), *Culture Theory. Essays on Mind, Self, and Emotion*. Cambridge, UK: Cambridge University Press, pp. 123-36.

Gehlen, Arnold 1980: *Man in the Age of Technology*. New York: Columbia University Press.

Gergen, Kenneth J. 1987: Toward Self as Relationship. In Krysia Yardley and Terry Honess (eds), *Self and Identity*. London: John Wiley & Sons, pp. 53-63.

Gerth, H. H. and Mills, C. Wright 1977: *From Max Weber. Essays in Sociology*. London: Routledge.

Giddens, Anthony 1993: *The Transformation of Intimacy*. Stanford, CA: Standford University Press.

Gill, Robin 1993: *The Myth of the Empty Church*. London: SPCK.

Gill, Robin 2002: *Changing Worlds: Can The Church Respond?* London: Continuum.

Gill, Robin 2003: *The 'Empty' Church Revisited*. Aldershot, UK: Ashgate.

Gill, Robin, Hadaway, C. Kirk and Marler, Penny Long 1998: Is Religious Belief Declining in Britain? *Journal for the Scientific Study of Religion*, 37 (3), pp. 507-16.

Gilliat-Ray, Sophie 2003: Nursing, Professionalism, and Spirituality. *Journal of Contemporary Religion*, 18 (3), pp. 335-49.

Gilligan, Carol 1982: *In a Different Voice: Psychological Theory and Women's Development*. Cambridge, MA: Harvard University Press.

Gilligan, Carol 2002: *The Birth of Pleasure: A New Map of Love*. London: Chatto and Windus.

Gimlin, Debra L. 2002: *Body Work. Beauty and Self-Image in American Culture*. Berkeley: University of California Press.

Griffith 1997: God's Daughters: Evangelical Women and the Power of Submission. Berkeley: University of California Press.

Gross, Martin 1979: *The Psychological Society*. New York: Simon and Schuster.

Guest, Mathew 2002: Negotiating Community: An Ethnographic Study of an Evangelical Church. Lancaster, UK: Lancaster University Library.

Hadaway, C. Kirk and Marler, Penny Long 1993: All in the Family: Religious Mobility in America. *Review of Religious Research*, 35 (1), pp. 97-116.

Hadaway, C. Kirk and Marler, Penny Long 1998: Did You Really Go to Church This Week? Behind the Poll Data. *The Christian Century*, May 6, pp. 472-5.

Hadaway, C. Kirk and Marler, Penny Long 2003: How Many Americans Worship Each Week? An Alternative Measurement Strategy. Paper presented at ISSR 'Religion and Generations' Conference, Turin, 21-25 July.

Hadaway, C. Kirk, Marler, Penny Long and Chaves, Mark 1993: What the Polls Don't Show: A Closer Looks at U.S. Church Attendance. *American Sociological Review*, 58 (4), pp. 741-52.

Hadaway, C. Kirk, Marler, Penny Long and Chaves, Mark 1998: Over-reporting Church Attendance in America: Evidence that Demands the Same Verdict. *American Sociological Review*, 63 (1), pp. 122-30.

Hadden, Jeffrey K. and Cowan, Douglas E. (eds) 2000: *Religion on the Internet: Research Prospects and Promises*. Amsterdam: JAI.

Hall, Peter A. 1999: Social Capital in Britain. *British Journal of Politics*, 29, pp. 417-61.

Hamilton, Clive 2003: *Downshifting in Britain. A Sea-Change in the Pursuit of Happiness*. Discussion Paper Number 58. Canberra: The Australia Institute.

Hammond, Phillip E. 1992: *Religion and Personal Autonomy: The Third Disestablishment in America*. Columbia: University of South Carolina Press.

Harrington, Anne 1996: *Reenchanted Science. Holism in German Culture from Wilhelm II to Hitler*. Princeton, NJ: Princeton University Press.

Harris Interactive Service Bureau 2003: Yoga in America. <http://www.yogajournal.com/about_press061603.cfm>.

Harrison, Judy and Burnard, Philip 1993: *Spirituality and Nursing Practice*. Aldershot, UK: Avebury.

Heald, Gordon 2000: *Soul of Britain*. London: The Opinion Research Business.

Hedges, Ellie and Beckford, James A. 2000: Holism, Healing and the New Age. In Steven Sutcliffe and Marion Bowman (eds), *Beyond New Age: Exploring Alternative Spirituality*. Edinburgh: Edinburgh University Press, pp. 169-87.

Heelas, Paul 1996: *The New Age Movement*. Oxford: Blackwell.

Heelas, Paul 1998: New Age Authenticity and Social Roles: A Response to Steve Bruce. *Journal of Contemporary Religion*, 13 (2), pp. 257-64.

Heelas, Paul 2002a: The Spiritual Revolution: From 'Religion' to 'Spirituality'. In Linda Woodhead (ed.), *Religions in the Modern World*. London: Routledge, pp. 357-77.

Heelas, Paul 2002b: Work Ethics, Soft Capitalism and the 'Turn to Life'. In Paul du Gay and Michael Pryke (eds), *Cultural Economy*. London: Sage, pp. 78-96.

Heelas, Paul and Seel, Benjamin 2003: An Ageing New Age? In Grace Davie, Paul Heelas and Linda Woodhead (eds), *Predicting Religion. Christian, Secular and Alternative Futures*. Aldershot, UK: Ashgate, pp. 229-47.

Hicks, Douglas A. 2003: *Religion in the Workplace: Pluralism, Spirituality, and Leadership*. Cambridge, UK: Cambridge University Press.

Hirst, Rob 2003: Social Networks and Personal Beliefs: An Example from Modern Britain. In Grace Davie, Paul Heelas and Linda Woodhead (eds), *Predicting Religion: Christian, Secular and Alternative Futures*. Aldershot, UK: Ashgate, pp. 86-94.

Hobsbawm, Eric 1995: *Age of Extremes*. London: Abacus.

Hochschild, Arlie R. 1983: *The Managed Heart: Commercialization of Human Feeling*. Berkeley and London: University of California Press.

Hochschild, Arlie R. 1989: *The Second Shift: Working Parents and the Revolution at Home*. New York: Viking.

Hochschild, Arlie R. 1997: *The Time Bind. When Work Becomes Home and Home Becomes Work*. New York: Metropolitan Books.

Hochschild, Arlie R. 2003: *The Commercialization of Intimate Life. Notes from Home and Work*. Berkeley, Los Angeles and London: University of California Press.

Hofstede, Geert 2001: *Culture's Consequences*. London: Sage.

Hoge, Dean R. 1974: *Commitment on Campus: Changes in Religion and Values over Five Decades*. Philadelphia: Westminster Press.

Hoge, Dean R. 1979: National Contextual Factors Influencing Church Trends. In Dean R. Hoge and David A. Roozen (eds), *Understanding Church Growth and Decline 1950-1978*. New York: The Pilgrim Press, pp. 94-122.

Hoge, Dean R. with McGuire, Kenneth and Stratman, Bernard F. 1981: *Converts, Dropouts, Returnees: A Study of Religious Change Among Catholics*. Washington, DC: U.S. Catholic Conference; New York: Pilgrim Press.

Hoge, Dean R., Johnson, Benton and Luidens, Donald A. 1994: *Vanishing Boundaries: The Religion of Mainline Protestant Baby Boomers*. Louisville, KY: Westminster/John Knox Press.

Hoge, Dean R. and Roozen, David A. (eds) 1979: *Understanding Church Growth and Decline 1950-1978*. New York: The Pilgrim Press.

Hollinger, Franz and Smith, Timothy B. 2002: Religion and Esotericism among Students: A Cross-Cultural Comparative Study. *Journal of Contemporary Religion*, 17 (2), pp. 229-49.

House of Lords 2000: *Science and Technology – Sixth Report*. <www.parliament. the-stationery-office.co.uk/pa/ ld199900/ldselect/ldsctech/123/12301.htm>.

Hout, Michael and Greeley, Andrew 1998: What Church Officials' Reports Don't Show: Another Look at Attendance Data. *American Sociological Review*, 63 (1), pp. 113-19.

Houtman, Dick and Peter Mascini 2002: Why do Churches become Empty, While New Age Grows? Secularization and Religious Change in the Netherlands. *Journal for the Scientific Study of Religion*, 41 (3), pp. 455-73.

Hunter, James Davison 1987: *Evangelicalism: The Coming Generation*. Chicago: The University of Chicago Press.

Iannaccone, Laurence 1994: Why Strict Churches Are Strong. *American Journal of Sociology*, 99 (5), pp. 1180-1211.

Inglehart 1977: *The Silent Revolution: Changing Values and Political Styles Among Western Publics*. Princeton, NJ: Princeton University Press.

Inglehart, Ronald 1990: *Culture Shift in Advanced Industrial Society*. Princeton, NJ: Princeton University Press.

Inglehart, Ronald 1997: *Modernization and Postmodernization: Cultural, Economic and Political Change in 43 Societies*. Princeton, NJ: Princeton University Press.

Inglehart, Ronald, Basanez, Miguel and Moreno, Alejandro 1998: *Human Values and Beliefs: A Cross-Cultural Sourcebook*. Ann Arbor: University of Michigan Press.

James, William [1902]1960: *The Varieties of Religious Experience*. London: Fontana.

Järvinen, Margaretha 1993: *Of Vice and Women: Shades of Prostitution*. Oslo: Scandinavian University Press.

Johnson, Douglas W., Picard, Paul R. and Quinn, Bernard 1974: *Churches and Church Membership in the United States 1971: An Enumeration by Region, State and County Based on Data Reported for 133 Church Groupings*. Washington, DC: Glenmary Research Center.

Jones, Constance A. 2003: Students in Ramtha's School of Enlightenment: A Profile from a Demographic Survey, Narrative, and Interview. In Mikael Rothstein and Reender Kranenborg (eds), *New Religions in a Postmodern World.* Aarhus, Denmark: Aarhus University Press, pp. 257-85.

Jones, Dale E., Doty, Sherri, Grammich, Clifford et al. 2000: *Religious Congregations and Membership in the United States 2000: An Enumeration by Region, State and County Based on Data Reported for 149 Religious Bodies.* Washington, DC: Glenmary Research Center.

Kelley, Dean M. [1972]1995: *Why Conservative Churches Are Growing.* Macon, GA: Mercer University Press/Rose.

Kelner, Marrijoy and Wellman, Beverly 1997: Health Care and Consumer Choice: Medical and Alternative Therapies. *Social Science Medicine,* 45 (2), pp. 203-12.

Keynes, John Maynard 1931: *Essays in Persuasion.* London: Macmillan.

Kleinig, John 1991: *Valuing Life.* Princeton, NJ: Princeton University Press.

Lambert, Yves 1999: Religion in Modernity as a New Axial Age: Secularization or New Religious Forms? *Sociology of Religion,* 60 (3), pp. 303-33.

Langford, Wendy 1999: *Revolutions of the Heart: Gender, Power and the Dimensions of Love.* London: Routledge.

Lau, Kimberly J. 2000: *New Age Capitalism: Making Money East of Eden.* Philadelphia: University of Pennsylvania Press.

Leonardo, Micaela di 1987: The Female World of Cards and Holidays: Women, Families and the World of Kinship. *Signs,* 12 (3), pp. 440-53.

Lindner, Eileen W. 2003: *Yearbook of American and Canadian Churches 2003.* New York: National Council of the Churches of Christ in the U.S.A.

Löwendahl, Lena 2002: *Med Kroppen som Instrument.* Lunds Universitet: Lund Studies in History of Religions.

Luckmann, Thomas 1967: *The Invisible Religion.* London: Collier-Macmillan.

Luckmann, Thomas 1990: Shrinking Transcendence, Expanding Religion? *Sociological Analysis* 50 (2), pp. 127-38.

Lukes, Steven 1973: *Individualism.* Oxford: Basil Blackwell.

Lynch, Gordon 2002: *After Religion: 'Generation X' and the Search for Meaning.* London: Darton, Longman and Todd.

Mann, Horace 1854: *Religious Worship in England and Wales, Census of Great Britain, 1851.* London: George Routledge and Co.

Marler, Penny Long and Hadaway, C. Kirk 1999: Testing the Attendance Gap in a Conservative Church. *Sociology of Religion* 60 (2), pp. 175-86.

Marler, Penny Long and Hadaway, C. Kirk 2000: Attendance. In Wade Clark Roof (ed.), *Contemporary American Religion,* vol. 1. New York: MacMillan, pp. 40-2.

Marler, Penny Long and Hadaway, C. Kirk 2002: 'Being Religious' or 'Being Spiritual' in America: A Zero-Sum Proposition? *Journal for the Scientific Study of Religion* 41 (2), pp. 289-300.

Marler, Penny and Roozen, David A. 1993: From Church Tradition to Consumer Choice: The Gallup Surveys of the Unchurched American. In David A. Roozen and Kirk C. Hadaway (eds), *Church and Denominational Growth*. Nashville, TN: Abingdon Press, pp. 253-77.

Marsden, George 1991: *Understanding Fundamentalism and Evangelicalism*. Grand Rapids, MI: W. B. Eerdmans.

McCullers, Carson 1973: *The Member of the Wedding*. New York: Bantam Books.

McGuire, Meredith, with Kantor, Debra 1988: *Ritual Healing in Suburban America*. New Brunswick, NJ: Rutgers University Press.

McGuire, Meredith B. 1997: Mapping Contemporary American Spirituality: A Sociological Perspective. *Christian Spirituality Bulletin* 5 (1), Spring, pp. 1-8.

Mercer, Calvin and Durham, Thomas W. 1999: Religious Mysticism and Gender Orientation. *Journal for the Scientific Study of Religion*, 38 (1), pp. 175-82.

Miller, Donald E. 1997: *Reinventing American Protestanism: Christianity in the New Millennium*. Berkeley and Los Angeles: University of California Press.

Mills, Simon and Budd, Sarah 2000: *Professional Organisation of Complementary Medicine in the United Kingdom 2000*. Centre for Complementary Health Studies, University of Exeter.

Mitchell, Arnold 1983: *The Nine American Lifestyles*. New York: Macmillan.

Mitroff, Ian I and Denton, Elizabeth A. 1999: *A Spiritual Audit of Corporate America*. San Francisco: Jossey-Bass.

Moore, R. Laurence 2003: *Touchdown Jesus: The Mixing of Sacred and Secular in American History*. Louisville, KY: Westminster John Knox.

Mudie-Smith, Richard (ed.) 1904: *The Religious Life of London*. London: Hodder.

Mulgan, Geoffrey 1994: *Politics in an Antipolitical Age*. Cambridge, UK: Polity.

Nietzsche, Friedrich [1883-5]1981: *Thus Spoke Zarathustra*. Harmondsworth, UK: Penguin.

Norman, Edward 2002: *Secularisation*. London: Continuum.

Nussbaum, Martha C. 2003: *Upheavals of Thought: The Intelligence of Emotions*. Cambridge, UK: Cambridge University Press.

Nussbaum, Martha and Glover, Jonathan (eds) 1996: *Women, Culture, and Development: A Study of Human Capabilities*. Oxford: Oxford University Press.

Orchard, Helen (ed.) 2001: *Spirituality in Health Care Contexts*. London: Jessica Kingsley.

Ostwalt, Conrad (2003), *Secular Steeples: Popular Culture and the Religious Imagination*. Harrisburg, PA: Trinity Press International.

Partridge, Chris 2004: Alternative Spiritualities, New Religions and the Re-enchantment of the West. In James R. Lewis (ed.), *Oxford Handbook of New Religious Movements*. New York: Oxford University Press, pp. 39-67.

Penning, James M. and Corwin E. Smidt 2002: *Evangelicalism: The Next Generation*. Grand Rapids, MI: Baker Academic.

Percy, Martyn 1996: *Words, Wonders and Power*. London: SPCK.

Percy, Martyn 2003: A Place at High Table? Assessing the Future of Charismatic Christianity. In Grace Davie, Paul Heelas and Linda Woodhead (eds), *Predicting*

Religion: Christian, Secular and Alternative Futures. Aldershot, UK: Ashgate, pp. 95-108.

Perrin, Robin, D., Kennedy, Paul and Miller, Donald E. 1997: Examining the Sources of Conservative Church Growth: Where are the New Evangelical Movements Getting their Numbers? *Journal for the Scientific Study of Religion,* 36 (1), pp. 71-80.

Perry, Everett and Hoge, Dean 1981: Faith Priorities of Pastor and Laity as a Factor in the Growth or Decline of Presbyterian Congregations. *Review of Religious Research* 22 (3), pp. 221-32.

Pickering, W. S. F. 1975: *Durkheim on Religion.* London: Routledge and Kegan Paul.

Pilgrim, Gay 2003: The Quakers. Towards an Alternate Ordering. In Grace Davie, Paul Heelas and Linda Woodhead (eds), *Predicting Religion: Christian, Secular and Alternative Forms.* Aldershot, UK: Ashgate, pp. 147-58.

Poloma, Margaret M. and Hoelter, Lynette F. 1998: The 'Toronto Blessing': A Holistic Model of Healing. *Journal for the Scientific Study of Religion,* 66, pp. 257-71.

Poster, Mark (ed.) 1988: *Jean Baudrillard: Selected Writings.* Cambridge, UK: Polity.

Presser, Stanley and Stinson, Linda 1998: Data Collection Mode and Social Desirability Bias in Self-Reported Religious Attendance. *American Sociological Review* 63 (1), pp. 137-45.

Princeton Religion Research Center 1978: *The Unchurched American.* Princeton, NJ: Princeton Religion Research Center.

Princeton Religion Research Center 1988: *The Unchurched American Ten Years Later.* Princeton, NJ: Princeton Religion Research Center.

Pringle, Rosemary 1989: *Secretaries Talk: Sexuality, Power and Work.* Sydney: Allen and Unwin.

Putnam, Robert D. 2000: *Bowling Alone.* New York: Simon & Schuster.

Puttick, Elizabeth 2003: New Age Publishing: Reflecting or Creating the Trends. Paper delivered to the Alternative Spiritualities and New Age Studies Conference, The Open University, Milton Keynes, 30 May–1 June.

Quinn, Bernard, Anderson, Herman, Bradley, Martin, Goetting, Paul and Shriver, Peggy 1982: *Churches and Church Membership in the United States 1980: An Enumeration by Region, State and County Based on Data Reported by 111 Church Bodies.* Atlanta, GA: Glenmary Research Center.

Ray, Paul H. and Anderson, Sherry Ruth 2000: *The Cultural Creatives.* New York: Three Rivers Press.

Reeves, Thomas C. 1996: *The Empty Church: The Suicide of Liberal Christianity.* New York: Free Press.

Richter, Philip and Francis, Leslie J. 1998: *Gone but not Forgotten: Church Leaving and Returning.* London: Darton, Longman and Todd.

Rieff, Philip 1987: *The Triumph of the Therapeutic*. London: Chatto and Windus.

Roberts, Dan and Kelleher, Ellen 2004: Alternative Therapy. US Companies Search for Radical Ways to Cut the Spiralling Cost of Employee Healthcare. *Financial Times*, 19 March, p. 11.

Roof, Wade Clark 1993: *A Generation of Seekers: The Spiritual Journeys of the Baby Boom Generation*. New York: HarperSanFrancisco.

Roof, Wade Clark 1999: *Spiritual Marketplace: Baby Boomers and the Remaking of American Religion*. Princeton, NJ: Princeton University Press.

Roof, Wade Clark and McKinney, William 1987: *American Mainline Religion: Its Changing Shape and Future*. New Brunswick, NJ: Rutgers University Press.

Roozen, David A. and C. Kirk Hadaway 1993: *Church and Denominational Growth*. Nashville, TN: Abingdon Press.

Rose, Nikalas 1999: *Inventing Our Selves: Psychology, Power and Personhood*. Cambridge, UK: Cambridge University Press.

Rose, Stuart 1998: An Examination of the New Age Movement: Who is Involved and What Constitutes its Spirituality. *Journal of Contemporary Religion*, 13 (1), pp. 5-22.

Rousseau, Jean-Jacques [1781]1971: *The Confessions of Jean-Jacques Rousseau*. London: Penguin.

Salamon, Karen 2000: No Borders in Business: The Managerial Discourse of Organisational Holism. In Timothy Bewes and Jeremy Gilbert (eds), *Cultural Capitalism*. London: Lawrence & Wishart, pp. 134-57.

Salamon, Karen 2001: 'Going Global from the Inside Out': Spiritual Globalism in the Workplace. In Mikael Rothstein (ed.), *New Age Religion and Globalization*. Aarhus, Denmark: Aarhus University Press, pp. 150-72.

Salamon, Karen 2002: Prophets of a Cultural Capitalism: An Ethnography of Romantic Spiritualism in Business Management. *Folk. Journal of the Danish Ethnographic Society*, 44, pp. 89-115.

Sargeant, Kimon Howland 2000: *Seeker Churches: Promoting Traditional Religion in a Non-Traditional Way*. New Brunswick, NJ: Rutgers University Press.

Scott, Robert Owens 2001: Are you Religious or are you Spiritual? *Spirituality & Health*, Spring Issue, pp. 26-31.

Schwartz, Shalom and Huismans, Spike 1995: Value Priorities and Religiosity in Four Western Religions. *Social Psychology Quarterly*, 58 (2), pp. 88-107.

Sennett, Richard 1977: *The Fall of Public Man*. Cambridge, UK: Cambridge University Press.

Sharma, Ursula 1995: *Conplementary Medicine Today: Practitioners and Patients*. London: Routledge.

Sharma, Ursula and Black, Paula (1999): *The Sociology of Pampering: Beauty Therapy as a Form of Work*. Working paper. University of Derby: Centre for Social Research.

Shibley, Mark A. 1996: *Resurgent Evangelicalism in the United States: Mapping Cultural Change Since 1970*. Columbia: University of South Carolina Press.

Silk, Mark 1998: *Unsecular Media: Making News of Religion in America*. Urbana and Chicago: University of Illinois Press.

Simmel, Georg 1997: *Essays on Religion*. New Haven, CT: Yale University Press.

Singer, Peter 1993: *Practical Ethics*. Cambridge, UK: Cambridge University Press.

Smith, Christian 1998: *Evangelicalism: Embattled and Thriving*. Chicago: University of Chicago Press.

Smith, Christian 2002: *Christian America? What Evangelicals Really Want*. Berkeley: University of California Press.

Smith, Christian (ed.) 2003: *The Secular Revolution: Power, Interests and Conflict in the Secularization of American Public Life*. Berkeley: University of California Press.

Smith, Dorothy E. 1974: Women's Perspective as a Radical Critique of Sociology. *Sociological Inquiry*, 44 (1), pp. 7-13.

Sointv, Eeva 2004: *The Wellbeing Society*. Lancaster: Lancaster University Library.

Stacey, Jackie 2000: The Global Within: Consuming Nature, Embodying Health. In Sarah Franklin, Celia Lury and Jackie Stacey, *Global Nature, Global Culture*. London: Sage, pp. 97-145.

Stanley, Liz and Wise, Sue 1983: *Breaking Out: Feminist Consciousness and Feminist Research*. London: Routledge.

Stark, Rodney 1985: Europe's Receptivity to Religious Movements. In Rodney Stark (ed.), *Religious Movements*. New York: Paragon House, pp. 301-39.

Stark, Rodney and Finke, Roger 2000: *Acts of Faith: Explaining the Human Side of Religion*. Berkeley: University of California Press.

Tamney, Joseph B. 2002: *The Resilience of Conservative Religion: The Case of Popular, Conservative Protestant Congregations*. Cambridge, UK: Cambridge University Press.

Taylor, Charles 1989: *Sources of the Self: The Making of the Modern Identity*. Cambridge, UK: Cambridge University Press.

Taylor, Charles 1991: *The Ethics of Authenticity*. Cambridge, MA: Harvard University Press.

Taylor, Charles 2002: *Varieties of Religion Today*. Cambridge, MA: Harvard University Press.

Thomas, K. J., Nicholl, J. P. and Coleman, P. 2001: Use and Expenditure on Complementary Medicine in England: A Population Based Survey. *Complementary Therapies in Medicine*, 9, pp. 2-11.

Thompson, Wayne L., Carroll, Jackson W. and Hoge, Dean R. 1993: Growth or Decline in Presbyterian Congregations. In David A. Roozen and C. Kirk Hadaway (eds), *Church and Denominational Growth*. Nashville, TN: Abingdon Press, pp. 188-207.

Thrift, Nigel 1997: Soft Capitalism. *Cultural Values*, 1 (1), pp. 29-57.

Tipton, Steven M. 1982: *Getting Saved from the Sixties*. Berkeley: University of California Press.

Trilling, Lionel 1974: *Sincerity and Authenticity*. London: Oxford University Press.

Troeltsch, Ernst 1931: *The Social Teaching of the Christian Churches*. London: Allen and Unwin.

Veroff, Joseph, Douvan, Elizabeth and Kulka, Richard 1981: *The Inner American: A Self-Portrait from 1957 to 1976*. New York: Basic Books.

Walter, Tony 1996: Developments in Spiritual Care of the Dying. *Religion*, 26 (4), pp. 353-63.

Walter, Tony 2002: Spirituality in Palliative Care: Opportunity or Burden? *Palliative Medicine*, 16 (2), pp. 133-140.

Warner, R. Stephen 1993: Work in Progress Toward a New Paradigm for the Sociological Study of Religion in the United States. *American Journal of Sociology* 98 (5), pp. 1044-93.

Watts, Alan 1973: *In My Own Way. An Autobiography 1915-1965*. London: Jonathan Cape.

White, A. and Ernst, E. 2000: The BBC Survey of Complementary Medicine Use in the UK. *Complementary Therapies in Medicine*, 8, pp. 32-37.

Wolffe, John 1994: *God and Greater Britain: Religion and National Life in Britain and Ireland, 1843-1945*. London and New York: Routledge.

Woodhead, Linda 2004: *Introduction to Christianity*. Cambridge, UK: Cambridge University Press.

Woodhead, Linda and Heelas, Paul (eds) 2000: *Religion in Modern Times: An Interpretive Anthology*. Oxford: Blackwell.

Woodward, James 1995: *Encountering Illness: Voices in Pastoral and Theological Perspective*. London: SCM.

Wootton, J. C. and Sparber, A. 2001: Surveys of Complementary and Alternative Medicine. Part 1. General Trends and Demographic Groups. *Journal of Alternative and Complementary Medicine*, 7 (2), pp. 195-208.

Wraight, Heather and Brierley, Peter (eds) 1999: *UK Christian Handbook, 2000-2001*. London: Harper Collins.

Wright, Andrew 2000: *Spirituality and Education*. London: Routledge.

Wuthnow, Robert 1976 *The Consciousness Revolution*. Berkeley: University of California Press.

Wuthnow, Robert 1996: *Sharing the Journey: Support Groups and America's New Quest for a Community*. London: The Free Press.

Wuthnow, Robert 1998: *After Heaven. Spirituality in America Since the 1950s*. Berkeley: University of California Press.

Wuthnow, Robert 2003: *All in Sync: How Music and Art are Revitalizing American Religion*. Berkeley, Los Angeles and London: University of California Press.

Yankelovich, Daniel 1981: *New Rules*. New York: Random House.

Yafai, Faisal al 2003: Failing Health. *The Guardian*, 23 July, pp. 2-3.

Yip, Andrew K. T.: 2000: Leaving the Church to Keep My Faith: The Lived Experiences of Non-Heterosexual Christians. In Leslie J. Francis and Yaacov J. Katz (eds), *Joining and Leaving Religion: Research Perspectives.* Leominster, UK: Gracewing, pp. 129-45.

Young, Iris Marion 1990: *Throwing it Like a Girl and Other Esssays in Feminist Philosophy and Social Theory.* Bloomington and Indianapolis: Indiana University Press.

Zaleski, Jeff 1997: *The Soul of Cyberspace.* New York: HarperCollins.

Zinnbauer, Brian J., Pargament, Kenneth I., Cole, Brenda et al. 1997: Religion and Spirituality: Unfuzzying the Fuzzy. *Journal for the Scientific Study of Religion*, 36 (4), pp. 549-64.

Index

Note: Page references in italics indicate tables and figures; those prefaced by *Pl.* indicate plates. Where more than one sequence of endnotes appears on one page, notes of the same number are distinguished by the addition of 'a' or 'b'.

activities, associational 8, 12–13, 25–9,
33, 82–3, 125–6
  growth 43–5, 47–8, 54
  numbers involved 8, 33–40, 45–8,
    52–8, 135–6
  small groups 66–7
  and subjectivization thesis 129
  voluntary groups 80, 112, 127
acupressure *156*
acupuncture 28, 44, *156*
Adkins, Lisa 101, 170 n.19
Adorno, Theodore 160 n.5
advertising, subjective-life 80, 84–5,
  87, 88, 166–7 n.4
affluence, and subjective
  wellbeing 130–1
age
  and congregational domain 140
  and involvement in holistic milieu
    107–10, 132–3, 134, 136, 137
Alexander Technique 24, 43–4, *156*
Allport, Gordon 125
Alpha Course 147

Ammerman, Nancy 61, 65
Anglicanism *see* Church of England
Arnold, Matthew xii
aromatherapy 7, 24, 26, 37, 138, *156*
  numbers involved 52, 58, 89
art therapy *156*
association *see* activities, associational
Astin, John A. 163 n.6
astrology 26, 43–4, *156*
authority:
  in congregations of difference 19,
    20, 61, 145
  in congregations of experiential
    difference 63, 67, 145
  of God-in-humanity 18
  in life-as religion 2–5, 6, 10, 13, 14,
    15–16, 19–20, 22–3, 31, 81,
    113–15, 141
  of subjective experience 11, 17, 28–9,
    65–6, 82–3, 85, 87, 95–6, 118–19
autonomy 95–7, 105, 115, 120, 130,
  135
  and men 106–7

baby-boomers
    and life-as religion 115, 117–19
    and subjective-life spirituality 57–8,
        112, 132–3
Backström, Anders 165–6 n.23
Baha'i faith 160 n.4b
Balmer, Randall 65
Baptists 61, 62
Barna Research Online 2001 73
Baudrillard, Jean 166 n.4
Bauman, Zygmunt 125
belief, popular, and spiritual
        revolution 50, 73–4, 75, 89, 98,
        126
Bell, Emma and Taylor, Scott
        165 n.18
Bellah, Robert N. et al. 79, 96, 159 n.1
Benson, Paddy and Roberts, John 47
Berger, Peter 49
Berger, Peter, Berger, Brigitte and
        Kellner, Hansfried 159 n.1,
        167–8 n.9
Best, Ron 165 n.19
Bible, as authoritative 15, 19, 20, 23,
        61, 145
body, concern for 15–16, 104–5
books
    mind body and spirit 42, 68, 69–70,
        136
    wellbeing 87
Bookseller 70
Bradley, Martin B. et al. 56, 64
Brahma Kumaris 161 n.4
Brannen, Julia and Moss, Peter 101,
        170 n.19
Brierley, Peter 41, 47, 51–2, 54, 62,
        65–6, 70, 129, 139–40, 146–7
Britain, and spiritual revolution 23,
        50–5, 149
Brown, Callum 47, 117
Brown, Michael F. 168 n.11,
        169 n.13

Bruce, Steve 2, 9, 36, 42, 54–5, 72,
        135, 139, 165 n.21, 168 n.11,
        173–4 n.7
Buddhism 24, 156, 160 n.4b
    number of groups 43, 44
    Theravada 28
Bunting, Madeleine 125, 166 n.3
business culture 71, 79–80, 88,
        130

CAM (complementary and alternative
        medicine) 73, 80, 99, 167 n.5
    in Kendal 44, 52–3
    in USA 58–9
Campbell, Colin 2, 9, 55, 73, 166 n.4,
        172–3 n.2
CancerCare Group 24, 156
Cancian, Francesca M. 101,
        169 n.15
capital
    cultural/social 136, 142
    sacred 133, 134, 148
capitalism
    sanctified Pl. 13
    'soft' 71, 84, 130, 138, 169 n.12,
        Pl. 12
    and subjectivity 81, 172–3 n.2
Capouya, John 138
care
    in congregations of humanity 18, 22,
        64–5, 143
    and gender 101, 103–4, 116–17,
        170–1 n.20
Carlyle, Thomas 125
Carrette, Jeremy and King,
        Richard 165 n.18
Carroll, Jackson and Roof, Wade
        Clark 115
case studies 152–3
Casey, Catherine 165 n.17
Celtic spirituality 65
Census 2001 53, 55, 136

Census of Religion (1851) 41, 45,
  139
chakra 71
Chambers, Robert 166 n.2
channelling 161 n.3
chaplaincy, hospital 73
charismatic renewal 19, 20–1, 64, 78,
  146
Chaves, Mark and Cavendish, James C.
  56
Cheshire, Andrea 68
'chi' 27, 38, 71
children
  and congregational decline 119, 140,
    146
  and holistic milieu 136
Chinese College of Physical
  Culture 157
chiropractice 156
CHOICE (Complementary Health
  Options in a Caring Environment)
  44
Chopra, Deepak 87
Christadelphians, decline 62
Christianity
  congregational domain 8, 13–23, 54
  declining influence 1–2, 10, 49,
    139–41
  and education-culture 71–2
  future prospects 139–48
  newspaper coverage 70
  and purchasing-culture 68–9
  revival 147–8
  and spiritual revolution 2, 60–8
  and spirituality 5–6, 65, 158
church, as authoritative 15, 16, 19
church attendance
  bottoming-out 141–8
  decline 41–2, 45–8, 51–2, 55–7,
    59–60, 65, 111–12
  future prospects 129, 131, 149
  in Kendal 33–5, 160–1 n.1b, Pl. 6

and occasional offices 143
  post-war 112
  reasons for leaving 81–2, 120–3
  in USA 55–7, 59–60, 65
Church of England
  attendance figures 160–1 n.1b
  declining attendance 41–2, 46, 65,
    122, 145
  and holistic milieu 46
churches, new paradigm 62–4, 147,
  Pl. 4
Cimino, Richard and Lattin,
  Don 171 n.21
circle dancing 24, 156
Cline, Sally and Spender, Dale 102
Coleman, John A. 49, 59
Collins, Sylvia 103, 110, 121
common good, in congregational
  domain 14, 18, 113
conformity
  and congregational domain 14, 22,
    31, 114–15
  in congregations of difference 20,
    61
  in life-as 3–4, 6
congregational domain 8, 13–23, 31,
  154–6
  and age profile 118–20, 140
  and bottoming-out 141–8
  decline 40–2, 45–8, 51–2, 55–7, 59,
    75, 77, 81–2, 110–25, 127, 131,
    139–41
  future prospects 129, 131, 139–48,
    149
  and holistic milieu 31–2, 60–8,
    Pl. 17
  and life-as religion 50, 60, 111
  numbers involved in 33–5, 45–6, 51,
    77, 139, 149
  reasons for leaving 81–2, 120–3
  returnees 115, 119
  and revival 147–8

and sexual revolution 117–18
and small groups 22, 66–7
and spirituality 121–2
and subjective-life 14–17, 22–3,
    60–8
and subjectivization thesis 81,
    111–25, 126, 143–5, 146–7
and transmission 119, 140, 146
unity-in-variety 13–17
in USA 55–6, 59–60
variety-in-unity 17–23, 60, 75–6,
    125
congregations of difference 15–16, 17,
    18–20, 22–3, 31, 155, *Pl. 8*
areas of growth 123–4
and authority 19, 20, 61, 145
decline 41–2, 62, 75
future prospects 143, 145–7
and subjectivization 61–2, 123–4,
    143
congregations of experiential
    difference 17, 18–19, 31, 41, 155,
    Pl. 4, *Pl. 9*
and authority 63, 67, 145
future prospects 143, 145, 148, 149
growth 63–4, 75–6, 124
and subjectivization 23, 62–4, 67,
    75, 124–5, 143, 146–7
and worship 21–2
congregations of experiential
    humanity 17–18, 31, 155–6
future prospects 143–4
and subjectivization 21–2, 23, 65–6,
    75, 113, 124–5
and worship 21–2
congregations of humanity 19, 154–5
decline 41–2, 65, 75
future prospects 142–3, 144–5,
    148
and God-in-humanity 17, 18
and humanitarian care 18, 22, 64–5,
    143

reasons for leaving 121
and self-sacrifice 22, 64
and subjectivization 64–5
and worship 17, 18, 64
conversion 19, 20, 63, 145
Conway, Janet 28
counselling *156*
counter-culture
    conservative Christian 123–4, 143
    1960s 43, 54, 112, 118–19, *119*,
        132, 133–4
    see also sixties revolution
craniosacral therapy 29, *156*, *Pl. 10*
crystal healing 44
culture
    and church attendance 140
    education-culture 5, 71–2, 80, 84–5,
        126, 130, 134, 137–8
    health-culture 5, 73, 85, 130, 134,
        138
    life-as elements 128
    production-culture 5, 71–2, 84,
        134
    purchasing-culture 5, 68–71, 84,
        134
    and spiritual revolution 50, 68–73,
        75
    subjective turn *see* subjectivization
        thesis
    and subjectivization thesis 78–82,
        84, 111–12
    wellbeing culture 83–94, 124, 130,
        132, 134, 136–7, *Pl. 14*, *Pl. 15*,
        Pl. 16
Cupitt, Don 33, 71
Currie, Robert, Gilbert, Alan and
    Horsley, Lee 174 n.11

Davie, Grace 49
Dawson, Lorne L. and Hennebry,
    Jenna 165 n.17
Day, Abby 152

De Beauvoir, Simone 170 n.18
De Michaelis, Elizabeth 162–3 n.1
deference, in congregational
    domain 15, 31, 81
Delphy, Christine and Leonard,
    Diana 101, 102
difference *see* congregations of
    difference
direction, spiritual 69
discipline, in life-as religion 20
domain, congregational, *see*
    congregational domain
downshifting
    and age profile of holistic milieu 107–9
    and quality of life 93, 131
    and relationality 108, 110
dualism, in congregational
    domain 15–16
Durkheim, Emile 1, 96, 148, 159 n.1,
    166 n.1

education
    and involvement in holistic milieu
        93–4, 136
    and subjectivization 5, 71–2, 80,
        84–5, 126, 130, 134, 137–8
Eisenberg, David M. et al. 58, 163 n.6
Elizabeth II, HM Queen 1
Emerson, Ralph Waldo 66
emotions, in life-as religion 17, 19,
    20–1; *see also* feelings
energies
    'blocked' 104
    and subjective-life spiritualities 25,
        26–7, 29, 38
    'subtle' 25, 135
energy management workshops *156*
enlightenment, and subjective-life
    spirituality 30, 167 n.6
ethic of subjectivity 80, 85, 130
ethnography of religion 7
European Values Surveys 114

evangelicalism
    American 124
    charismatic 19, 20–1, 64, 78, 146
    and congregations of difference 15,
        18, 61, 147
    and subjectivization 61
    and testimony 19–20
experience, subjective
    as authoritative 11, 17, 28–9, 65–6,
        82–3, 85, 87, 95–6, 118–19
    economy of 172 n.2
    enhancement 29–30
    and the sacred 31, 143, 145–6
    and small group involvement 67
experiential difference *see* congregations
    of experiential difference
experiential humanity *see* congregations
    of experiential humanity

Faith Communities Today 64
family values 63, 79, 111, 142–3, 146–7
Farias, Miguel 99, 114
feelings
    and subjectivization 80, 146
    and wellbeing culture 85–6
Fellside Centre, Kendal 24, 43
feng shui 71
Festival for Mind Body Spirit 162 n.1
Field, Clive D. 51
Finke, Roger and Stark, Rodney 2, 49,
    123, 163–4 n.8
flower essences therapy 24, *156*
foot massage *156*
Foucault, Michel 160 n.5
Francis, Leslie J., Lankshear, David W.
    and Jones, Susan H. 64
Frankfurt School 160 n.5
freedom, and subjective-life 82–3, 95,
    115, 120
Frisk, Liselotte 168 n.11, 169 n.13
Fromm, Erich 160 n.5
Fuller, Robert C. 92, 163–4 n.8

Gallup, George Jr. and Jones,
    Timothy 49, 74, 120
Gallup, George Jr. and Lindsay, D.
    Michael 56, 73–4, 168 n.11
Gallup polls
  and church attendance 55, 56
  and popular beliefs 74
  and Sunday School attendance 72
Geertz, Clifford 96
Gehlen, Arnold 159 n.1
gender
  and involvement in congregational
    domain 116-17
  and involvement in holistic
    milieu 94–5, 98, 102–7, 108–10,
    136
  and moral individualism 95
  and relationality 98–102, 103–5,
    108–10, 117
  roles 63, 116–17, 142, 170 n.18
  see also men, women
General Social Surveys (USA), and
    church attendance 55, 56
Gergen, Kenneth J. 169 n.125
Giddens, Anthony 79, 98, 169 n.15
Gill, Robin 139, 140, 160–1 n.1b
Gill, Robin, Hadaway, C. Kirk and
    Marler, Penny Long 73
Gilliat-Ray, Sophie 165 n.20
Gilligan, Carol 101, 170 nn.18, 19
Gimlin, Debra L. 99, 166 n.4
Glenmary Institute 56, 66, 164 n.10
gnosticism, subjective-life spirituality
    as 62
God
  in humanity 17–18
  and masculinity 15
  in popular beliefs 73–4
Gomes, Jaquetta 27–8
Green Spirit group 157
Griffith, 124, 164 n.9
Gross, Martin 79

groups, holistic 24, 27–8, 36
  growth 43–5, 47
  numbers involved 38–40, 52, 57–9
growth
  personal 26, 92, 170 n.16
  spiritual 49, 61, 69, 71–2, 74, 92,
    114, 173–4 n.7
Guest, Mathew 174 n.13

Hadaway, C. Kirk and Marler, Penny
    Long 56, 164 n.10
Hadaway, C. Kirk, Marler, Penny Long
    and Chaves, Mark 55–6, 57, 163
    n.2, 164 n.10
Hadden, Jeffrey K. and Cowan,
    Douglas E. 165 n.17
Hall, Peter A. 166 n.2, 171 n.24
Hamilton, Clive 107, 109, 131
Hammond, Phillip E. 67, 73, 115, 118
harmony 26, 27
  and gender 104
Harrington, Anne 172–3 n.2
Harris Interactive Service Bureau 137,
    163 n.7, 163–4 n.8, 168 n.11, 169
    n.13
Harrison, Judy and Burnard, Philip 165
    n.20
Heald, Gordon 51, 73, 92, 106, 108,
    134
healing
  and congregations of experiential
    difference 19, 172 n.29
  in life-as religion 19
  in subjective-life spirituality 25–8,
    44, 157
  see also CAM
health
  and age 108–9
  and subjectivization 5, 73, 80, 126,
    130, 138
  and wellbeing culture 84, 92, 109,
    130

heartlands activities 8–9, 12–32, 152
    change over time 40–5, 116–20
    numbers involved in 33–40
    see also congregational domain;
        holistic milieu
Hedges, Ellie and Beckford, James
    A. 170 n.16
Heelas, Paul 154, 159 n.1, 161 n.4,
    162 n.1, 165 nn.18, 22, 173 n.7,
    174 n.12
Heelas, Paul and Seel, Benjamin 89,
    110, 171 n.21, 173 nn.3, 5
herbalism 157
Hicks, Douglas A. 165 n.17
hierarchy
    in congregational domain 15, 20, 64,
        111, 116
    in management 79–80
Hirst, Rob 119
Hobsbawm, Eric 5
Hochschild, Arlie 101, 102, 108,
    170–1 n.20
Hofstede, Geert 100, 171 n.25
Hoge, Dean R. 114
Hoge, Dean R., Johnson, Benton and
    Luidens, Donald A. 115, 120
Hoge, Dean R., McGuire, Kenneth and
    Stratman, Bernard F. 115, 120–1,
    124, 172 n.28
Hoge, Dean R. and Roozen, David
    A. 115, 120, 172 n.28
holistic milieu 156–8
    age profiles 107–10, 132–3, 134,
        136, 137
    and Christian background 133
    and congregational domain 31–2,
        60–8, Pl. 17
    and educational background 93–4,
        136
    future prospects 129, 131–8, 149
    and gender 94–5, 98, 102–7,
        108–10, 136

growth 42–5, 47–8, 54, 59, 60, 75,
    81–2, 88–90, 107
    mapping 37–8, 43, 152, 161 n.3
    newspaper coverage 70
    numbers involved 7, 36–40, 45–6,
        52–5, 57–8, 77, 135–6, 149
    practitioners 24, 26–9
    reasons for involvement 29, 30, 39,
        52, 89–92, 91
    small groups 66–7
    and subjective-life spirituality 8, 11,
        13, 23–30, 31
    and subjectivization thesis 77, 78,
        81, 82–110, 137
    transmission 135–6
    in USA 49, 57–8, 60, 99, 137
    and wellbeing culture 86–90
Hollinger, Franz and Smith,
    Timothy 137
Holy Spirit, and subjective
    experience 6, 17, 20, 21, 23,
        62–3, 144–5, 146
homeopathy 24, 27–8, 44, 52, 87, 89,
    157
hospices, and holistic spirituality 73,
    80, 84, 85
hospitals, and holistic spirituality 73,
    126
Hout, Michael and Greeley, Andrew
    56
Houtman, Dick and Mascini, Peter 95,
    110, 115, 127, 137–8, 165–6
    n.23, 168 n.11, 169 n.13
humanity see congregations of humanity
Hunter, James Davison 61, 67
hypnotherapy 157

Iannaccone, Laurence 123
Indian head massage 157
individualism, and subjectivism 95–7,
    98–100, 106, 135, 148, 170 n.16
individualization

and congregational domain 14,
    115–16
and subjectivization 11, 90, 95–7
Inglehart, Ronald 5, 79, 86, 93–4,
    110, 114, 120, 131, 172 n.30
Inglehart, Ronald, Basanez, Miguel and
    Moreno, Alejandro 115, 169 n.14
integration, and subjective-life
    spirituality 26, 86
inter-faith group 157
Iona group 157

James, William 148–9, 159 n.1
Järvinen, Margaretha 101
Jehovah's Witnesses 46, 161 n.5
Jesuits 3
Jesus Christ, devotion to 15
Johnson, Douglas W, Picard, Paul R.
    and Quinn, Bernard 56
Jones, Constance A. 168 n.11, 169 n.13
Jones, Dale E. et al. 66

Kelley, Dean M. 62, 123–4
Kelner, Marrijoy and Wellman,
    Beverly 168 n.11, 173–4 n.7
Kendal 53, 68-9, 151, Pl. 1
Kendal Cancer Care 24, 156
Kendal College 24, 44, 53, 165 n.19
Kendal Leisure Centre 24, 29, 152, Pl.
    11
Kendal Project xiii–xiv, 8, 12–32
    age profile 107–10, 132–3, 134,
        136
    congregational domain 13–23,
        113–14, 116, 121–2, 140, 144,
        146–7, 154–6, Pl. 3, Pl. 6
    definitions of spirituality 98
    feasibility study 8, 12–13, 151
    gender profile 94–5, 103–6, 136
    research strategies 151–8
    and spiritual revolution 9, 12–13, 32,
        33–48, 50

subjective-life spirituality 23–30,
    131–2, 133–4, 135–6, 156–8, Pl.
    7, Pl. 10
    team xiii, 152, Pl. 2
    see also questionnaire
Kenton, Leslie 169 n.12
Keynes, John Maynard 129, 130–1
kinesiology 26, 28, 29, 87, 157

Lakeland College of Homeopathy 24,
    43–4
Lambert, Yves 127
Langford, Wendy 110
language of subjective-life spirituality 1,
    70–1
Lau, Kimberly J. 164 n.12
Leonardo, Micaela di 101
liberalism, religious
    and church growth 172 n.28
    and congregations of humanity 18,
        64–5, 145
life
    in-relation 4
    life-as 3, 70
    life-itself 25, 127
    as site of worship 33, 38
    subjective-life 3–5, 6, 8–9, 25, 33,
        50, 61–3, 68, 80, 82–4, 87,
        149
    see also life-as spirituality; subjective-
        life spirituality; religion, life-as
life trainers 80
life-as spirituality 6–7, 8–9, 22, 31
    and decline 6–7, 9–10, 12, 23, 60,
        111, 131
    and external authority 2–5, 6, 10,
        13, 14, 16, 61–3
    and subjective-life spirituality 60–8,
        75
Lindner, Eileen W. 56, 64
Loop Cottage, Kendal 24, 37, 44
Löwendahl, Lena 162 n.6, 169 n.13

Luckmann, Thomas 2, 9, 55, 73,
    159 n.1
Lukes, Steven 96, 159 n.2, 169 n.15
Lynch, Gordon 110, 121

management culture, and
    subjectivization 71, 79–80, 88, 130
Mann, Horace 41, 45, 139
Marler, Penny Long and Hadaway,
    C. Kirk 56, 166 n.24
Marler, Penny Long and Roozen,
    David A. 119
Marsden, George 145
masculinity, and God 15
massage 24, 28, 44, 87, 89, 138, *157*
massage retreats 69
materialism, and church attendance 114
McCullers, Carson 11, 97
McGuire, Meredith 1–2, 168 n.11, 169
    n.13, 171 n.21, 172 n.29
media *see* press; television
medicine, complementary and
    alternative *see* CAM
meditation 7, 136
    Christian 65, 144
    Transcendental Meditation 43, 122
megachurches, and experiential
    difference 62–4, 147
men
    and individuated
        subjectivism 98–100, 106–7
    involvement in holistic milieu 95,
        106–7
Mercer, Calvin and Durham, Thomas
    W. 100, 168 n.11
meridian therapy *157*
metamorphic technique *157*
Methodist Church
    declining attendance 65, 139
    and holistic milieu 46, 54
methodology *see* case studies;
    questionnaire

Miller, Donald 62–3, 67, 124
Mills, Simon and Budd, Sarah 52
Mingins, Rosemary 152
Mitroff, Ian I. and Denton, Elizabeth
    A. 165 n.18
Moore, R. Laurence 165 n.17
moralism, and life-as religion 16–17,
    18, 145
Mudie-Smith, Richard 34
Mulgan, Geoffrey 166 n.2
mysticism, Christian 6, 65, 144

naturopathy 24, *157*
New Age *see* holistic milieu; subjective-
    life spirituality
new paradigm churches 62–4,
    147
new religious movements 167 n.8
newspapers *see* press
Nietzsche, Friedrich 77
Norman, Edward 65
Nussbaum, Martha 166 n.4
Nussbaum, Martha and Glover,
    Jonathan 166 n.2
nutritional therapy 29, *157*

obedience, in congregational
    domain 15
Orchard, Helen 165 n.20
osteopathy 24, 38, 138, *157*
Ostwalt, Conrad 165 n.17

paganism 7, *157*
palm reading *157*
Partridge, Chris 71
Penning, James M. and Smith,
    Corwin E. 61
Pentecostal Christians, and holistic
    milieu 54
Percy, Martyn 146, 172 n.29
Perrin, Robin D., Kennedy, Paul and
    Miller, Donald E. 64, 147

Perry, Everett and Hoge, Dean R.
    172 n.28
pilates 161 n.4
Pilgrim, Gay 66
play therapy *157*
pluralization 130
politics, subjectivization 166 n.2
Poloma, Margaret M. and Hoelter,
    Lynette F. 172 n.29
post-materialism 79, 114, 115, 131,
    148, 169 n.14, 172 n.30
practitioners, holistic 24, 26–7, 36–8
    age profile 107, 132–3
    female 94
    numbers 53, 59
    numbers attending 39–40, 57, 58
    relationships with participants 27–9,
        88, 90, 98
press
    and holistic activities 59, 70,
        162–3 n.1
    and wellbeing culture 84
Presser, Stanley and Stinson, Linda
    57
Princeton Religion Research
    Center 120, 121–2
Pringle, Rosemary 101
prosperity, and congregations of
    experiential difference
    172 n.29
psychic consultancy *157*
psycho-drama 43
psychosynthesis 28, *157*
psychotherapy *157*
Putnam, Robert D. 101–2, 142,
    166 n.2
Puttick, Liz 69–70

Quakers *see* Society of Friends
questionnaire
    congregational domain 14, 113–14,
        153

holistic milieu 25, 30, 39–40, 46,
    91–3, 94, 98, 105–6, 107–8, 133,
    136, 153, 157–8
Quinn, Bernard et al. 56, 66

Rainbow Cottage, Kendal 24, 29, 37,
    44, 152, *Pl. 5*
Ray, Paul H. and Anderson, Sherry
    Ruth 99, 163 n.7
rebirthing 7, 29, 87, *157*
recognition, in holistic milieu 105
Redfield, James 70
Reeves, Thomas C. 65
reflexology 7, 24, 89, 138, *157*
number of practitioners 52
reiki 7, 24, 26, 29, 87, 138, *157*
relationality
    and downshifting 108, 110
    and gender 98–102, 103–5, 108–10,
        117
    and subjectivism 96–7, 135
relationships
    and subjective-life spirituality 27–8,
        95–7, 98
    and wellbeing culture 85–6, 88, 90,
        103
relaxation therapy *157*
religion, life-as 5, 6–7, 8–9, 31, 50,
    125–6, *Pl. 8*
    decline 6–7, 9–10, 12, 23, 48, 75–7,
        81, 126–7, 131, 149
    and education-culture 71–2
    future prospects 131, 139–47
    growth areas 123–4
    and life-as life forms 160 n.4a
    and life-as values 114–15, 141–3,
        146–7
    new religious movements 167 n.8
    and production-culture 71
    and purchasing-culture 68–71
    and spirituality 2, 5–6,
        12–32

religion, life-as (*cont'd*)
  and subjectivization thesis 77, 78,
    111, 113
  subjectivized 23, 62–3
  see also congregational domain
religion, and spirituality 5–6, 73–4
research
  qualitative 7, 8, 114
  quantitative 7, 8
retreats, Christian 69, 144
revolution, sixties, *see* sixties revolution
revolution, spiritual 1–2, 6–9
  in Britain 23, 50–5
  and Christianity 2, 13–23, 60–8
  and cultural transformation 50,
    68–73, 75
  evidence for 7–9, 49–76
  future prospects 75, 148–50
  and holistic milieu 6–7, 23–30, 31,
    138
  and Kendal Project 9, 12–13, 32,
    33–48
  mini-revolutions 46–8, 54, 149
  and new paradigm churches 62–4
  and personal beliefs 50, 73–4, 75,
    89, 98, 126
  and subjectivization 60–8
  in USA 49–50, 55–60, 165 n.21
Richter, Philip and Francis, Leslie 120,
    121–2, 172 n.28
Rieff, Philip 79
Roberts, Dan and Kelleher, Ellen
    138
roles, life-as 14, 30, 62, 67, 78, 104,
    111–12, 116–17, 139, 142
Roman Catholicism
  declining attendance 65
  and holistic milieu 1, 15, 46
  Jesuit Spirituality Centre 164 n.13
  and returnees 115
  and subjectivization 61
  in USA 57

Romanticism, and culture of wellbeing
    172–3 n.2
Roof, Wade Clark 57–8, 77, 118–19,
    119, 159 n.1, 168 n.11
Roof, Wade Clark and MacKinney,
    William 164 n.10
Roozen, David A. 114
Roozen, David A. and Hadaway,
    C. Kirk 62, 64, 164 n.10
Rose, Nikolas 81
Rose, Stuart 169 n.13
Rousseau, Jean-Jacques 11

sacralization 6, 9–10, 33, 77
  and subjective-life 31, 82–3
  and subjectivization thesis 81–110
Sai Baba group *157*
Salamon, Karen 165 n.18
Salvation Army 35
Sargeant, Kimon Howland 63
Schwartz, Shalom 114
Schwartz, Shalom and Huismans,
    Spike 114, 115
Scott, Robert Owens 166 n.24
Sea of Faith group *157*
secularization 9–10, 33, 48, 55, 62, 77
  and subjectivization thesis 81–2,
    111–25, 127
self
  autonomous 95–7, 105, 115, 120,
    130, 135
  in-relation 2, 11, 105
  life-as 18, 141–7
self-realization 81, 86
  and life-as religion 15, 22, 121
self-sacrifice 3, 14, 15, 20, 61, 81
  in congregations of humanity 22, 64
Sennett, Richard 70, 169 n.15
sexuality, in life-as religion 16, 63
Sharma, Ursula 168 n.11, 171 n.24
Sharma, Ursula and Black, Paula 99
shiatsu 27, 29, 138, *157*

Shibley, Mark A. 62, 64, 65, 67, 124, 163 n.3
shops, and holistic spirituality 68–9
Silk, Mark 164 n.15
Simmel, Georg 148–9, 159 n.1
Simmha, Anton 87
Singer, Peter 166 n.4
sixties revolution:
  and holistic milieu 43, 54, 132, 133–4
  impact on churches 112, 117–19, *119*
  see also counter-culture
Smith, Christian 67, 124
Smith, Dorothy 102
Social Attitudes Survey (1997) 50–1
Society of Friends:
  declining attendance 41–2, 66
  and experiential humanity 21, 65, 143–4
  growth in attendance 66
Sointu, Eeva 105
Soul of Britain Survey (2000) 51, 73, 134
Southern Baptist Convention (US) 62
spinal touch therapy *157*
spirituality:
  Christian 5–6, 65, 121–2, 144–5
  immanent 57
  life-as 6–7, 8–10, 74
  meaning 1–2, 74
  and relationality 98–102, 135
  and religion 2, 5–6, 12–32
  significance 1–2, 173 n.7
  small-group 66–7
  see also life-as spirituality; subjective-life spirituality
Stacey, Jackie 33, 99
Stark, Rodney and Finke, Roger 123
Steindl-Rast, David 169 n.15
Stelfox, Margaret 152
stress, and holistic milieu 27, 29, 30, 39, 52, 92, 104

subjective-life spirituality 5–7, 8–9
  in congregational domain 14–17, 22–3, 60–8
  in congregations of experiential difference 23, 62–4
  in congregations of experiential humanity 21–2, 23, 65–6
  in congregations of humanity 19–20, 22, 23
  and culture 68–73
  and education-culture 5, 71–2, 126, 130, 137–8
  and enlightenment 30, 167 n.6
  future prospects 131–2
  as gnosticism 62
  growth 1, 9–10, 12, 42–5, 47–8, 54, 60, 75, 77, 81–2, 126–7, 149
  and subjectivization thesis 77, 78, 81, 82–110, 137
  in USA 49, 54, 59, 65
  irreplaceabilities 10
  numbers involved 36–40, 52–5, 57–8, 135–6
  and personal beliefs 25, 73–4, 89, 98, 126, 137
  in press and media 70–1
  and purchasing-culture 5, 68–71, 84, 134
  and subjectivization thesis 77, 78, 81, 82–110
  in USA 49, 57–60
  see also holistic milieu
subjectivism, individuated/relational 2, 96–7, 98–100, 106, 170 n.16
subjectivization
  in Christianity 60–8, 144
  and individualization 11
subjectivization thesis 2–5, 9–10, 31–2, 75, 77, 149
  and age 107–10, 132–3, 137

subjectivization thesis (*cont'd*)
  and congregational domain 81,
    111–25, 126, 130–1, 143–5
  counter-evidence 123–4
  and cultural change 2–5, 78–82,
    111–12, 116
  cultural momentum 130–2
  and future of associational
    activities 129–50
  and gender 94–107
  and growth of holistic milieu 77, 78,
    81, 82–110, 137
  and wellbeing culture 83–94,
    124
Sufism 161 n.4
Sunday Schools, decline 72, 133
Sweden, church attendance 129, 141,
  143

tai chi 7, 24, 26, 29, 37, 43, 69, 138,
  152, *157*
  non-spiritual practice 52
  numbers involved 53
Taizé singing *157*
Tamney, Joseph B. 64, 65, 67, 78,
  124
tarot card reading *157*
Taylor, Charles 2–3, 5, 77, 79, 97,
  159 n.1
television, reality shows 80
Tennyson, Alfred Lord 3, 77
territory, associational 8, 12–13, 33
testimony, evangelical 19–20
Theravada Buddhism 28
Thomas, K. J., Nicholl, J. P. and
  Coleman, P. 58, 99, 163 n.6,
  167 n.5
Thompson, Wayne L., Carroll,
  Jackson W. and Hoge, Dean
  R. 172 n.28
Thrift, Nigel 165 n.18

Tipton, Steven M. 67, 124, 159 n.1
traditionalism 3, 114
transcendence, in Christianity 3, 6, 10,
  14, 22, 142, 145
Transcendental Meditation 43, 122
transmission, intergenerational
  congregational domain 119, 140,
    146
  holistic milieu 135–6
Trilling, Lionel 95, 126
Troeltsch, Ernst 148–9, 159 n.1
True Vision group *157*
'Turning Point' shop 44

uniqueness, human 11, 13
  and congregations of experiential
    difference 62–3
  and congregations of humanity 18
  and subjective-life spirituality 4, 30,
    31, 50, 75, 78, 87, 135
  and wellbeing culture 81, 82–5,
    87
Unitarianism, and experiential
  humanity 21, 31, 65–6,
    143–4
United Reformed Church, declining
  attendance 65
Universal Peace dancing 43, *157*
USA
  church attendance 55–7, 59–60, 65,
    120, 147, 174–5 n.14
  congregations of difference 123
  and education-culture 165 n.19
  growth in small groups 66–7
  growth in subjective-life
    spirituality 49, 54, 59, 65
  and holistic milieu 49, 57–8, 60, 99,
    137
  and life-as values 114–15
  media 164 n.15, 165 n.16
  and popular beliefs 73–4

and spiritual revolution 49–50,
  55–60, 165 n.21
and wellbeing culture 86

values, life-as 113–16, 126, 141–3,
  146–7
Veroff, Joseph et al. 5, 79, 86, 100,
  166 n.2, 168 n.11
vision therapy *157*

Walter, Tony 73
Warner, R. Stephen 49
Watts, Alan 118
Weber, Max 77
wellbeing
  and Christian retreats 69
  in congregational domain 121,
    124–5
  and gender 98–107
  and holistic milieu 29, 86–90, 124,
    132, 136, *Pl. 10, Pl. 14*
  and purchasing-culture 68–71
  as quality of life 84, 86, 87, 89, 94,
    103, 131–2, 166 n.2
  and subjectivization thesis 81,
    83–94, 124–5, 130
White, A. and Ernst, E. 163 n.6
wholeness, and subjective-life
  spirituality 26–8, 30, 105
wicca 7
Wilber, Ken 133
Wild Women group *157*
women
  involvement in congregational
    domain 116–17
  involvement in holistic milieu 94–5,
    102–7, 108–10, 136, *157*
  and relationality 98–102, 103–5,
    108–10, 117
Women's Aglow movement
  164 n.9

Women's spirituality group *157*
Woodhead, Linda 144, 152, 154, 159
  n.1
Woodhead, Linda and Heelas, Paul 17,
  159 n.1
Woodward, James 72
Woolf, Virginia 80
Wootton, J. C. and Sparber, A. 99, 168
  n.11, 169 n.13, 171 n.21
World Values Surveys 114, 131
worship
  alternative forms 174 n.13
  in congregations of experiential
    difference 20–1
  in congregations of experiential
    humanity 21–2
  in congregations of humanity 17, 18,
    64
  numbers involved 34–5, 140–1
Wraight, Heather and Brierley,
  Peter 174 n.11
Wright, Andrew 71
Wuthnow, Robert 33, 55, 56, 59, 62,
  66–7, 74, 118, 159 n.1

Yafai, Faisal al 138
Yankelovich, Daniel 79, 168 n.11
*Yearbook of American and Canadian
  Churches* 56
Yeats, W. B. xii
Yip, Andrew K. T. 171 n.27
yoga 24, 26–7, 69, *157, Pl. 11*
  growth in groups 43–4, 59
  non-spiritual practice 29, 30, 39,
    52
  numbers involved 46, 53–4, 58, 89,
    136, 137, 162–3 n.1
  and relationality 170 n.17
  seen as spiritual 7, 173–4 n.7
  and younger people 137–8
Young, Iris Marion 170 n.19

young people
   in congregations of experiential
      difference 147
   and decline in church
      affiliation 118–20, 140–1

and holistic milieu 134, 137–8

Zaleski, Jeff 165 n.17
Zinnbauer, Brian J. et al. 165 n.24

Index compiled by Meg Davies (Registered Indexer, Society of Indexers)

MAKE IT SCREAM, MAKE IT BURN

ALSO BY LESLIE JAMISON

NONFICTION

The Recovering: Intoxication and Its Aftermath
The Empathy Exams: Essays

FICTION

The Gin Closet

MAKE IT
SCREAM,
MAKE IT
BURN

ESSAYS

LESLIE JAMISON

GRANTA

Granta Publications, 12 Addison Avenue, London W11 4QR

First published in Great Britain by Granta Books, 2019
Originally published in the United States in 2019 by Little, Brown and Company,
Hachette Book Group, New York

Quotations from John Masefield's poem 'Sea Fever' on pages 163 and 170 reproduced by
kind permission of the Society of Authors as the Literary Representative of the Estate of
John Masefield.

The essays in this book previously appeared, sometimes in significantly different form, in the
following publications: "Up in Jaffna" (as "The Two Faces of Paradise") in *Afar*; "52 Blue" in
The Atavist; "Sim Life" in *The Atlantic*; "We Tell Ourselves Stories in Order to Live Again"
(as "Giving up the Ghost") in *Harper's*; "No Tongue Can Tell" in the *Los Angeles Review
of Books*; "The Long Trick" (as "Saudades") in the *Mississippi Review*; "Rehearsals" in *The
Nervous Breakdown*; "Daughter of a Ghost" (as "In the Shadow of a Fairy Tale") in the *New
York Times Magazine*; "Make It Scream, Make It Burn" in the *Oxford American*; and
"Maximum Exposure" (as "Going Back") and "Museum of Broken Hearts" (as "The Breakup
Museum") in the *Virginia Quarterly Review*.

A CIP catalogue record for this book is available from the British Library.
1 3 5 7 9 10 8 6 4 2

ISBN 978 1 78378 155 3
eISBN 978 1 78378 157 7

Offset by Avon DataSet Ltd, Bidford on Avon, B50 4JH
Printed and bound by CPI Group (UK) Ltd, Croydon, CR0 4YY
www.granta.com

For my father,
Dean Tecumseh Jamison

When do our senses know any thing so utterly as when we lack it?

— Marilynne Robinson, *Housekeeping*

CONTENTS

I: LONGING

    52 Blue   3

    We Tell Ourselves Stories in Order to Live Again   28

    Layover Story   49

    Sim Life   58

II: LOOKING

    Up in Jaffna   87

    No Tongue Can Tell   99

    Make It Scream, Make It Burn   106

    Maximum Exposure   124

III: DWELLING

    Rehearsals   155

    The Long Trick   159

    The Real Smoke   173

    Daughter of a Ghost   196

    Museum of Broken Hearts   215

    The Quickening   238

Acknowledgments   *257*

— I —

LONGING

52 Blue

December 7, 1992. Whidbey Island, Puget Sound. The world wars were over. The other wars were over: Korea, Vietnam. The Cold War was finally over, too. The Whidbey Island Naval Air Station remained. So did the Pacific, its waters vast and fathomless beyond an airfield named for an airman whose body was never found: William Ault, who died in the Battle of the Coral Sea. This is how it goes. The ocean swallows human bodies whole and makes them immortal. William Ault became a runway that sends other men into the sky.

At the Naval Air Station, the infinite Pacific appeared as finite data gathered by a network of hydrophones spread along the ocean floor. Initially used to monitor Soviet subs during the Cold War, these hydrophones had since been turned toward the sea itself, transforming its formless noises into something measurable: pages of printed graphs rolling out of a spectrograph machine.

On that particular December day in 1992, petty officer second class Velma Ronquille heard a strange sound. She stretched it out on a different spectrogram so she could see it better. She couldn't quite believe that it was coming in at 52 hertz. She beckoned one of the audio technicians. He needed to come back, she said. He needed to take another look. The technician came back. He took another look. His name was Joe George. Velma told him, "I think this is a whale."

Joe thought, *Holy cow*. It hardly seemed possible. The sound pattern looked like the call of a blue whale, but blue whales usually came in somewhere between 15 and 20 hertz—an almost imperceptible rumble, on the periphery of what the human ear can detect. Fifty-two hertz was off the charts. But here it was, right in front of them, the audio signature of a creature moving through Pacific waters with a singularly high-pitched song.

Whales make calls for a number of reasons: to navigate, to find food, to communicate with one another. For certain whales, including humpbacks and blues, songs also play a role in sexual selection. Blue males sing louder than females, and the volume of their singing—at more than 180 decibels—makes them the loudest animals in the world. They click and grunt and trill and hum and moan. They sound like foghorns. Their calls can travel thousands of miles through the ocean.

Because this whale's frequency was unprecedented, the folks at Whidbey kept tracking him for years, every migration season, as he made his way south from Alaska to Mexico. They figured it was a he, as only males sing during mating season. His path wasn't unusual, only his song—along with the fact that they never detected any other whales around him. He always seemed to be alone. This whale was calling out high, and apparently to no one—or at least, no one seemed to be answering. The acoustic technicians called him 52 Blue. A scientific report would eventually acknowledge that no other whale calls with similar characteristics had ever been reported. "It is perhaps difficult to accept," the report conceded, that "there could have been only one of this kind in this large oceanic expanse."

*   *   *

The drive from Seattle to Whidbey Island took me through the plainspoken pageantry of Washington State industry: massive stacks of cut lumber, rivers clogged with tree trunks like fish trapped in pens, towers of candy-colored shipping containers near Skagit port, and a collection of dirty white silos near Deception Pass Bridge, its steel span looming majestically over Puget Sound—hard-sparkling water glinting with shards of sunlight nearly two hundred feet below. On the far side of the bridge, the island felt pastoral and otherworldly, almost defensive. LITTER AND IT WILL HURT, one sign read. Another said, SPACE HEATERS NEED SPACE. Whidbey Island often calls itself the longest island in America, but this isn't strictly true. "Whidbey is long," the *Seattle Times* observed in 2000, "but let's not stretch it." It's long enough to hold a kite festival, a mussel festival, an annual bike race (the Tour de Whidbey), four inland lakes, and a yearly murder-mystery game that turns the entire town of Langley, population 1,035, into a crime scene.

Joe George, the technician who first identified 52 Blue, still lives in a modest hillside home perched on the northern end of Whidbey, about six miles from the air station. When I visited, he answered the door smiling—a burly man with silver hair, no-nonsense but friendly. Though he hadn't worked at the air station for twenty years, he was still able to get us past security with his Navy ID. He told me he uses it whenever he comes back to the base to drop off his recycling. Outside the officers' club, men in flight suits were drinking cocktails on a wooden deck. The coastline was ragged and beautiful beyond—waves crashing onto dark sand, salt wind moving through the evergreens.

Joe explained that when he worked at the air station, his team—the team responsible for processing audio data from the hydrophones—was fairly disconnected from the rest of the base. It was a question of security, he said. When we reached his old building, I saw what he meant. It was surrounded by double fences topped with razor wire. He told me that some of the other servicemen on base used to think his building was some kind of prison. They never knew what it was for. When I asked him what he had thought those strange sounds had been, back in 1992, before he realized they were whale calls, he said, "I can't tell you that. It's classified."

Back at his house, Joe pulled out a sheaf of papers from his days spent tracking 52 Blue. They were computer maps documenting nearly a decade of migratory patterns, the whale's journey each season marked by a different color—yellow, orange, purple—in the crude lines of mid-'90s computer graphics. Joe showed me charts of 52's song and explained the lines and metrics so I could compare its signature with more typical whale noise: the lower frequencies of regular blues, the much higher frequencies of humpbacks. Blue-whale songs hold various kinds of sounds—long purrs and moans, constant or modulated—and 52 Blue's vocalizations showed these same distinctive patterns, only on a wildly different frequency, one just above the lowest note on a tuba. The brief recorded clip of 52 he played me, sped up for human hearing, sounded ghostly: a reedy, pulsing, searching sound, the aural equivalent of a beam of light murkily visible through thick fog on a moonlit night.

Joe clearly enjoyed explaining his charts and maps. It seemed to have something to do with his love for organization and order. As he proudly showed me the fruits of his various and somewhat surprising hobbies—his impressive collection of carnivorous plants and the bees he raised to feed them, or the pristine musket he'd built from a kit for one of his eighteenth-century fur-trapper rendezvous reenactments— a clear penchant for care and conscientiousness emerged. He had a deep desire to be accurate and meticulous about everything he did. As he showed me the cobra lilies, his favorite plants, he explained how their translucent hoods trick trapped flies into exhausting themselves by flying toward the light—evidently impressed by the economy and ingenuity of their design—and then carefully fixed a frost cloth over their curled green backs to protect them from the cold.

I sensed that Joe enjoyed the chance to pull out his old whale charts. They took him back to the days when the story of 52 was still unfolding, and he was right in the middle of it. Joe told me he'd arrived at Whidbey after several years of what was technically classified as "arduous duty" on a base in Iceland, though he explained that those years weren't particularly arduous at all; his kids built snowmen by the Blue Lagoon. Joe was a good candidate for Whidbey. He was already trained as an acoustic technician, already prepared for the work that happened in his squat little bunker behind the razor-wire fences.

The hydrophone tracking program—also known as the Sound Surveillance System, or SOSUS—was a bit of a "bastard child," Joe told me. After the Cold War ended, without Soviet submarines to listen to, the Navy needed more convincing about how the expensive hydrophone array could earn its keep. The work that emerged surprised even the ones who started doing it. Darel Martin, an acoustic technician who worked with Joe at Whidbey, described it like this: "We went from being experts on sharks of steel to tracking living, breathing animals." He said: "It's just endless what you can hear out of the ocean." Now the mystery of one particular whale survives as a man sitting at his kitchen table, pulling out weathered folders to point out the ordinary-looking graph of an extraordinary song.

July 2007, Harlem, New York. Leonora knew she was going to die. Not just someday, but soon. She'd been suffering from fibroids and bleeding for years, sometimes so heavily that she was afraid to leave her apartment. She grew obsessed with blood: thinking about blood, dreaming about blood, writing poems about blood. She stopped working as a case supervisor for the city, a job she'd held for more than a decade. At that point, Leonora was forty-eight years old. She had always been a self-sufficient person; she'd been working since she was fourteen. She'd never been married, though she'd had offers. She liked to know that she could support herself. But this was a new level of isolation. One family member told her, "You are in a very dark place," and said she no longer wanted to see her.

By summer things had gotten worse. Leonora felt truly ill: relentless nausea, severe constipation, aches across her whole body. Her wrists were swollen, her stomach bloated, her vision blurred with jagged spirals of color. She could hardly breathe when she was lying down, so she barely slept. When she did sleep, her dreams were strange. One night she saw a horse-drawn hearse moving across the cobblestone streets of another century's Harlem. She picked up the horse's reins, looked it straight in the eye, and knew it had come for her. She felt so convinced she was going to die that she unlocked her apartment door so her neighbors wouldn't have trouble removing her body. She called her doctor to tell her as much—*I'm pretty sure I'm going to die*—and her doctor got pissed, said she needed to call the paramedics, that she was going to live.

As the paramedics were wheeling Leonora away from her apartment on a gurney, she asked them to turn around and take her back so she could lock the door. This was how she knew she'd regained faith in her own life. If she wasn't going to die, she didn't want to leave her door unlocked.

That request, asking the paramedics to turn around, is the last thing Leonora can remember before two months of darkness. That night in July was the beginning of a medical odyssey—five days of surgery, seven weeks in a coma, six months in the hospital—that would eventually deliver her, in her own time and her own way, to the story of 52 Blue.

* * *

During the years when Joe and Darel were tracking 52 Blue, they worked under the supervision of Bill Watkins, an acoustic expert from Woods Hole who came across the country to Whidbey Island every few months to hear about what they'd found. Everyone who told me about Watkins spoke of him in almost mythic terms. The number of languages he spoke kept changing every time I heard it: six, twelve, thirteen. One of his former research assistants claimed it was twenty. He'd been born to Christian missionaries stationed in French Guinea. According to Darel, Watkins had hunted elephants with his father when he was a kid. "He could actually hear twenty hertz, which is extremely low for any human," Darel told me. "You and I can't hear that...but he could actually hear the elephants in the distance. And he would tell his dad which way to go."

Over the course of his career, Watkins developed much of the technology and methodology that made it possible to record and analyze whale songs: whale tags, underwater playback experiments, location methods. He developed the first tape recorder capable of capturing whale vocalizations.

For Joe and Darel, 52 Blue's unusual frequency was interesting mainly because it made him easy to track. You could always distinguish his call, so you always knew where he was traveling. Other whales were harder to tell apart, their patterns of motion harder to discern. The possibility of particularity—*this* whale, among all whales—allowed for an ongoing relationship to 52 as an individual creature, while other whales blurred into a more anonymous collective body.

52's particularity, as well as his apparent isolation, lent him a certain sheen of personality. "We always laughed when we were tracking him," Darel told me. "We said, 'Maybe he's heading to Baja for the lady blues.'" Darel's jokes echoed with the familiarity of affectionate condescension, the way frat brothers might talk about the runt of a pledge class who never had much luck with girls: *52 struck out, looked again, tried again. 52 never let up with that song.* It was something more than a job. Darel bought his wife a whale necklace during the years he spent tracking 52, and she still wears it.

Joe had his own fixations. "One time he disappeared for over a *month*," he said of 52, his inflection registering a mystery that clearly still engaged him. And at the end of the month, when they finally picked him up again, he was farther out in the Pacific than he'd ever been. Why was there that gap? Joe wondered. What had happened during that time?

Watkins was the driving force behind the whale tracking, but he couldn't keep it running forever. After 9/11, Joe explained, all the money disappeared for good.

As it turned out, however, the saga of 52 was just beginning. After the Woods Hole researchers published their findings about 52 Blue for the first time—in 2004, three years after the funding dried up—they started getting inundated with notes about the whale. Bill Watkins had died a month after the paper was accepted, so it was his former research assistant, a woman named Mary Ann Daher, who found herself receiving this flood of letters. They weren't typical pieces of professional correspondence. They came, as *New York Times* reporter Andrew Revkin wrote at the time, "from whale lovers lamenting the notion of a lonely heart of the cetacean world" or from people who identified with the whale for other reasons: because he seemed restless or independent, because he sang his own song.

After Revkin's story ran that December, headlined "Song of the Sea, a Cappella and Unanswered," more letters flooded Woods Hole. (One marine-mammal researcher quoted in the story, Kate Stafford, may have inadvertently fanned the flames: "He's saying, 'Hey, I'm out here.' Well, nobody is phoning home.") These letters came from the heartbroken and the deaf; from the lovelorn and the single; the once bitten, twice shy and the twice bitten, forever shy—people who identified with the whale or hurt for him, ached for whatever set of feelings they projected onto him.

A legend was born: the loneliest whale in the world.

In the years since, 52 Blue—or 52 Hertz, as he is known to many of his devotees—has inspired numerous sob-story headlines: not just "The Loneliest Whale in the World" but "The Whale Whose Unique Call Has Stopped Him Finding Love"; "A Lonely Whale's Unrequited Love Song"; "There Is One Whale That Zero Other Whales Can Hear and It's Very Alone: It's the Saddest Thing Ever, and Science Should Try to Talk to It." There have been imaginative accounts of a solitary bachelor headed down to the Mexican Riviera to troll haplessly for the biggest mammal babes alive, "his musical mating calls ringing for hours through the darkness of the deepest seas…broadcasting a wide repertory of heartfelt tunes."

A singer in New Mexico, unhappy at his day job in tech, wrote an entire album dedicated to 52; another singer in Michigan wrote a kids' song about the whale's plight; an artist in upstate New York made a sculpture out of old plastic bottles and called it *52 Hertz*. A music producer in Los Angeles started buying cassette tapes at garage sales and recording over them with 52's song, the song that was quickly becoming a kind of sentimental seismograph suggesting multiple story lines: alienation and determination; autonomy and longing; not only a failure to communicate but also a dogged persistence in the face of this failure. People have set up Twitter accounts to speak for him, including @52_Hz_Whale, who gets right to the point:

Hellooooooo?! Yooohoooooo! Is anyone out there? #SadLife

I'm so lonely. :'(#lonely #ForeverAlone

* * *

11

Leonora woke up in St. Luke's–Roosevelt Hospital in September 2007, in the aftermath of a seven-week coma but still near the beginning of the medical odyssey that would deliver her to 52 Blue. Across the course of five days of surgery, the doctors had removed nearly three feet of her intestines in order to cut out all the necrotic tissue that had rotted around a severe intestinal blockage. Then they'd put her in the coma to help her recover more efficiently. But so much recovery remained ahead of her. She couldn't walk. She had trouble remembering words, and she could barely speak anyway—her trachea was so scarred from all the tubes that had been thrust down it during her coma. She couldn't count past ten. She couldn't even quite count to ten. But she pretended. She didn't let on. She didn't want other people to see her struggling.

Leonora had grown up around struggle, raised mostly by her grandmother, a determined and resourceful woman, four feet eleven and blind from diabetes, who'd come to the States from Chennai by way of Trinidad. She'd always told Leonora that her people back in India thought America was full of golden sidewalks. But Leonora remembers the part of Harlem where she grew up, a neighborhood near Bradhurst Avenue, as something of an urban war zone during her high-school years in the mid-'70s, with its own police task force and sky-high murder rates. When Leonora got interested in photography one summer, people started calling her Death Photographer because so many of her subjects ended up as victims of violence.

Leonora was determined to leave, eventually saving enough bartending money to fund a trip to Paris, where she spent a blurry year walking up and down the Boulevard Saint-Michel with a corkscrew in her hand; taking a trip to Capri, where she and a friend met a pair of amorous lifeguards, broke into an abandoned villa, and ate bread and jam off the dusty kitchen table. Back in New York, Leonora met a man she almost married, but when they went to the courthouse, she got such terrible cramps that she had to go to the bathroom and realized it was her body telling her: *Don't do this*. She listened. She stayed in the bathroom until the offices closed; a police officer had to get her out.

She got a job as a case manager for the city, working with clients on food stamps or welfare, but grew increasingly isolated in her personal life. By the time she was hospitalized in July 2007, she'd retreated from the world so much that her time in the hospital felt less like an abrupt rupture and more like the continuation of her descent.

For Leonora, the hardest part of the recovery process was losing her self-sufficiency, realizing that she could no longer be independent or take care of herself. As she regained her voice, she started to grow more comfortable asking for what she needed. When she eventually realized the source of a stench she'd grown aware of—that it was her own hair, matted with blood—she demanded that one of the doctors cut it, and it turned out looking pretty good. They joked that the doctor might have a second career as a hairdresser.

During the six months she spent at the hospital and various rehab facilities, Leonora felt abandoned. She didn't have many visitors. It seemed like everyone in her life was fleeing her damage, pushing her away because they didn't want to be around her sickness. She assumed her illness made them uncomfortable because it reminded them of their own mortality. When people did visit, she perceived a dark energy coming from them; it nauseated her. When her father came to see her, he told her over and over that she looked like her mother—a woman he hadn't spoken about in many years. She felt that her illness raised long-buried emotions of anger and loss in him.

Leonora was cut off from others, and from the world itself. She couldn't even watch television because it gave her headaches. It was late one night, alone and trolling the internet, that she came upon the story of 52 Blue. By then the story of the whale had been floating around the internet for several years. But it resonated for Leonora with a particular urgency. "He was speaking a language that no one else could speak," she told me. "And here I was without a language. I had no more language to describe what had happened to me...I was like him. I had nothing. No one to communicate with. No one was hearing me. No one was hearing him. And I thought: *I hear you. I wish you could hear me.*"

Like the whale's, she felt that her own language was adrift. She was struggling to come back to any sense of self, much less find the words for what she was thinking or feeling. The world seemed to be pulling away, and the whale offered an echo of this difficulty. She remembers thinking, *I wish I could speak whale*. She found a strange kind of hope in the possibility that 52 Blue knew he wasn't alone. "I was like: Here he is. He's talking. He's saying something. He's singing. And nobody's really understanding, but there are people listening. I bet he knows people are listening. He must feel it."

The hunt for an elusive whale is the most famous story in the history of American literature. *Hast thou seen the White Whale?* But as much as *Moby-Dick* is about the quest for an animal, or for revenge, it's also about the quest for metaphor—the attempt to understand what can't be understood. Ishmael calls the whiteness of the whale "a dumb blankness, full of meaning." Full of many meanings, actually: divinity and its absence, primal power and its refusal, the possibility of revenge and the possibility of annihilation. "Of all these things the Albino whale was the symbol," Ishmael explains. "Wonder ye then at the fiery hunt?"

When I first began looking into the story of 52 Blue, I reached out to Mary Ann Daher at Woods Hole, hoping she could help me understand how the story of this whale had jumped the bounds of science and become something more like a rallying cry. Her role in the story was curious. She'd become the unwitting confessor for a growing flock of devotees simply because her name was on a paper recounting work for which she'd been a research assistant years before. "I get all sorts of emails," she told one reporter at the time, "some of them very touching—genuinely; it just breaks your heart to read some of them—asking why I can't go out there and help this animal." Eventually the media attention started to grate on her. "It's been pretty painful," she told another reporter in 2013. "You name the country and I've had a phone call, wanting to get information. And I haven't worked on this since 2006 or so...and...oh God, [Watkins would] be dismayed, to put it mildly."

I was eager to speak with Daher anyway. I pictured the two of us at Woods Hole, meeting by the sea, locking eyes, nursing cups of coffee in the salt air. How did it feel to get those letters? I'd ask her. And she'd tell me about the tug on her heart each time, her in-box turned into confessional booth. Perhaps she'd recite one from memory, the one that had moved her the most: *He is hope and loss at once.* I'd hear some break in her voice, and I'd copy her words. I'd copy the break. I'd make note of her scientific neutrality showing the strain at its seams, nearly torn open by a lonely stranger's helpless wonder.

It could have gone like that. Perhaps there is another world in which it did. This world, however, holds only her refusal to return my emails. The Woods Hole media-relations representative made it very clear: Daher was done talking about the whale; done refusing to make assumptions about the whale; done correcting other people's assumptions about the whale. She'd already said everything she had to say.

The last journalist Daher agreed to talk to was a writer named Kieran Mulvaney. The transcript of their conversation gives a sense of her wariness and aggravation. "We don't know what the heck it is," she said, when asked about the cause of 52's odd song. "Is he alone? I don't know. People like to imagine this creature just out there swimming by his lonesome, just singing away and nobody's listening. But I can't say that...Is he successful reproductively? I haven't the vaguest idea.

Nobody can answer those questions. Is he lonely? I hate to attach human emotions like that. Do whales get lonely? I don't know. I don't even want to touch that topic."

Daher never agreed to speak to me. She never agreed to pass along the letters she'd received from all the people who had been moved by this animal. So I went looking for them on my own.

At first, they were just voices out of the digital ether: a Polish tabloid photographer, an Irish farmers' cooperative employee, an American Muslim woman who associated 52 Blue with the Prophet Yunus. They congregated at a Facebook page dedicated to the whale, where most of the messages converged on two themes: feeling bad for 52 and wanting to find 52. Denise posted one message—"find 52 hertz"—over and over and over again one morning: at 8:09, 8:11, 8:14, 8:14 (a second time), and 8:16. A woman named Jen wrote, "Just want to give it a hug."

Shorna, a twenty-two-year-old in Kent, England, told me that learning about 52 gave her a way to understand the isolation she felt after her brother was killed when she was thirteen—the abiding conviction that her grief was nothing anyone else could ever understand. Her family didn't want to talk about it. Therapists were telling her what she should feel. The whale never told her what to feel. It just gave a shape to what she already felt, which was that she was "on a different wave length to other people." Juliana was a nineteen-year-old English major at the University of Toronto who told me she understood the whale as "the epitome of every person who's ever felt too weird to love." For her, he represented anyone "wandering alone," or anyone, herself included, "trying to find someone who accepts us for our weaknesses and faults."

Zbigniew, a twenty-six-year-old photo editor at the biggest daily tabloid in Poland, decided to get the outline of 52 Blue tattooed across his back after the end of a six-year relationship:

> i was deeply in love. but as it came out she was treating me like a second category person in relationship...i was devastadem mainy becose i have given her everything i could, and i thought she would do the same for me. [Because] of her i lost connection with important friends. View of the wasted time made me sad...Story of 52 hz whale made me happy. For me he is symbol of being alone in a positive way...He is like a steatement, that despite being alone he lives on.

For Zee, as he calls himself, 52 came to represent the lonely days after the breakup, watching sad movies alone at home with his two cats, Puma and Fuga. "For long time i was 'singing' in other frequency then everybody around," he wrote to me. But for him the whale also represented resilience: "this is what my life looks like for last 2 years. im swiming slowly through my part of ocean, trying to find poeple like me, Patient, going past life being sure that im not crippled but special in positive way."

The tattoo was a way for Zee to honor what the whale had meant to him, and to communicate that meaning—to sing at a frequency that might be understood. It stretches across his upper back, the "only place on my body huge enough to make it look awesome." Behind a detailed rendering of Moby-Dick, another one of Zee's fixations, there is a second whale, a ghost whale: just a negative space of bare skin defined by an outline of ink. Rather than illustrating 52 Blue, Zee's tattoo evoked the fact that he hadn't ever been seen.

Sakina, a twenty-eight-year-old medical actor living in Michigan, associates 52 with a different kind of loss—a more spiritual struggle. I first saw her in a YouTube video, wearing a hijab, describing how the story of 52 immediately made her think of the prophet Yunus, who was swallowed by a whale. "It makes sense that the loneliest whale feels lonely," she says. "Because he had a prophet with him, inside of him, and now he doesn't." I met Sakina in a coffee shop in downtown Ann Arbor, where she told me that learning about 52 Blue had evoked certain lonely periods of her childhood. (She grew up Muslim in New Mexico.) But she hadn't imagined the whale hungry for love so much as for a sense of purpose, craving a prophet to swallow or a prophecy to fulfill. She wondered: "Is he aching for the divinity again?"

David, an Irish father of two, identified with 52 Blue more deeply after he lost his job at Waterford Crystal, where he had been working for more than two decades. He wrote a song lamenting that he'd "followed sorrow like Whale 52 Hertz," and then moved to Galway with his wife to forge a new life. "I am told by everyone that Galway will be good for me," he wrote to me at the time. At the age of forty-seven, he was starting with a singing group and going back to school. "I have taken the discovery of the Whale as a signal from the depths that I am close to discovery...All I really know is that the 52 Hertz Whale is out there singing and that makes me feel less alone."

Six months later, David wrote to tell me that his wife had left him after twenty-five years of marriage. They could barely speak to each other. Life in Galway wasn't what he'd expected. His singing group had been a bust. But he still found solace in the whale. "I know that she's still out there," he wrote, imagining her as a female, perhaps as a soul mate. "I see others searching. Maybe I won't be alone for much longer."

The natural world has always offered itself as a screen for human projection. The Romantics called this the pathetic fallacy. Ralph Waldo Emerson called it "intercourse with heaven and Earth." We project our fears and longings onto everything we're not—every beast, every mountain—and in this way we make them somehow kin. It's an act of humbling and longing and claiming all at once. Often, we're not even aware that we're doing it. Decades after amateur astronomer Percival Lowell claimed to have seen canals on Mars and shadowy "spokes" on Venus, interpreting both as signs of alien life, an optometrist figured out that the settings on Lowell's telescope—its magnification and narrow aperture—meant that it was essentially projecting the interior of his eye onto the planets he was observing. The spokes of Venus were the shadows of his blood vessels, swollen from hypertension. He wasn't seeing other life; he was seeing the imprint of his own gaze.

When Emerson claimed that "every appearance in nature corresponds to some state of the mind," he understood this correspondence as a kind of completion. "All the facts in natural history taken by themselves have no value but are barren, like a single sex," he argued, suggesting that human projection effectively fertilized the egg. It not only brought meaning to the "barren" body of natural history, Emerson suggested, but offered sustenance to man himself, becoming "part of his daily food."

Though Emerson celebrated this process, he also interrogated its implications. "We are thus assisted by natural objects in the expression of particular meanings, but how great a language to convey such pepper-corn informations!" he wrote. "We are like travelers using the cinders of a volcano to roast their eggs." He wondered whether it robbed the natural world of its integrity to deploy it as metaphor: "Have mountains, and waves, and skies, no significance but what we consciously give them, when we employ them as emblems of our thoughts?" Roasting an egg on volcano cinders might be an apt way of describing what it means to use a giant whale to embody dorm-room homesickness or post-breakup ennui. *Is he lonely? I hate to attach human emotions like that.*

There used to be a name for the kind of people who like to tell tall tales about animals: nature fakers. Teddy Roosevelt himself issued a scathing public condemnation of what he called "yellow journalism of the woods." These syrupy accounts of the natural world projected human logic onto animal behaviors, spinning tales of wild fowl setting their own broken legs in mud-made casts, or crows convening schoolrooms for their young. "I know as President I ought not do this," he wrote, but criticized them anyway. "He is not a student of nature at all who sees not keenly but falsely, who writes interestingly and untruthfully, and whose imagination is used not to interpret facts but to invent them." Roosevelt was especially concerned about "fact-blindness": the possibility that telling fake stories about nature might blind us to the true ones. This is the danger of making the whale lonely or prophet-hungry, asking the duck to set a mud cast for his own broken leg—the possibility that feeling too much awe about the nature we've invented will make us unable to appreciate the nature in which we live.

Roosevelt's argument finds a strange modern echo in a Twitter account called @52Hurts, whose bio imagines the whale protesting his own symbolic status: "I am no symbol, no metaphor. I am not the metaphysics you feel stirring in you, no stand-in for your obsessions. I am a whale." Many of his tweets are nonsense—"Ivdhggv ahijhd ajhlkjhds"—but something about them seems honest. They are the tweets of a whale that doesn't know why he's on Twitter, whose jumbled language protests the projection of language onto him at all. His gibberish is more interested in what *isn't* legible than in forcing the unknown into false legibility. It's more interested in acknowledging the gaps than in voicing the projections we hurl across them.

When I first reached out to Leonora, she responded immediately to welcome me into the "vast vibrational pool" of 52 devotees. We met in Harlem's Riverbank State Park on a March afternoon caught between winter and spring. The wind was chilly off the Hudson.

Leonora moved carefully and chose her words with the same deliberate attention. Riverbank was clearly a special place for her. She was eager to explain that the park had been built on top of a sewage-treatment facility. She seemed proud of how it had turned ugly necessity into possibility. Riverbank had also been an important part of her rehabilitation process. It was the place she'd practiced walking after coming out of her coma. She'd been embarrassed at the thought of her home-care aide watching her stumble at every step, so she went to the park instead. The park didn't judge. It just let her practice.

As we walked past a row of withered garden plots, Leonora told me she hadn't gotten a cold all winter because of her vitamins. She'd been taking a "barrage" of them ever since she died. That's how she described her illness and coma: as a process of dying and coming back to life. "My ticket back came with conditions," she said. She had to learn to take care of herself—hence the vitamins, the art classes, and the desire to start growing her own vegetables this spring. She was hoping to get one of the small gardens that the park association was going to auction off before summer. The plots were down by the running track, full of the residue of winter: shriveled stalks, leaves withered to a crisp, bent lattices that had once held tomatoes and would hold them again. Leonora said she wanted to plant peppers and parsley, a small crop perched above a sewage plant. It would be a way of saying, *We do what we can with what we have.* She'd come back from her coma in pieces. She was still putting those pieces back together into a life.

A red-bellied robin hopped across one of the garden plots, right in front of us, and Leonora couldn't believe we were seeing it. It was too early in spring. She told me we needed to wish on it. This was part of her three-day rule: when she asks the universe a question, she always gets an answer in three days, in a dream or a visitation—maybe an animal or something as simple as the smell of lavender. She is open to messages from everything, all the time, in languages that aren't even recognizable as languages at all.

We walked inside and settled at the snack bar, by the ice rink, where an elementary-school hockey team was practicing. The Squirts. Leonora told me this was the last place in New York where you could still get coffee for a dollar. This was her home turf. The guys behind the counter knew her order before she ordered it. The guy riding by in a motorized wheelchair said hello. The guy lurking by the register wanted her to sign a petition for a candidate for parks superintendent.

At our table, Leonora pulled out a large notebook to show me some of her pen and pencil sketches of 52 Blue. "He obsesses me," she explained. "I was trying to get a sense of what he looks like." But she told me her early drawings were "muddled." So she looked at photographs of other whales. "But I still wasn't finding *him*. He's so elusive." She kept sketching him anyway. She was working on a painting of 52 for the final exhibition of an art class she was taking at the park's recreation center.

The first time Leonora ever listened to 52's song, she told me, she played it back at least fifty times. She once dreamed about swimming with him: he was in a pod of whales, no longer alone, and she was moving with them at what felt like a hundred miles per hour—her head huge, her body sleek and hairless. Her coma recovery was full of dreams about water, always rivers and oceans rather than lakes or ponds. The water needed to be in motion, rather than stagnant or still. After her dream about 52, she woke up astonished. "I was moved by it," she said. "All I could do was just lie there and think, *What was that? What was that?*"

Leonora's sense of connection to 52 had always been about two things at once: communication and autonomy. He represented her difficulties in recovery—her failed attempts to speak—but also the independence that these difficulties had taken away. While others saw the whale as heartbroken, because he couldn't find a companion, Leonora saw him as a creature that didn't need one. He was a representation of her own capacity to live alone. It was a capacity she cherished, and it was precisely what her illness had imperiled.

It bothered Leonora that people conflated 52's aloneness with loneliness. It bothered her that people conflated *her* aloneness with loneliness. Apropos of very little, she told me, "I haven't been in a relationship since the last century. I haven't been on a date." She said it worried other people in her life, friends and family members who tried to set her up. "It's like a woman is not a whole person until she has a man." But it didn't worry her. "I've never felt lonely. There is not this lonely factor. I am *alone*. But I am not lonely, okay? I go over to a friend's, I buy cases of wine, I have people over, I cook."

It was hard not to hear a hint of *doth protest too much* in her insistence. But I was also hearing an argument for the importance of humility: Don't assume the contours of another person's heart. Don't assume its desires. Don't assume that being alone means being lonely. Leonora told me that she hopes 52 is never found. "I pray they don't. I like to believe that I'll see him in my dreams."

I just don't know what it is, the fascination with this whale," Joe George told me, while we sat at his dining room table. "To me it's just science." Which made the tray of cookies that sat between us even more charming—all of them shaped like whales, with frosted tails, various pastel shades of green and pink and periwinkle, and "52" written in matching shades of icing. Joe's daughter had made them for us. He was pleased to offer them to me but also seemed a bit sheepish. They were complicit in the whimsy of a phenomenon he couldn't quite wrap his mind around.

He told me it felt odd to have funding for the whale tracking cut so suddenly and unequivocally—to feel like no one cared about what they were doing—and then to see his whale resurface so many years later in such a strange, refracted form. Suddenly *everyone* cared, but for reasons that didn't really make sense to Joe, a man more worried about doing his job right than mining it for metaphor.

At a certain point, Joe told me, the whale called 52 Hertz stopped coming in at 52 hertz. The last time they tracked him, his call was more like 49.6 hertz. It could have been a kind of delayed puberty, or else a function of size, his growing form pulling his vocalizations down into lower frequencies.

It's another lesson in humility—the possibility that an elusive animal might stop flashing its old calling card, that the physical creature might render all our mythical projections moot. It's as if we have tuned our hearts to a signal that no longer exists. Which means there is no way to find what we've been looking for, only—perhaps—a way to find what that creature has become.

After a spring spent getting to know Leonora, I went back to Riverbank State Park for her class's final art show. It was an early summer day of celebration. The beginning keyboard class played "When the Saints Go Marching In" under giant beige industrial fans. A group of elderly women did a synchronized dance to bubblegum-pop, waving matching fans and wearing white capri pants with bright sapphire and coral-pink shirts. One of the park staff leaned close to whisper in my ear, "These are our seniors. They like to get down."

Leonora, wearing lavender pants and a pink scrunchie, was taking photos and rolling around a shopping cart full of her artwork. She showed me her painting of 52 Blue hanging on a hallway wall: a whale painted in flat acrylics, flying over a rainbow, over an ocean. The decoupaged figure of a woman was riding him—or flying with him, it wasn't entirely clear—and Leonora said it was a photograph of her taken years ago, though she'd obscured the face so it wouldn't be just *her*. It could be anyone. The woman's head was ducking close to the whale, as if she were listening to something he was saying. "Someone asked me, 'Is the whale kissing you?'" Leonora told me. "And I said, 'Maybe he is.'"

When a young woman wearing the green shirt of park staff walked by, Leonora explained to her, without apology or introduction: "This is 52 Hertz. Just how I imagined him." As if everyone would know the whale, or should—as if the project of imagining his distant body should be familiar to us all.

Over the course of our conversations during the previous few months, I'd come to understand Leonora's attachment to the whale as something her whole life had been building toward. If she thought of her medical crisis as a culmination—the intestinal blockage as an accretion of traumas from all across her life, experiences she endured but never let herself cry or talk about, until they cluttered her insides and finally made her ill—then it seemed the whale offered another kind of gathering: a vessel in which the accumulation of a lifetime of longings might reside. She had a deep desire to understand her life as something structured by patterns, woven through with signs and signals and voices. She was hungry for a logic that might arrange all the isolated points of her experience into a legible constellation. During one of our talks, she told me she thought of me whenever she saw a robin, because we'd seen one together. I told her that two weeks after we saw that robin, I'd met the man I wanted to marry. It wasn't three days, but still. It was something.

During another one of our visits at the rec-center snack bar, Leonora told me she believed the whale might be the last of his kind—as she would be the last of hers, in a way, because she doesn't have any kids. She hated how people considered her childlessness an insufficiency.

Her artwork was the closest thing she had to progeny, and that was okay with her. It didn't seem like an accident that she used the words "resurrection," "rebirth," and "second birth" to describe her coma and its aftermath, or that we kept coming back to the subject of babies, to having them or not having them. It didn't seem like coincidence that birth was such a big part of how she thought about all this. She'd bled for years. And at the end of all that blood, when she came back from death, it was like she gave birth to herself.

As I left Riverbank State Park that last day, Leonora handed me a small painting: a robin with a red breast, tiny claws, and a single beady eye. She said the red on his breast symbolized activation. I thought of the man I'd met after I saw that robin. I felt the contagion of magical thinking. Life becomes a series of omens. I wanted them to imply the presence of some organizing spirit, or at least compose a story.

"*Vaya con Dios,*" Leonora told me. "You should have a baby someday."

When Emerson lamented that "the material is degraded before the spiritual," he was referring to the ways we have "transferred nature into the mind, and left matter like an outcast corpse." The actual body of 52 Blue has become the outcast corpse, the matter left over once our machinations are done. This alchemy holds both violence and beauty. Emerson understood both parts. "Every spirit builds itself a house, and beyond its house a world; and beyond its world, a heaven," he wrote. "What we are, that only can we see."

Wondering aloud about the whale, Leonora once asked me: "How do you know that he wasn't sent here to heal us, and his song is a healing song?"

Maybe every song is a healing song if we hear it in the right mood — at the end of the right seven weeks, or the worst ones, the ones lost to us forever. Maybe desire and demand are just the same song played at different frequencies. At one point, Leonora told me, simply, "The whale is everything."

52 Blue suggests not just one single whale as a metaphor for loneliness, but metaphor *itself* as salve for loneliness. Metaphor always connects two disparate points; it suggests that no pathos exists in isolation, no plight exists apart from the plights of others. Loneliness seeks out metaphors not just for definition but for the companionship of resonance, the promise of kinship in comparison. Now there's an entire coterie gathered around this particular kinship, people tracking the same pulse of a minivan-sized heart. You might say it's a community formed around an empty center. When we pour our sympathy onto 52 Blue, we aren't feeling for a whale, exactly. We're feeling for what we've built in his likeness. But that feeling still exists. It still matters. It mattered enough to help a woman come back from seven weeks at the edge of death.

At one point during our conversation on Whidbey Island, I mentioned Leonora to Joe. At first I wasn't sure he'd heard me, but near the end of our visit he turned to me and said, "That woman you mentioned, the one who was in the coma." He paused. I nodded. "That's really something," he said.

Joe was right when he said that the whale is just a whale. And so was Leonora when she said the whale is everything. What if we grant the whale his whaleness, grant him furlough from our metaphoric employ, but still allow the contours of his second self—the one we've made—and admit what he's done for us? If we let the whale cleave in two, into his actual form and the apparition of what we needed him to become, then we let these twins swim apart. We free each figure from the other's shadow. We watch them cut two paths across the sea.

We Tell Ourselves Stories
in Order to Live Again

In April 2000, a Louisiana toddler named James Leininger started having nightmares about plane crashes. Whenever his mother came to his bedroom to comfort him, she would find his body contorted, his arms and legs flailing as if he were struggling to extricate himself from something. He repeated the same phrases again and again: "Airplane crash! Plane on fire! Little man can't get out!"

Over the next few years, an increasingly specific story emerged from these dreams. James eventually told his parents they were memories from another life. He said he'd been a pilot shot down by the Japanese. He started using proper nouns that his parents couldn't account for. He'd flown a Corsair. He'd taken off from a ship called the *Natoma*. His parents hadn't ever talked to him about World War II and couldn't imagine where these visions were coming from. James told them about his friends on the ship: a man named Jack Larsen, and guys named Walter and Billy and Leon, who had all been waiting for him in heaven. He named his G.I. Joes after them. His mom, Andrea, became convinced that James was remembering another life. His father, Bruce, was more skeptical.

But when Bruce started doing some research, he found pieces of information that made it hard for him to stay that way. An aircraft carrier called the *Natoma Bay* had been deployed near Iwo Jima in 1945. Its crew included a pilot named Jack Larsen and another named James Huston, who was shot down near Chichi-Jima on March 3 of that year. The crew of the *Natoma Bay* also included Walter Devlin and Billie Peeler and Leon Conner, all of whom perished not long before Huston himself. How would a little boy have known about these men, let alone the name of their ship and the sequence of their deaths?

In 2002, Bruce went to a *Natoma Bay* reunion and started asking questions. He wasn't about to tell anyone what his son claimed to remember; he told everyone that he was writing a book on the history of the ship instead. Andrea, meanwhile, wasn't worried about the military history. She just wanted to end her son's nightmares. She told James that she believed him but that his old life was over. Now he had to live this one.

Seeking closure was the idea behind a trip the family took to Japan when James was eight years old. The plan was to hold a memorial service for James Huston. They rode a fifteen-hour ferry from Tokyo to Chichi-Jima, then a smaller boat to the approximate spot in the Pacific where Huston's plane had gone down. That's where James tossed a bouquet of purple flowers into the ocean. "I salute you, and I'll never forget," he said. Then he sobbed into his mother's lap for twenty minutes straight.

"You leave it all here, buddy," his father told him. "Just leave it all here."

When James finally looked up and brushed away his tears, he wanted to know where his flowers had gone. Someone pointed to a distant spot of color on the water: there they were, far away but still visible, still floating, drifting away on the surface of the sea.

*　　*　　*

On a sunny January day in 2014, I visited the offices of a small research institute in Virginia called the Division of Perceptual Studies (DOPS). I was there to interview a child psychiatrist named Jim Tucker, who had spent the past fourteen years compiling a database of children who claimed to remember prior lives. By the time I met Tucker, his database included more than two thousand families, but he called James Leininger his strongest case.

I was interviewing Tucker on assignment for a glossy New York magazine, and I knew my editors expected a debunking. When I told people I was writing a story about the DOPS, whose research focused on past-life memories, near-death experiences, and extrasensory perception, they often said, "Wait, WHAT?" It lent itself to easy jokes. But I felt defensive of reincarnation from the start. It wasn't that I necessarily believed in it. It was more that I'd grown deeply skeptical of skepticism itself. It seemed much easier to poke holes in things—people, programs, systems of belief—than to construct them, stand behind them, or at least take them seriously. That ready-made dismissiveness banished too much mystery and wonder.

The beliefs themselves are hardly unusual. We've all wondered what happens after we die. A 2018 Pew study found that 33 percent of Americans believe in reincarnation, and a 2013 Harris Poll estimated that 64 percent believe in the more loosely defined "survival of the soul after death." Back home in New York, whenever I rode the subway, I saw photos of the thirteen-year-old autistic boy who had gone missing that October. The boy was from Queens; there was no Queens-bound train his face wasn't on. I was irrationally convinced they would find him, or that he was somehow safe, wherever he was—and if that conviction made me foolish, I wanted to be a fool.

When Tucker welcomed me into the DOPS offices, housed in a

stately brick building in downtown Charlottesville, he didn't seem like a kook or a mystic. He was a personable, lucid, clearly intelligent guy—middle-aged and losing his hair, but lithe and trim, like your high-school best friend's marathon-running dad. He was self-possessed, with a courtly formality. He chose his words carefully but unapologetically as he explained how mediums channeled the spirits of the dead and birthmarks could testify to injuries sustained during prior lives. It was a bit like listening to a geologist on acid matter-of-factly describe the composition of the soil.

Founded in 1967, the DOPS is technically affiliated with the University of Virginia but is financed mainly by private donations, including an original million-dollar bequest from the man who invented Xerox technology, Chester Carlson, whose wife believed she had some skill at ESP. After a cover story about its research ran in the University of Virginia alumni magazine in 2013, the online comments were full of reactions from readers who found its existence ridiculous, or were "appalled" to learn about its connection to the university.

As Tucker showed me around their offices, I scribbled a catalog of odd details in my notebook, the low-hanging fruit of institutional quirk. A framed photo showed one former director handing a copy of his book, *The Handbook of Near-Death Experiences*, to the Dalai Lama, who knew a thing or two about reincarnation himself. The bulletin boards were papered with inspiring quotes ("Our notions of mind and matter must pass through many a phase as yet unimaginable") and flyers describing ongoing research projects ("Investigation of Mediums Who Claim to Give Information About Deceased Persons," "Mystical Experiences in Epilepsy"). We passed the "shielded room," designed for experiments on extrasensory perception: a grim-looking cave with a La-Z-Boy recliner where subjects waited to receive messages from "senders" elsewhere in the building. Tucker explained the mechanics of the room as an afterthought—its walls covered in metal sheeting

31

to block cell-phone cheating—as if I probably already knew how ESP chambers worked.

Touring the DOPS, I often felt like a teenager trying to keep from giggling in sex-ed class. But my humor reflex didn't feel entirely authentic. It felt more like channeling an internalized sense of collective judgment, some anonymous "sensible" perspective that told me I'd be a fool if I took any of this stuff seriously; or else like the nervous laughter that erupts from us in the face of what we can't entirely understand.

The DOPS library contained an impressive glass case holding weapons from all over the world—a Nigerian cutlass, a Thai dagger, a Sri Lankan sword—that corresponded to injuries supposedly transferred across lives. The placard beneath a gong mallet from Myanmar told the story of a monk who was struck on the head by a deranged visitor and allegedly came back a few years later as a boy with an unusually flattened skull. In a nearby aisle, stacks of pamphlets documented various DOPS studies, including one titled "Seven More Paranormal Experiences Associated with the Sinking of the *Titanic*." We passed two spoons mounted on the wall, one twisted as if it had been melted over flames. When I asked Tucker about them, his reply was nonchalant. "Those?" he said. "Bent-spoon experiments."

Then there was the lock. When Ian Stevenson, the founding director of the DOPS, died, in 2007, he left behind a lock whose combination was known only to him. The idea was that he'd find a way to send it back if his soul survived death. Tucker and his colleagues had received several call-in suggestions from strangers, but they hadn't gotten the lock open yet. When he told me about the lock, Tucker finally allowed a certain wry playfulness into his voice. But during most of our visit, he kept himself on limited rations when it came to reincarnation jokes. At dinner that night, he told me he'd once tried his hand at writing fiction, and when I asked if he'd ever thought about picking it up again, he smiled. "Maybe in another life."

Tucker told me that having a career as a credentialed child psychiatrist alongside his DOPS work made him feel like he was inhabiting a split self. "My child-psychiatry work has been my mild-mannered Clark Kent identity," he said. "But then there's a secret identity, completely connected to another world." He outlined the makeup of his database: Most of his cases were children between the ages of two and seven, and their memories, which often took the form of vivid dreams, were suffused with a wide range of emotions—fear, love, grief. Most were from foreign countries, and many were children Tucker himself had never met, though he regularly went to interview new families who contacted him with their claims. He referred to a case as "solved" whenever a plausible prior life had been identified, usually someone in the family; though occasionally it was a stranger, as it had been for James.

Tucker seemed like a sensible straight man who had somehow found himself playing Hamlet to the Horatios of the world: *There are more things in heaven and earth...than are dreamt of in your philosophy.* He'd grown up Southern Baptist in North Carolina and hadn't given much thought to reincarnation until his second marriage. His second wife, Chris, also academically trained, believed in psychic abilities and reincarnation, and being with her had opened him up to considering things he never had before. Tucker eventually grew to regard his child-psychiatry practice as "rewarding but not fulfilling." It was gratifying to see kids getting better with treatment, but ultimately it was just "one appointment after another. There was no big picture." His work with past-life memories felt more expansive. It was about following the hazy patterns of a picture that stretched far beyond the limits of his vision.

Weeks later, when I listened to recordings of our interviews, I was embarrassed to hear myself repeatedly declaring to Tucker my "openness to mystery." This insistence had been in earnest, but I could also hear in my voice the shrill and overeager tones of self-convincing, and the savviness of strategy. On some level, I'd been trying to persuade Tucker that I wasn't just another skeptic. Janet Malcolm has famously described the journalist as "a kind of confidence man, preying on people's vanity, ignorance, or loneliness, gaining their trust and betraying them without remorse." And in my interviews with Tucker, I could hear myself confessing to him in advance: "You can never tell the story about somebody that's precisely the story he would have told about himself."

By the time I visited Tucker at the DOPS, I'd been involved in 12-step recovery for more than three years. I'd found that its grace required extinguishing, or at least suspending, many forms of skepticism at once: about dogma, about clichés, about programs of insight and pre-fabricated self-awareness, about other people's ostensibly formulaic narratives of their own lives. In recovery, we were asked to avoid "contempt prior to investigation," and writing a piece about reincarnation—visiting the DOPS and its bent spoons—seemed like another test of this willingness to keep an open mind.

Coming of age as a writer, I had always loved Joan Didion's essay "The White Album," which famously begins, "We tell ourselves stories in order to live," and less famously ends in pretty much exactly the same place, with Didion reiterating her suspicions about all of these "stories" and their false coherence as if it wasn't a point she'd already made several times. Eventually, I started to have my doubts about her doubt. I hated its smugness—how she positions herself as a knowing skeptic in a world full of self-delusion. I started to believe there was an ethical failure embedded in skepticism itself, the same snobbery that lay beneath the impulse to resist clichés in recovery meetings or wholly dismiss people's overly neat narratives of their own lives.

In my own work, I found myself increasingly addicted to writing about lives or beliefs that others might have scoffed at: people who claimed to suffer from a skin disease most doctors didn't believe in, or self-identified outsiders who felt a spiritual kinship to an elusive whale. But if I was honest with myself, this affinity also carried the faint whiff of self-righteousness. Maybe I liked telling myself I was defending underdogs. Or maybe it was cowardice. Maybe I was too scared to push back against the stories people told themselves in order to keep surviving their own lives.

In this case, it wasn't that I was convinced by Tucker's ostensibly "physics-based" account of how reincarnation worked: a theory grounded in a series of experiments drawn from the history of physics that one physicist I interviewed called "cherry-picked" and selectively misinterpreted. Tucker was a psychiatrist, after all, not a physicist. It was more that I felt emotionally, spiritually, and intellectually allergic to a certain disdainful tone that implied it knew better, that it understood what was possible and what wasn't. It seemed arrogant to assume I understood much about consciousness itself—what it was, where it came from, or where it went once we were done with it.

D own in Virginia, I accompanied Tucker on interviews with two families. Both had teenagers who'd remembered prior lives as children. At a large house overlooking bare winter woods, a twenty-year-old college student named Aaron told me that when he was young he'd remembered being a tobacco farmer. He'd had visions of a farm, a mean sister, a fire. He pretend-smoked whatever he could get his hands on: twigs and straws and Popsicle sticks. He was obsessed with tattoos and motorcycles and wouldn't wear anything but cowboy boots. He even wore them to the pool with nothing but his bathing suit.

His mother, Wendy, told me that learning about Aaron's "old soul" helped explain why he often struggled to make friends his own age. She always wanted to throw him birthday parties, but never knew whom to invite. "Not to hurt your feelings, son," she told him, "but you never fit in anywhere." Aaron himself attributed his more recent dating troubles to the same old soul. While the girls around him seemed mainly interested in partying, he explained, he wanted to settle down and start a family. As we spoke, we could see a man through the window standing at the edge of the woods, throwing sticks for a bristling trio of dogs. When he turned around to come inside, Wendy asked me not to mention anything about reincarnation. Her boyfriend was a jet mechanic, she explained. He found all of this absurd.

At a smaller house in a more working-class neighborhood, with a lawn full of deflated plastic reindeer, a mother named Julie explained that her daughter Carol had started speaking late and didn't say much once she'd started. When Julie finally asked Carol why she was so quiet, at the age of four or five, Carol at last mentioned her other family: long-haired parents who grew herbs and owned a mint-green rotary phone. Carol found it confusing that she didn't live with them. She missed them. Julie recalled, "I felt like I had to tell her, 'I really am your mother.'" She worried Carol might share her past life with her classmates at show-and-tell and get teased for it.

More than a decade later, Carol—almost twenty—told me and Tucker that she had recently started culinary school to learn how to decorate cakes for people with food allergies, and Julie speculated that her daughter's creative tendencies may have also carried over from her prior existence. She explained that one of Carol's strongest past-life memories was of drawing at a kitchen table. The association felt charged with the willed electricity of a horoscope: almost anything can fit into the puzzle of your life if you want it to.

After a beat, Carol gently corrected her mother's story. In her memory, she hadn't been drawing at a kitchen table but painting at an easel inside a glass-walled skyscraper. The conversation paused. We all dwelled in the blurry zone between Carol's memories and the stories Julie had told herself about these memories—where the kitchen had replaced the skyscraper and the drawing had replaced the easel, where the kaleidoscope of memory had reshuffled its glimmering shards.

M y flight home got canceled by a rare Virginia blizzard, and I spent two nights killing time at a corporate hotel near the airport, drinking seltzer after seltzer at the lobby bar. The bartender and I exchanged pained glances as the TV delivered endless doomsday news: corruption, molestation, dead dolphins bloodying the saltwater of a secret Japanese cove. In some deep unspoken part of my psyche, I'd convinced myself that agnosticism and acceptance were moral virtues unto themselves, but in truth I wasn't so sure. Maybe I wasn't doing anyone any favors by pretending that my belief system was tolerant enough to hold everything as equally valid. Maybe there were experiences I couldn't relate to and things I might never believe.

Why did I want to defend these tales of prior lives, anyway? It had less to do with believing I could prove that reincarnation was real and more to do with investigating why it was appealing to believe in it. If we told ourselves stories in order to live, what did we get from stories that allowed us to live again? It was about something more than buffering against the terrifying finality of death. It had to do with recognizing the ways we're shaped by forces we can't see or understand.

On the television screen at the airport hotel bar—in the middle of that blizzard, just before I went to bed—I saw the face of Avonte Oquendo, the missing boy from Queens. His remains had been discovered in the East River. Back when they thought they might still find him alive, the police had played a recording that his mother had made, in order to help him trust them: "Avonte. This is your mother. You are safe. Walk toward the lights."

*   *   *

Driving down Louisiana back roads a few weeks later, on my way to the Leiningers' home in Lafayette, I passed forests webbed with pockets of glistening water, and shotgun shacks collapsing under their own weight. The radio in my rental car spoke to me about demons. "I believe in the spiritual enemy," a man said. "He works by way of substitution."

Before coming down, I'd interviewed a child psychiatrist named Alan Ravitz about the possibility of past-life memories, and he'd been less immediately dismissive than I'd expected. "Who the hell knows?" he said. "Anything is possible." He admitted that Tucker had found "certain sorts of phenomena that are just difficult to explain," and stressed that many of these reported past-life memories weren't "the typical kind of imaginative material that kids would come up with." But Ravitz posited that "past lives" like these could also emerge from a subtle process of reinforcement. When a kid tells a story—or recounts an odd memory or a weird dream that felt real—and gets any kind of attention for it, it's only natural for the child to keep expanding it.

These dynamics of reinforcement—maybe operating for parents and children alike—were part of what fascinated me about these cases. We tell stories about why we're lonely, or what we're haunted by, and these stories about absence can define us as fully as our present realities. Kids build identities around ghosts. A mother believes that her son has trouble making friends because the soul of an old man lives inside him. Stories about past lives help explain this one. They promise an extraordinary root structure beneath the ordinary soil of our days. They acknowledge that the realities closest to us—the rhythms of our lives, the people we love most—are shaped by forces beyond the edges of our sight. It's thrilling and terrifying. It's expansion and surrender at once.

Down in Louisiana, I was renting a cabin out in Arnaudville, past the daiquiri drive-through and the biker barn saloon on I-49, past the church marquee that said JESUS IS A HUGGER and the hand-painted sign advertising USED SUGAR KETTLES FOR SALE, past tiny streets with speed signs in bright purple: 7½ MILES PER HOUR. The cabin was a wooden shack set back among pecan and magnolia trees, with an old wooden sign for DR. KILMER'S SWAMP ROOT above the toilet and a brass lamp beside a bed where I imagined sleeping with all the men I wasn't sleeping with anymore. Their ghosts crowded the shack, vessels for all the selves I used to be.

The Leiningers lived in a modest house shadowed by river birches draped in Spanish moss. When Bruce answered the door, he offered me a cup of coffee and a slice of banana bread, then—almost immediately—offered to show me his gun collection. I could tell it made him wary to see me writing in my notebook. "I'm not a gun nut," he said, holding a gun in each hand. After I used the bathroom, I emerged to find a collection of bullets spread across his comforter. I didn't want to touch them, but I mentally recorded them as a "telling detail." The tattoo that ran along my arm was posing questions about this man, this moment, and these bullets. *Homo sum: humani nil a me alienum puto*, it said. "I am human: nothing human is alien to me." Had I been foolishly unwilling to acknowledge that some people *were* alien to me? Did I need to identify with all the gun-loving men of this world? Was it naïve or even ethically irresponsible to believe I should find common ground with everyone, or that it was even possible?

In preparation for my arrival, Bruce had pulled out his material about the *Natoma Bay* and its pilots—more than a decade's worth of research. The dining room table was covered with notebooks and folders, but it was "only a fraction," he said, of what he had in his closets. He had compiled a separate notebook for every single soldier who died on the ship, crammed with as much biographical information and as many military after-action reports as he could assemble. There was a wooden champagne crate full of microfiche reels that the ship's historian had sent him. Bruce freely admitted: "I was obsessed." Everything was labeled PROPERTY OF BRUCE LEININGER / RESEARCH MATERIAL FOR 'ONE LUCKY SHIP' ©. *One Lucky Ship* was the book that Bruce was writing about the *Natoma Bay,* the book that would finally make good on the story he'd told its veterans years earlier, in order to gain access to their inner circle. Now he sent the families of dead pilots any information he'd gathered about how their loved ones had fought and died, specifics they had almost never gotten from the military. Bruce told me he believed that James Huston had returned in the body of his son for a reason—so that he and Andrea could recover this sliver of American history, one that might otherwise have been lost to obscurity.

Bruce showed me the office closet that James had once pretended was his cockpit, jumping out wearing a canvas shopping bag on his back like a parachute. Then he brought out some of the artifacts he'd gathered over the years, including a vial of soil from Iwo Jima and a piece of melted engine from the kamikaze plane that flew into the *Natoma Bay* in 1945—a metal hunk coated in melted tar and bits of redwood from the ship's deck. Bruce handled it like a holy relic.

After years of research, Bruce had finally managed to locate Anne Huston Barron, James Huston's sister, whom he initially befriended under the auspices of his usual cover story. About six months after making contact, however, he and Andrea decided to tell Anne the actual reason for their interest in her brother. They were nervous. They started the phone call by suggesting that she might want to pour herself a glass of wine. They had the number of her local EMT service on hand in case the news was too much of a shock. As Bruce and Andrea shared these details—the glass of wine, the EMT number—I heard echoes of *Soul Survivor,* their 2009 book about James's past-life memories. Their witty asides had become part of a well-worn story. Even its grooves of self-deprecation held the uneasy echoes of lines performed effectively and often.

As for Anne? She wasn't sure what to make of their revelation at first—she was shocked—but eventually she came to embrace the idea that their son was her brother reincarnated. Perhaps there was something comforting about the possibility that her James was not entirely gone. Bruce showed me one of her letters. "All of this is still overwhelming," she'd written. "One reads about it, but never expects it to happen to you." And in her neat, orderly print, an unequivocal affirmation: "But I believe."

When I met James, he struck me as a pretty well-adjusted teenager. He seemed polite but vaguely bored, and evinced close to zero interest in talking to me. Here was yet another stranger curious about past-life memories that he hadn't remembered in years, not since that ceremony on the sea. It was easier to draw him out on other subjects: his commitment to jujitsu, his advice on how to tell if your gator meat had been decently prepared. He wasn't at all defensive, but I sensed he was a bit tired of the whole past-life production, and perhaps a bit sheepish about the publicity circus these memories had yielded— the book and the interviews—the way you might amiably tolerate the public antics of an embarrassing sibling. He no longer wanted to be a Navy fighter pilot like James Huston; now he wanted to be a Marine. But he also spent much of the afternoon playing a video game that involved shooting from a simulated cockpit, and his bedroom was still full of the model airplanes Bruce had built for him, dangling from the ceiling.

The hardest part about spending time with the Leiningers was how much I liked them. As we ate dinner together at a local creole restaurant, shadowed by a twelve-foot taxidermy alligator, I knew I wasn't writing the story they wanted me to write about their family. Once again, Janet Malcolm had articulated my guilt before I'd even felt it: "Like the credulous widow who wakes up one day to find the charming young man and all her savings gone, so the consenting subject of a piece of nonfiction writing learns—when the article or book appears—*his* hard lesson." And yet, it seemed too easy to narrate the Leiningers as hucksters of petty mystery, parents who had turned their son's alleged past life into something like a cottage industry: a best-selling memoir and another book in the works, a slew of television specials and speaking gigs. Their motives never struck me as entrepreneurial. It seemed more like they had encountered something genuinely mysterious in their son—a force they couldn't explain—and that their explanation had become a narrative engine of its own, a story that granted them a sense of purpose: to excavate one forgotten corner of human history, and—more broadly—to testify to the world that a soul could travel from one body to another.

Of course, the story of their son also gave them a way to be special: to sell a book, to be interviewed on television. I'd started to notice an abiding irony embedded in stories of reincarnation. Even as they replaced a belief in the uniqueness of the self with an idea of interchangeability—suggesting that your soul had belonged to others before it belonged to you—they also provided an extraordinary explanation for deeply ordinary things: a shy daughter, a son with no friends, a toddler with nightmares. They turned quotidian experiences into symptoms of an exotic existential phenomenon.

Near the end of our visit, the Leiningers offered to show me some of the television specials they had been featured in. Together we watched *The Ghost Inside My Child* and *Science of the Soul*. We watched a Japanese special with a voiceover that had never been translated; the

Leiningers still didn't know what it said. It was this TV special that had funded their trip to Chichi-Jima and its cathartic farewell. We watched the B-roll footage, in which the Leiningers sit in a boat for hours, waiting for the ritual. I would see James weep, his parents promised, almost as an implicit challenge: *Try not to believe after you've seen how hard he cried.*

Andrea left the house as we watched, insisting that she needed to buy a printer cartridge but also confessing that it made her too emotional to watch James weep. Bruce wanted to skip past his own "silly speech" on the boat, but I asked him not to. It turned out to be an earnest homage to the bravery of James Huston, and to the beauty of his final resting place—those blue waters off a remote Japanese island where, as Bruce said on camera, "my own son's journey began."

People on the show kept asking James how he was feeling. "Okay," he said. "Good."

I couldn't help wondering whether these initial responses had disappointed his family, or the filmmakers—if it had been frustrating to stage an elaborate memorial on the other side of the world, and have no tears to show for it.

On-screen, however, Bruce gave no sign of disappointment. "I'm glad you don't feel anything," he told his son. "You've suffered for so long."

It was only after the eulogy was done and the tribute paid, when Andrea finally said that it was time to say goodbye to James Huston, that her son started crying. And then he kept going. He just couldn't stop.

Offscreen—years after that day, on his living room couch—Bruce got quiet. He told me that it still upset him to consider what had been going through his son's mind that day. At one point, a camera guy crept into the frame to give James a hug. Then he embraced Bruce too.

"They were just in pieces," Bruce said, meaning the whole Japanese crew. At this point, their tears had become an inextricable part of the story, proof of their investment and belief. But I wondered what it must have been like for them, sitting beside the ostensible reincarnation of a soldier who'd fought against their country.

Andrea rejoined us later to watch some of the other documentaries. She said she especially liked the one that didn't make her look a million years old. The friendliest of the family's four cats climbed onto the couch with us, but turned away from the screen. I sensed that she, too, had seen these shows before.

Bruce mouthed the words he said on-screen before he actually said them. "Bullshit!" he whispered to himself, a moment before he barked out the word on the television. He had been re-creating his own skepticism for the interviewer, playacting an earlier version of himself from the days before he'd come to believe in James's memories. Bruce enjoyed performing his former disbelief because it wasn't something that ran counter to his current faith; it was actually a necessary part of the same narrative arc, suggesting to other skeptics that their doubt was perfectly reasonable but ultimately wrong.

For her part, Andrea seemed less interested in other people's relationships to James's memories and more interested in how James himself had experienced them. She showed me a stack of his young drawings: messy circles meant to show the motion of propellers, peppery dots meant to represent anti-aircraft flak, everything broken and splintered and covered with rashes of red-marker blood. She showed me his stick-figure parachutists falling through the sky. Some of their chutes had bloomed into arcs above their bodies; others, less lucky, had chutes collapsed into straight lines above them.

From across the room, where he was still watching the TV, Bruce mentioned that according to an after-action report he'd found, James Huston once shot down a parachuting Japanese pilot. Andrea was shocked; she hadn't known that. "I just got chills," she said. "That's probably why James was always drawing them—because he shot one down."

Meanwhile, on the TV screen, Bruce sat on a tiny boat and placed a hand on his son's back. "You're such a brave soul and spirit," he said.

In that moment, beneath the sensational story of reincarnation, there was a simpler story at work: a father trying to make his son feel better. These were two parents who wanted to believe their love could fill the gap between what they couldn't explain and the explanations they sought anyway. Love is not immune from the human hunger for narrative. It's a hunger I experience constantly myself. It's the hunger from which I make my living. For this family, that hunger had built an intricate and self-sustaining story, all of it anchored by the desire to care for a little boy in the dark.

Before I left, Andrea handed me a composition James had written in seventh grade called "Nightmares":

The burning torture of fire and smoke hit me every single night for five years... The nightmares were not dreams, but something that actually happened: the death of James M. Huston. His soul was brought back in the human form. He was brought back in my body and he chose to come back to Earth for a reason; to tell people that life is truly everlasting.

The specter of skepticism haunted this crescendo, and James was wise to it:

You can think I am a fool for knowing this, for believing these things. But when my parents wrote the book about me and my story, people who were deathly ill or had incurable diseases sent me e-mails that said, "Your story helped me and made me not afraid to die."

At the bottom of James's composition his teacher had written just one word, three times in red: *Wow. Wow. Wow.*

*   *   *

A few months after I returned from Louisiana, I got a letter from my aunt. She had just spent the afternoon with my grandfather, a former chemical engineer a few months shy of his hundredth birthday. They had been talking about the possibility of reincarnation. For my grandfather—the first in his family to go to college, and a deeply rational man his whole life—the question of what came next was no longer abstract. He and my aunt had eaten salmon and potatoes—solid foods, foods that reminded you that your body was still yours—while he sketched out his vision of living and dying: "We pick up a piece of consciousness when we are born, and when we die it goes back to where it came from."

That same week, a magazine fact-checker was filling my in-box with his skepticism every day. He informed me that more than one World War II aircraft carrier had a Walter and a Leon and a Billy on its crew, so the names were probably just coincidence, and that no Corsairs had ever flown from the *Natoma Bay*. Some part of me wanted to get into it, to tell him that maybe there never were Corsairs flying from the *Natoma*, but James Huston had been one of only twenty pilots flying Corsairs as part of an experimental team earlier in the war. "There's photographic evidence!" I wanted to shout, like a proper Bruce Leininger acolyte, but my defensiveness had never really been about the facts. It had always been about the vision.

The most compelling question for me had never been "Is reincarnation real?" It had always been "What vision of the self does reincarnation ask us to believe in?" I found something appealing about the vision of selfhood it suggested: porous and unoriginal. It was deeply related to what I loved about recovery—that it asked me to understand myself as interchangeable, to see my dilemmas as shared and my identity as something oddly and inescapably connected to distant strangers. Recovery was another story of reincarnation, after all: the sober self reborn from its drunken past. It was as if reincarnation made explicit the philosophical premise underneath recovery itself. If recovery said, "Your soul isn't this special thing," then reincarnation said, "Your soul isn't even yours." If recovery said, "You could have been this other person," then reincarnation said, "You actually *were* this other person."

And if reincarnation is a story some people find comforting, then it's also true that the soul is just a story, too: the notion of an essential, singular self in each of us. Reincarnation both buffers this belief and disrupts it: what we call our soul doesn't die, but perhaps it was never ours. Ultimately this is what appealed to me about the story of reincarnation, that it asked me to believe in a self without rigid boundaries—a self that had lived before and would do it again. In this way, it was a metaphor for what I was struggling to accept about living at all: that nothing we lived was unique, that we were always—in some sense—living again.

Reincarnation is an assertion of contingency: *I could have been anyone. Maybe I was a nurse or a hitman or a mean guy or a hero. Maybe I was a colonial explorer, a colonized subject, a queen or a sailor.* It's humble and it's the opposite of humility, the same way people can read my tattoo as empathy or arrogance: "Nothing human is alien to me." In all my wrestling with reincarnation, I'd been looking for a way to get humble in the face of consciousness, to be the teacher writing, "Wow. Wow. Wow," rather than giving a letter grade.

Reincarnation struck me as an articulation of faith in the self as something that could transform and stay continuous at once—in sobriety, in love, in the body of a stranger. This faith believes a thirteen-year-old boy in Queens might not be lost for good. This faith says, "Come back." Come back to Lafayette, to Virginia, to Myanmar. Come back with scars telling a story no one understands, to a lawn full of crumpled plastic reindeer or a house overlooking skeletal winter trees, to a jet mechanic throwing sticks for the dogs, a man who refuses to believe you were ever a lost boy in Long Island City. Come back to some suburb off the interstate, some condo, some row house. Come back remembering, so you can tell us where you've been. We want to know. We watch a little boy wear his cowboy boots to the pool. We watch a little man who can't get out. We watch the past fill the present like smoke: the memory of sisters and parachutes and flames. We say, *Wow*. We say it again. We stay humble. We can't know for sure until the body turns up in the river—and even then, it might not be the end. We walk toward the lights. We are safe, or else we aren't. We live, until we don't. We return, unless we can't.

Layover Story

This is the story of a layover. Who tells that story? I'm telling it to you now. One January evening, my flight got delayed out of Louisiana, where I'd been talking to people about their past lives, and I missed my connection in Houston. I had a night there. Trying to have a travel experience near the Houston airport is like trying to write a poem from the words on a yeast packet. Don't try to make it beautiful. Just let it rise. Let the freeways run like unspooled thread into the night. Blink against the neon signs of chain stores. Take shelter where you can.

I take shelter at the salmon-pink hotel where I am sent. On our shuttle from the airport, I hear the voice of a difficult woman coming from the front row. She can't believe the bus will run only hourly the next morning. She can't believe her dinner voucher is for so little money. She needs someone to take her bag into the lobby. She'll also need someone to fetch it tomorrow. Later, at the hotel restaurant, her voice is there again at the table behind me: She wants her bag placed where she can see it. She wants her water without ice. She doesn't want to be a pain but she really needs to know if the veggie wrap is absolutely 100 percent vegetarian. She wants to know about the other stranded people sitting around us, especially Martin the German, and the Penn State math major. The math major loves Pi Day. The woman with the voice wants to know if she bakes pie for Pi Day? No, she just eats pie for Pi Day. What kind of pie does she like? All kinds. What kind of math does she like? All kinds. Well, okay. She especially likes patterns and sequences. The woman with the voice wants to know how she feels about i to the i? The undergrad doesn't know about i to the i. "Oh, girlfriend," says the woman with the voice. "Go look up i to the i."

When she finally turns to me, the woman with the voice turns out to be a woman with curly black hair. She asks what I do for a living. She loves that I'm a writer. Turns out she's coming from a vacation in Cabo. Turns out she's on my flight back to Newark. She suggests we protest the hourly shuttles together. The 4:00 a.m. departure is too early for our flight, but the 5:00 a.m. is too late. We should campaign for a 4:40, or a 4:45. She is a difficult woman from New York trying to convince me that we should be difficult women from New York together. But I'm not a difficult woman from New York. I'm not any kind of person from New York. I just happen to live there. I just want to take the 4:00 a.m. shuttle and stop talking about it. It embarrasses me to be associated with her request, with her sense of entitlement, with these justifications—*I hurt more, I need more*—perhaps because I recognize myself in them.

It's only when the woman and I walk to the front desk to check on the shuttle that I notice how she walks. The woman with the voice is also a woman with a body. She's limping. Once I notice her limp, I feel guilty about leaving her to make the shuttle request alone—as if it would be an act of abandonment, in her hour of need, to refuse her my company. She tells the clerk she needs help with her bags, and in the morning she will need help again. She explains that she was in a wheelchair at the airport. I bet she has one of those nebulous pain conditions where the pain is always moving somewhere else. I bet she felt like a victim before she ever started hurting. I am actually thinking these things, and I am someone who has written indignantly about the world's tendency to minimize the pain of women in precisely these ways, for precisely these reasons.

We don't get our 4:40 shuttle. She's going to speak to a manager, she tells me. She'll call me when she gets this sorted out. She takes my number. We trade our names.

Back in my room, I google the name she's given me. It's fairly unusual and involves a body part. The first ten hits are all the same porn star; the next hit is an article about a stabbing spree in New York. A homeless man lunged at several strangers with a half scissors. The face of the woman with the voice is one of the five faces. I enlarge her on my screen. I try to remember her limp, which part of her was hurting.

When I see her in the morning, I won't tell her what I know. The etiquette of our era demands that we pretend we are still unknown to each other, though she will know I probably googled her, and I will know she probably googled me. But I find myself reframing everything I've seen her do—every complaint, every demand, every annoying attempt at small talk—as if a victim couldn't also be a solipsist. Now I want to read everything about her more generously, in order to compensate her for the indignity of becoming a character in my story, *the woman with the voice*, when she was already another kind of character, in another story entirely.

The next morning, I try to help the woman with the voice as best I can. I carry her bags through the Houston airport. I offer to stay with her while she waits for her wheelchair. I barely grimace when she speaks rudely to the airport staff. She's been *stabbed*. She asks me to preboard the plane with her and get her bag stowed above her seat. She asks if I'd help her get from Newark to the city, once we arrive—if I can get her through the airport train station in New Jersey, through New Jersey Transit, then through Penn Station itself, in New York—all those stairs and escalators and platforms and doorways and crowds and crowded baggage racks. I say *yes, yes, yes*. Yes to all of it! She has a story and now I'm part of it. I'm swollen with virtue. I'm so swollen with virtue I can hardly believe it when the man sitting next to me on the flight wants to have a conversation. Doesn't he understand? My virtue has already found its object; I have none left for small talk with strangers. The woman with the voice is sitting in the front of the plane, probably making someone wish they were sitting in the back.

The man next to me starts talking about driving his sister out to Texas, where she was moving for work. She's a traveling nurse and they drove through an ice storm in Atlanta and I really couldn't care less. This guy is just a kid, complaining about the Houston airport not having enough vending machines. I feel like his mother, as if I should offer him a snack. On the tiny monitors above us a nature documentary plays: a baby bison is getting cornered by a pack of wolves. What will happen next? Only one thing, we all know. Back home in Brooklyn, no one is waiting for me. I'm newly single and not-so-newly thirty and leaving lots of crumbs between my couch cushions from dinners made of crackers that don't seem like the dinners of an adult.

Now this guy is talking about his tour in Iraq. He says he got used to desert skies. *Oh.* His life is a little different than I'd thought. I don't know how to ask him about the war. But I ask him anyway. I ask him about the guys he was there with—that seems safe, possible. He shakes his head: the best crew of guys ever. "Now here I am," he says, nudging his duffel bag. "Flying home with an army bag full of hermit-crab shells." I ask how many are in there. Maybe fifty, he says. He has a daughter and she has four pet hermit crabs. I ask if they have names. "They've got so many names I can't keep track," he says. "Their names are always changing." Right now there is one named Clippers and the others are Peaches. All three of them? Yep. Just Peaches and Peaches and Peaches. He says they need a bottomless buffet of shells. They keep getting bigger, so they keep needing new ones.

So the shells in his bag aren't hermit-crab shells because they were made *by* hermit crabs, but because hermit crabs might someday use them? Yes, he says. That is correct.

Perhaps there is profundity in this. We claim something not by making it, but by making it useful. What we squat inside can begin to constitute us. And now he's saying something else, something about the new aquarium he's building for Clippers and the Peaches. He's using old shower doors from his construction company. He has over twenty large sheets of glass, he says, and more than fifty smaller ones. And I'm trying to run the meaning-making logic over this one too: *we have the big and the small; we have more than we can use.* But it doesn't yield; Houston all over again. And how big will his crab aquarium be, anyway? An entire city block? This guy can't decide whether to be interesting or not—like someone who is mostly late but every once in a while, unaccountably, on time. Why would I possibly believe he owed me interest, anyway? Other lives are shells I want to scavenge only when the mood strikes right, only when the shells are good enough.

For now, I want to know what these crabs eat. He says they'll eat pellets, but they prefer fresh fruit. What kind of fruit? Pineapples, he says. They love pineapples. He explains they have a lot of preferences. For example, they need salt water *and* fresh water.

What about when they live in the ocean? I ask. How do they get fresh water then?

He doesn't know. He says, "That's what I'm still trying to figure out."

This man punctures me. I felt like his mother until he said he was a father. I think of all the fear he's known—the guilt, and loss, and boredom—and how I don't know any of it. His endlessness is something I receive in finite anecdotes: big desert skies, a little girl poking crabs. Sometimes I feel I owe a stranger nothing, and then I feel I owe him everything; because he fought and I didn't, because I dismissed him or misunderstood him, because I forgot, for a moment, that his life—like everyone else's—holds more than I could ever possibly see.

It makes me think of that David Foster Wallace commencement speech, "This Is Water," the one that everyone finds inspiring except the people who think it's unbearably trite and find it pathetic that everyone else is so inspired by it. I'm so inspired by it. Wallace talks about the tedium of standing at a supermarket checkout counter, irritated by the other people in line, "how stupid and cow-like and dead-eyed and non-human they seem." But, he says, you can choose to see them differently. You can regard the woman who just yelled at her kid and admit that for all you know she might have just stayed up three nights straight with a husband dying of bone cancer. Maybe she just helped your spouse get through some tangle at the DMV. Maybe the annoying woman on the bus just got stabbed by a deranged stranger on her morning jog. If you learn to pay attention, he says, "it will actually be within your power to experience a crowded, hot, slow, consumer-hell type situation as not only meaningful, but sacred, on fire with the same force that lit the stars."

*   *   *

he Newark airport train station in the middle of a blizzard does not feel on fire with the same force that lit the stars. I am helping the woman with the voice and the injured body get onto a train headed into the city. We get hot chocolate at the tiny station café, and wait on the outdoor platform, in the Jersey cold, while the snow comes down. I'm tired of benevolence, ready for my own apartment. She tells me it was stupid, how she got hurt. It was her own fault.

I'm a little bit confused. Is this a confession of privilege guilt? Guilt at her complicity in the systems that oppressed the homeless man who stabbed her? Is she going to tell me that he had a story too? Because he did: untreated mental illness, a life spent moving from shelter to shelter. He got sentenced to more than twenty years in prison, where most likely his mental illness remains untreated still. One of his victims was a toddler. This is the kind of story with an easy victim and an easy villain; except maybe it's not so easy—maybe we are all the villains, maybe that's what the woman with the voice is trying to tell me. She is also telling me she is tired of standing, though I cannot make her a chair.

Anyway, she says, she was dancing down in Cabo, and her knee started hurting, but she kept dancing anyway. It was "Mamma Mia." How could she not keep dancing? That's how she hurt herself. She looks at me and I nod. How indeed.

But inside I'm feeling robbed, like something has been stolen from me: the story in which I carried the bags of a woman still recovering from a stabbing attack. Now I'm in a story about a woman who danced too hard on the Mexican Riviera. It's a story about putting bags in overhead compartments and waiting in the bitter Jersey cold, about getting to the ugliest train station in the world and weaving through its maze of underground tunnels with three suitcases to emerge into the grim bustle of a purgatory between Midtown and Koreatown.

In a way I can't explain, I've started to feel attached to this woman, weirdly protective. It's like we've been on some kind of odyssey together, and it has less to do with the night in Houston or the blizzard in Jersey and more to do with all her shapeshifting in my internal narrative. First she was a tyrant, then a saint, and finally just a tourist, dancing.

We part ways by the cabstand. The woman with the voice thanks me for my kindness. She'll take a taxi home. I'll take the subway to my empty apartment, where I'll read another article about the stabbing, full of eyewitness quotes. In another photograph of the woman with the voice, she's being carried by a police officer. She has one hand wrapped around his neck, the other hand pressed against her own throat. I will never hear what her voice sounded like when she was crying out, in broad daylight, for help; when she was just a difficult New York woman asking her city to save her.

This is how we light the stars, again and again: by showing up with our ordinary, difficult bodies, when other ordinary, difficult bodies might need us. Which is the point—the again-and-again of it. You never get to live the wisdom just once, rise to the occasion of otherness just once. You have to keep living this willingness to look at other lives with grace, even when your own feels like shit, and you would do anything to crawl inside a different one; when you would claw one Peaches out of the way, and then another, and then a third, just for a shot at some shell of respite. A 3:30 a.m. wake-up call in Houston isn't the respite shell. New Jersey public transit the day after a New Jersey Super Bowl isn't the respite shell. The blizzard is no respite shell for anyone; it makes the hurt knee throb harder.

Does graciousness mean you want to help—or that you don't, and do it anyway? The definition of grace is that it's not deserved. It does not require a good night's sleep to give it, or a flawless record to receive it. It demands no particular backstory.

You thought the story kept changing, but the most important part never did. She was always just a woman in pain, sitting right in front of you. Sometimes it hurts just to stand. Sometimes a person needs help because she needs it, not because her story is compelling or noble or strange enough to earn it, and sometimes you just do what you can. It doesn't make you any better, or any worse. It doesn't change you at all, except for the split second when you imagine that day when you will be the one who has to ask.

Sim Life

G idge Uriza lives in an elegant wooden house overlooking a glittering creek, its lush banks lined with weeping willows. Nearby meadows twinkle with fireflies. Gidge keeps buying new swimming pools because she keeps falling in love with different ones. The current specimen is a teal lozenge with a waterfall cascading from its archway of stones. Gidge spends her days lounging in a swimsuit on her poolside patio, or else tucked under a lacy comforter, wearing nothing but a bra and bathrobe, with a chocolate-glazed doughnut perched on the pile of books beside her. "Good morning girls," she writes on her blog one day. "I'm slow moving, trying to get out of bed this morning, but when I'm surrounded by my pretty pink bed it's difficult to get out and away like I should."

In another life, the one most people would call "real," Gidge Uriza is Bridgette McNeal, an Atlanta mother who works eight-hour days at a call center and is raising a fourteen-year-old son, a seven-year-old daughter, and severely autistic twins who are thirteen. Her days are full of the daily demands of raising children with special needs: giving her twins baths after they have soiled themselves (they still wear diapers, and most likely always will), baking applesauce bread with one to calm him down after a tantrum, asking the other to stop playing the *Barney* theme song slowed down until it sounds, as she puts it, "like some demonic dirge." One day, she takes all four kids to a nature center for an idyllic afternoon that gets interrupted by the reality of changing an adolescent's diaper in a musty bathroom.

But each morning, before all that—before getting the kids ready for school and putting in eight hours at the call center, before getting dinner on the table or keeping peace during the meal, before giving baths and collapsing into bed—Bridgette spends an hour and a half on the online platform Second Life, where she lives in a sleek paradise of her own devising. *Good morning girls. I'm slow moving, trying to get out of bed this morning.* She wakes up at half past five in the morning to inhabit a life in which she has the luxury of never getting out of bed at all.

What is Second Life? The short answer is that it's a virtual world that launched in 2003 and was hailed by many as the future of the internet. The longer answer is that it's a controversial landscape—possibly revolutionary, possibly moot—full of goth cities and preciously tattered beach shanties, vampire castles and tropical islands and rain-forest temples and dinosaur stomping grounds, disco-ball-glittering nightclubs and trippy giant chess games. In honor of Second Life's tenth birthday, in 2013, Linden Lab, the company that created it, released an infographic charting its progress: 36 million accounts had been created, and their users had spent 217,266 cumulative years online, inhabiting an ever-expanding territory that comprised almost seven hundred square miles composed of land units called "sims." People often call Second Life a game, but two years after its launch, Linden Lab circulated a memo to employees insisting that no one refer to it as that. It was a *platform*. This was meant to suggest something more holistic, immersive, and encompassing.

Second Life has no specific goals. Its vast landscape consists entirely of user-generated content, which means that everything you see has been built by someone else—an avatar controlled by a live human user. These avatars build and buy homes, form friendships, hook up, get married, and make money. They celebrate their "rez days," the online equivalent of a birthday: the anniversary of the day they joined. At church, they cannot take physical communion—the corporeality of that ritual is impossible—but they can bring the stories of their faith to life. At their cathedral on Epiphany Island, the Anglicans of Second Life summon rolling thunder on Good Friday, or the sudden illumination of sunrise at the moment in the Easter service when the pastor pronounces, "He is risen." As one Second Life handbook puts it: "From your point of view, SL works as if you were a god."

In truth, in the years since its zenith in the mid-2000s, Second Life has become something more like a magnet for mockery. When I told friends that I was working on a story about it, their faces almost always followed the same trajectory of reactions: a blank expression, a brief flash of recognition, then a mildly bemused look. *Is that still around?* Second Life is no longer the thing you joke about; it's the thing you haven't bothered to joke about for years.

Many observers expected monthly-user numbers to keep rising after they hit one million in 2007, but instead they peaked there—and have, in the years since, stalled at about eight hundred thousand. And an estimated 20 to 30 percent are first-time users who never return. Just a few years after declaring Second Life the future of the internet, the tech world moved on. As a 2011 piece in *Slate* proclaimed: "Looking back, the future didn't last long."

But if Second Life promised a future in which people would spend hours each day inhabiting their online identity, haven't we found ourselves inside it? Only it's come to pass on Facebook, Twitter, and Instagram instead. As I learned more about Second Life and spent more time exploring it, it started to seem less like an obsolete relic and more like a distorted mirror reflecting the world many of us actually live in. Perhaps Second Life inspires an urge to ridicule not because it's unrecognizable, but because it takes a recognizable impulse and carries it past the bounds of comfort, into a kind of uncanny valley: the promise of not just an online voice but an online body; not just checking Twitter on your phone, but forgetting to eat because you're dancing at an online club; not just a curated version of your real life, but a separate existence entirely. It crystallizes the simultaneous siren call and shame of wanting a different life.

I n Hinduism, the concept of an avatar refers to the incarnation of a deity on earth. In Second Life, it's your body: an ongoing act of self-expression. From 2004 to 2007, an anthropologist named Tom Boellstorff inhabited Second Life as an embedded ethnographer, naming his avatar Tom Bukowski and building himself a home and office called Ethnographia. His immersive approach was anchored by the premise that the world of Second Life is just as "real" as any other, and that he was justified in studying Second Life "on its own terms" rather than feeling obligated to understand people's virtual identities primarily in terms of their offline lives. His book *Coming of Age in Second Life,* titled in homage to Margaret Mead's classic about adolescent girls in Samoa, documents the texture of the platform's digital culture. He finds that making "small talk about lag [streaming delays in SL] is like talking about the weather in RL," and interviews an avatar named Wendy, whose creator always makes her go to sleep before she logs out. "So the actual world is Wendy's dream, until she wakes up again in Second Life?" Boellstorff recalls asking her, and then: "I could have sworn a smile passed across Wendy's face as she said, 'Yup. Indeed.'"

One woman described her avatar to Boellstorff as a truer manifestation of her interior self. "If I take a zipper and pull her out of me, that's who I am," she told him. Female avatars tend to be thin and impossibly busty; male avatars are young and muscular; almost all avatars are vaguely cartoonish in their beauty. These avatars communicate through chat windows, or by using voice technology to actually speak. They move by walking, flying, teleporting, and clicking on "poseballs," floating orbs that animate avatars into various actions: dancing, karate, pretty much every sexual act you can imagine. Not surprisingly, many users come to Second Life for the possibilities of digital sex—sex without corporeal bodies, without real names, without the constraints of gravity, often with elaborate textual commentary.

The local currency in Second Life is the Linden Dollar, and recent exchange rates put the Linden at just less than half a cent. In the decade following its launch, Second Life users spent $3.2 billion of real money on in-world transactions. The first Second Life millionaire, a digital-real-estate tycoon who goes by Anshe Chung, graced the cover of *Businessweek* in 2006, and by 2007 the GDP of Second Life was larger than that of several small countries. In its vast digital Marketplace, you can still buy a wedding gown for 4,000 Lindens (just over $16) or a ruby-colored corset with fur wings for just under 350 Lindens (about $1.50). You can even buy an altered body: different skin, different hair, a pair of horns, genitalia of all shapes and sizes. A private island currently costs almost 150,000 Lindens (the price is fixed at $600), while the Millennium II Super Yacht costs 20,000 Lindens (just over $80) and comes with more than three hundred animations attached to its beds and trio of hot tubs, designed to allow avatars to enact a variety of bespoke sexual fantasies.

Second Life started to plateau just as Facebook started to explode. The rise of Facebook wasn't the problem of a competing brand so much as the problem of a competing model. It seemed that people wanted a curated version of real life more than they wanted another life entirely.

They wanted to become the sum of their most flattering profile pictures more than they wanted to become a wholly separate avatar. But maybe Facebook and Second Life aren't so different in their appeal. Both find traction in the allure of inhabiting a selective self, whether built from the materials of lived experience—camping-trip photos and witty observations about brunch—or from the impossibilities that lived experience precludes: an ideal body, an ideal romance, an ideal home.

Bridgette McNeal, the Atlanta mother of four, has been on Second Life for just over a decade. She named her avatar Gidge after what the bullies called her in high school. Though Bridgette is middle-aged, her avatar is a lithe twentysomething whom she describes as "perfect me—if I'd never eaten sugar or had children." During her early days on Second Life, Bridgette's husband created an avatar as well, and the two of them would go on Second Life dates together, a blond Amazon and a squat silver robot, while sitting together at their laptops in their study at home. It was often the only way they *could* go on dates, because their kids' special needs made finding babysitters difficult. When we spoke, Bridgette described her Second Life home as a refuge that grants permission. "When I step into that space, I'm afforded the luxury of being selfish," she said, invoking Virginia Woolf: "It's like a room of my own." Her virtual home is full of objects she could never keep in her real home because her kids might break or eat them—jewelry on dishes, knickknacks on tables, makeup on the counter.

In addition to the blog that documents her digital existence, with its marble pools and frilly, spearmint-green bikinis, Bridgette keeps a blog devoted to her daily "RL" existence as a parent. It's honest and hilarious and full of heartbreaking candor. Recounting the afternoon spent with her kids at the nature center, she describes looking at a bald eagle: "Some asshole shot this bald eagle with an arrow. He lost most of one wing because of it and can't fly. He's kept safe here at this retreat we visited a few days ago. Sometimes I think the husband and I feel a little bit like him. Trapped. Nothing really wrong, we've got food and shelter and what we need. But we are trapped for the rest of our lives by autism. We'll never be free."

When I asked Bridgette about the allure of Second Life, she said it can be easy to succumb to the temptation to pour yourself into its world when you should be tending to offline life. I asked whether she had ever slipped close to that, and she said she'd certainly felt the pull at times. "You're thin and beautiful. No one's asking you to change a diaper," she told me. "But you can burn out on that. You don't want to leave, but you don't want to do it anymore, either."

S econd Life was invented by a man named Philip Rosedale, the son of a U.S. Navy carrier pilot and an English teacher. As a boy, he was driven by an outsized sense of ambition. He can remember standing near the woodpile in his family's backyard and thinking, "Why am I here, and how am I different from everybody else?" As a teenager in the mid-'80s, he used an early-model PC to zoom in on a graphic representation of a Mandelbrot set, an infinitely recursive fractal image that kept getting more and more detailed as he got closer and closer. At a certain point, he realized he was looking at a graphic larger than the Earth. "We could walk along the surface our whole lives and never even begin to see everything," he explained to me. That's when he realized that "the coolest thing you could do with a computer would be to build a world."

Just as Rosedale was beginning to envision Second Life, in 1999, he attended Burning Man—the festival of performance art, sculptural installations, and hallucinogenic hedonism that happens every summer in the middle of the Nevada desert. While he was there, he told me, something "inexplicable" happened to his personality. "You feel like you're high, without any drugs or anything. You just feel connected to people in a way that you don't normally." He went to a rave in an

Airstream trailer, watched trapeze artists swing across the desert, and lay in a hookah lounge piled with hundreds of Persian rugs. Burning Man didn't give Rosedale the idea for Second Life—he'd been imagining a digital world for years—but it helped him understand the energy he wanted to summon there: a place where people could make the world whatever they wanted it to be.

This was the dream, but it was a hard sell to early investors. Linden Lab was proposing a world built by amateurs and sustained by a different kind of revenue model—based not on paid subscriptions, but on commerce generated in-world. One of Second Life's designers recalled investors' skepticism: "Creativity was supposed to be a dark art that only Spielberg and Lucas could do." As part of selling Second Life as a world rather than a game, Linden Lab hired a writer to work as an "embedded journalist." This was Wagner James Au, who documented the digital careers of some of Second Life's most important early builders: an avatar named Spider Mandala (who was managing a Midwestern gas station offline) and another named Catherine Omega, who was a "punky brunette...with a utility belt" in Second Life, but offline was squatting in a condemned apartment in Vancouver. The building had no running water and was populated mainly by addicts, but Omega used a soup can to catch a wireless signal from nearby office buildings so she could run Second Life on her laptop.

Rosedale told me about the thrill of those early days, when Second Life's potential felt unbridled. No one else was doing what he and his team were doing. "We used to say that our only competition was real life." He said there was a period in 2007 when more than five hundred articles a day were written about their work. Rosedale himself loved to explore Second Life as an avatar named Philip Linden. "I was like a god," he told me. He envisioned a future in which his grandchildren would see the real world as a kind of "museum or theater," while most work and relationships happened in virtual realms like

Second Life. "In some sense," he told Au in 2007, "I think we will see the entire physical world as being kind of left behind."

Alice Krueger first started noticing the symptoms of her illness when she was twenty years old. During fieldwork for a college biology class, crouching down to watch bugs eating leaves, she felt overwhelmed by heat. One day while she was standing in the grocery store, it suddenly felt as if her entire left leg had disappeared—not just gone numb, but disappeared. Whenever she went to a doctor, she was told it was all in her head. "And it *was* all in my head," she told me, forty-seven years later. "But in a different way than how they meant."

Alice was finally diagnosed with multiple sclerosis at the age of fifty. By then she could barely walk. Her neighborhood association in Colorado prohibited her from building a ramp at the front of her house, so it was difficult for her to go anywhere. Her three children were eleven, thirteen, and fifteen. She didn't get to see her younger son's high-school graduation, or his college campus. She started suffering intense pain in her lower back and eventually had to have surgery to repair spinal vertebrae that had fused together, then ended up getting multidrug-resistant staph from her time in the hospital. Her pain persisted, and she was diagnosed with a misalignment caused by the surgery itself, during which she had been suspended "like a rotisserie chicken" above the operating table. At the age of fifty-seven, Alice found herself housebound and unemployed, often in excruciating pain, cared for largely by her daughter. "I was looking at my four walls," she told me, "and wondering if there could be more."

That's when she found Second Life. She created an avatar named Gentle Heron, and loved seeking out waterslides, excited by the sheer thrill of doing what her body could not. As she kept exploring, she started inviting people she'd met online in disability chat rooms to join her. But that also meant she felt responsible for their experiences, and eventually she founded a "cross-disability virtual community" in Second Life, now known as Virtual Ability, a group that occupies an archipelago of virtual islands and welcomes people with a wide range of disabilities—everything from Down syndrome to PTSD to manic depression. What unites its members, Alice told me, is their sense of not being fully included in the world.

While she was starting Virtual Ability, Alice also embarked on a real-life move: to the Great Smoky Mountains in Tennessee from Colorado, where she'd outlived her long-term disability benefits. ("I didn't know you could do that," I told her, and she replied, "Neither did I!") When I asked her whether she felt like a different version of herself in Second Life, she rejected the proposition strenuously. Alice doesn't particularly like the terms *real* and *virtual*. To her they imply a hierarchical distinction, suggesting that one part of her life is more "real" than the other, when her sense of self feels fully expressed in both. She doesn't want Second Life misunderstood as a trivial diversion. After our first conversation, she sent me fifteen peer-reviewed scientific articles about digital avatars and embodiment.

Alice told me about a man with Down syndrome who has become an important member of the Virtual Ability community. In real life his disability is omnipresent, but on Second Life people can talk to him without even realizing he has it. In the offline world, he lives with his parents—who were surprised to see he was capable of controlling his own avatar. After they eat dinner each night, as his parents wash the dishes, he sits expectantly by the computer, waiting to return to Second Life, where he rents a duplex on an island called Cape Heron. He has turned the entire upper level into a massive aquarium, so he can walk among the fish, and the lower level into a garden, where he keeps a pet reindeer and feeds it Cheerios. Alice says he doesn't draw a firm boundary between Second Life and "reality," and others in the community have been inspired by his approach, citing him when they talk about collapsing the border in their own minds.

When I first began working on this essay, I imagined myself falling under the spell of Second Life: a wide-eyed observer seduced by the culture she had been dispatched to analyze. But being "in-world" made me queasy from the start. I had pictured myself defending Second Life against the ways it had been dismissed as little more than a consolation prize designed for people for whom "first life" hasn't quite delivered. Instead I found myself writing, *Second Life makes me want to take a shower.*

My respect deepened intellectually by the day. I talked with a legally blind woman whose avatar had a rooftop balcony from which she could see the view (thanks to screen magnification) more clearly than she could see the world beyond her computer. I heard about a veteran with PTSD who gave biweekly Italian cooking classes in an open-air gazebo. I visited an online version of Yosemite created by a woman who had joined Second Life in the wake of several severe depressive episodes and hospitalizations. She used an avatar named Jadyn Firehawk and spent up to twelve hours a day on Second Life, devoted mostly to refining her curated digital wonderland—full of waterfalls, sequoias, and horses named after important people in John Muir's life—grateful that Second Life didn't ask her to inhabit an identity entirely contoured by her illness, unlike internet chat rooms focused on bipolar disorder that were all about being sick. "I live a well-rounded life on SL," she told me. "It feeds all my other selves."

But despite my growing appreciation, a certain visceral distaste for Second Life endured—for the emptiness of its graphics, its nightclubs and mansions and pools and castles, their refusal of all the grit and imperfection that make the world feel like the world. Whenever I tried to describe Second Life, I found it nearly impossible—or at least impossible to make it interesting—because description finds its traction in flaws and fissures. Exploring the world of Second Life was more like moving through postcards. It was a world of visual clichés. Nothing was ragged or broken or dilapidated—or if it was dilapidated, it was because that particular aesthetic had been carefully cultivated.

Of course, my aversion to Second Life—as well as my embrace of blemishes and shortcomings in the physical world—testified to my own good fortune as much as anything. When I moved through the real world, I was buffered by my (relative) youth, my (relative) health, and my (relative) freedom. Who was I to begrudge those who had found in the reaches of Second Life what they couldn't find offline?

One day when Alice and I met up as avatars in-world, she took me to a beach on one of the Virtual Ability islands and invited me to practice tai chi. All I needed to do was click on one of the poseballs levitating in the middle of a grassy circle, and it would automatically animate my avatar. But I did not feel that I was doing tai chi. I felt that I was sitting at my laptop, watching my two-dimensional avatar do tai chi.

I thought of Gidge in Atlanta, waking up early to sit beside a virtual pool. She doesn't get to smell the chlorine or the sunscreen, to feel the sun melt across her back or char her skin to peeling crisps. Yet Gidge must get something powerful from sitting beside a virtual pool—pleasure that dwells not in the physical experience itself but in its anticipation, its documentation, and its recollection. Whatever categories of "real" and "unreal" you want to map onto online and offline worlds, the pleasure she finds in going to Second Life is indisputably actual. Otherwise she wouldn't wake up at half past five in the morning to do it.

From the beginning, I was terrible at navigating Second Life. "Body part failed to download," my interface kept saying. Second

Life was supposed to give you the opportunity to perfect your body, but I couldn't even summon a complete one. For my avatar, I'd chosen a punk-looking woman with cutoff shorts, a partially shaved head, and a ferret on her shoulder.

On my first day in-world, I wandered around Orientation Island like a drunk person trying to find a bathroom. The island was full of marble columns and trim greenery, with a faint soundtrack of gurgling water, but it looked less like a Delphic temple and more like a corporate retreat center inspired by a Delphic temple. The graphics seemed incomplete and uncompelling, the motion full of glitches and lags. I tried to talk to someone named Del Agnos but got no response. I felt surprisingly ashamed by his rebuttal, transported back to the paralyzing shyness of my junior-high-school days.

On that first day in-world, I teleported to a deserted island where there was supposed to be an abandoned mansion and a secret entrance to a "bizarre circus in the sky," but all I found was a busted lifeguard station perched on stilts in the sea, where I was (once again!) ignored by a man who looked like a taciturn cross between a WWF wrestler and a Victorian butler, with a silver-studded dog collar around his neck. I ended up falling off a wooden ledge and bobbing in the gray rain-pocked waves, under a permanently programmed thunderstorm. This wasn't exactly the frustration of lived experience, in all the richness of its thwarted expectations, but something else: the imperfect summoning of its reductive simulation. It was like a stage set with the rickety scaffolding of its facade exposed.

Each time I signed off Second Life, I found myself weirdly eager to plunge back into the obligations of my ordinary life. Pick up my stepdaughter from drama class? Check! Reply to my department chair about hiring a replacement for the faculty member taking an unexpected leave? I was on it! These obligations felt real in a way that Second Life did not, and they allowed me to inhabit a particular version of myself as someone capable and necessary. It felt like returning to the air after struggling to find my breath underwater. I came up gasping, desperate, ready for entanglement and contact: *Yes! This is the real world! In all its vexed logistical glory!*

At my first Second Life concert, I arrived excited for actual music in a virtual world. Many SL concerts are genuinely "live" insofar as they involve real musicians playing real music on instruments or singing into microphones hooked up to their computers. But I was trying to do too many things at once that afternoon: reply to sixteen dangling work emails, unload the dishwasher, reload the dishwasher, make my step-daughter a peanut-butter-and-jelly sandwich before her final rehearsal for a production of *Peter Pan*. The concert was taking place on a dock overlooking an expansive bay of sparkling blue water. With my jam-sticky fingers, I clicked on a dance poseball and started a conga line—except no one joined my conga line; it just got me stuck between a potted plant and the stage, trying to conga and going nowhere. My embarrassment, more than any sense of having fun, was what made me feel implicated and engaged. In wondering what other people thought of me, I felt acutely aware—at last—of sharing a world with them.

When I interviewed Philip Rosedale, he readily admitted that Second Life has always presented intrinsic difficulties to users—that it is hard for people to get comfortable moving, communicating, and building; that there is an "irreducible level of difficulty associated with mouse and keyboard" that his team "could never make easier." Peter Gray, Linden Lab's director of global communications, told me about what he called the "white-space problem"—having so much freedom that you can't be entirely sure what you want to do—and admitted that entering Second Life can be like "getting dropped off in the middle of a foreign country."

When I spoke with long-term users, however, the stubborn in-accessibility of Second Life seemed to have become a crucial part of their assimilation narratives. They looked back on their early embarrassment with nostalgia. Gidge told me about the time someone convinced her that she needed to buy a vagina, and she'd ended up wearing it on the outside of her pants. (She called this a classic #SecondLifeProblem.) A Swedish musician named Malin Östh—one of the performers at the concert where I'd started my abortive conga line—told me about attending *her* first Second Life concert, and her story wasn't so different from mine. When she'd tried to get to the front of the crowd, she'd ended up accidentally flying onto the stage. Beforehand, she'd been sure the whole event would seem fake, but she was surprised by how mortified she felt, and this made her realize that she actually felt like she was among other people. I knew what she meant. If it feels like you are back in junior high school, then at least it feels like you are somewhere.

One woman put it like this: "Second Life doesn't open itself up to you. It doesn't hand you everything on a silver platter and tell you where to go next. It presents you with a world, and it leaves you to your own devices, tutorial be damned." But once you've figured it out, you can buy a thousand silver platters if you want to—or design the yacht of your dreams, or build a virtual Yosemite. Rosedale believed that if a user could survive that initial purgatory, her bond with the world of Second Life would be sealed for good. "If they stay more than four hours," he told me, "they stay forever."

Neal Stephenson's 1992 cyberpunk novel, *Snow Crash*, with its virtual "Metaverse," is often cited as Second Life's primary literary ancestor. But Rosedale assured me that by the time he read the novel he'd already been imagining Second Life for years. ("Just ask my wife.") The hero of *Snow Crash*, aptly named Hiro Protagonist, lives with his roommate in a storage locker, but in the Metaverse he is a sword-fighting prince and a legendary hacker. No surprise he spends so much time there: "It beats the shit out of the U-Stor-It."

In one study of reported life satisfaction among Second Life users, researchers concluded that because users reported such a large gap in satisfaction between their virtual lives and their real ones, it made sense that "some people may be strongly motivated to take refuge in digital life rather than try to change their real life." But if you inhabit a happier Second Life, does that make it harder to find satisfaction offline—if that actual life is constantly competing with a realm in which all fantasies are possible?

Hiro's double life in *Snow Crash* gets at some of the core fantasies of Second Life: that it could invert all the metrics of real-world success, or render them obsolete; that it could create a radically democratic space because no one has any idea of anyone else's position in the real world. Many residents of Second Life understand it as a utopia connecting people from all over the world—across income levels, across disparate vocations and geographies and disabilities—a place where the ill can live in healthy bodies and the immobilized can move freely. Seraphina Brennan, a transgender woman who grew up in a small coal-mining community in Pennsylvania and could not afford to begin medically transitioning until her mid-twenties, told me that Second Life had given her "the opportunity to appear as I truly felt inside," because it was the first place where she could inhabit a female body.

In his book *The Making of Second Life,* Wagner James Au tells the story of an avatar named Bel Muse, a classic "California blonde" who is played by an African American woman. She led an early team of build-ers working on Nexus Prime, one of the first Second Life cities, and told Au that it was the first time she hadn't encountered the prejudices she was accustomed to. In the offline world, she said, "I have to make a good impression right away—I have to come off nice and articulate, right away. In Second Life, I didn't have to. Because for once, I can pass." But this anecdote—the fact that Bel Muse found respect more readily when she passed as white in Second Life—confirms the persistence of racism more than it suggests the possibility of any liberation from it. Although many users see Second Life as offering an equal playing field, free from the strictures of class and race, its preponderance of slender white bodies, most of them outfitted with the props of the leisure class, simply reinscribes the same skewed ideals that sustain the unequal playing field in the first place.

Sara Skinner, an African American woman who has always given her avatars complexions similar to her own, told me the story of trying to build a digital black-history museum in a seaside town called Bay City. Another avatar (playing a cop) immediately built walls and eventually, ironically, a courthouse that blocked her museum from view. The cop avatar claims it was a misunderstanding, but so much racism refuses to confess itself as such—and it's certainly no misunderstanding when white men on Second Life tell Sara that she looks like a primate after she rejects their advances; when someone calls her "tampon nose" because of her wide nostrils; or when someone else tells her that her experience with bias is invalid because she is a "mixed breed." She plans to rebuild her museum somewhere else.

Au told me that though he was initially deeply excited by the premise of Second Life, particularly the possibilities of its user-generated content, he ended up disappointed by the fact that most people turned out to be primarily interested in clubbing like twentysomethings with infinite money. Rosedale told me he thought the landscape of Second Life would be hyper-fantastic, artistic, and insane—full of spaceships and bizarre topographies, Burning Man on virtual steroids—but what emerged looked more like Malibu. People were building mansions and Ferraris. "We first build what we most covet," he told me, and cited an early study by Linden Lab that found the vast majority of Second Life users lived in rural rather than urban areas. They came to Second

Life for what their physical lives lacked: the concentration, density, and connective potential of urban spaces—the sense of things *happening* all around them, and the possibility of being part of that happening.

S wedish entrepreneur Jonas Tancred joined Second Life in 2007, after his corporate headhunting company folded during the recession. Jonas was graying and middle-aged, a bit paunchy, but his avatar, Bara Jonson, was young and muscled, with spiky hair and a soulful vibe. What Jonas found most compelling about Second Life was not that it let him role-play a more attractive alter ego; it was that Second Life gave him the chance to play music, a lifelong dream he'd never followed. (He would eventually pair up with Malin Östh to form the duo Bara Jonson and Free.) Offline, Jonas might stand in front of a kitchen table covered with a checkered oilcloth, playing an acoustic guitar connected to his computer. But in Second Life, Bara would be rocking out in front of a crowd of supermodels and Mohawked bikers.

Before a performance one night, a woman showed up early and asked him, "Are you any good?" He said, "Yes, of course," and played one of his best gigs yet, just to back it up. This woman was Nickel Borrelly; she would become his (Second Life) wife and eventually, a couple of years later, the mother of his (real-life) child.

Offline, Nickel was a younger woman named Susie who lived in Missouri. After a surreal courtship full of hot-air-balloon rides, romantic moonlit dances, and tandem biking on the Great Wall of China, the pair had a Second Life wedding on Twin Hearts Island—at "12 p.m. SLT," the electronic invitations said, which meant noon Standard Linden Time. During their vows, Bara called it the most important day of his life. He did not specify which life he meant, or if the truth of his statement reached across both of them.

After he and Nickel got married, Bara's Second Life musical career started to take off. Eventually he was offered the chance to come to New York to make a record, one of the first times a Second Life musician had secured a real-life record deal. It was on that trip that Jonas finally met Susie offline. When their relationship was featured in a documentary a few years later, she described her first impression: "Man, he looks kinda old." But she said that getting to know him in person felt like "falling in love twice."

Susie and Jonas's son, Arvid, was born in 2009. By then Jonas was back in Sweden because his visa had run out. While Susie was in the delivery room, he was in his club on Second Life—at first waiting for news, and then smoking a virtual cigar. For Susie, the hardest part was the day after Arvid's birth, when the hospital was full of other fathers visiting their babies. What could Susie and Jonas do? Bring their avatars together to cook a virtual breakfast in a romantic enclave by the sea, holding steaming mugs of coffee they couldn't drink, looking at actual videos of their actual baby on a virtual television, while they reclined on a virtual couch.

Susie and Jonas are no longer romantically involved, but Jonas is still part of Arvid's life. He Skypes with them frequently and visits the States as often as he can. Jonas believes that part of the reason he and Susie have been able to maintain a strong parenting relationship in the aftermath of their separation is that they got to know each other so well online before they met. In this framing, Second Life wasn't an illusion but a conduit that allowed them to understand each other better than a real-life courtship would have. Jonas describes Second Life as a rarefied version of reality, rather than a shallow substitute for it. As a musician, he feels that Second Life hasn't changed his music but "amplified" it, enabling a more direct connection with his audience, and he loves the way fans can type their own lyrics to his songs. He remembers everyone "singing along" to a cover he performed of "Mmm Mmm Mmm Mmm" by the Crash Test Dummies, when so many people typed the lyrics that their *Mmm*s eventually filled his entire screen. For Jonas, the reality and beauty of his creations—the songs, the baby—have transcended and overpowered the vestiges of their virtual construction.

O f the more than thirty-six million Second Life accounts that had been created by 2013, only an estimated six hundred thousand people still regularly use the platform. (Approximately two hundred thousand more people try out the platform each month but don't come back.) That's a lot of users who turned away. What happened? Au sees the simultaneous rise of Facebook and the plateau in Second Life users as proof that Linden Lab misread public desires. "Second Life launched with the premise that everyone would want a second life," Au told me, "but the market proved otherwise."

When I asked Rosedale whether he stood behind the predictions he'd made during the early years of Second Life—that the locus of our lives would become virtual, and that the physical world would start to seem like a museum—he didn't recant. Just the opposite: he said that at a certain point we would come to regard the real world as an "archaic, lovable place" that was no longer crucial. "What will we do with our offices when we no longer use them?" he wondered. "Will we play racquetball in them?"

I pressed him on this. Did he really think that certain parts of the physical world—the homes we share with our families, for example, or the meals we enjoy with our friends, our bodies leaning close across tables—would someday cease to matter? Did he really believe that our corporeal selves weren't fundamental to our humanity? I was surprised by how rapidly he conceded. The sphere of family would never become obsolete, he said, or the physical home, where we choose to spend time with the people we love. "That has a more durable existence," he said. "As I think you'd agree."

*   *   *

Alicia Chenaux lives on an island called Bluebonnet, a quaint for-ested enclave, with her husband, Aldwyn (Al), to whom she has been married for six years, and their two daughters: Abby, who is eight, and Brianna, who is three, although she used to be five, and before that she was eight. As a family, they live their days as a parade of idyllic memories, often captured as digital snapshots on Alicia's blog: scouting for jack-o'-lantern candidates at the pumpkin patch, heading to Greece for days of swimming in a pixilated sea. It's like a digital Norman Rock-well painting, an ideal of upper-middle-class American domesticity—an utterly unremarkable fantasy, except that Abby and Brianna are both child avatars played by adults.

When Alicia discovered in her early thirties that she couldn't have biological children, she fell into a prolonged depression. But Second Life has offered her a chance to be a parent. Her virtual daughter Abby endured a serious trauma in real life at the age of eight (the specifics of which Alicia doesn't feel the need to know), so she plays that age to give herself the chance to live it better. Brianna was raised by nannies in real life—her parents weren't particularly involved in her upbringing—and she wanted to be part of a family in which she'd get more hands-on parenting. Perhaps that's why she kept wanting to get younger.

Alicia and her family are part of a larger family-role-play community on Second Life, facilitated by adoption agencies where children and potential parents post profiles and embark on "trials," during which they live together to see whether they are a good match. Sara Skinner, the would-be founder of a virtual black-history museum, told me about parenting a four-year-old son played by a man deployed in the armed ser-vices overseas. He often logged on with a patchy connection, just to hang out with Sara for a few hours while his service flickered in and out.

Sometimes adoptive parents will go through a virtual pregnancy, using "birth clinics" or accessories called "tummy talkers," package kits that supply a due date and body modifications, including the choice to make the growing fetus visible or not; as well as play-by-play announcements ("Your baby is doing flips!") and the simulation of a "realistic delivery," along with a newborn-baby accessory. For Second Life parents who go through pregnancy after adopting in-world, it's usually with the understanding that the baby they are having is the child they have already adopted. The process is meant to give both parent and child the bond of a live birth. "Really get morning sickness," one product promises. "Get aches." Which means being informed that a body-that-is-not-your-corporeal-body is getting sick. "You have full control over your pregnancy, have it EXACTLY how you want," this product advertises, which does seem to miss something central to the experience: that it subjects you to a process largely beyond your control.

In real life, Alicia lives with her boyfriend, and when I ask whether he knows about her Second Life family, she says, "Of course." Keeping it a secret would be hard, because she hangs out with them on Second Life nearly every night of the week except Wednesday. (Wednesday is what she calls "real-life night," and she spends it watching reality television with her best friend.) When I ask Alicia whether she gets different things from her two romantic relationships, she says, "Absolutely." Her boyfriend is brilliant but he works all the time; Al listens to her ramble endlessly about her day. She and Al knew each other online for two years before they got married (she says his "patience and persistence" were a major part of his appeal), and she confesses that she was a "total control freak" about their huge Second Life wedding. In real life, the man who plays Al is a bit older than Alicia—fifty-one to her thirty-nine, with a wife and family—and she appreciates that he has a "whole lifetime of experiences" and can offer a "more conservative, more settled" perspective.

After their Second Life wedding, everyone started asking whether Alicia and Al planned to have kids. (Some things remain constant across virtual and actual worlds.) They adopted Abby in 2013 and Brianna a year later, and these days their family dynamic weaves in and out of role-play. When Brianna joined their family, she said she wanted more than "just a story," and sometimes the girls will interrupt role-play to say something about their adult lives offline: guy trouble or job stress. But it's important to Alicia that both of her daughters are "committed children," which means they don't have alternate adult avatars. While Alicia and Al share real-life photos with each other, Alicia told me, "the girls generally don't share photos of themselves, preferring to keep themselves more childlike in our minds."

For Christmas a few years ago, Al gave Alicia a "pose stand," which allows her to customize and save poses for her family: she and Al embracing on a bench, or him giving her a piggyback ride. Many of Alicia's blog posts show a photograph of her family looking happy, often accompanied by a note at the bottom. "Btw, if you want to buy the pose I used for this picture of us," one says, "I put it up on Marketplace." In another post, beneath a photograph of her and Al sitting on a bench, surrounded by snowy trees, cuddling in their cozy winter finery, Alicia admits that she took the photo after Al had gone to bed. She logged his avatar back on and posed him to get the photo just as she wanted.

To me, posing illuminates both the appeal and the limits of family role-play on Second Life. It can be endlessly sculpted into something idyllic, but it can never be sculpted into something that you have not sculpted. Though Alicia's family dynamic looks seamless—a parade of photogenic moments—a deep part of its pleasure, as Alicia described it to me, seems to involve its moments of difficulty: when she has to stop the girls from bickering about costumes or throwing tantrums about coming home from vacation. In a blog post, Alicia confesses that her favorite time each evening is the "few minutes" she gets alone with Al, but even invoking this economy of scarcity—appealing for its suggestion of obligation and sacrifice—feels like another pose lifted from real-world parenting.

Last year Alicia and Al adopted two more children, but found it problematic that the new kids wanted "so much, so fast." They wanted to call Alicia and Al "Mom" and "Dad" right away, and started saying "I love you so much" from the very beginning. They had a desire for intense, unrelenting parenting, rather than wanting to weave in and out of role-play, and they constantly did things that demanded attention—losing their shoes, jumping off the roof, and climbing trees they couldn't get down from. Basically they behaved more like actual kids than like adults pretending to be kids. The adoption lasted only five months.

There's something stubbornly beautiful about Alicia's Second Life family, all four of these people wanting to live inside the same dream. And there's something irrefutably meaningful about the ways Alicia and her children have forged their own version of the intimacies they've been denied by circumstances. But their moments of staged friction (the squabbling, the meltdowns) also illuminate the claustrophobia of their family's perfection. In their ability to court the ideals of domesticity too easily, Second Life families effectively short-circuit much of the difficulty that constitutes domestic life. Your virtual family will never fully reach beyond your wildest imagining, because it's built only of what you can imagine.

One evening during the earliest days of my Second Life exploration, I stood with my husband outside a barbecue joint in (offline) Lower Manhattan and asked him: "I mean, why isn't Second Life just as real as 'real life'?" At first, he said nothing. He just reached over and pinched my arm. (Quite hard, actually.) Then he said: "That's why it's not as real."

His point wasn't just about physicality—the ways our experiences are bound to our bodies—but about surprise and disruption. So much of lived experience is composed of what lies beyond our agency and prediction, beyond our grasp, beyond our scripts. So much dwells in surprise, in otherness, in missteps and unforeseen obstacles and the textures of imperfection: the grit and grain of a sidewalk with its cigarette butts and faint summer stench of garbage and taxi exhaust, the possibility of a rat scuttling from a pile of trash bags, the lilt and laughter of nearby strangers' voices. Second Life promises another reality but can't fully deliver the rifts and fissures that give reality its grain. In Second Life, landscapes often look like Thomas Kinkade paintings, sex exists in the imagination, parenting happens when you choose to log on. A 2011 study found that people attributed more idealized personality traits to their Second Life partners than to their offline partners—ranking them higher in extroversion, con-scientiousness, agreeableness, and openness. Intimacy between two avatars isn't "unreal," but its reality is different from what happens when two people find themselves enmeshed in a relationship in the physical world—when the self has to stand behind the words she has spoken or the secrets she has disclosed, when she has to inhabit the daily constancy of her home.

In the perfected landscapes of Second Life, I kept remembering what a friend had once told me about his experience of incarceration. Having his freedom taken from him meant not only losing access to the full range of the world's possible pleasures, but also losing access to the full range of his own possible mistakes. Maybe the price of a perfected world, or a world where you can ostensibly control everything, is that much of what strikes us as "experience" comes from what we cannot forge ourselves, and what we ultimately cannot abandon. Alice and Bridgette already know this, of course. They live it every day.

In Second Life, as elsewhere online, *afk* stands for "away from keyboard," and during the course of his ethnographic research, Tom Boellstorff sometimes heard residents saying that "they wished they could 'go afk' in the actual world to escape uncomfortable situations, but knew that this was not possible; 'no one ever says "afk" in real life.' " This sentiment inspired what Boellstorff calls the "afk test": "If you can go 'afk' from something, that something is a virtual world." Perhaps the inverse of the afk test is a decent definition of what constitutes reality: something you can't go afk from—not forever, at least. Philip Rosedale predicted that the physical world would become a kind of museum, but how could it? It's too integral to our humanity ever to become obsolete, too necessary to these imperfect, aching bodies we use to lumber through it.

Did I find wonder in Second Life? Absolutely. When I sat in a wicker chair on a rooftop balcony, chatting with the legally blind woman who had built herself a house overlooking the crashing waves of Cape Serenity, I found it moving that she could see the world of Second Life better than our own. When I rode horses through a virtual Yosemite, I knew that the woman leading me through the pines had spent years on disability, isolated from the world, before she found a place where she no longer felt sidelined. That's what is ultimately liberating about Second Life—not its repudiation of the physical world, but its entwinement with that other world, their fierce exchange. Second Life recognizes the ways that we often feel more plural and less coherent than the world allows us to be.

Some people call Second Life escapist, and often its residents argue against that. But for me the question isn't whether Second Life involves escape. The more important point is that the impulse to escape our lives is universal, and hardly worth vilifying. Inhabiting any life always involves reckoning with the urge to abandon it—through day-dreaming; through storytelling; through the ecstasies of art and music, hard drugs, adultery, a smartphone screen. These forms of "leaving" aren't the opposite of authentic presence. They are simply one of its symptoms—the way love contains conflict, intimacy contains distance, and faith contains doubt.

— II —

LOOKING

Up in Jaffna

I t was early evening when I arrived in Colombo. We'd leapfrogged a day from New York, and everything felt half-dreamed. On my first flight, to Dubai, old men had peered out the bulkhead windows to check for the first lines of dawn, then dropped to the cabin floor in prayer. Dessert was apricot cake draped in cream. A teenage girl wore a bright pink T-shirt that read NEVER LOOK BACK. The *Gulf Times* was full of Middle Eastern justice—"Woman to be lashed for insulting morality police," "Arrest of atheist bloggers urged"—and chilling dispatches from my own country: "Tear gas and baton rounds can't keep the peace in Missouri."

I'd come to Sri Lanka on assignment for a travel magazine. The premise of the feature was that the magazine paid you to fly somewhere for a week but told you only twenty-four hours in advance where you were going. It was the kind of assignment that made other people jealous, but there was also something a bit shameful about it, as if it had distilled a certain colonial arrogance into a jaunty journalistic lark: *I'll just show up ignorant and narrate this place!* But had I turned down my free trip halfway around the world? I had not.

The next morning, I was planning to head north to the Jaffna Peninsula along the A9 highway, through the vast northern scrublands known as the Vanni. This was the territory controlled for many years by the Liberation Tigers of Tamil Eelam, better known as the Tamil Tigers, until they were finally defeated by Sri Lankan government forces, in 2009, near the shores of the Nanthikadal Lagoon. Thousands of civilians died during that final siege. One U.N. report put the number at forty thousand.

It's impossible to understand what it means to go north in Sri Lanka without a basic map of the fault lines that catalyzed the civil war—a Sinhalese Buddhist majority in the south; a Tamil minority concentrated in the north, with the Tigers fighting for a separate state—and some sense of that war's enduring aftermath: the damaged infrastructure and persistent ethnic tensions in a territory still thick with military presence.

In frantic preparation, I'd been reading deeper into the conflict. Every time I thought I'd found its beginning, I found another beginning that came earlier. Maybe the war started with Black July, in 1983, when anti-Tamil ethnic riots killed as many as three thousand in Colombo; or it began when the Tigers killed thirteen Sri Lankan soldiers in the ambush that prompted those riots; or it began in the 1950s when Sinhalese was designated the country's only official language. Every beginning was preceded by an earlier beginning, and the civil war itself had an ending that seemed, to many, like no ending at all. Two things became increasingly clear: there had been tremendous brutality that the government was not fully willing to own, and the country's ruptured populations did not agree on the narrative of their rupturing.

That first night in Colombo, I went to dinner with a Sri Lankan journalist. He picked me up at my hotel, the Galle Face: an old-school affair on the water, all teak angles and verandas, overlooking the rest-less slate-gray sea beyond. It was a room the magazine had booked for my first night, and I felt self-conscious about staying there, with its whiff of corroded English power. I told the journalist I was going north and asked him what he thought of how the government had been rebuilding since the war. He said the simplest way to put it was this: they hadn't done anything right. Government attempts to investigate wartime civilian disappearances had been largely token efforts. The Tamils were still carrying the burden of the struggle: military surveillance, a population of war widows. But he also told me, more than once, that it was dangerous to think of these citizens in the north exclusively or primarily as victims. They were also survivors, actively rebuilding their lives and communities.

He told me that Sri Lankans from the south were increasingly traveling north to visit parts of their country they'd never seen, and that the army had started running its own resorts, including a converted prison fort and a villa on the shores of the same Nanthikadal Lagoon where so many civilians had died. Later that night, I found the resort's Facebook page: "Enjoy a soothing holiday and the cool breeze of Nanthikadal Lagoon."

The journalist told me it bothered him to hear the way travelers talk about the north, especially its beaches—*pristine, unspoiled, undiscovered*. Those beaches aren't unspoiled, he told me. There are skeletons in the sand.

I asked how recently he'd been up there himself, and he just shook his head. Not recently, he said. He didn't have to go. He already knew. He wouldn't go just to *look,* he said. That would make him uncomfortable. He'd go only if he thought he could be useful.

About a year before I landed in Sri Lanka on assignment, I'd saved up enough adjunct-teaching money to travel to Cambodia on my own dime so I could visit a good friend living there. One of the first things I did in Phnom Penh was visit Tuol Sleng, the old Khmer Rouge prison: three concrete buildings whose box rooms still held rusting metal bed frames, old shackles, voltage boxes used to deliver electric shocks. It had been a school before it became a prison, or before it became whatever you call a place where fourteen thousand people came and seven survived. There were stains on the floors, but no plaques to tell us the names of the people whose bodies had bled there. Barbed wire gleamed from upper-level balconies. Many tuk-tuk drivers didn't like coming around at night, because they thought the place was thick with ghosts.

My guidebook had said: "No visit to Phnom Penh would be complete without a visit to Tuol Sleng." I wondered what they meant by *complete*. It seemed to suggest that you needed to pay your dues to history — to the wounds of the land — before you could earn the right to drink rum from wooden buckets on the umbrella-studded beaches of Sihanoukville, or shoot sepia-stained Instagram albums at Angkor Wat.

When I visited, everyone was snapping photos of the palm trees and the barbed wire. Everyone was sweating. It was a thick heat and the soda stand was doing good business. I was thirsty but refused to carry a Diet Coke through those halls of death. Whether I bought the soda or not, there was no escaping the inevitable affront. We were all going to look at these things, and then stop looking, and then keep on living just like we ever did. Genocide tourism turns public history into private commodity. The past is parceled into ticket stubs and photographs, into the souvenir of experience itself, so it can be taken home.

The Khmer Rouge documented their own practices obsessively, which made it easier to expose their atrocities. They'd effectively built themselves in effigy: all these photographs; the cisterns where prisoners had been dunked with their heads underwater; the gallows where they had been hanged. I told myself that it was better to have seen this place than it would have been to move over this land with no knowledge of its wounds at all; that it was better to see the slanted wooden plank studded with shackles, and the watering can beside it, to remember Christiane

Amanpour arguing with one of George W. Bush's speechwriters about whether waterboarding counted as torture. I told myself it was better to see the rows of photographs mounted on poster board on the ground floor of Building A: faces of people just after arriving, and then—thinner, gaunter, hollow-eyed—just before dying, or leaving, which usually meant transport to the killing fields, which just meant dying somewhere else. After the graves became too full around Tuol Sleng, prisoners were loaded onto buses in the middle of the night and driven to a place called Choeung Ek, on the outskirts of town: the killing fields.

Choeung Ek was essentially a meadow and a generator and a toolshed full of ways to kill someone. By the time I visited, it was a meadow full of bones. This was not lyrical truth but literal fact. I watched my own shoes picking between and stepping over them. The dead were not done with us yet. There was a recognizable kind of reverence summoned by the experience of approaching the stupa, a Khmer burial monument—a glass tower full of skulls and femurs and ribs—when I removed my shoes and bowed my head, my body on one side of the glass, those bones on the other. That was a ritual whose rules I knew how to follow. But walking among bones was something else—stepping between the shards of a dead man's ribs, between scraps of old clothing and shoe rubber. It felt disrespectful to walk over the dead but also honest. We are always doing it anyway.

It wasn't particularly easy to get to Jaffna, the largest city in the north and the cultural center of the Tamil minority. Though the train lines bombed out by the Tamil Tigers had been largely rebuilt, the final leg to Jaffna wasn't open yet. I could have taken a plane from Colombo for a lot of money, or an overnight bus for much less, but I didn't want to travel by air or by night. Because I didn't want to see just Jaffna; I wanted to see the Vanni itself, the shift from south to north, the landscape of the war and what had been built since its end.

I found a driver who could take me all the way from the capital, an eight-hour journey by car. He seemed confused about why I was headed north, though he was eager to assure me I'd be safe there. "Danger before," he said. "One hundred percent okay now." He repeated this a few times over the course of the day: *One hundred percent okay, one hundred percent okay.* He was from a town on the southern coast, Ambalangoda, where he had been staying with his mother when the 2004 tsunami hit. He survived by holding on to a coconut tree. His mother died.

The early drive took us past bustling commercial towns, Kurunegala and Dambulla, and smaller, single-industry villages: a village full of pineapples, a village full of cashews, a village full of hubcaps. We passed tuk-tuks with their Che Guevara stickers—HE LOVE YOUR REBEL—weaving through the heavy traffic of all this capitalism: True Lover Shop, Hotel Cool Bar, Hotel Tit 4 Tat. Farther north on the A9, past the district capital of Vavuniya, the shops grew more scarce and ramshackle, makeshift huts strung with bags of potato chips, and the land opened up—more like plains, less like jungle. We passed shelled-out buildings, one after another, roofs blown off and walls blown ragged. Many had been people's homes. Now they were naked to the sky. My driver explained that Tigers had been hiding inside them; that's why they got bombed. *One hundred percent okay.* We seek narratives that will make it so. Violence becomes a necessity, or gets turned into a resort, a soothing holiday.

In Kilinochchi, the old Tiger capital, we stopped at an overturned water tower: ruins tall as a house, concrete cracked and crumbling, rebar jutting out, a tiny DANGER sign hanging off the side like a punch line in poor taste. We passed fields marked by faded skull-and-crossbones signs, where little concrete mounds covered unexploded mines. We hit the bleak expanse of Elephant Pass, a thin strip of land connecting the Jaffna Peninsula to the rest of the island, and stopped at an improvised tank, an armored bulldozer, enshrined in honor of Gamini Kularatne, who died thwarting a Tiger suicide mission. We watched a busload of visitors — presumably up from the south — buy orchids to place before his statue, flanked by soldiers standing as still as the bronze itself. Nearby display cases held Gamini's old uniform, his dishes, his sheets.

At a war memorial a few kilometers farther on, there was no one but me and my driver and a soldier who explained what the sculpture meant: its exploding shell with a lotus blooming from it, the two hands below shaking in peace. These meanings were offered in fragments of skewed translation, and they rang hollow. Whatever you might say about the end of the war — were there war crimes? how many? what kind? by whom? — it certainly wasn't a peaceful handshake. It wasn't anything like that.

In Jaffna there were soldiers everywhere. There were soldiers by the gleaming white library with its sculpted domes, and soldiers by the hardware stores, and soldiers by the cricket field. There were soldiers at every intersection. The journalist had told me Jaffna had recently gotten its first stoplight, but I didn't see it. I saw only soldiers directing traffic.

I stayed in a single bed in a white room just down the road from the Nallur Temple, where barefoot worshippers walked circular paths around the premises. There were soldiers here, too, though they stood barefoot in the sand as well. I'm not sure I saw another tourist anywhere. Schoolgirls slowed on their bikes to say hello. Each time I left the hotel, I encountered the same boy in a wheelchair who wanted to shake my hand. Every time we shook, I smiled wide enough to feel the stretch and strain of my own skin. I owed him more than a smile. I owed him something I couldn't name. I kept thinking of what the journalist had said: "I would go there only if I felt I could be useful." I kept thinking of the Elizabeth Bishop poem "Questions of Travel": "Is it right to be watching strangers in a play / In this strangest of theatres?" I kept thinking of my tattoo. I'd gotten it with heartfelt intentions the year before, as an expression of kinship and curiosity, but now my own arm admonished me. Perhaps it was better to accept that not everything human was something I could know.

People like me—which is to say, people who've had the privilege to travel, and to think of traveling as a part of their identity—often like to travel where others like themselves haven't already gone, often like to think of this travel as more "authentic" and less "touristic." But in Jaffna, being away from other tourists didn't make me feel *less* like a tourist. Just the opposite. I was looked at, sussed out, wondered about, and rightly so, because what was I doing there, anyway? I felt my own lack of use.

In my room, there was a can of Pringles on the mini-fridge and three mangoes in a basket on the desk. Nathan, the de facto concierge, was eager to manage my experience. He kept calling the phone in my room: *You have had dinner? You have had lunch? You are going where today?* Nathan showed me pictures of his daughters. He said his Hindu family no longer spoke to him, because he'd converted to Christianity for his wife.

Walking through the buildings east of the old fort, I saw where the war damage was thickest: crumbling walls, empty chambers full of shrubs and climbing tendrils. Pink walls with strips of peeling paint enclosed stairs leading straight to the sky. A little boy chased a kitten into the damage. The roads by the water were a tight grid full of fishermen's shacks with blue mesh nets flung over their fences. A man squatted in the dusty road, mending one of them with twine. Baby goats were suckling outside the fuchsia doors of a tiny hospital. I tried to walk with purpose but clearly didn't have one. I ended up at the end of a cul-de-sac where a rainbow-colored house was pulsing noise from some interior boom box. I turned around, still trying to look purposeful, still failing. A round of firecrackers startled me—not because of what it was but because of what it wasn't. Men said *hello hi how are you,* asked where was I from, was I lost, what did I want, what did my arm say, pointing at my tattoo.

I skirted the barbed-wire edges of an army enclosure, long barracks with flung-open windows showing bare cots and racks of well-ironed uniforms. A man holding a machine gun watched me scrape bird shit off my shoe with a waxy green leaf. His smile said what he wasn't saying: *Where was I from, was I lost, what did I want?* In the courtyard behind him, another soldier was throwing big stones at a little dog. She held her ground. He kept throwing. The other soldier kept holding his gun. Birds kept shitting, above me and everywhere. I bent down again to keep wiping. After a few more minutes, the dog skulked away beneath the barbed wire.

I'd begun to feel increasingly frustrated by the nature of my own assignment. There's a notion that spontaneity permits authenticity, liberating us from the freight and tangle of too much context, too much research, too much intention. But this kind of spontaneity didn't seem to permit anything but ignorance. Looking at this place without knowing its history wasn't any kind of vision at all. Seeing the Jaffna library—its regal white spires, its security guard so proud to show me the second floor—would have been hollow without knowing it was rebuilt from the ruins of its predecessor, burned in 1981 by an anti-Tamil mob. It had been one of the largest libraries in Asia. Manuscripts were destroyed in that fire that existed nowhere else, that the world will never have again. The ghost of that destruction haunted the white spires I saw. What kind of authenticity comes from looking at a library and knowing nothing about the wreckage it emerged from? That's nothing but deficit. At least I knew enough to know how little I knew.

I had started reading about the war on my flight to Dubai, and kept reading as we touched down in Colombo—as I fell asleep on hotel beds, as I ate my breakfast of egg hoppers, their quivering yolks cupped by thin pancakes of fermented rice, as I described this "local specialty" in my notes before returning to descriptions of field-hospital amputations during the war. Was I blocking the place out when I read my book instead of walking through town? Or was I blocking it out when I walked through town without having read the book? The first was what I'd been trained to believe, but the second was starting to seem more like the truth.

On the overnight bus back to Colombo, I sat perfectly still while the elderly woman beside me arranged her orange sari carefully around her seated body. The bus was supposed to leave at 7:30. We got out of Jaffna around 10:00. We stopped to pick people up; we stopped to drop people off; we stopped to let someone purchase a television; we stopped so our driver could walk into a roadside Hindu shrine, place his palms together, and bow in worship. He came back clutching two fistfuls of flower petals. I wondered if he'd been praying for our journey, and I hoped so, because we kept screeching to avoid hitting things—a tractor piled high with rusty machinery, a van creaking along, turtle-slow and determined. As we finally rolled out of town, we passed one last soldier standing with his machine gun silhouetted against the clouds, and then a graveyard full of headstones catching the moonlight on their broad faces.

Around three in the morning we stopped for half an hour in the middle of the road while our conductor ran his flashlight over one side of the bus. Who knows what was getting fixed, or wasn't. We kept moving through the dark until it was finally dawn. We left the north behind: the hero and his orchids, the lagoon and its skeletons. What good had it done, in the end, that I'd seen anything at all? I was still an outsider to the damage.

True statement: Sri Lanka is paradise. Also true: every paradise is made possible by blindness.

G etting from New York to Dubai to Colombo had taken twenty hours, and getting from northern Sri Lanka to its southernmost point took seventeen: an overnight bus and then a coastal train past the Galle Fort—beside the pulsing green hills of the interior, not just green but *greens,* lime and mint and deep sage darkening into brown—and then a tuk-tuk ride to the town of Mirissa, where the bright blue sea flashed into view between wooden stands piled with glistening stacks of silvery fish.

Mirissa was where I did the things my magazine wanted in my article, exotic experiences to string like miniature anecdotes on a charm bracelet: swimming in a teal pool on a stone terrace, smelling roti sizzling on a griddle in the shadows, watching monkeys chase each other around the edges of ponds full of floating lotus blossoms. Mirissa was where I whale-watched in the rain, or whale-*sought* in the rain, while our boat hit waves as tall as houses and their spray left me storm-drenched and salt-soaked and blinking against the sting, sitting in the prow beside a woman who clenched the railing with one hand and a plastic baggie of her own vomit with the other. Mirissa was where I found the Sri Lanka you see in guidebooks, with white sand beaches and palms swaying in the rain, sweet lime water by candle-light and vanilla ice cream drizzled with treacle from the trees, passion fruits sliced open to show their bright pink flesh. Mirissa was where I ate dal so good I wanted to travel back in time and tell prior versions of myself, versions of myself that thought I'd eaten dal, that I'd never eaten dal at all. Not really.

The war was nowhere to be seen. But it was everywhere. The dead were everywhere.

What else can I tell you about the south? On the train, I sat next to a boy who was headed home to Matara. He seemed fifteen, maybe sixteen. He wanted to know about the phrase on my arm, what did it say? *Nothing human is alien to me,* I would have told him, except I couldn't, because some things are alien to me, like the Sinhalese language. He offered me his spicy peanuts and wanted to know if maybe I had a local mobile-phone number, which was amusing to me because I felt old enough to be his mother. He wanted to switch seats with me because maybe I wanted the window? He could tell I was hungry for beauty, that this was my role in the landscape—to consume it, to admire the plural greens. His smile was so big it showed his gums. I asked if he was a student somewhere.

He shook his head. "I am a soldier," he told me. "Up in Jaffna."

Then he showed me his tiny military portrait—no gums in sight. Just his green fatigues. I smiled, thumbs-up, and gave it back to him.

No, he said. He wanted me to keep it.

No Tongue Can Tell

O n October 20, 1862, a year and a half into the Civil War, the *New York Times* reviewed the first public display of photography from the conflict: an exhibit of Mathew Brady's prints documenting the carnage at Antietam. "Mr. Brady has done something to bring home to us the terrible reality and earnestness of war," the *Times* reported. "If he has not brought bodies and laid them in our dooryards and along the streets, he has done something very like it." This praise implies a faith in photography's ability to offer immediate access, but it's an anxious faith, haunted by the persistent gap between actuality and representation: *something very like it*. The loss can be brought closer, but never close enough to touch. As Emerson once wrote about the death of his son: "I cannot get it nearer to me."

"No tongue can tell, no mind conceive, no pen portray the horrible sights I witnessed," a Union captain named John Taggart wrote to his brother after Antietam. His assertion of futility isn't the refusal of expression so much as its fiercest realization: insisting that it's impossible to describe war becomes the best way of describing it. The bodies can *never* arrive in the dooryards, Taggart suggests, at least not by the old means of expressive transport: text, language, tongue.

When a massive exhibition of Civil War photography opened at the Metropolitan Museum of Art a century and a half later in 2013, it was bracketed by these two sentiments: the *Times*'s assertion that Brady's photography had managed to evoke the "terrible reality and earnestness of war," and Taggart's denial that any mind could conceive of it. One voice insisted on the potential of representation, the other on its limits. By marking the beginning and the conclusion of the exhibit, they worked like conceptual bookends, making explicit the questions lurking behind portraits of rouge-cheeked soldiers and vistas of bloody battlefields: Can photographs offer what other forms of expression cannot manage? Can they offer what the mind can't fully hold? Are there certain kinds of horror that cannot ever be fully known?

America's war with itself marked a singular intersection of aesthetic experimentation and national trauma: a new art was being deployed to document an unprecedented tragedy. The Civil War changed the history of photography by giving it an unimaginable task, and photography, in turn, changed our very notion of war by giving it a previously inconceivable level of representation.

The rooms of the Met's exhibit, *Photography and the American Civil War*, held photos showing the brick skeletons of ravaged Southern factories and the outlined ribs of starving soldiers. They showed the lush grassy ravines of deep Virginia valleys, and "the scourged backs" of runaway slaves, another kind of landscape, where the whip had created its own lines and furrows. These juxtapositions suggested unspoken, unbearable stories: a group of young recruits eating dinner at camp, holding their forks high around a campfire, and then the bloated bellies of bodies on a battlefield. One could feel how quickly the boys became the corpses, how easily their bodies slid from one photograph to the next. Soldiers posing proudly with their weapons for studio portraits became the faceless amputees in clinical medical shots two rooms away. Private Robert Fryer, a teenager recently returned from battle, is shown holding his hand over his chest, with three fingers missing; it looks eerily like the way a younger boy might turn his hand into a make-believe gun, two longest fingers as barrel, to play at war.

War photography acknowledged death and protested it at once. Studio portraits of departing soldiers were meant to grant them several kinds of immortality: as talismans, they might prevent them from dying; as relics, they could preserve their memory once they were dead. Other images were plucked from the middle of the fray: photographers set up shop on battlefields still fuming with smoke or studded with rotting bodies. The forward march of technology—the desire to utilize new techniques and new effects, to make everything as real as possible, even *realer than real*—meant that some photos verged into various shades of the surreal. Soldiers wore the garish blush of hand-tinted color on their cheeks; stereoscopes created the crude 3-D effect of corpses emerging from rubble. These effects feel less like realism and more like the performances of actors trying too hard, their effortful urgency like a plea: *here, please, look at this dead man*—another body almost delivered to the dooryard, limbs pressed close to a pair of eyes pressed close to the stereoscopic viewer.

I n *Regarding the Pain of Others,* Susan Sontag articulates the shame of finding beauty in horror:

> That a gory battlescape could be beautiful—in the sublime or awe-some or tragic register of the beautiful—is a commonplace about images of war made by artists. The idea does not sit well when ap-plied to images taken by cameras: to find beauty in war photographs seems heartless. But the landscape of devastation is still a landscape. There is beauty in ruins.

There is certainly beauty in the ruins of these Civil War photographs—ruined industry and ruined woods and ruined bodies, crumbling factories against Georgia skies, fog lifting off corpse-riddled fields—but it's a dangerous beauty if it distracts us from the brute fact of all that death, and the long-standing structural brutality that gave rise to it: the institution of slavery itself.

The beauty of these photographs is more ethically productive as a kind of Trojan horse. It seduces us with awe, then lodges inside us as enduring horror. It also reminds us that the photo was once framed by someone. The ghost of the photographer looms. We are seeing everything through his eyes.

That sense of being haunted is part of what accounts for the appeal of what Sontag calls "anti-art" photography: "For the photography of atrocity, people want the weight of witnessing without the taint of artistry, which is equated with insincerity or mere contrivance." They want the weight of witnessing without the ghost of the witness, without his fingerprints obscuring their view.

That desire for witnessing without artistry was part of why people felt betrayed when they learned that certain photos from the Civil War had been staged: props placed, bodies moved, limbs arranged. Alexander Gardner's *Home of a Rebel Sharpshooter, Gettysburg*—which shows a Confederate corpse tucked into his ironic "home" between boulders—became the most famous object of this ire, after it came to light that Gardner most likely moved the corpse away from the battle-field and into the more "scenic" framing of this rocky ravine. As Sontag notes, the "odd" thing isn't that this photograph may have been staged, "it is that we are surprised to learn [it has] been staged," and not only surprised, but "disappointed." Our desire for the absolutely *un*altered photograph testifies to a collective delusion that the unmoved body would somehow offer an unmediated vision of reality.

Conspicuous forms of distortion, however, only force us to confront the truth that all photos are inevitably mediated, inevitably constructed, inevitably distancing. Once the bodies arrive in the dooryard, they aren't bodies anymore: they've been run through chemical solutions; they've been flattened, framed, and fitted.

If the taint of artistry is all over these photographs of the war, this taint is also the residue of something deeply authentic—the longing to glorify, to immortalize, to preserve. There's a way to look at the so-called taints of mediation and artistry not as traces of deception—the body wasn't *really* there, the soldier didn't *really* use that gun—but as truthful records of a ferocious desire to convey the courage and horror of war as powerfully as possible. It's the honesty of exaggeration, the truth of whatever desire—to command awe or indignation or sympathy—made us exaggerate in the first place. Perhaps the part of us that feels betrayed by prop guns and relocated bodies is continuous with, rather than betrayed by, the desire to move those bodies at all. Both rearrangement and its indignant backlash grow from a shared anxiety about the limits of representation. There is no way to photograph the soldier's body—moved or unmoved—that will communicate the whole truth of his life, and of his death.

Once you have peeled away the fantasy of photography as unconstructed truth, you can start to explore the fascinating story of its construction. "The camera is the eye of history," Mathew Brady once said, but behind the eye of the camera there was always the eye of a man (often Brady himself), and behind the man there was usually a team, and behind the team there was always some funding. Civil War photography was spurred and nourished by the marketplace: competing galleries funded photographers in the field, eager for the best shots, and profit-driven studios sold portraits to ordinary civilians. Emancipated slave Sojourner Truth sold her own portrait to raise money for other freed slaves. As she put it: "I Sell the Shadow to Support the Substance." For Truth, photography inverted the terms of ownership she had always suffered under. She "used to be sold for other people's benefit," she wrote; now she sold herself, for her own.

At the Met, guards kept saying "No photographs" inside hallways full of photographs, but people kept trying anyway, slyly lifting their cell phones, Instagramming all those captured corpses. The same hungers that made people take the photographs in the first place now made other people—strangers living a century and a half later—want to photograph them all over again: the desire to preserve and to possess, to carry forth, to hold close.

In a photograph called *Woman Holding Cased Portraits of Civil War Soldiers,* the young woman's face is stoic, unflinching. Her cheeks have been rouged so brightly—tinted in a studio, after the fact—that they no longer belong to her expression. She holds a double-sided frame displaying the faces of two men: one looks overexposed, the other shadowed. She grips the photos tightly. She wants something from those faces—and I wanted something from hers, when I stood before her portrait. I studied her expression to find out *what*. What did I want? Some feeling from her image, long faded but not yet gone. A trim curatorial label can't tell us what we're seeking from images of the dead. We want to remember things that never happened to us. We want to sense grief we never felt.

A friend who came with me to the exhibit—a photographer, incidentally—struggled to feel anything about its photographs of war. He wondered: How could you feel saddened by images that were supposed to make you feel sad? Didn't this expectation of pathos deaden their impact? How could we find ourselves overwhelmed by a feeling we know we are supposed to have? And when I spent hours in the exhibit, scrutinizing its photographs, maybe I was trying to get around that problem by thinking myself into grief. But you can't *think* the bodies through the dooryard gates. They can truly arrive only when you're surprised by their arrival.

For me, it wasn't a battlefield panorama that ended up delivering them. It wasn't a splay of corpses bloated on the grass, their pockets turned out by robbers. It wasn't even a shot of soldiers before battle: their forks stuck into crocks of beans, their crooked smiles, the sharp sting of their aliveness when I knew that many of them would soon be dead.

For me, it was a studio shot. The bodies arrived in the dooryard as three men posed in suits, with sleeves folded and pinned at the elbows: two standing, one seated, all stiff. In the photo, their faces are regal and stoic, two gazing into unknown middle distances, while the third has two black hollows—empty sockets—where his eyes should be. His face is also regal, also stoic. He is staring at nothing; he'll never stare at anything again.

When I saw this photograph, all the fascination that had been carrying me through the exhibit parted suddenly, like some great sea, to make way for feeling. It had something to do with the solemnity of its staging, how that care suggested a hunger for order amid the great chaos of war. And it had something to do with the expressionless faces of those men, how their refusal to show sadness invited me to fill the gap, make up the difference, obey the hydraulics of compensatory sympathy. It had something to do with the blind man's *mouth*, in particular, set in a rigid line whose affect I couldn't parse—determined? angry? hopeful?—because I couldn't read the expression in his eyes, because he had no eyes to read.

All these dissections of my sudden sympathy are accurate, but it would be more honest to say simply: Something *happened*. When I looked at that photo, something happened. A body arrived. It had no eyes. It belonged to William R. Mudge, Union soldier. Before the war, in Massachusetts, he worked as a photographer.

Make It Scream,
Make It Burn

In the summer of 1929, after completing his freshman year at Harvard, James Agee headed west to spend a few months working as a migrant farmhand. As he wrote to Dwight Macdonald—his fellow Exeter alum, longtime friend, and eventual boss at *Fortune* magazine—he had grand visions for what the summer would hold:

> I'm going to spend the summer working in the wheat fields, starting in Oklahoma in June. The thing looks good in every way. I've never worked, and greatly prefer such a job; I like to get drunk and will; I like to sing and learn both dirty songs and hobo ones—and will; I like to be on my own—the farther from home the better—and will.

It's an amusing letter. Agee has never worked, but knows he'll enjoy it. He *has* gotten drunk, and he knows he'll enjoy that too. There's a sense of manifest destiny in his hypnotic syntax, a grammatical insistence on the fulfillment of desire: *I like to . . . and will; I like to . . . and will; I like to . . . and will.* He fantasizes about camaraderie and distraction. He wants to be delivered from his own interior life. He's done too much hard time with too many sonnet writers in Harvard Yard. He wants out. The thing looks good in every way. As it turned out, it wasn't.

"Kansas is the most utterly lousy state I've ever seen," he wrote Macdonald on "maybe August 1st." He continued: "Am now working at hauling and scooping grain on a 'combine' crew...I rammed a pitchfork into my Achilles tendon." Agee paints a vivid portrait of himself suffering under the heartland heat—hobbling along a dusty road, raising grain-dusted fingers to put scare quotes around his newly inherited life—but it's also clear he took pleasure in the hardship he described, or at least he took pleasure in describing it. He signs off: "Have to tackle a load now, Jim."

At that point in his life, Agee's manual labor didn't have much to do with his creative work back home. At Harvard in the fall, he'd been focused mainly on getting elected to the editorial board of the *Advocate*, the campus literary magazine, and composing dubious love lyrics to his long-distance girlfriend, to whom he was (painfully, it seems) trying to remain faithful: "I murdered joy, that your love might abide; / A precious skeleton lies at my side."

It was largely anxiety about this girlfriend—and their joy-murdering relationship—that had made Agee so eager to work the fields in the first place. "It will be hellishly bad work," he wrote, "so for once I won't have a chance to worry and feel like hell all summer." His letter imagines hard labor as liberation. It's absurd, of course, but Agee acknowledges his own absurdity before anyone else could possibly call him out on it. "I'm afraid it sounds a little as if I were a lousy bohemian and lover of the Earth Earthy, but I assume I'm nothing so foul, quite, as that." He is aware of how naïve he sounds as soon as he sounds that way. This preemptive self-excoriation would eventually become one of his hallmarks.

Agee's early letters bear so many traces of his later voice: a fascination with worlds far removed from his own; an anguished reeling between judging and valorizing his encounters; and an abiding obsession with the relationship between hard labor and interior life. How does feeling reside inside a body that works all day long? Does that kind of brutal monotony banish consciousness? Is it degrading to suggest that it does? To deny it?

The thing looks good in every way. Seven years later, Agee would indict the thing from every angle possible.

Researched in 1936 and eventually published in 1941, *Let Us Now Praise Famous Men*—Agee's sui generis work of sprawling lyric reportage—wrestles with the material lives of three sharecropper families in rural Alabama. The book describes their homes and the necessities of their daily labor. It catalogs their clothes and meals and physical possessions, their illnesses and their expenses. But it also forces us into the anguish of Agee's attempt to do this describing, as if his attempt were another house, a labyrinthine architecture of thwarted narratives and self-sabotaging journalism, built of convoluted syntax and tortuous abstractions, charged by feelings of attachment and—beyond and beneath all else—guilt. The book is exhaustive and exhausting. It is tormented about what it finds beautiful. Sometimes it doesn't even want to exist. "If I could do it, I'd do no writing at all here," Agee announces at the start of the book. "It would be photographs; the rest would be fragments of cloth, bits of cotton, lumps of earth, records of speech, pieces of wood and iron, phials of odors, plates of food and of excrement...A piece of the body torn out by the roots might be more to the point." He'd do no writing at all, besides the four hundred pages he ended up writing. He hadn't worked, but knew he'd like it. Now he *had* worked—at writing this book, a thankless job—and knew he didn't like what his labor had made, but offered it anyway, because what else could he do? This was what he'd done.

The project of *Praise* began when *Fortune* sent Agee to Alabama on assignment during the summer of 1936. He traveled with Walker Evans, whose accompanying photographs would become as famous as Agee's words. "Best break I ever had on *Fortune*," Agee wrote in a letter. "Feel terrific personal responsibility toward story; considerable doubts of my ability to bring it off; considerable more of *Fortune*'s ultimate willingness to use it as it seems (in theory) to me." Evans described how this sense of "terrific personal responsibility" shaped Agee's research: "Agee worked in what looked like a rush and a rage. In Alabama he was possessed with the business, jamming it all into days and the nights. He must not have slept."

Agee's doubts about his "ability to bring it off " only deepened once the business itself was done. As he wrote to Father James Harold Flye, a teacher at his Episcopal boys' school in Sewanee and one of his great lifelong mentors: "Everything there was unpredictable from day to day, I was half crazy with the heat and diet... The trip was very hard, and certainly one of the best things I've ever had happen to me. Writing what we found is a different matter. Impossible in any form and length *Fortune* can use; and I am now so stultified trying to do that, that I'm afraid I've lost the ability to make it right in my own way."

Agee was on staff at *Fortune*, outfitted with an office in the Chrysler Building back in Manhattan, where he went on all-night whiskey benders turning out copy about cockfighting and the Tennessee Valley Authority. But he was right to doubt their "ultimate willingness" to publish. The magazine killed the piece in late 1936. At that point, Agee began looking for other ways to write and publish the material. He applied for a Guggenheim grant, calling his project "An Alabama Record" and describing it as an attempt "to tell everything possible as accurately as possible [with] as total a suspicion of 'creative' and 'artistic' as of 'reportorial' attitudes and methods," and (humbly) "likely to involve the development of some more or less new forms of writing." He didn't get the grant. Eventually he got a small advance from a publishing house, so he holed up in New Jersey and began expanding his original article into the glorious sprawl that would eventually become *Praise*. The book was published to little fanfare in 1941, sold about six hundred copies, a few hundred more in remainders, and was, in Macdonald's words, "a commercial failure in every sense."

Not until its 1960 rerelease did the book catch fire, fueled by the energy of the civil rights movement and appreciated by a readership primed for the rich narrative texture of the New Journalism. Lionel Trilling would eventually call *Praise* "the most realistic and most important moral effort of our American generation," arguing not only for its cultural stature but also for the ways in which it could shift our expectations about what "realism" might mean, and the kinds of messy emotive texture that "realistic" portraits of human existence might require. In the meantime, it was generally believed that the original manuscript of Agee's magazine article had been destroyed, or lost for good—until his daughter discovered it in a collection of manuscripts that had been sitting in his Greenwich Village home for years: a thirty-thousand-word typescript titled simply "Cotton Tenants."

Reading this carefully structured original draft, alongside the un-spooling book it eventually became, offers a split-screen glimpse into the process of witnessing itself. How does the morally outraged mind begin to arrange its materials? And then—once it begins to doubt itself—how does it rearrange them all over again?

A t first blush, it's tempting to understand "Cotton Tenants" and *Praise* in binary opposition: the unpublished article and the published book; one bound by capital, the other liberated by form. But there were no binaries in Agee's process, only the unfolding and self-frustrated quest to capture what he had seen, to do it justice—which he knew he would never do, and which he kept attempting anyway. *Praise* deploys more swollen syntax, more convolution, more metaphoric opacity, more soaring upsurges into song, but these differences are ultimately symptomatic of a deeper divergence in subject. The article documents the lives of others, while the book documents the process of documentation itself.

In some sense, *Praise* is nothing but an endless confession of everything Agee felt and thought and questioned as he tried to tell the story of these Alabama families. We see much of the material in the original article reproduced, but its nodes of physical particularity—descriptions of houses and objects and clothing and meals—are hopelessly enmeshed in the overpowering dilemma of a tyrannical narrative consciousness: Agee's bottomless but ever-thwarted desire for proximity. Imagine a director's cut five times as long as the film itself, with the camera constantly turning to gaze at the face of the director himself—explaining how it felt to film each scene, how he'd hurt the actors' feelings or how even the extended film you're watching now isn't nearly as good as the one he'd imagined.

While a glance at the table of contents in *Cotton Tenants* suggests a framework whose rules are already familiar—chapters titled "Shelter," "Food," "Health," and so on—the table of contents in *Praise* throws up its hands from the start, its sections odd and disordered. Three "Parts" are interspersed with unparallel sections: "(On the Porch: 1" and "(On the Porch: 2," both cupped by mysteriously unclosed parentheses—as if half-parenthetical, half-included—alongside a section called "Colon" and a section called "Intermission: Conversation in the Lobby," all of these preceded by several attempts at throat clearing: opening prologues called "Verses," "Preamble," and "All Over Alabama." This table of contents calls itself "Design of the Book," suggesting an inescapable self-awareness: this artifact is the product of much hand-wringing about how such an artifact could or should be put together, its various sections can't ever claim a full view, and its refusal to streamline them into consistency is an insistence on making the difficulty of its own construction legible.

The two texts offer starkly different visions of journalistic access: in *Tenants* it's implicit, while in *Praise* it's understood as constantly polluted. In *Tenants* we sense the physical bodies of Agee's subjects—wide-eyed and weary, sorghum-stuffed and boil-strewn—but in *Praise* we have to contend with Agee's body as well. An outraged and outrageous "I" is giving us everything we see, and giving it slanted, awed. We hear about Agee's emotional relationship to his subjects ("I am fond of Emma, and very sorry for her"), and we hear declarations of personality that often feel gratuitous. When Agee confesses, "I am the sort of person who generalizes," we think, *Yes, we know*. We recognize the Agee who went "half-crazy with the heat and diet," whose throat and gut protested the food he was served, whose skin protested the bed he was offered. When he describes spending the night with one of his families, sleeping on their porch, he lapses into the second-person "you," as if speaking to a separate self who slept there:

> Waking, feeling on your face the almost slimy softness of loose cotton lint and of fragile, much washed, torn cotton cloth, and immediately remembering your fear of the vermin it might be harboring, your first reactions were of light disgust and fear, for your face, which was swollen and damp with sleep and skimmed with lint, felt fouled, secretly and dirtily bitten and drawn of blood, insulted.

This visceral reeling is typical of the narrative voice in *Praise*. The speaker emerges as a set of nerve endings, disgusted and disgusted by his own disgust, cataloging physical particularity anyway, unafraid of banality and repetition in his descriptions ("loose cotton lint...torn cotton cloth"), feeling violated by the very place he wants to enter.

He understands himself as fouled and faraway at once. He begins the sentence with something external, the texture of linens, and ends up deep inside his own interior life, "insulted," the declaration isolated at the end of the sentence—a moment of pause, an experiential cul-de-sac.

The shape-shifting "I" of *Praise* was foreshadowed by a wobbly "you" in *Tenants* that shifts from reader to writer to subject. It often works as an imperative invitation. "It's a very unusual year when you do well with your most important crops," Agee writes, making farmers of his readers. Here, he describes a plague of pests: "They web up in the leaves and become flies; the flies lay eggs; the eggs become army worms by the million and you can hear the rustling of their eating like a brushfire." You can hear them eating—not just *can* but *must*. It's a moral command by way of pyrotechnic sorcery. The fire rages all around you.

Elsewhere, Agee uses "you" to make his readers occupy another position: his own. Observing the sharecroppers' children, he seems to shy away from the force of his reaction: "You will possibly get the feeling that they carry around in them like the slow burning of sulphur a sexual precocity." It is, of course, not *you* but Agee himself who has noticed this "sexual precocity," but Agee isn't ready to confess the sexual charge of his own attention. He isn't ready to own the "I" just yet.

When he finally does inhabit this "I" in *Praise*, he is often punishing it or pointing out its failures. Part of the claustrophobia of *Praise* is its suggestion that every strategy of representation is somehow flawed or wrong. It's a kind of paralysis. What to say if nothing will be good enough? We see an interesting prefiguration of this skepticism in *Tenants*, where Agee continually imagines problematic ways someone else could react to the same material. He keeps defining his voice by articulating what it's not. He spots a tinted photograph of Roosevelt in a frame on a mantel and imagines that a "Federal Project Publicizer" could "flash out some fine copy about the Ikon in the Peasant's Hovel"; he disputes a "stupid" but widely believed "exaggeration about child labor in the cotton fields"; he describes a "'rustically' bent" settee but puts "rustically" in ironic quotes. All of these dismissals evoke ways another witness might have witnessed wrongly: by flashing copy, exaggerating tragedy, or romanticizing poverty. Agee wants to establish that his documentary work isn't doing PR for Roosevelt or his New Deal; he wants to push back against the beautification of poverty; he wants to avoid sensationalizing the brutality of agricultural life so that its actual brutality can be better appreciated.

Here we find another important difference between article and book: In *Tenants*, Agee projects problematic reactions onto hypothetical observers; in *Praise*, he claims them as his own. He discards one sense of realism—the illusion of presenting truths unmediated and unaltered—and replaces it with another: confessing all mediation, all doctoring, all artifice and subjectivity, the inescapable contagion of the one doing the documenting—himself.

If Sontag wondered at the public hunger for "the weight of witnessing without the taint of artistry," then Agee measures the "weight of witnessing" in every way possible. He rails against the fantasy of objectivity. He maps the "taint of artistry" by exposing himself as an author disgusted and betrayed by his own representational materials. He rejects the strategies of both narrative fiction (plot, character, pacing) and standard journalism (the illusion of objectivity, or an "I" submerged to invisibility). Agee resists turning his characters into glorified archetypes by suggesting that poverty is "inevitably destructive" of consciousness as we understand it. He resists dramatic narrative by continually stressing the monotony of his subjects' lives. And amid his thousand-and-one metaphors, he suggests the inadequacy of metaphor itself.

Describing the departure of Emma—a young married woman to whom he has become attached and attracted, who is moving away with her husband——he gives us a paragraph-long sentence that recedes from comprehension just as Emma recedes from sight. We lose Emma just like Agee does. Starting midstream, we find Agee watching Emma's truck disappear into the distance:

> ...steadily crawling, a lost, earnest, and frowning ant, westward on red roads and on white in the febrile sun above no support, suspended, sustained from falling by force alone of its outward growth, like that long and lithe incongruous slender runner a vine spends swiftly out on the vast blank wall of the earth, like snake's head and slim stream feeling its way, to fix, and anchor, so far, so wide of the strong and stationed stalk: and that is Emma.

The closing beat reads like mockery: *and that is Emma.* But what is *that?* Is Emma the *slender runner,* the *snake's head,* the *slim stream,* the *strong and stationed stalk?* Is the *stationed stalk* the family she's being removed from? Does her departure hold hope or simply loss? If she is a *snake* and a *slim stream* and a *slender runner* all at once——the sibilance itself spreading like a long and lithe thing across the tongue——this heap of figurations suggests a kind of frantic clutching, layer upon layer, as if they will never be enough to bring Emma back, or to settle on the *that* of who she is, the *that* of any life.

At times, Agee invokes photography as a counterpoint to the failures of language and its inevitable distortions, suggesting that photos are "incapable of recording anything but absolute, dry truth," though this is just another straw-man mythology: all photographs are constructed by framing and selection. For the photographs he took with Agee in Alabama, Evans removed and rearranged objects in the sharecroppers' cabins, placing rocking chairs in natural light or removing clutter to coax a pleasing austerity from others' hardship, the same way Gardner moved the body of a Rebel sharpshooter to create a more aesthetically powerful tableau of tragedy. The cabins were rough drafts that Evans revised into iconic tableaux: a pair of boots standing picturesque on soil, a spare kitchen framed by angled wooden planks, a hanging white washcloth echoing bits of bright light reflected off the glass bulb of an oil lamp.

In a review of Evans's photographs called "Sermon with a Camera," the poet William Carlos Williams—who was himself, by his own declaration, "obsessed by the plight of the poor"—praised Evans's work not for its "absolute, dry truth" but for the ways it summoned universality by drawing eloquence and despair from its raw materials. "It is ourselves we see, ourselves lifted from a parochial setting...ourselves made worthy in our anonymity," Williams writes. "What the artist does applies to everything, every day, everywhere to quicken and elucidate, to fortify and enlarge the life about him and make it eloquent—to make it scream, as Evans does."

A re things 'beautiful' which are not intended as such, but which are created in convergences of chance, need, innocence, or ignorance?" Agee asks. In letters, he worries continually about his tendency to glorify poverty, troubled by his own "form of inverted snobbery...an innate and automatic respect and humility toward all who are very poor." Sometimes he confesses this snobbery ("I cannot unqualifiedly excite myself in favor of Rural Electrification, for I am too fond of lamplight") and sometimes he simply enacts it, noticing a "pure white mule, whose presence among them in this magic light is that of an enslaved unicorn." Agee's voice is full of sentiment and its backlash. He means his unicorns and doesn't. His eye for beauty turns his stomach, but he honors it anyway, insisting that "the partition wall of the Gudgers' front bedroom IS importantly, among other things, a great tragic poem."

Though it might be intuitive to assume that the lyrical excess of *Praise* became possible for Agee only once he had been unmoored from the financial anchor of *Fortune* and its straitlaced aesthetic, this isn't actually true. In fact, *Fortune* generally encouraged a certain brand of metaphoric abandon. Its owner, media magnate Henry Luce, founded the magazine on the belief that it would be easier to teach poets how to write about business than it would be to teach businessmen to write. Agee devoted plenty of real estate to melodramatic lyricism in his original unpublished article, describing flies "vibrating to death in the buttermilk" and vegetables "cooked far beyond greenness to a deep olivecolored death." Dinner isn't just *fatty*, it's *sepulchral*. Collard greens aren't just *fried*, they're *martyred*.

Only in *Praise* do we see Agee explicitly question his own lyrical excess. But if *Praise* questions the metaphoric prerogatives of poetry and resists the aesthetic techniques of narrative fiction, it openly deplores the strategies of journalism. As the Guggenheim committee already knew, Agee had a "suspicion" of creative, artistic, and reportorial methods alike. In *Praise* he critiques many isms—capitalism, consumerism, Communism, optimism—but his critique of journalism feels most pointed. It carries the sense of a spurned child rejecting his absentee parents. "The very blood and semen of journalism," Agee writes, "is a broad and successful form of lying." Elsewhere, his critique is more specifically pointed at *Fortune:*

It seems to me curious, not to say obscene and thoroughly terrifying, that it could occur to an association of human beings drawn together through need and chance and for profit into a company, an organ of journalism, to pry intimately into the lives of an undefended and appallingly damaged group of human beings, an ignorant and helpless rural family, for the purpose of parading the nakedness, disadvantage and humiliation of those lives before another group of human beings...and that these people could be capable of meditating this prospect without the slightest doubt of their qualification to do an "honest" piece of work, and with a conscience better than clear.

While *Praise* is still doing exactly what it condemns the journalistic establishment for soliciting—this "parading" of "nakedness, disadvantage and humiliation"—it certainly doesn't orchestrate this parade with a "conscience better than clear." It's in his deliberately muddied conscience that Agee distinguishes himself from the journalistic establishment. It's as if he accumulates moral debt by writing about a vulnerable population, then wants to repay it by confessing his own trespass. The strong emergence of the "I" in *Praise* is perhaps less a failure to get outside the self, or an unwillingness to grant textual real estate to otherness, than it is a deliberate formal choice to avoid the moral failures of journalism. And the drama of Agee's vexed relationship to the possibility of moral failure, more than the plight of the families themselves, is the closest thing to a plot that his book ever attempts.

The documentary "I" rarely documents without doing some damage. *How the Other Half Lives,* that classic text of social exposé, recounts a time when Jacob Riis, one of Agee's godfathers in the American poverty canon, breaks from civic sermon to make room for a brief revelation of ineptitude: "Some idea of what is meant by a sanitary 'cleaning up' in these slums may be gained from the account of a mishap I met with once, in taking a flash-light picture of a group of blind beggars in one of the tenements down here. With unpractised hands I managed to set fire to the house."

Riis published *How the Other Half Lives* in 1890, just a few years after the emergence of the portable (so-called "detective") camera. But instead of simply celebrating this new tool, Riis's narrative confesses a moment in which taking photos threatened to destroy what they were trying to capture. We imagine the bumbling witness igniting flash-lights on a frying pan and firing cartridges from a revolver, so eager to save these people that he almost kills them. "I discovered that a lot of paper and rags that hung on the wall were ablaze," Riis continues. "There were six of us, five blind men and women who knew nothing of their danger, and myself." Riis's confession carries the stink of paternalism even as it admits fault: he makes it clear that he "smother[ed] the fire" himself "with a vast deal of trouble." He is the agent of trouble, but he's also the only one who can see it—and the only one who has the power to repair it. He elucidates. He makes it scream. He makes it burn. He puts it out.

Agee never burned down any houses, but his prose betrays a constant preoccupation with the possibility of doing harm—more specifically, with the possibility that his reportage might betray his subjects, the ones whose pain he spins into lyric. He always felt the force and peril of his own intrusion. One of Evans's photographs shows the sign hanging above a fireplace mantel: *PLEASE BE quite Every body is Welcome*. And Agee did his best to stay quiet. He describes listening to the Gudger family waking at dawn:

When at length I hear the innocence of their motions in the rear of the hall, the noise of the rude water and the dipper, I am seated on the front porch with a pencil and an open notebook, and I get up and go toward them.

In some bewilderment, they yet love me, and I, how dearly, them; and trust me, despite hurt and mystery, deep beyond making of such a word as trust.

It is not going to be easy to look into their eyes.

119

Here, Agee's guilt attaches to the "innocence" of his subjects and to the threat of his own pencil—the open notebook like a confessional between them—and his invocation of something "deep beyond making of such a word as trust" betrays his fear that trust itself can't ever apply, and neither can love. No matter how close he feels to his subjects ("how dearly"), Agee also confesses the shadow-side of this intimacy. It is not going to be easy to look into their eyes.

If he can't look into their eyes, Agee wants to do other things to them. He wants to eat their food and sleep on their beds. He wants to "embrace and kiss their feet." He wants to know them, and understand them, and explain them, to be loved by them and love them back; he even wants—at times—to make love to them. At one point, he imagines having a multiday orgy with Emma, the young bride who eventually disappears down a long dirt road:

> If only Emma could spend her last few days alive having a gigantic good time in bed, with George, a kind of man she is best used to, and with Walker and with me, whom she is curious about and attracted to, and who are at the same moment tangible and friendly and not at all to be feared, and on the other hand have for her the mystery or glamour almost of mythological creatures.

The fantasy of an orgy is so striking in its own right that it can be easy to gloss over its timing—"her last few days alive"—which seems to suggest that Agee cannot imagine a different kind of life for Emma, only a different kind of role she might play in his. Agee not only confesses his own desire but also projects this desire onto Emma, imagining what she thinks of him, betraying an amusing sliver of humility in placing "almost" before "mythological creatures."

For Agee, this orgy represents an alternative to grim procreation (he calls every conception in a sharecropper marriage a "crucifixion of cell and whiplashed sperm") and a consummate journalistic closeness: subject and object of the portrait finally joined. Agee fantasizes that this consummation could grant Emma, cloistered and degraded by circumstance, some liberty and bliss. "Almost any person, no matter how damaged and poisoned and blinded," Agee writes, "is infinitely more capable of intelligence and of joy than he can let himself be or than he usually knows." Sex represents the ultimate access. It resurrects capacity. It blooms against damage. But sexual intimacy also summons its opposite: the peril of defilement. It's no mere coincidence that Agee found deception in the "semen" of journalism. If Agee conjures the orgy as a fantasy of reciprocity and closeness, he also fears that journalism is more like onanistic spillage, an observer getting off at the expense of his subject.

When Agee finally does spend a night at the home of his subjects, it's not much of an orgy at all. "I tried to imagine intercourse in this bed," Agee writes, and (unsurprisingly), "I managed to imagine it fairly well." But this sexual fantasy quickly gives way to bodily reality: "I began to feel sharp little piercings and crawlings all along the surface of my body." This is something closer to the "insult" of violation, in which he is the one being preyed upon.

Imagination and insult are never far apart for Agee. The latter haunts the former as guilt and specter. After the impossible orgy, he knows, everyone would still be separated by the old subject/object divide, and Agee can't bring himself to imagine the "gigantic good time" without imagining what would happen once it finished: "how crazily the conditioned and inferior parts of each of our beings would rush in, and take revenge." Whatever fleeting pleasure or closeness an orgy could provide, it would inevitably be followed by the betrayal of returning context. Agee would once again be the journalist; Emma would once again be the subject. They couldn't stay in bed forever.

*   *   *

Jacob Riis describes how he once fought the impulse to cry out at a city-planning meeting when a builder called for designing more humane apartments. "I wanted to jump in my seat at that time and shout Amen," Riis writes. "But I remembered that I was a reporter and kept still." He wrote *The Other Half* instead. It was his way of trying to make the world a place that could deserve an *Amen*—an accusation and an exhortation, a prayer directed at the entire city.

Praise is a prayer, but it is also an admonishment. To read it, says writer William T. Vollmann, "is to be slapped in the face." Agee wasn't thinking just about himself—his own guilt, his own love, his own arms flung hopelessly around his subjects—he was thinking about you, reading his words, what you could see and what you couldn't. He wanted to throw a pile of excrement on your open notebook and let you figure it out. The dilemma of impotence—the quest to keep speaking, and the inability to ever say enough—is one of Agee's great legacies. It choked and spurred his speech.

But Agee's legacy isn't merely his sublime articulation of futility. His legacy isn't just journalistic skepticism. It is his attempt to find a language for skepticism and to rewrite journalism in this language—to insist upon a sincerity that lies on the far side of self-interrogation. In the four hundred–odd pages of *Praise* we find a lot of guilt, but we also find a lot of research. The rough draft of *Tenants* helps us remember this. It lets us witness what Agee made first, and examine it alongside the epic it became once it got digested by the organs of an endless self-loathing.

In *Tenants* we have the first failure in a long line of failures—all of them filled with rush and rage, all of them beautiful. We have the first record of eloquence before it learned to scream. *Tenants* summons a *you*, and it extends an invitation that becomes a command: You can look. You must. Look at what Agee wrote when he remembered he was a reporter, and wouldn't keep still, wouldn't keep *quite*. Look what happened when he sought an *Amen* and found these words instead. Now look closer. You can feel him getting restless. You can hear the rustling of his guilt like the beginning of a brushfire.

Maximum Exposure

On a warm autumn day in 1993, two women met near a shanty-town in Baja California. Annie was an American photographer on vacation, staying in a friend's trailer with her girl-friend. María was hiking up a hill in the noon heat with her two young daughters, bringing lunch to her husband, Jaime, a bricklayer, who was digging clay from the hillside. She was nearly eight months pregnant. Her girls had just found a discarded sketchpad in the bushes. Annie gave them her pencils. She felt an immediate connection to María that had something to do with her warmth and her energy with her daughters, and also something to do with the jarring splendor of the land around them: their shantytown against the glimmering Pacific, that jolt of poverty alongside beauty, neither canceling the other.

Annie had brought only a point-and-shoot camera with her on the trip, but she asked María if she could take a few photos of her anyway. María said yes. This part might not seem important: the asking, and the saying yes. But that tether of request and consent was the core of everything that unfurled between these two women over the decades that followed. *Can I take this moment of your life and make my art from it?* Annie photographed María standing with her daughters against the brown, grassy horizon, and then the whole family at the door of their two-room adobe house—parents weary, kids grinning.

Annie wasn't the first white woman who had asked to photograph María. But she was the first one who returned. Back home in Los Angeles a few weeks after they first met, stuck in gridlock traffic on her way to a gig taking school photos, Annie had a realization. It took the form of a panic attack. It wasn't just about the fact that she was going to miss the school job—one of her first paying jobs as a photographer—it was that the world seemed to be falling apart. The radio was talking about ethnic cleansing in Bosnia. Her best friend from art school had recently been killed in a hit-and-run after returning from taking photographs in Kuwait. Everything seemed fragile and heavy at once. On that congested highway, pounding the steering wheel in frustration, Annie was determined not to waste any more time. She found her mind traveling back to the family she'd met in Mexico. She promised herself—on that day, in that rush-hour traffic—that she would keep photographing them for ten years.

Ten years became fifteen, then twenty, then twenty-five, until Annie had made twenty-six trips over the course of the next quarter century.

The first time Annie returned to Baja, María came to the door of their adobe in a panic, saying her baby was sick. She had diarrhea and a fever. María was afraid she'd die. This was Carmelita, whom she'd been carrying when she and Annie met on the hill. Annie didn't understand María's panic until she learned that another one of her babies had died after being ill with diarrhea several years before.

María and Carmelita on the beach, 1994

It would be like this whenever Annie returned—she was plunged right into the stream of their lives. Proof sheets from her early visits show all the detritus and glory of everyday existence: a wheelbarrow full of dirty dishes, a box spring propped up as a fence, two girls sitting atop a tower of bricks as tall as a two-story house, a boy waiting behind a market table full of screwdrivers. Her photos excavate the vexed feelings simmering beneath ordinary moments: a mother laughing, inadvertently showing a glimpse of the rotten teeth she is ashamed of; a father lighting his cigarette against the wind off the ocean, laying bricks at four o'clock in the morning; the same father bathing himself with a mug and a plastic bucket, looking sheepish, or nuzzling his infant daughter's neck, punch-drunk with love.

During one early visit, Annie watched the kids do their homework by candlelight after the neighbor had cut off their illegal electricity, then bartered prints of her own photos to coax that neighbor to restore the wiring. During another trip, Jaime was helping Annie jump-start her Oldsmobile—the one they all called the red donkey, *burro rojo*—when the cops arrived, frisked Jaime, and put him in their van. When Annie protested, saying he'd only been helping her, they said they knew exactly who he was. Taking photos was the only way Annie knew how to protest his arrest, but her photos didn't keep the police from hauling him away.

"Don't take pictures of us, little bird," they told her over their car speakers, as they drove past the edge of her frame. But she took them anyway, for twenty-five years.

You could call Annie committed, or you could call her obsessed. Obsessed with seeing María and her family evolve across the decades, and obsessed with the elusive horizon of a complete gaze. She

127

kept visiting as the toddlers became children, then teenagers, and then parents with toddlers of their own. She kept visiting as Jaime started drinking more and hitting María; after a fire ravaged their two-room adobe and Jaime switched from booze to heroin; after María left him and moved to the city where her mother lived; after she found a new partner and a new home, a new job in a factory making sandals.

Jaime, washing, 1995

Twenty-five years was long enough for humanity and too long for sainthood. It was long enough for children to slough off the snakeskins of their innocence—to get booze habits, get into fights, get pregnant, get across the border. Over and over again, Annie was forced to see her subjects in more complicated terms. The day that Jaime was arrested, for instance, Annie raced up the hill to tell María he'd been taken away, and María told her that she had been the one who called the cops. Jaime had struck her across the face with his belt buckle during an argument about Carmelita's baptism.

Annie's documentary work is a process of intimate entanglement. When she says, "I photograph from where my heart lives," her phrasing is built upon decades of road trips and plane flights and time off her day jobs; decades of fleabites and bellyaches and fevers and sleeping on floors and learning slingshot strategy from four-foot experts; decades of counseling a woman through two abusive relationships; decades of finding the right moment, the right dusk light, the right gaze from mother to child; or not finding the right moment and showing up again anyway. "Now that I think about it," she told me once, "this work has survived and thrived almost twice as long as my longest love affair."

Annie Appel isn't famous, but her work is part of a powerful documentary tradition. It's a lineage that extends from W. Eugene Smith's seminal 1951 photo-essay in *Life,* about a black South Carolina midwife ministering to rural patients, to Mary Ellen Mark's photographs of homeless teenagers in 1980s Seattle. It stretches back to the "folk studies" of North Carolinian Bayard Wootten, a single mother who borrowed a camera in 1904 to take photos to support her two sons, and reaches forward to the contemporary portraits that Galician photographer Lua Ribeira has taken of spice addicts on the streets of Bristol. "I have become close to some of them," Ribeira said of her subjects, "but...that clash, it is painful and complicated." These are all photographers who take ordinary people as their subjects and insist on the importance of "ordinary" lives, who are not interested in telling fairy tales about their photographs as redemptive or their gazes as objective, who forge intense emotional relationships with their subjects and create images shaped by that intensity. Ribeira once remarked of her homeless subjects, "In this structure we exist in, they have to be *there* for us to be *here,*" and her photographs momentarily collapse that distance—not to pretend that it has been bridged, but to insist on looking across it.

In many ways, Annie claims the identity of an outsider artist with pride. Her work has been exhibited mainly at small galleries around

San Pedro, the Los Angeles port town where she lives in an apartment tucked behind the storefront dance studio in which her wife teaches tango lessons. For a decade, Annie has had a day job as the supervisor of a photo lab in order to support her projects: traveling across the country to make portraits of Occupy protesters; photographing a cloistered nun in a Hollywood monastery; setting up a portable studio on the grass of Pershing Square in downtown Los Angeles—inviting anyone to sit for portraits, including the homeless, persuading the police to let her stay when they arrived to send her away—then coming back twenty-three years later to repeat the project. But for nearly three decades, the cornerstone of her creative life has been the Mexico project. Every time Annie calls her mother to say she's heading back to Mexico, her mother asks, always gently, some version of the same question: "Again? Don't you have enough pictures of that family yet?" Always following up with a mother's concern: "Is anyone paying you?"

The fact that Annie hasn't gotten substantial institutional support for her work only brings her own investment into sharper focus. She has not only devoted herself to her Mexico project for a quarter century in the absence of serious official recognition, she has also devoted herself to funding it—and to fighting for her work, over and over again.

When the Smithsonian acquired a series of her Occupy portraits for its permanent collection in 2015, it was a powerful lifeline of affirmation. Annie flew the photographs to Washington, D.C., herself, committing to memory how it felt to carry her portfolio into the museum, and the giddy, floating sensation of carrying an empty portfolio out the door. It meant so much to her that the world had finally said: *Your work matters.*

Her work does matter. It matters because her photographs are full of human life in its mess and complexity, because they illuminate intimacy as a compost heap smoldering with layers of fear and distance and longing. Her work matters because it evokes the ways that daily life simultaneously holds tedium and astonishment, drudgery alongside sudden surges of wonder.

Doña Lupe caring for grandchildren, 2003

In a 2003 photo of Doña Lupe, María's mother, sitting with three of her grandchildren, so much is visible at once: the strain of caring for these children, and the love that fuels her care. Lupe sits on a stool, holding her youngest granddaughter's wrist, with a pile of dishes on the counter behind her. The features of the children's faces are lit by sunlight, exposed in their ordinary holiness. Lupe's grandson Joelle looks gangly and hopeful in a striped shirt and baggy jeans, holding a pigeon in both hands, its feathers peeking out between his fingers. It's as if he's offering this bird to the person behind the camera as a gift, something precious squirming in his hands that might fly away at any moment. His expression is full of fragile hope and tentative uncertainty. He is poised just at the far edge of youth, not yet ashamed to find the world wondrous.

But what makes the photo truly extraordinary is precisely what feels *un*-wondrous about it. A more predictable cropping of the shot might have been framed more fully around Joelle and the bird—making the image more lyric, more iconic, and more symbolic, the young boy with this symbol of hope and flight—but Annie's composition does something else. She frames the photo so that it includes not just Joelle and the bird but also his grandmother and two of his young cousins, alongside the mess of the kitchen behind them: a bag of trash blurry in the foreground, a broomstick drawing our eyes toward a corner of the frame; all of these visual elements making it hard for the eye to know where to land. It's akin to what we might have seen if Walker Evans had not rearranged the homes of his sharecropper subjects to evoke from their poverty an uncluttered restraint, all clean lines and simplicity. Annie refuses to do that. She insists on letting the clutter of daily life into her frame alongside the soulful surges. She insists that each is part of the other.

Many of her images are compositionally off-kilter, as the photographer Ryan Spencer pointed out to me, in a way that makes them more visually surprising, caught in a purgatory between being centered and uncentered. It's a visual manifestation of Annie's interest in capturing in-between moments, not necessarily moments of high drama but moments of ordinary humanity. This jarring quality summons the French aesthetic of *jolie laide:* the idea that something is beautiful because of its imperfections, not in spite of them. In one photo of María's daughter Angelica and her four kids, the composition vibrates with humanity not despite the fact that Angelica's youngest baby is crying, but *because* he is crying. The frame is electrified by that disruption.

Angelica and her four children, 2007

These elements of Annie's work—her irregular compositions and her willingness to let in visual chaos—are formal manifestations of her commitment to portraying life in all its complexity, just as the duration of her project manifests her commitment to allowing the human complexity of her subjects to unfold across decades. Once you become obsessed with documenting, it can seem impossible to stop. No ending feels honest or defensible. What does it mean to make art from other people's lives? What distinguishes exploitation from witnessing, and when is that witnessing complete? Is it ever? It's the problem of Borges's imagined map: In order to show every detail of the world, a map would have to be as large as the world itself. It would have no edges. It would never be done. Which is to say: A family keeps living; you keep witnessing. A woman keeps getting older. Her kids keep getting older. Her kids have kids of their own. You keep witnessing. The woman you're witnessing gets upset with you. You keep witnessing. Her life seems like it's falling apart. Your life feels like it's falling apart. You keep witnessing. It's endless. That's the problem, and the point.

Annie grew up in El Paso during the 1960s and '70s, directly across the border from Ciudad Juárez. "Born and raised in twin cities divided by a river," as she describes it. From her childhood home on Thunderbird Drive—way up the mountain on the west side of town, in one of the wealthiest parts of the city—Mexico was a distant horizon. Nana, her family's live-in housekeeper, went back across the border every weekend to be with her own family. Whenever Nana got detained on her way back to El Paso, she'd be gone for days. If she was outside when the green immigration car cruised down Thunderbird Drive on a weekday, she would duck into the house.

The border was always there, and Annie was always aware of being on one side of it—her life built on the guilt of privilege, the abiding shame she calls "my age-old apology for being born into a well-to-do household in El Paso." Whenever Annie's relatives visited from the East Coast, they all went across the border to buy embroidered dresses and cheap liquor. Annie and her brother crossed the border to buy a bag of what turned out to be loco weed—the stuff gringos got tricked into paying for. Annie didn't know that girls were disappearing from Juárez when she rode across the border as a fourteen-year-old tomboy, with a group of older friends, to get drunk on tequila in bars where all you had to do to get a drink was be tall enough to reach the counter. One of Annie's teachers explained that El Paso had the highest traffic-fatality rates in the nation because of immigrants running across the highway. During driver's-ed lessons, Annie was told to watch for them. As soon as she turned sixteen, she started driving housekeepers in her neighborhood to the bus stop on Fridays for their weekend trips across the border.

As a child, Annie would squint at Juárez across the river whenever her family drove down the interstate, hoping to see an actual person amid its cardboard-roofed shacks. But it was too far away. The scale wasn't right. "At night, without electricity, the darkness on their side of the river was complete," she remembers. "It was as if I were staring into the empty horizon over open seas." But the horizon wasn't empty. Annie knew that as a kid, and she has spent twenty-six trips and twenty-three thousand frames rejecting that delusion. She's been forcing exposures instead.

For the entirety of her Mexico project, Annie has carried the same three cameras: all Nikon, all fully manual; one loaded with color film, two with black-and-white. She never uses zoom or telephoto lenses. For a close-up, she has to get close. She never uses a flash, only ambient light. She never crops her images in the studio, which means forcing herself to trust the way her eye composes the photo in the moment of its capture.

Annie's rules function like formal constraints in a poem, supplying generative boundaries that animate her creative impulse. But they also evoke the procedures of ritual. For Spencer, photographers are "the art-world equivalent of pitchers on the mound," because all their super-stitions about process remind him of baseball players wearing unwashed hats or kissing their gold crosses, chewing a particular brand of tobacco or drawing lucky figures in the dirt with their toes.

Annie's formal constraints create the texture of immediacy in her compositions, but they wouldn't be possible without the emotional commitments embedded in her process: her deep immersion in the lives of her subjects, the long-term arc of building these relationships. Annie only learned the phrase *participant observer* after she'd already been one for years. She can't plan her photos; she just has to be there when the right moment shows up—which means being there for all the other moments, too. Every great shot isn't just about its particular light or angle or composition, it is also about all the years that came before, the ones that delivered Annie and her subjects to that instant in time.

What do her photos show? A boy holding a pigeon. A girl holding her grandmother's hand. A group of kids playing tag with bloody hands, after sticking their fingers in a still-wet bull skull perched on a wheelbarrow, its dead tongue lolling. Her photos show Carmelita as an infant, as a sullen schoolgirl, then as a teenager at her first job—putting up a market stall, its orange tarp filtering the sunlight like the veined skin of an internal organ. Annie's photos don't remove her subjects from their circumstances, but they don't reduce them to their circum-stances, either. She doesn't conscript them into serving easy moralizing arguments about inequality or guilt. She lets their faces occupy her frames in many different ways: sometimes so large that their particular features blur their background entirely, sometimes vague in the dim light, sometimes pushed partially out of view.

In one photo of María's son Carlos, taken on a bus in Mexico, Carlos is looking straight at the camera—his gaze disarming and penetrating, his face in crisp focus while those of his fellow passengers are blurred. This composition captures the essence of Annie's whole project because it highlights the way she observes her subjects in situations of anonymity, like an ordinary bus ride, in order to dramatize the illumination of their particular humanity—in this case, Carlos's gaze brought into startling clarity.

Carlos on the bus, 2007

*   *   *

One early photograph from 1995 shows Annie sitting with María and Jaime at their kitchen table. Jaime is eating, his hand hovering over the beans. There's a stack of tortillas in the foreground, a bottle of Coke mostly drunk, a portrait of Jesus regarding everyone. On the wall behind Jaime, eight holes are visible from nights he punched through the plaster during drunken rages. Annie looks exhausted, a bit bleary, but not nervous or uncomfortable. She isn't putting on a performance of affection or closeness. Two of her cameras rest beside her on the table.

What strikes me most about the kitchen-table photo is the fact that these three people aren't looking at each other. They are looking past one another, in a way that suggests both familiarity and slippage. Annie's photos are interested in making room for these unvarnished moments, for the ways people see past each other—how they can't quite make eye contact because they are too tired to connect, too wary to trust fully, too depleted to reveal themselves. Her photos refuse reductive tales of connection that elide these sly, persistent, constitutive gaps between people. Instead, they claim the world of what *is*—in which these ruptures are as much a part of intimacy as an embrace.

This kitchen-table shot is also, of course, a photograph of the photographer—her cameras resting on the table. Another photo shows Annie's shadow falling across a stack of bricks, and this image feels like a confession: I was *there*. She was part of it. Her photographs insist upon the mess of subjectivity, the tangle of caring and caring *for*, of getting angry and coming back. In a 2000 photograph taken at Doña Lupe's house, Annie crouches in front of Carlos with a camera held up to her face as he laughs and the rest of the family watches. She is at the center of the frame, but of all the people in the photo, hers is the only face you cannot see — as if she is confessing her desire to erase herself, as well as her understanding that this cannot ever fully happen.

Self-portrait with María and Jaime, 1995

Annie has transcribed her Mexico journeys in a series of diaries that now total more than a thousand pages. They describe long naps on the couch with the youngest baby, Viviana, sleeping on her chest, feeling her tiny heart beat twice as fast as her own; or sweltering afternoons spent at the river with Carlos, watching him catch a two-inch fish in an empty can of Orange Fanta, letting him sling green algae at her forehead and then getting him back by smearing it between his shoulder blades. These diary entries are a reminder that the documentarian was also, always, a woman drying her socks on the windowsill and getting eaten alive by the "night shift" of mosquitoes, a woman who got irritated and tired, who drank cold beers alone when she was exhausted by the relentless communion she craved, who was heartbroken by a lover's betrayal back in California or by her father's death in

Texas—who brought those griefs with her. They soften the diary pages like humidity.

Annie always knew how absurd it was to arrive in Baja or San Martín or Tijuana and complain about her "grumpy boss" alongside everything María and her kids were facing. Her journals confess how the lens sometimes felt like a necessary buffer between their lives and her own guilt: "No electricity, for some reason, at Lupe's tonight, so I was officially excused from picture-taking, and couldn't stomach hanging out in her house without the distraction of work to keep me from thinking too much about how impossible the way they live is." It wasn't always romantic to watch the kids do homework by candlelight.

Getting involved never felt sufficient, but it started to seem necessary. After María's youngest brother, Guillermo, came across the border with his family, Annie kept taking photographs of their new life in the States. And when Guillermo faced deportation, Annie wrote a letter on his behalf and helped his wife, Gloria, look for a house to rent in a different town. After taking photographs of Gloria at work—picking grapes in a vineyard, her scarf-wrapped face almost hidden among the vines—Annie purposefully tracked muddy footprints across the floor of the vineyard's upscale tasting room. She wanted to bring dirt into a room that had forgotten the hands picking the grapes outside, or had never cared at all—had never cared about the woman who'd crossed a desert pregnant, who supported an infant daughter with a chronic lung disease while living with the daily terror that her husband might get deported. Annie understood her own muddy footprints as an act of insistence, the ways her photographs were an act of insistence: that this woman existed, that her life mattered.

It can be easy to believe that a documentary project requires absence in order to do its work most effectively: that the writer or photographer or filmmaker should step out of the frame in order to leave room for her subjects. Early in her Mexico project, Annie fantasized about this kind of invisibility: "relinquishing self 100% so as to become a blank canvas of sorts, on which I can record the true colors of the situation at hand." But for me, Annie's work succeeds because it fails at making her absent. She's at the kitchen table. Her shadow falls across the bricks. Her photos are saturated by the full range of her feelings: admiration of Jaime's curiosity, rage at his drunken violence. Her presence isn't cumbersome baggage, but part of the work itself. "Self" and "other" are not forces caught in a zero-sum game. Annie's failure to remove herself entirely doesn't obstruct what she documents, it widens the scope of what she's documenting: not just her subjects but the emotional complexity of photographing them. She confesses her own residue. She owns the taint of artistry.

Self-portrait with the family at Doña Lupe's house, 2000

*   *   *

The language of photography conjures aggression and theft: You *shoot* a picture. You *take* a photograph. You *capture* an image or a moment. It is as if life—or the world, or other people, or time itself—has to be forcibly plundered, or stolen.

If you take a photograph, what do you give in return? In the early years, Annie knew that a single paycheck from her day job could pay for a year of textbooks for María's kids, or even a few months' rent. She gave what she could: cash, art supplies, backpacks, new shoes, bananas, beans. Her budgets list the pesos she spent on each trip: for a waterpark trip with María's sons, for jicama and toothpaste, for mangoes and tortillas, for a birdcage for Doña Lupe, for tickets to the hypnotist and popcorn at the show. Each time she returned, she brought back prints for everyone in the family, giving them back to themselves.

When María needed to get one of her rotten front teeth pulled—it made her too self-conscious to smile—she asked Annie for the money to get it done. Annie said she would give her the money to fix her teeth if María would start smiling for her photographs. It was a joke, and also something more complicated than a joke—an acknowledgment of the ongoing transaction that framed their deepening intimacy.

When Annie finally gave María the money, María didn't use it for her teeth. Five years later, María asked again, and got the money again, and didn't use it for her teeth again. Annie felt betrayed both times, and judged herself—both times—for feeling that way.

What did María use the money for? Clothes for the kids. Tortillas. Propane.

After Jaime switched from tequila to heroin, and his abuse grew intolerable, María asked Annie for the money to leave him. Years later, Annie recalled their talk this way:

María called to ask me for help after she'd finally decided to flee Jaime's violence against her and the children. One hundred dollars for six bus tickets and a thirty-six-hour bus ride home. Was it right? And if I'd denied her request for help? A different life for them all. I've wondered if I did the right thing for ten years now. Looking at photos from that time, I identified a bottle in Jaime's hand for a majority of the images. I'd forgotten that part, like the feeling of fear when he beat her in front of me that time.

Once Annie had gotten close enough to María and her family, *not* doing anything started to feel like doing something, too. When María's elder daughters accused her second partner, Andres, of beating them when they refused his sexual advances, Annie thought about giving María a month's rent so she could get a place of her own. "Discovered that a house the size of María's current place runs $30 U.S. a month," Annie wrote in her journal. "Thought I could pay her rent in advance if she wants to leave this abusive man...What should I do? What shouldn't I do?" She didn't end up offering rent for a new place, but she did tell Andres she was aware of his abuse, and willing to defend María: "I stood a foot away from him, and face to face I whispered, 'Should I hit you with my new belt? Which end should I use—the metal buckle, or the smooth side? Show me how to do it properly, Andres.'"

In one journal entry, Annie instructs herself, "Always say yes," but her diaries also confess the times she didn't: the time she didn't pay for Doña Lupe's propane tank, the time she didn't give María her favorite green sweater, the times she needed to be alone for the day. She never gave anyone in the family her address because she knew if they ever crossed the border and showed up at her home, she wouldn't be able to turn them away.

When photographer Mary Ellen Mark and her husband, Martin Bell, were making their 1983 documentary *Streetwise*, centered on a thirteen-year-old Seattle prostitute named Tiny, they were constantly torn about how much help to offer. It can feel inhuman to document pain without trying to ameliorate it. But a documentary project can become unsustainable when it claims the additional responsibility of aid. And it's also true that for some subjects no amount of aid will ever feel like enough. Mark and Bell never gave the kids they were filming money, but they did give them food, jackets, and shoes. When they went back to New York after they were done shooting, they offered to take Tiny with them — "to adopt her, essentially," as Bell put it. The only condition was that she go to school, which she didn't want to do, so she didn't go with them. They stayed in touch with her for decades, and nineteen years later, she told them: "I think about it all the time. The fact that I didn't come."

In 1993, while South African photojournalist Kevin Carter was taking photographs of the rebels in Sudan, he captured an image that would become famous: a skeletal toddler crawling on the dirt toward a feeding station while a vulture perched behind him. Carter crouched down carefully — not wanting to disturb the bird, so he could get the best possible shot — then waited twenty minutes for the bird to fly off; when it didn't, he shooed it away and let the boy continue on his journey. Carter didn't bring the boy food. He didn't take him to the feeding station. He simply sat under a tree, and smoked, and wept. "He was depressed afterward," one friend reported. "He kept saying he wanted to hug his daughter." Fourteen months later, the photograph won him a Pulitzer Prize. "I swear I got the most applause of anybody," he wrote to his parents after the ceremony, but two months later he killed himself at the age of thirty-three. In the note he left behind, he said: "The pain of life overrides the joy to the point that joy does not exist."

In her diaries, Annie interrogates all the mythic versions of herself that she has wanted to believe in. "What truths shall I tell?" she wonders. "Paint myself as savior?" For decades, she has struggled against her desire to become one. In one entry she describes herself as a "naked, vulnerable, egotistical, self-absorbed artist masquerading as a well-intentioned 'do-gooder,' such an effective mask I'd even convinced myself." After years, she finally told herself, "Not my job to play karma cop."

I first discovered Annie's work five years ago, when she wrote me an email saying she felt a kinship between her photographs and my writing—in particular, an essay I'd written about James Agee and his expansive, relentless, guilt-ridden book about sharecropper families in Alabama. When Annie described the duration of her own documentary project, I felt humbled. At that point, it already comprised more than twenty visits. It made me ashamed of the ways I'd written about the lives of others after knowing them for a year, or even a month. How meager that seemed in the face of Annie's ongoing gaze. The ethical divide between showing up and coming back loomed large; it made me feel accused. This was respect, I thought: to look and *keep* looking, not to look away as soon as you'd gotten what you needed. Respect meant letting your subjects get older, letting them get more complicated, letting them subvert the narratives you'd written for them. It meant having enough stamina and humility to say: *I'm not done. I haven't seen enough.* In one diary entry, nine years into her project, Annie wrote: "I understand nothing."

From the beginning, Annie's Mexico project struck me as a spiritual descendant of *Let Us Now Praise Famous Men,* not only because both projects involved privileged white artists documenting impoverished families, but because both projects were fueled by a persistent sense of their own incompleteness. When it came to ongoingness, Annie had Agee beat. While he'd reported for months, she'd been coming back for decades. But both of them were hounded by the suspicion that no matter how much they said or showed, it would never be enough to conjure their subjects fully. The part of Annie that confessed she understood nothing could have been speaking directly to the part of Agee that worried his efforts would be failures, or at least wanted that confession contained within his project; the part of him that worried his words were not enough, that wanted to offer broken plates and excrement instead of sentences and paragraphs.

As I kept corresponding with Annie, I frequently felt flooded by her desire for connection and communion. For every note I sent to her, I got three back; for every reply, three more. (After I mentioned that to her, I got an email from her with the subject line *My third reply.*) It didn't feel foreign to me, her hunger, but deeply intuitive: it spoke to the part of me that had stayed on the phone with my high-school girlfriends for hours each night, even though we'd already spent the entire day together; that thrill of feeling no borders between us, the futile attempt to reach a saturation state of closeness in which there was nothing we hadn't shared.

The first time Annie and I met in person, it was for coffee in a hotel lobby, and I arrived to find she had brought two huge suitcases and started unloading their contents across several coffee tables. It was an array of her own prints alongside a spread of books that had inspired her. She'd set up a light stand so she could take my portrait. It was excessive. It was taking up room. I loved it. She was an agile, quick-moving woman with sandy blond hair cropped short around her ears. She radiated momentum and appetite.

In one of her letters to me, Annie said she missed in herself "a sense of inner boundaries that I have longed to understand since childhood." Over the years, I've started to suspect that whatever force prevents these boundaries from finding purchase inside her—her unquenched curiosity, her porousness, her hunger for fuller exchange—is also precisely what carries her back to Mexico over and over again. She once told me about her fascination with the construction crew that perpetually painted and repainted the Long Beach bridge. She could see them from her studio window. They would spend a year repainting one side, then a year repainting the other, in a never-ending loop. "All these years later I can see my early obsession with the idea of 'process' taking shape," she told me, remembering her fascination with those painters and their endless job. "Little did I know at the time this would one day describe me too."

When I finally wrote about Annie's work, in a brief essay to accompany a magazine portfolio of her Mexico photos, the piece upset her. I wondered if the critical distance of writing about her rather than *to* her felt like a boundary erected between us. She said the writing had made her feel betrayed and exposed, and she articulated that reaction as a kind of abandonment, as if I'd left her by removing too much of my own subjectivity. "Where are you in this, Leslie?" she wrote. "It does not even sound like your voice." Apologizing a few months later, she said: "It was my own inability to handle the intensity of your gaze, and the naked truth."

I have spent much of my life as a writer chasing poet C. D. Wright's suggestion that we try to see people "as they elect to be seen, in their larger selves." But it's an impossible dream. Making art about other people always means seeing them as *you* see them, rather than mirroring the way they would elect to be seen. And yet I felt defensive of Annie. In the face of the ways others might dismiss her obsessiveness as pathology or excess, I felt protective of her relentless drive toward connection and her compulsion to make herself vulnerable, to communicate fully, to say *everything*, to document everything, to capture every nuance, every complexity. At a certain point, I started to suspect that my ongoing obsession with Annie's obsession stemmed partially from a savior complex of my own—my attempt to defend an outsider artist who was almost stubbornly uncool in her methods and her affect, who was gloriously unrestrained and sentimental, who didn't apologize for being earnest. Sometimes the relationship between artist and subject can get messy and overwhelming. Agee knew it, and so did Annie, and so did I.

Annie's impulse to keep expanding her project plays out a certain fantasy I've felt in my own work: to put no boundaries around my evocation of my subjects, to make them infinite, to let them keep going forever. Representing people always involves reducing them, and calling a project "done" involves making an uneasy truce with that reduction. But some part of me rails against that compression. Some part of me wants to keep saying: *there's more, there's more, there's more.* It's why I often write ten thousand more words than I was assigned.

It's back to the Borges problem: in order to do justice to the world, the map has to reproduce the world in its entirety. But does more of a thing always make it truer? If the average length of a photographic exposure is one-sixtieth of a second, Spencer observed, that means Annie has cumulatively captured only about six minutes of her subjects' lives. But the force of Annie's work isn't the achievement of a complete gaze. It's the yearning for completion. Her work succeeds most fully not as a comprehensive account of a family but as an account of her longing to know them—as a testimony, more broadly, to the human desire to witness other people.

There is something contagious about her obsession. It has certainly infected me—her sense that no account can ever be complete, or *enough*. If Annie feels it about María and her family, then I've come to feel it about her. Her appetite has started to seem ecstatic, her drive toward connection almost Whitmanesque: a generative superpower. And I'm convinced that the fulfillment of her longing would only take away the engine of her art.

Carmelita and Diego, 2017

*   *   *

E very time I hear from Annie, she tells me that the Mexico project has gotten larger: another trip, another set of photographs, another series of entries in her ever-expanding diary. In recent years many of these trips have involved visiting María's brother Guillermo and his family in the various American cities where they have lived, and on each trip she plunges right into the grain of their lives: going to church with Guillermo to pray he won't get deported, helping Gloria straighten out a tax reimbursement, listening to their daughter tell stories about her Tinker Bell doll and to their son talk about wanting to go to medical school because he has been so deeply affected by his younger sister's lung disease. Even though Annie initially decided it wouldn't be wise to give Guillermo her home address, she eventually ended up not only giving him her address but inviting him to visit her in San Pedro.

When I called Guillermo to ask him directly about his relationship with Annie, I reached him in the midst of work. He'd just purchased a van to start up a portable mechanic's shop and was headed to a junkyard to pick up an engine. He could still remember the first time he'd met Annie, back in the early '90s, when he'd come home to find a stranger standing outside his house, taking photographs, and had no idea what she was doing there. He hadn't seen a lot of Americans. The first thing he ever said to her was "Someday, I'm going to get to your country."

Now that Guillermo was here, he still insisted that—even under Trump—it was a better life for his children. "We are a little bit afraid," he told me, and then I heard Gloria say something in the background, and he corrected himself: "We are a lot afraid." Whenever he left the house, he said, Gloria would make the sign of the cross for his safety, and he would tell her, "If I don't come back, you'll know why."

When I asked Guillermo how his relationship with Annie had

evolved over the years, he paused for so long I wondered if the connection had dropped. But eventually he said, "I think...too much," and I realized he was struggling to describe a relationship that felt so encompassing. Annie had photographed his entire life. "When I don't remember something about my life," he told me, "I ask Annie, because she has probably photographed it."

On her visits, he explained, she was constantly taking photographs. "When we are eating, she photographs us eating. When we are working, she photographs us working. All the time. All the moments." He could look at her photographs and see his children as infants, or himself as a child, living in poverty in San Martín. When he was just a teenager, Annie gave him the money he needed to move away from his hometown. She had always been there for him to talk to. She had always told him he would be able to live his dreams. As we spoke, I kept waiting for darker notes to creep into his voice—for any suggestion that perhaps sometimes he felt invaded by Annie's attention, or betrayed by it. But I never heard those notes. Those were simply the tensions I'd conjured when I'd imagined the narrative for myself.

When I asked Guillermo what single thing he would want someone to know about Annie and her relationship with his family, he said: "She is a good person." And then: "She is my sister." Not *like*, but *is*. And to his kids, she is *Tía Anita*. *Tía Anita*. He didn't say it once, but several times. He wanted me to understand.

Annie calls her work a form of love, and considers love a form of focused attention. In the academic programs where I've studied and taught, where bromides are kryptonite and emotion is expected to footnote its own presence, it is always risky to use the word *love* without cautionary quotes. But that's part of why I keep coming back to Annie: there's no room for scare quotes in how she speaks. She owns the heart in her work. It's another kind of transgression.

And if Annie's work is fueled by love, then it's a form of love that doesn't blunt or distort her gaze. Her love sharpens her sight. Her work has helped me trust that an enduring emotional investment—even in all its mess and mistakes, *because* of its mess and mistakes—can help you see more acutely. It can sensitize your gaze to the competing vectors of emotion churning beneath ordinary moments: the particular angle of a woman's body over her laundry; a father's bewilderment as he stares down at his crying daughter; the posture of a man at the doorway of his new home, grinning as he holds his tired son, right before carrying him across the threshold.

When I look at Annie's early proof sheets, from her first visits to Baja, I see some version of what she saw then: a mother with her infant, a father with his encyclopedias and his tequila bottles and his towering stacks of bricks. But I also see the long shadows cast by everything that hasn't happened yet: years of day jobs and rejected grant applications and ruptured love affairs; fights with mothers and unexpected pregnancies; addictions and fires and bus rides to new lives. I see the lurking horizons of a project that would keep leaving Annie humbled, more confused than when she'd begun. After nine years: *I understand nothing*. In those early negatives, I see cornflakes and cigarettes and stubborn wind and sudden laughter. I see everything the photos knew alongside everything they didn't know yet, and this unknowing is one more definition of love: committing to a story you can't fully imagine when it begins.

— III —

DWELLING

Rehearsals

Weddings are holiness and booze, sweat under the dress, sweet icing in the mouth. A whaler's church in the afternoon, sunlit and salted, gives way to the drunken splendor of a barn, and an entire island is suddenly *yours*, yours and everyone's. You feel the lift of wine in you, you feel the lift of wine in everyone, and you're all in agreement—not to believe in love, but to want to. This, you can do. You dance with a stranger and think, *We have this in common, this wanting to believe.* In what, again? In the possibility that two people could actually make each other happy, not just today but on ten thousand days they can't yet see.

Weddings are hassle. Hassle is spending money you don't have to celebrate the lives of people who have more money than you do. Hassle is finding yourself booked on a round-trip flight, Boston to Tulsa, and wondering, *How did this happen?* Hassle is driving to an Oklahoma conference center in the middle of the night. Hassle is getting stuck in traffic on the Brooklyn Bridge and listening to your friend's boyfriend talk about getting his pilot's license. Hassle is taking the PATH train to Hoboken at two in the morning, shoulder to shoulder with the drunkest bridge-and-tunnel crowd, thinking, *"Bridge-and-tunnel" is such a demeaning phrase*, and also, *These people are really drunk!* Weddings are taking a plane, a train, a bus, a ferry, and then setting down your bulky backpack in a little internet café to check your email and finding a note from your new boyfriend saying he just talked about you with his father for the first time. This makes the wedding ahead feel swollen with possibility. You're someone who might someday be loved. You're in the game.

Weddings are getting dropped at a post office on a dusty road in the middle of the Catskills and waiting for a ride to the lodge. There's always a lodge. There's always cocktail hour at the lodge, and group activities at the lodge, and a hurried hunt for a bridesmaid's missing shoes at the lodge. We go distances to celebrate the love of people we love, but sometimes it hurts the heart to stand alone on an empty road and think, *What am I doing here?*

Everyone talks about weddings as beginnings but the truth is they are also endings. They give a horizon of closure to things that have been slowly dissolving for years: flirtations, friendships, shared innocence, shared rootlessness, shared loneliness.

Weddings are about being single and wondering about being in love, and being in love and wondering about being in love—what it's like for other people, and whether it hurts as much as it sometimes does for you. At every wedding, all of a sudden, all bets are off and everyone is asking when your boyfriend is planning to propose, and you are watching your boyfriend talk to the girl at the cheese table, and the wine in you wants to fight, and the wine in you thinks, *You will never love me like I need you to.*

You thought you knew drunk crying before you went to weddings. You'd gotten tipsy on cheap wine in the middle of the afternoon, alone, and cried rereading emails ex-boyfriends sent before they were ex-boyfriends. But you didn't know this kind of drunk crying: alone in the bathroom at your brother's wedding, or your other brother's wedding. And you couldn't even explain it properly, because you were happy for them, you were, but you were also feeling something else, only you'd gotten too drunk to remember what it was. You learned there was a kind of crying that was okay, and another kind of crying that wasn't—a violent, angry crying—and without quite noticing, you'd crossed from one to the other.

Sometimes the best weddings are the weddings of strangers. You are only a date. No particular feelings are required. You cry as a groom remembers his mother, who died of cancer years earlier, and even though you've never met this guy, he'd once been in a band with your boyfriend, you can see the way he looks at his wife, and you think his mother must have loved him well. When you step outside the barn, it's sunset in early June and there are fields of something under the light, and you think of that Sting song, the one you were always embarrassed to love, except maybe it's not embarrassing to love it here. You have a little quiche in your palm, and you feel your boyfriend's arms wrap around you from behind—he has only one suit, you know its crispness well—and this moment might be a little too sweet, like wedding cake, but it's yours. You summon your most primal, shameful dreams—for some kind of life you learned to love in magazines—and feed them tiny quiches, these dreams, and hope that these will be enough.

You wonder what they feel, people who get married, at the precise moment they commit to their vows. Is it only bliss, or also fear? You hope for fear. Because mostly you can't imagine feeling anything else. Except when you can summon the edge of a man's suit against your back, familiar, his hand on your arm, his voice in your ear.

By *you*, of course, I mean *I*. I wonder about fear. I don't want to be afraid.

At thirteen I took a flight from Los Angeles to San Francisco and wondered what my father loved in the woman he was about to marry, and what he'd loved in my mother, and if there was anything he *still* loved in my mother, and how these circles might overlap, if laid across one another. At the airport my mother hugged me and tried her best to pretend she didn't feel betrayed that I'd chosen to go, that she wasn't buckling under the weight of thirty years ending. Or maybe she was going to buckle once I left. I could see it. I took it with me.

At the wedding I cried what my mother hadn't cried in front of me. I cried in a room full of the relatives of my father's new wife. I was that terrible stepdaughter, the one from terrible movies, *making a scene* in front of everyone. I sat in the corner of a dim banquet hall and my brothers patted me on the back so I wouldn't feel so fully out of place, so fully without an anchor. They didn't have wives yet then. I didn't want anyone to look at me. That was part of why I started crying even harder, which of course must have seemed like just the opposite: a plea for everyone's attention.

When my parents first separated, my father had moved into a dark apartment in a corporate-looking building facing a grove of eucalyptus trees. I remember he got an ice-cream maker so we could make ice cream together. I remember the ice cream tasted like ice crystals. I remember finding a photograph of a beautiful woman with a blurry face on his dresser. I remember thinking the whole place felt incredibly lonely. I remember feeling sorry for him.

Months later, when he told me he was getting married, to a woman I hadn't yet met, I thought of the woman in the photograph and realized that his loneliness had lied to me. It wasn't his but mine, my own loneliness reflected in the cage of his new life, a space in which I felt I had no place.

When I cried at his wedding, I cried for the betrayal of that dim apartment—how I'd imagined him lonely when in fact he was happy, and how my sympathy had made a fool of me in the end.

The Long Trick

When my grandfather died, I lost a man I'd never really known. I was nearly thirty and I'd seen him maybe three times in my life. He existed mainly as legend: a drunk and a pilot. He was a colonel in the Air Force, stationed in Brazil during World War II, and for the rest of his life he claimed that country as a second home: bought a tract of land in the jungle, off the grid, and eventually got sober in Natal. He raised my father and my two aunts before he quit drinking and started taking lithium; after doing these things he got married again and had two more daughters. Over the years, I came to realize he'd been a very different father to them.

When I was young, my father used to tell me stories about going to the airfield with his dad when he was a boy. He loved watching Marshall inspect his plane, circling the tires and checking the glass canopy for cracks. These stories didn't make me feel close to my grandfather so much as they made me feel close to my father. They brought me into his awe. Once, I asked my dad if he'd been proud that his dad knew how to fly a plane. He was quick to specify: not just a *plane*, a bomber jet. That meant yes, he'd been proud. That meant he still was.

His voice got soft when he spoke about the way Marshall held his helmet case like a briefcase in his hand, like any regular businessman going to work, except his office was an airfield, and his business was in the sky.

My father never learned to fly a plane, but he spent a lot of time in flight. For my whole childhood, his work took him all over the world. The casual ease with which he mentioned a round-trip to Beijing was thrilling, his voice gravelly with authority and elusiveness, his presence electrified by the fact that he always had commitments elsewhere. His passport was a patchwork of entry stamps and visas. He always had to order extra pages.

I grew up worshipping the men in my family, my father and my two older brothers, but once I turned nine, they all started leaving. My brothers went to college. My father moved across the country for work. I don't remember being angry about it. He was gone so often anyway. I knew his work was important, but I didn't know why. I didn't know why my parents got divorced when he got back. I didn't get angry about that either. Instead, I got angry that my middle brother, Eliot, went to college, two years after Julian, my oldest. These ordinary departures carried the full weight of betrayal. They made me realize I wasn't as central to their lives as they were to mine.

The house was very quiet in those days. It was just me and my mother. A few months into Eliot's freshman year, I made a drawing on our computer, using an early-'90s graphics program that made everything look like an Etch A Sketch. It was a self-portrait of me sitting on his bed with big fist-sized teardrops pasted under my eyes. I called it *Jealous Sorrow*.

I used to call Eliot in his faraway dorm room and refuse to get off the phone until he told me he loved me. *I love you,* I'd say. *I love you I love you I love you.* I'd say it until he said it back. Sometimes he did. Sometimes he didn't. Sometimes there was just silence. I felt so wronged. Really, of course, I felt wronged by my father. Really, of course, pleading to that quiet line, I was talking to my father.

Before my brothers were gone, and before my father was gone, my grandfather was gone. He was the original absent man. The distance between him and my father—the fact that they saw each other so rarely—was almost never discussed. But decades later, when my grandfather was dying of cancer, my father asked me to come to the small fishing town on the Chesapeake Bay where Marshall lived with his second wife. Eliot and I sat with our father at a seafood shack about a ten-minute drive from the house where his own father was dying. He'd camped out there over a dish of crab cakes because he wanted to grant his stepmother and his half sisters their privacy. It made me sad to think my father thought he would be intruding on his own father's death.

Marshall died with his youngest grandson, just one month old, tucked into the crook of his arm. When I saw his body an hour later, still lying on the bed, he looked frail and jaundiced: a smooth wax statue, yellow face capped with a pale blue beanie, eyes partway open.

During the days after his death, life in his house felt physical and proximate: soft blankets on chairs, soup on the stove, babies crying. My father's stepmother, Linda, and his half sisters, Danica and Kelda, were gracious in their grief. They welcomed us into a home that smelled like shampoo and cooking oil and diaper cream. They read us the poem they had read to Marshall as he was dying: *I must go down to the seas again, to the vagrant gypsy life, / To the gull's way and the whale's way where the wind's like a whetted knife.* Both of my aunts had newborn sons who remained oblivious in the face of mortality: they got hungry, got gassy, got confused and amazed by every little thing. Danica told me that for days life in that house had been all about bodies: nursing her son, turning her father in bed so he wouldn't get sores, helping him get to the bathroom when he was able to walk, then changing his bedpan when he wasn't.

Eliot was reserved—he was almost always reserved—but he was comfortable holding the babies. His posture with them summoned his whole life back home: everything he had built, the kind of father he had chosen to become. Back in Vancouver, he had a wife and two young sons and a split-level house and a job in infrastructure: bridges and railroads and highways. Nothing in the air. He hit suburban playgrounds on weekends. He wasn't afraid of presence. That's what I told myself back then. Now I think maybe he was afraid of presence, just like the rest of us, and kept showing up anyway. He carried a briefcase but it held no helmet. He stayed on land.

On the other side of the continent, in Connecticut, I was smoking cigarettes on my stoop and feeling sorry for myself by replaying arguments I'd had with my boyfriend before we broke up. At the tail end of my twenties, newly sober and newly single and still regularly commuting to other people's weddings, I had just broken the lease on the apartment I'd shared with my ex and moved into a one-room studio with a fridge full of seltzer water and a dryer whose indoor vent laced the humid air with tiny particles. It always smelled like mint from the extract I'd sprinkled everywhere to repel the mice that kept coming back anyway. The loneliness of that apartment seemed like apt punishment for fleeing my relationship instead of working on it harder—for being fickle, unstable, and uncertain; for being needy but unable to reciprocate the love I needed. My mother wanted me to have children, and some part of me wanted that also—a part of me buried deep beneath the fear of being constantly accountable to another person.

It was bracing to show up at this old wooden house in Virginia where two people had been married for decades, settled here in a little fishing town at the tip of a peninsula. The local catch was Atlantic menhaden, which was not a kind of fish that people ate but a kind of fish that people ground into chicken feed. The local processing plant was called Omega Protein. Eliot had learned all this on Wikipedia. We joked about the name *Omega Protein*. It sounded sinister. But it moved me, somehow, that Eliot had gone to the trouble of looking up this town. He wanted to know something about this place besides *someone died here.* I got that. I wanted to know something about my grandfather that wasn't about his death, or the mythology of his life. And it wasn't just him I wanted to know better, but also the traces of him left in the men of my family. His ghost seemed like a way of understanding those parts of them that had always been mysterious and opaque—that had always felt far away, even when they were right in front of me.

The Portuguese word *saudade* is infamously untranslatable, but I've always loved how it describes something more mysterious than sheer nostalgia. It's a longing not for what you've lost but for what you've never had. It's something like homesickness, but it could mean homesick for a place you've never been. It's at home in Brazil, where Marshall went when he wasn't with his family. It usually takes a grammatical construction that suggests possession or company: you have *saudades*, or you can be with them. As if longing could become a kind of company. As if it could compensate for absence itself. *Saudade* is a name for the ache I feel when I conjure that image of my father and his father on the airfield: a little boy in awe of the sky-bound pilot kneeling next to him, eager to help him check the cockpit for cracks. I miss that airfield, even though I've never been there. It's a memory that pulses inside me, even though it's not mine. It glows with my desire to know the man and boy who live inside it.

*   *   *

When I was six years old and couldn't fall asleep at night, Eliot started to sleep on my empty bottom bunk. We called it sleep insurance. It helped just to know that his body was in the darkened room with mine.

I can't remember a time when I wasn't obsessed with Eliot's life. He told me so little about it. I kept his senior-prom photo framed on my bureau for years, his date in a gold lace dress with gold pumps. (This was 1992.) It was endlessly fascinating to me, the question of what kind of woman he found beautiful. Bruce Springsteen was his favorite singer, so I listened to "Human Touch" on repeat for clues about his inner life. (It wasn't until years later that I realized it *might* not be his favorite song.) He played on the varsity tennis team and I loved to watch him practice with his doubles partner, Amir, while I called out commentary from the sidelines. "Eliot rips a winner down the line!" I'd say, or, "Amir slaps another unforced error into the net!" I remember Amir asking, "Is she going to do this all day?" I left his actual tennis matches with my palms covered in red crescents from where I'd dug my nails into the skin from game-point nerves.

My mom once told me that when I was a baby, Eliot often cried when I cried. He was nine years old. He couldn't calm down until I did. As an adult, he'd come to keep his feelings studiously private, as if he'd already done all the crying he planned to do in his lifetime. But I needed to remember: he had once cried for me. It was proof that I had the power to move him.

When my parents fell in love, my father was already engaged to another woman. He and my mother were working together in Brazil—a research project my grandfather had put together, focused on rural education—and my childhood vision of their affair gleamed with the luster of myth: kissing on rugged Brazilian beaches, swimming in the wild, frothing Atlantic. I even loved the part of the story about my father's fiancée getting so angry she threw the birthday cake she'd baked for him in his face. When I was a kid, I focused on Brazilian beaches because it was easier to imagine those postcard vistas than it was to imagine my father's fiancée asking herself what she could have done to make him love her enough to stay. I wanted to imagine the story of my own origins as an epic passion rather than an ordinary betrayal. In truth, of course, it was both. I identified with my mother in the story, because she was my mother. But for years I would be the one wondering—with my father, my brothers, my boyfriends— *What can I do to make him love me more?*

For a long time, I was angry at my father for his restlessness, his absences, and his countless infidelities. But by the time Marshall died, I'd begun to acknowledge how many similarities existed between us. We both liked our work. We both liked our wine. I was not entirely unlike him in what I sought from the world—what I felt I was owed, or didn't owe anyone. I had always sworn I wouldn't repeat the mistakes that had run roughshod over my family, but I found myself more than capable of cheating on boyfriends—there I was, the first time, mouth tasting like cigarettes and orange soda and liquor, waking up next to an Irish guy who had just ridden his motorcycle all the way across Latin America. It was almost liberating that I could no longer judge my father for all the times he'd done something like this too. It's not that seeing yourself becoming your parents doesn't mean you can't still be angry at them. In fact, it can make you even angrier. *You made me this way!* But it nagged at my judgment like a hair caught on the back of my tongue.

If I spent my twenties becoming more like my father, Eliot had already spent his twenties becoming his opposite: a committed monogamist with a career in investment banking and designs on a house with a white-picket fence. I saw Eliot's identity as an inverted inheritance—this desire to become the things his father had not been.

A month before Eliot's wedding—when he was in his early thirties, and I was in my early twenties—we had a conversation about relationships, one of the most revealing talks we'd ever had. I told him my white-room theory: I wanted to find a guy with whom I could spend three days in an empty white room and not get bored. I'd just ended a relationship in the way I had begun to end relationships, the way I would keep ending relationships: getting out once I got bored. Once I wanted out of the white room. My invitation to Eliot's wedding had my ex-boyfriend's name on it, because we'd been together when it was sent, but I was going to the wedding alone—and *proud* of going alone—because going alone meant I wasn't settling, and I thought settling was one of the worst things that could happen to a human being.

That day we talked, before Eliot's wedding, I asked him what he wanted. Why was he marrying the woman he was marrying? He said they had similar visions for the life they wanted to build; they had compatible values and like-minded approaches to practical things like finances. When I was twenty-one, that sounded like the opposite of romance: *similar visions for the life we wanted to build*. Looking back, at thirty-five, it seems like everything.

They had their wedding in Yosemite, and I ended up delaying the ceremony by half an hour because my bridesmaid's corset tore as I was zipping it up. My future sister-in-law was gracious. We'd fix it, she said. And we did. Another bridesmaid was a seamstress; I was literally sewn into my outfit. Even though I told everyone I was mortified at delaying the ceremony, secretly I was a little proud. I was a force for chaos, for disruption, for whatever the opposite of settling was. I was unsettled, hard to contain, recently single, breaking seams.

In truth, the ceremony was beautiful. I remember seeing how happy my brother looked, and my sister-in-law; realizing how little I knew of other people's hearts, how little I knew of my own. At their reception they served apple pies instead of wedding cake because they both preferred pie. Another shared vision. When I cried that night, brimming with vodka and chardonnay, I kept mentioning my ex's name in conversation just so everyone would know that coming alone was a choice I'd made. I used the toe of my sparkly party shoes to grind cigarette butts into the redwood planks of a deck that overlooked rippling green meadows gone dusky in the twilight. It was so beautiful. I was so drunk.

Back then, life existed most forcefully for me in evenings like those: bleary nights when I confronted the difficulty of love—my broken heart! my ex's broken heart!—and felt existentially alone, and drank enough Absolut to tell everyone I was feeling that way. But as the years unfolded, life started to seem less like something that crystallized in these cinematic moments—weeping in bathrooms, or gesticulating with a glowing cigarette tip against the backdrop of a darkening summer sky—and more like something that accumulated across broad swaths of ordinary days: morning commutes, school pickups, the heat of my little nephews' bodies pressed against mine on couches, listening to *The Lorax*, asking for apple pie instead of cake on their birthdays.

A few years after his wedding, I asked Eliot to lend me enough money so I could take a two-month trip to Bolivia. He said no. "I have enough money for the trip," I explained helpfully. "I just need money to pay rent when I get back." He still said no. I felt judged, I told him. He said that I shouldn't ask for a favor unless I was okay with hearing *no*. I started crying—*I'm sad at you*, I used to say to my brothers when I was young—because some part of me knew he was right. It wasn't needing the money that made me cry so much as the thought that I had disappointed him. I'd spent so much of my life straining toward his praise like a houseplant leaning into sunlight, begging for something from that voice on the other end of the line—not just love, but the assurance that I deserved it.

* * *

When Marshall was dying, nearly two decades after my parents had divorced, my mother wrote him a card that she asked me to read over his body. "Thank you thank you thank you thank you," she wrote—one thanks for my father, and one for each of the children they'd had together. Her words created a solid surface around the hollowness in me where grief should have been. "I've always admired your willingness to dream big dreams," she wrote. His body on the bed seemed so unbelievably small. I touched his arm and held his hand, but could not bring myself to touch his face.

Beneath my feet, his basement was full of the detritus of his ongoing projects, their uneasy marriage of mania and brilliance: a library of sandpaper so he could make his own nail files, index cards scribbled with to-do lists, *Send Israel-Palestine Resolution to Senator Warner; Finish Afghanistan Exit Plan.* He could make you see the wonder in anything, my aunts told me, even a little bug or a weed. The poem they read to him as he was dying—with its gull's way, its whale's way—didn't end with the whetted knife of wind or the vagrant gypsy life. It ended with rest: *And all I ask is a merry yarn from a laughing, fellow-rover, / And quiet sleep and a sweet dream when the long trick's over.*

The day after he died, I made brunch for everyone, fried oysters, palming the glistening ovals of muscle and crusting them with bread crumbs, willing them to become something edible. I wanted to be useful. I wanted to feed the bereaved. I'd bought these oysters from a gas station near Rappahannock, where the man behind the counter sold me a glass jar full of their slippery bodies and then announced to me, for no apparent reason, that he wanted a root beer and a moon pie. The world seemed full of desires that couldn't always be explained, but could sometimes—in surprising ways—be met.

Over oily breaded oysters, Kelda told us Marshall had always talked easily about the early years of his life—his childhood, his service in the Air Force—but there were thirty years he rarely spoke about at all: the years of raising his first family. When my father heard that, his face showed no expression. Later that day, when I saw an empty wine bottle in his hotel room, I thought of his face at the table. What lay behind it? His empty bottle summoned all the empty wine bottles that I'd dumped in neighbors' recycling bins during the months my grandmother was dying, many decades after she and Marshall had divorced, when I was living in her home and caring for her imperfectly, as best I could. My grandfather was the only other person in my family who'd ever gotten sober, but I didn't know anything about what sobriety had been like for him. Had he also drunk seltzer water straight from the bottle? Had he also spent days in an apartment that smelled like too much toothpaste, remembering his bungled love affairs? Probably not. He'd had his own, worse journeys.

Among other things, sobriety was teaching me that I loved nothing better than telling inflated stories about my own ordinary dysfunction. And maybe I'd corralled the men in my family into another one of these tales: the story of a little girl yearning for elusive men—the pilot, the frequent flier, the silent voice at the other end of the line—whose bodies and attention were often directed somewhere else. But the story was more complicated than that. Because at some point I'd developed an attachment to the state of yearning itself. I no longer desired presence; in fact, I often had no idea what to do with men when they stuck around. It was like staying at my father's apartment for a single night after months away from him. Everything was uncomfortable. There was no food for my school lunch, only chardonnay in the fridge. I just wanted to go home. It was easier to miss him than to have him close.

It was years before I discovered the second definition of the word *saudade*. In this meaning, *saudade* doesn't describe longing for any particular object, but longing for that very state of yearning. As critic

F. D. Santos writes: "It is no more the Loved One or the 'Return' that is desired. Now, Desire desires Desire itself." This kind of desire doesn't know what to do with being met. It has trouble with the proximity of white rooms. It can't see the ways in which elusive men sometimes show up. It has trouble fitting their presence into the frame.

The truth is, the elusive men in my family also showed up plenty of times. Marshall built a second family and loved his daughters well. Sometimes he escaped to Brazil, and sometimes he escaped to his basement projects, but through it all he built a thirty-year life in an old wooden house by the Chesapeake Bay. My father was often gone, but there were plenty of times he was there—making me ramen and popcorn for dinner when my mom was out of town, or waiting in the hospital cafeteria during my heart surgery, years later. If I was attached to stories about my restless father and his restless father, then maybe once my grandfather died I could let him live as something more than myth, more than godhead; and maybe I could let my father live as something more complicated and contradictory as well, which is to say: devoted, imperfect, trying his best. Maybe I could start to see that while I had been longing for him, he'd been longing for me as well.

Two days after our grandfather died, Eliot and I woke up early to go running in the rain. "I love running in the rain," I told him, even though I didn't. I just wanted to be a person who loved running in the rain: stoic, unflappable. Eliot asked if I had a rain jacket. I didn't. He gave me his. I got soaked anyway. We both did. He got more so. Our shoes slapped sodden on the dirt road and brown grass, then on the asphalt two-lane highway, past wooden farmhouses. I resolved to run until Eliot suggested we turn around, which meant we kept going. Eliot regularly ran marathons. I'd already traded my running regimen for a smoking habit. Once we got back to the house where we were staying,

I asked Eliot how far he thought we'd gone. He guessed four miles and I guessed seven. It's always been this way: He undersells himself and stays in it for the long haul. I want credit and tire easily.

Before we got back, however, before we even turned around, we followed the highway turnoff for Omega Protein. We followed asphalt through the trees until we spied the plant itself: a collection of squat towers—huge boiling vats, probably—and a posse of forklift trucks, a few rusted boats. "What if we were spies from a rival fish-processing plant?" I asked him. "How would we take this place down?" We speculated about angles of approach, scaling chain-link fences, spoiling tanks of fish with something rotten. I have always liked laughing with Eliot because the way we laugh remains somehow untouched by the differences between the lives we've built. Eliot was one of the first people in the world I ever found hilarious.

We passed a tiny airfield at the edge of the Omega complex. It was patchy with grass and soggy with rain. It wasn't a mythic airstrip. It was more like an abandoned soccer field. It insisted on the muddy ground more than it suggested the possibility of leaving it behind. Who knew who flew there, or why? It was a field where fish were ferried to the sky in boneless lumps; where men who would someday be grandfathers did things they would someday tell their grandchildren about: carried brief-cases full of Atlantic menhaden or documents they would or wouldn't send to congressmen, documents that would or wouldn't save the world. The world would keep on needing saving. We kept on running. The sky kept on raining. We knew the sky would keep pulling men into the clouds and sending them back underground. We knew that life was a long trick that ended with a dream; living was a gull and a whale and a whetted knife of wind.

Everyone had always told me about Marshall and the sky. It was the perfect metaphor: he was a restless pilot. But on that day, the sky felt too easy. It turned everything weightless. It felt more honest to stare at a closed place below it: the patchy grass surrounded by a chain-link fence, at the fish plant, in the rain.

Each time I try to write an elegy for my grandfather, it ends up becoming a thank-you letter to my brother instead. I want to tell him: Thank you for having sons in fleece pajamas. Thank you for being a good father, and for refusing me that loan—or at least thank you for telling me I needed to be okay with it. Thank you for staying married and not needing your marriage to be a white room in which you're always entertained. Thank you for showing me that settling was just a story I told myself about other people's lives. Thank you for crying when I cried, when you were young and I was younger, and for understanding why I didn't cry at our grandfather's deathbed. Thank you for giving me your rain jacket and your prom photo and your apple pies, and for sleeping in a bed below my bed, years ago, when I didn't know how to get through the night.

The Real Smoke

Two years into sobriety, I found myself ordering a mocktail at the heart of the Vegas Strip. This was in a three-story cocktail lounge enclosed by a giant chandelier made from two million crystal beads, their sparkling curtains wrapped around a secret place called Level 1.5, where you could order real drinks with names like the Forbidden Fruit and the Infinite Playlist. I got something that tasted like raspberry sherbet. It came in a cosmopolitan glass with coarse sugar crystals around the rim.

I'd been flown out to give a reading at a writing program in town. It was one of the first times I'd ever been flown anywhere; even the syntax felt glamorous, thrillingly passive. It seemed like proof of being wanted, though it had brought me to a city that was all about degrading yourself by wanting too much, too rashly, without any hope of getting even a fraction of what you'd fantasized. Back in New Haven, I'd been reeling from the end of a four-year relationship that I still felt constituted by. My life with Dave had cut right to the core of me and burrowed there. It wouldn't give up residence for a long time. I could say I didn't know that then, but I did. I knew. Every time I said something to anyone, I was still trying to say it to him.

After my reading, my hosts said they wanted to take me to the Strip. We were all young, none of us tired, all of us buzzed on the prospect of having an ironic experience of the city's relentless pageantry. My hosts were grad students who said they never went to the Strip unless they were taking someone from out of town, except for one woman who worked there as a cocktail waitress to supplement her financial aid.

On nights like that one, sobriety still felt like deprivation. With strangers, drinking had always been the way I'd let the night unravel into something we couldn't see the edges of. Without it, I was stuck inside a container with visible boundaries. Now I was stuck inside a three-story chandelier. When someone suggested getting a mocktail, I recoiled. I had no interest in the simulated version of the actual experience of getting drunk. But then I thought, Why not? The most authentic Vegas experience was simulated experience anyway.

As it turned out, my mocktail tasted great. I was drinking juice in the land of two million crystal beads. The night was just getting started. We went to a secret pizza joint hidden behind the slot machines, deep in the interior of the interior, far from any windows or clocks. We went to a humid greenhouse where golden trees sprouted golden coins from their branches. Red lanterns flickered in the shadows. The snails were made of roses. We passed an electronic billboard that said WE RESPECT YOUR OPINION OF ASPARAGUS BUT DISAGREE WITH IT and then HAVE A SAFE TRIP HOME! But we weren't going home. We were going to the Bellagio fountains. We watched the water dance to an instrumental version of the *Titanic* theme song. Those illuminated surging plumes stirred the part of me—deep inside—that wanted to find beauty in what other people found absurd.

One of my hosts, a man named Joe—handsome in his hipster jeans, with curly blond hair and a perpetually wry, bemused expression on his face—asked if there was anything else I wanted to see. There *was* something, I told him. I wanted to buy a onesie. It was for one of my best friends, who was about to have a baby. She was possibly the classiest woman I knew. She had an elegant West Village apartment, an elegant dog, and an elegant chef husband who made elegant farm-to-table food. I wanted to buy her the tackiest onesie I could find.

"I know a place," Joe said, and took me to the biggest souvenir shop in the world. It was closed. Nothing was supposed to be closed. He said, "I know another place." It didn't have what we were looking for. He said, "This isn't done."

It turned out the only thing better than finding the onesie was not finding the onesie, because then we got to keep looking. It felt good to cruise the mild winter night in Joe's Jeep, to see the neon blurring and dazzling around us, dispensing enchantment like an IV drip. You got it in your bloodstream and things started to hum. This night felt more like the first night I'd done cocaine than anything had since.

We cruised the clutch of all-night wedding chapels that connected the Strip to downtown. We passed the Chapel of the Flowers, the Chapel of the Bells, Graceland Wedding Chapel, and A Wee Kirk o' the Heather, as well as the grande dame, with its humble name: A Little White Chapel, where Frank Sinatra and Michael Jordan and Rita Hayworth had each gotten hitched, all their ghosts sheltered under a towering Elvis in a gold lamé suit who promised, in cursive, *with love.* It was where Britney Spears had married her best friend at three in the morning, in a rented lime-green limo. "They were laughing, but crying, too," said the chapel's owner. "I thought it was a marriage that would last forever." They signed annulment papers the following afternoon. Reality was like that here: You ordered what you wanted, and then if you didn't want it anymore, you returned it. You could switch from Paris to Venice, from Luxor to New York, from the circus to the castle. These were the fruits of restlessness, the capitalist gospel of choice. You could get married. Then you could take it back.

Joe took me to the swimming pool at the Golden Nugget, where an enclosed glass waterslide curved through a massive aquarium full of ancient-bodied sharks circling their kingdom, cool as you please. We flirted beside the sharks, in the hotel corridors, in the parking lot. If the sensation of flirting were an interior landscape, it would be a cavern lit up like Vegas at night—flickering with possibility, sizzling like moths against neon.

We ended up finding our onesie on Fremont Street, in the shadow of forty-foot Vegas Vic, who smoked a neon cigarette between his neon lips. Once upon a time, that giant glowing cigarette had sent up actual puffs of smoke. Now Fremont Street had become the Fremont Street Experience: a pedestrian walkway covered by the massive canopy of a curving LED screen. This felt like a natural extension of the logic of the casinos, which kept you far away from windows—away from the rhythms of day and night, the vast otherness of sky. Now the sky had been banished completely. Strangers screamed above us on zip lines.

For the first time since the end of Dave, I was feeling the glimmering suggestion of what it might be like to fall in love with someone else. This feeling of anticipation was quite different from actually falling in love. It was arguably even better. Nothing was really at stake. It was more like opening a window without having to go outside and face the sky. I spent the ride home wondering if Joe would kiss me when we pulled up to my hotel in his Jeep. It was like being sixteen again. He didn't kiss me, but I knew—from the particular way he hadn't, from his pause—that someday he would.

In 1968 the Yale School of Architecture offered a seminar called the "Learning from Las Vegas Research Studio." The professors who designed it, Denise Scott Brown and Robert Venturi, believed that architecture had become too "socially coercive," imposing taste rather than responding to it, and they believed the Las Vegas Strip pushed back against this coercion as the "purest and most intense" manifestation of consumer desires. Their course centered on a ten-day trip to Vegas devoted to "open-minded and nonjudgmental investigation," seeking those truths that might dwell in the urban forms that other architects regarded with disdain.

It was an unusual venture: a couple of Yale professors and their students showing up on the Strip, freshly sprung from the Brutalist concrete palace of their architecture school back in New Haven. They stayed in free rooms at the Stardust. They got an invitation to the gala opening of the Circus Circus casino, where they showed up in Day-Glo castoffs from a local Salvation Army. After they asked for local funding, one headline read: "Yale Professor Will Praise Strip for $8,925." The implication was clear: these diplomats from the land of the highbrow would not deign to praise the lowbrow for free. But Venturi and Scott Brown didn't believe the highbrow and the lowbrow were separate. They wanted to put "A&P parking lot" and "Versailles" in the same sentence. They wanted them to share a lineage. Midway through the semester, the students started calling their course "The Great Proletarian Cultural Locomotive."

Decades later, I shared their impulse to frame Vegas as an underdog in the great games of taste. It's easy to call Vegas cheesy, but what is *cheesy*, anyway? Its current meaning is an ironic reversal of what it meant in the days of the British Empire, which was *fine* or *grand*, as in *the real chīz* (*chīz* being the Urdu word for *thing*). Now it means something inauthentic and unsubtle, something that tries too hard. All of Vegas tries too hard. But is it inauthentic? I've never thought so. If inauthenticity depends on pretending you are something you're not, then Vegas has always been adamantly honest. It is all fake, all the time.

Vegas gets it. There's no escape from artifice. You can pretend you aren't performing, or you can admit you're performing, but either way you are always performing.

"Let me confess my preference for the real fakery of Las Vegas over the fake reality of Santa Fe," writes art critic Dave Hickey. "For the genuine rhinestone over the imitation pearl." That night at the Chandelier Bar, Vegas was a genuine rhinestone. It followed its fakery so far that it ended up being radically honest. Even if it was trying too hard, it wasn't trying to be something it wasn't. Sure, it was lowbrow and absurd. Sure, it was tasteless. But fuck the snobs of taste. Why disdain Vegas for openly admitting what was already true everywhere? The whole world was making promises it couldn't keep. The whole world was out to scam you. Vegas was just upfront about it. It put marquee lights around it. To me, Vegas felt like the urban-planning equivalent of the homeless man we passed whose sign said: WHY LIE? I WANT BEER.

Maybe I was just drawn to the city because I liked finding beauty in what others found ugly. My awe at the Bellagio fountains wanted to believe it was compensating for someone else's disgust. Vegas understood that any time you were somewhere, there were a thousand elsewheres you might be longing for. So it jammed them together: New York–New York, Paris, the Tropicana, the Mirage. Its glaring neon landscapes were an articulation of collective longing. It acknowledged how much of our lives we spend looking toward illusory, impossible horizons. It suggested that this longing was not delusion, but one of our central truths. It constituted us.

When I got back to my New Haven winter, Joe and I started writing to each other. We turned our lives into stories and lobbed them back and forth. He told me about breaking into the Circus Circus midway after hours and playing free Skee-Ball in its empty aisles. He told me about shattering a bunch of empty bottles by throwing them off his balcony one night. I imagined his glowing city from the middle of my Connecticut blizzards. When I told my friends about him, I started calling him Vegas Joe. This wasn't dismissal, exactly. It was more like an acknowledgment of the ways that I had already cast him as a character in the story I was trying to write about this next chapter of my life. He was the mascot of Possibility in Aftermath.

We agreed to meet in Boston, at the massive annual writers' conference that I annually dreaded attending. That year I was desperate to get there. I dug my car out of three feet of snow and fishtailed down icy highways. The swell of potential worked on me like a drug, blocking out everything else: the pelting sleet, the black ice, the road slipping under my tires. I cranked up my radio: "I'm living on such sweet nothing." Joe kept texting, "Don't die!" He texted: "When will you get here?"

We booked a room that night. Because the conference had filled the hotel, the only room left was the Presidential Suite. We got it cheap because it was already 10:00 p.m. and it wasn't occupied. It was huge, with three rooms and panoramic views of downtown Boston's glassy skyscrapers. It didn't even have a bed, because it was used exclusively for large corporate cocktail parties. It had a wet bar and sectional leather couches. We ordered a trundle bed and a bucket of seafood: crab legs, oysters, lobster tail. We didn't sleep much.

After that night we found ourselves in a state I knew well: the giddy rush of offering ourselves to each other. To start, we offered each other rough transcriptions of the ragged emotional arcs of our last long-term relationships. He wrote about driving out to a ghost town on the shores of the Salton Sea: the gutted homes full of plates, a flock of white pelicans. He wrote: "Here's to unbland wellness," a phrase I'd used in an essay about an author who'd been afraid that sobriety would make him bland for good. I wondered if I was falling in love. I wondered if I was built exclusively to fall in love. I worried, sometimes, that I was built more to *fall* in love than to *be* in love. But didn't everyone worry about that? You couldn't think your way past it. You just had to keep falling in love, over and over again, and hope that it stuck once, to prove it could.

A few weeks after getting back from Boston, I visited the Yale architecture library, looking for a book called *Every Building on the Sunset Strip*. Published in 1966 by the artist Ed Ruscha, it is an accordion style art book that unfolds to a length of twenty-five feet. As its title promises, it documents every building on the Sunset Strip between Doheny and Crescent Heights: motor inns, faux Tudor cottages, a big shed called Body Shop Burlesque, a smaller shed called Sea Witch, a café called the Plush Pup. The book had helped inspire the Yale Vegas seminar. When Venturi and Scott Brown took their students to Vegas in 1968, they drove the length of the Strip with a camera mounted on the hood of their car, just as Ruscha had done on Sunset two years earlier.

I was drawn to the premise of Ruscha's book for the same reason I'd been drawn to the premise of the Vegas seminar: both wanted to find beauty in the same bric-a-brac sprawl that others called the epitome of ugliness. This was part of my heritage. All my life I'd been told I didn't seem like a person from Los Angeles. But all my life I'd been a person from Los Angeles. The more frequently I was told I didn't seem to be from L.A., the more strongly I wanted to defend it. It was a place other people loved to call shallow or fake, but I found its strip malls and their parking lots oddly gorgeous: sunlight glimmering off gritty streets, palm trees silhouetted against smoggy sunsets.

Ruscha's book made me want to walk the Vegas Strip from north to south, four miles total, and take notes on all of it. I would find the blueprints of collective fantasy. The project started gathering the force of an ethical repo job. I'd salvage meaning from what others had called blight. But who was I kidding? I also wanted a reason to go see Vegas Joe.

I hatched a plan. A friend of mine was getting married at Zion

National Park in early July, just a three-hour drive from Vegas, and I would go out a few days early to stay with Joe and walk the Strip. Then he and I would go to her wedding together.

A few weeks before the visit, Vegas Joe told me he had bedbugs. He was trying to get rid of them by cranking his heater in 110-degree weather and opening all his windows. I knew it wouldn't work. You needed professional temperatures. But the longer his bedbug saga dragged on, the more I started to suspect he enjoyed something about the battle. Once it became clear that his bedbugs were ongoing, I booked a room for forty-nine dollars at the Flamingo. A few days before my flight, Vegas Joe sent me a photograph of his thigh with three dots of dried blood neatly aligned across his pale flesh. It was the signature trio of bedbug bites that the internet called "breakfast, lunch, and dinner." I recoiled from the image—not so much the image itself as the threshold crossing that it seemed to signify. We were no longer awestruck strangers watching a dancing fountain, or new lovers perched fifteen stories above Boston. Now we were talking about our bug infestations. His notes made me itch. It was as if his little bugs were powerful enough to reach my brick row house across the country. I was no longer sure I wanted him that close.

From the moment I stepped into Joe's Jeep, outside the baggage carousels at McCarran, I felt the whole endeavor suffocating under the weight of our expectations: four months of notes and daydreams, all built from one night by a shark tank and another spent in a skyscraper surrounded by the crystalline lights of office buildings. All that fervor had been the intimacy of two curated selves culled from the mess of two actual selves. But this was something else: the sweltering desert evening, the smell of him, the awkwardness of trying to speak to each other in his front seat after months of speaking to each other without our bodies hanging around. I tried to remember that first night in his Jeep but could access only a memory that gleamed like a sparkling awning, a night I'd already conscripted into personal mythology: *the night I knew I would survive my breakup.* As soon as I got into his car, I started wondering if it might be best for me to go to my friend's wedding alone.

We drove down Paradise Road, the street running behind the huge hotels like a desolate backyard. It had shops selling uniforms for casino dealers and costumes for strippers. It was full of the detritus that had fallen off the edges of the dream. One billboard asked: INJURED IN A HOTEL? and suggested www.injuredinahotel.com. A vasectomy ad bragged NO SCALPEL NO NEEDLE at www.ez-snip.com. At the airport, I had overheard a man telling a stranger about his battle with cancer. "They took out my bladder and made me a new one from a fifteen-inch piece of my small intestine," he'd said. "Everything works great now."

I kept imagining bedbugs in the back of the Jeep, folding their tiny bodies into the crevices of my suitcase zippers and pockets. I vaguely understood that Joe's bedbugs had become a kind of psychic stand-in for his actual and flawed humanity: all the parts of him that could not be sculpted and viewed from a comfortable distance, all the parts that were imperfect or vulnerable or struggling, trying to get his depression medications right.

He spent the night with me at the Flamingo. We lay together in a king bed that suggested certain stories—an illicit tryst between lovers, a drunken night between strangers, a wedding anniversary—but we lived another kind of story. Our bodies didn't touch at all.

* * *

W hat I saw when I finally walked the Strip: the Palazzo, the Venetian, the Mirage. Treasure Island, the Wynn, the Encore. Circus Circus. New York–New York. Mandalay Bay. Hooters in the distance. An animatronic Atlantis, drowning and rising every hour. A recovery meeting in a Riviera conference room that smelled like stale popcorn, where a man said it was tough for him to stay sober as an electronica DJ. What else? Jeff Koons's tulips with their own security guard. Signs advertising yoga with dolphins. A prize booth called the Redemption Center that I turned into my Twitter backdrop.

I saw a homeless man sitting in the triangular shade of a Catholic church who asked me what kind of God I believed in, then said he wanted to show me his scar but didn't want to give me nightmares. I saw a dad on crutches beside an aisle of carnival games, his wheelchair piled with the stuffed animals he'd won for his kids: a robot, a banana. I saw a T-shirt bearing the silhouette of a stripper that said I SUPPORT SINGLE MOMS, then overheard a mom telling her son, "We have to go to another branch of this fucking stupid-ass bank." A man exiting the Luxor, suspicious of the daylight, asked his friend: "Why are we going outside?" Beyond the casino doors, it was 110 degrees in the shade. A dry fountain eager to defend itself said DUE TO DROUGHT. Even illusion had its limits.

Vegas no longer seemed like a rhinestone unfairly victimized by highbrow snobbery. It was a machine designed to make money. Its cheesiness was the ultimate capitalist enterprise. Its profit margins came layered in curtains of crystals, millions of untenable promises: every bulb, every steak, every shark in every shark tank. Even if I admired the honesty of the homeless man whose sign told the truth—WHY LIE? I WANT BEER—I had no desire to defend the economic system that had made him homeless in the first place. But who was I to cry false consciousness on the strangers in two hundred thousand hotel rooms all around me, to say they didn't understand their own plight? What did it mean that everyone kept losing their money but believed they were having a good time?

After one of Siegfried & Roy's white tigers attacked Roy onstage at the Mirage in 2003, Roy kept telling everyone that Montecore hadn't meant him any harm. Montecore had just been trying to protect him. At first the live audience didn't know the attack had not been a planned part of the show. A ten-year-old British boy buried his face in his mother's sleeve. "I tried to tell him it would be okay and that it wasn't real, because this was supposed to be magic," she told one reporter. During the days afterward, her son kept saying: "You said it wasn't real, Mummy." In a land where everything was supposed to be fake, the arrival of reality functioned as the betrayal of a promise, an upending of the deal, a reversal of the plan.

D uring my days at the Flamingo, I woke up early each morning to work on copyedits for a book deadline. The dirty room-service dishes of strangers stayed in my hotel hallway for days, untouched: the fudge sauce–smeared remains of a brownie sundae, desolate lumps in a filmy puddle of melted ice cream. Had the people who'd ordered that sundae gotten what they wanted? I assumed everyone had been wounded by the same boom-bust cycle I'd let myself be disappointed by.

Lining up for coffee in the lobby casino at 6:30 in the morning, I stood exclusively with people who'd been up all night. The whole place smelled like coconut sunscreen and smoke. One man in line—strung out, dead tired—looked at me with pity. "Good luck," he said softly, gently touching my elbow. I took my coffee to the thick heat of the flamingo garden, where the air stank of birds and their shit. I felt so sad at the sight of a woman smoking—in such heat, so early in the morning, among flamingos—that it took me a moment to remember I was smoking, too.

While I was working on my copyedits by the hotel pool, in the blazing sun, a leathery man spotted a leathery woman across the field of plastic chaise longues. "You are a *beast!*" he yelled. "Get me a club soda." A thirteen-year-old boy wore a T-shirt down to his knees printed with two boxes marked TAKEN and SINGLE. The latter was checked. People measured the price of things in terms of blackjack hands: "I could lose that in six." At closing time, people at the pool got upset. A man threw his inflatable beach ball at a lifeguard. In a city that advertised twenty-four-hour-a-day pleasure, the next best thing to immortality, every closing time was a little death.

After he got off work, Joe took me to a fondue restaurant tucked inside the Forum Shops at Caesars Palace. Everything was simultaneously too much—chocolate-chip cookies, dipped in chocolate fondue—and not enough. I was irritated by the way Joe kept cutting me off in the middle of my sentences. His medication meant he had no appetite, and that irritated me, too. I was easily irritated. He was saying something about nihilism, how all meaning was subjective and constructed and there was no core from which... but I wasn't following, totally. I was watching the flames curl from pink crystals below the fondue pot, leaning so close my hair almost caught on fire. The waiter smiled at me knowingly. He said it happened every day. I told Joe that maybe he shouldn't come to the wedding with me after all. It was too much, too soon. What I couldn't say to him: *You were an idea. Now you're here.* He told me he was working on a novel about an alternate universe where all the Vegas hotels had been converted into prisons. I'd converted Joe into Vegas Joe, but it turned out he was an actual person. He was funny and handsome and kind but he was also struggling, he was also *real*—he needed things, he was unsure about others—and when I was around him there was a lump in my throat that I couldn't stop swallowing, a longing not for the man in front of me, but for the man who wasn't.

In the book that emerged from their Vegas seminar, Venturi and Scott

Brown argue that the signs on a commercial strip are more important than the buildings they advertise: "The sign at the front is a vulgar extravaganza; the building at the back, a modest necessity." This kind of persuasion is also the logic of long-distance daydreams. There can be truth in these dreams, in that signage—and even beauty. But the architecture of persuasion is also the opposite of proximity and inhabitance. Which is all to say: After pulling off the highway, I didn't know how to dwell in the building I'd chosen. Joe was the real smoke at the end of a fake cigarette, but I wasn't ready for another person's full humanity. We had been something far apart that we were not able to be together.

A t my friend's bachelorette party the next night—in a suite at the Venetian, fifteen floors above a chlorinated Grand Canal—other women took turns describing the annoying habits of their Sig Os and passed around glasses of cheap champagne. I no longer drank champagne, or had a Sig O to be annoyed by. After dark, we strolled out of the cloud-painted Venetian sky and into the Vegas night, wearing our sparkly tiaras, walking past what appeared to be a pile of bloody rags bunched against the curb, above a drain pipe.

At the "Thunder from Down Under" male revue, under glittering disco lights at the Excalibur, a firefighter, a construction worker, a doctor, a soldier, and a milkman peeled away their uniforms to show their glinting six-packs. Baby-oiled bodies in the strobe-lit darkness collapsed the distinction between being there ironically and just being there. The emcee had a huge sobriety tattoo inked across one of his biceps—GOD GRANT ME THE SERENITY—and made an old woman cup his balls through his shiny leather pants.

As we walked home along the Strip, an SUV full of women pulled up beside us. One leaned her head out the window and asked: "Which one's the bride?" We pointed her out—with the largest tiara, and the veil—and all the women started shouting: "Don't do it!" Before they sped away, they said: "We're all divorced!"

The next time I went to Vegas, I got married there. It was just fifteen months later. I'd moved to New York and fallen in love with a man who had grown up in Vegas, the son of two pawnbrokers. Everyone he met was surprised to learn that he'd actually grown up in Vegas—that anyone had. But he did. He spent his childhood rolling quarters in the back of his parents' shops, hearing them get called dirty Jews by angry customers, watching them work seven days a week for their entire lives to give their four kids more opportunities than they'd had themselves.

For Charles, Vegas wasn't an outsized metaphor for impossible dreams or their deflation. It was Saturday-morning cartoons, and Slurpees from the 7-Eleven melting in the ruthless desert sunlight. It was playing high-school basketball at the same courts where the Runnin' Rebels played pickup games, back in the days of Tark the Shark, the legendary UNLV coach who gnawed on a wet towel when he got nervous. Vegas was where Charles and his father had cruised up I-15 with the radio tuned to the prizefights at Caesars Palace. It was where he'd made his own backyard boxing ring out of paper strips—a child inspired by the particular materials of his world, because it was the world he knew.

Charles and I met at the workspace in downtown Manhattan where we both wrote. He introduced himself by asking me to translate my tattoo. He had eleven tattoos of his own, the most recent of which was his five-year-old daughter's name, scrawled in blue across his forearm. He'd promised her that after she wrote her name for the first time, he would get it printed permanently on his skin. I would come to understand that he was always good to his word.

When we first met, I already knew his work. I'd read his first book

187

years earlier, a big sprawling novel about Vegas that I loved for its tender evocation of outsiders: teen runaways sleeping on the streets, awkward adolescent boys who lived for their comic books, pawnbrokers mocked by their customers. And his own personal story was well known in our shared literary world. His wife had been diagnosed with leukemia when their daughter, Lily, was just six months old. She'd died just before Lily's third birthday.

The first time Charles and I talked, we talked for hours. It felt, as they say, like we could have talked forever. Except we couldn't talk forever, because Charles had to pick up Lily from after-school at five. During that first conversation, I told him about a ritual I'd taken part in a few months earlier, at a residency in Wyoming: on the night of a full moon, we'd all brought empty purses and wallets into an open meadow and asked the universe for something specific we wanted. I'd asked to care less about worldly success. At the time, this had seemed like a very enlightened thing to ask for. The guy who went after me asked for a motorcycle. Charles laughed at that, as I'd hoped—nervous—he would. When I asked Charles what he thought Lily would request during a full-moon ritual, he said she'd probably ask for a plastic ice castle. Then he paused and said, "Honestly, she would ask for a mom."

This was vintage Charles: willing to state the truth bluntly, jocular about pain because he'd lived it so fully, deeply aware of life as something simultaneously full of trauma and plastic ice castles. He asked if we could meet up again soon and do our own full-moon ritual in the communal kitchen of our workspace. I told him I would bring the empty purses if he supplied the full moon. The next time we met, at a little table by the coffee machine, he tacked up an illustration he and Lily had made together: three jagged mountains cut from brown construction paper, and a round yellow moon hanging above them.

On our first date, Charles took me out for a seven-course Italian meal, but we had to skip the last two courses so he could get back by the time he'd promised the sitter. Our second date was a midday tryst while Lily was at school. We made out in my apartment all morning and then got turkey sandwiches from the bodega at the end of my block, ate them on the grassy strip of Eastern Parkway with plastic bottles of lemonade and a box of the chicken-and-waffle crackers he loved as a child. Our third date was a road trip to the Catskills while Lily was staying with her grandmother. I booked a last-minute room at a tiny bed-and-breakfast where our room was full of animal prints and photographs of Siegfried & Roy, unmauled and beaming. Those days in the Catskills were full of morning walks down a muddy road, messy with spring thaw, to a tiny highway diner where we got eggs and bacon so salty it stung the tiny cut in my mouth. On that trip, we found bliss in all the smallest things. We bought the best snacks at gas stations: licorice and sour cherry balls. We wondered at the albino tigers on our walls. We could riff back and forth on a joke for ten minutes straight, then return to it a day later, riff a little more. Charles was candid about difficulty, and he was funnier than anyone I'd ever met.

In certain ways, the pattern of our early months—our passionate descent into love—looked like other relationships I'd had. But I trusted it more. From the start, our love was embedded in the business of daily living, in all its scattered rag dolls and bake sales and meltdowns and rubber toys under your feet before you flicked on the bathroom light in the middle of the night. Our romance wasn't charged by the possibility of total abandon; it was electrified by borders and edges. It was less about engaging with curated versions of each other and more about inhabiting ordinary days that summoned our whole selves: scattered, overwhelmed, trying. Our story wasn't about getting the skyscraper suite just because we felt like it. It was about finding pockets of effervescence in the midst of daily life—waking up on a red futon in his tiny rent-controlled apartment, kissing first thing in the morning in the shadow of a four-foot-high plastic dollhouse.

In the abstract, our love looked tethered by obligation and trauma; by the demands of raising a child, and the long shadow of loss. But there was another truth lurking under all that difficulty: a felt experience of love that didn't follow any of the scripts I'd spent my life craving. This love lived in fits of midnight laughter on a futon with a too-small blanket. It lived in an hourly motel near the Hudson, with a sitter at home and a mirror on the ceiling of our room. It lived in the shared language of days contoured by after-school pickup and ballet-class leotards, by Saturday-morning chocolate-chip pancakes and tuna melts at their favorite diner.

I'd somehow rocketed straight from single life—smoking alone on my stoop, lost to daydreams and self-pity—into this life of accountability and intimate beholdenness. It was as if I'd taken a shortcut on the banana-yellow path of the Game of Life, which we often played on the living-room carpet that Lily called "Snow Rug, Throw Rug"; as if I'd jumped straight to the family portion of the game board rather than stopping in my little plastic car and spinning the plastic wheel for my own plastic babies. Instead I'd jumped into someone else's plastic car. Now I was living out of a suitcase wedged into the corner of his crowded living room.

After barely six months together, Charles and I decided to elope to Vegas. Almost every way you looked at it, this was reckless. I had no idea what it meant to be a mother, much less what it meant to mother a child who'd lost her mother. But Charles trusted that I was capable of showing up for this life, and I wanted to show up for it—for him, and for Lily, and for myself. I trusted him because when I looked at him I saw a man who had been showing up for the people he loved, even through unimaginable pain, for years. It was our extraordinary ordinary life—this life made of actual days, striated by obligation—that we were committing to with our improbable wedding, our clandestine joy.

We got married at A Little White Chapel, under the glowing heart, beyond the Astroturf. Lily was having a sleepover at her cousin's house. We showed up at the cashier's desk—past the pink Cadillac, past the Tunnel of Love and the drive-through window—and said: "Marry us!" The woman at the register said we needed to go to City Hall for a license. What had I been expecting? One-stop shopping, I suppose, especially at a place that advertised its twenty-four-hour drive-through window. I asked the woman at the register how many people never came back once they found out they needed to go to the courthouse. She thought for a moment, then said, "Maybe fifty percent?"

When we returned with our license in hand, just before eleven, we did not purchase the flower package or the Elvis impersonator. We did not rent the pink Cadillac. We did not have our ceremony in the Chapel L'Amour, or the Crystal Chapel, or the gazebo. We did not drive our rental car under the cherubs painted across the ceiling of the Tunnel of Love. We did it old-school style, in the original chapel, while "Fools Rush In" played from speakers we could not see. The back wall looked like a quilted comforter, upholstered with white silk. Statues of cherubs held tumbling bouquets of fake white flowers. There were stained-glass windows showing roses, hearts, and doves. None of this felt wrong. It felt—weirdly, improbably—right. If I was hurling myself into something entirely unknown, with no idea what the terrain would look like, then it seemed appropriate to do it someplace so utterly strange. It was almost freeing, like an acknowledgment of all the ways I couldn't have predicted how my life would turn out.

By the end of the ceremony, we had tears in our eyes. The photographer was the witness. Father Someone quoted Nietzsche: "It is not a lack of love, but a lack of friendship, that makes unhappy marriages." He did not quote Nietzsche saying, "We ought not to be permitted to come to a decision affecting our whole life while we are in the condition of being in love."

We were in the condition. I wore a long blue-and-white dress that Charles had given me for my birthday that summer. It looked like clouds. My red nail polish was chipped. I tried to capture both our faces in a selfie with two painted turtles whose wrinkled necks stretched out from their shells so their small heads could touch.

Back at the Golden Nugget, where we were staying, we got cupcakes in the lobby. We ordered room-service steak. I told Charles that the sharks in the aquarium had once struck me as a symbol of wonder and possibility. He said their tank had been built on the land where his grandfather's first pawnshop once stood. When we tried to go swimming at the third-story infinity pool, we were told it was closing at midnight, in five minutes. A boy who looked sixteen told us so. "But we just got married!" we said. He looked unfazed. He probably heard that every night.

The next year we would have a ceremony in the woods, with a treasure hunt for a feral pack of blissful children. It would be like a postcard that day: all our people and their toddlers, wading into the glittering water. But that night we had only the absurdity of our little white chapel, our fever dream turned actual, with Father Someone consecrating our love. That night it was just us. It was just ours.

One definition of living might be the perpetual swapping of story lines. We trade in the scripts we've written for ourselves and get our real lives in return. This is what Vegas did to me—what it did *for* me. It swallowed up the story I'd written about falling in love one night by the Bellagio fountain, and gave me another story to live instead: the story of marrying a widower and helping him raise his daughter, a story in which heading back to Vegas meant visiting the in-laws and waking up to ordinary life. It meant spending more time downtown and less time on the Strip.

In that Vegas, we took Lily and her cousin Diamond to the arcade games at Circus Circus, where the Redemption Center was no longer an ironic Twitter backdrop but a physical place where I begged the woman behind the counter to replace the whoopee cushion Lily had lost beneath the twirling bodies of four Brazilian acrobats. In that Vegas, we ate soft serve in the parking lot of Luv-it Frozen Custard, while the girls pretended to hold mistletoe over our heads until we kissed. We got lost on the drive to Lake Mead, and never made it to the water: the girls grew bored in the back seat while the desert darkened around our wrong highway.

In that Vegas, Lily and I watched strangers ride on zip lines over the commotion of Fremont Street—full of panhandlers and buskers, men painted in silver and moving their limbs like robots, casinos blasting air-conditioning into sweltering summer heat—and I said, "Someday we'll do it ourselves," and Lily's small body pressed against mine, trembling with fear and desire. We spent hours waiting for a tow-truck driver after a German tourist named Wolfgang Hamburger sideswiped us near the base of the Stratosphere, in a rental car with tinted windows covered in love graffiti: *W. Hamburger* scribbled inside a big pink heart. He was in town to celebrate his twenty-fourth wedding anniversary. Vegas never made this shit up. It simply invited me to bring doughnuts to my mother-in-law at her pawnshop—its glass cases full of turquoise jewelry, dice clocks, and old war medals—where the walls were decorated with racing silks from a horse jockey her dad used to bet on, and the patchy carpet existed under the benevolent rule of a huge cat wandering among the furs hanging in back. In that Vegas, after five years of watching strangers on the zip lines, Lily and I finally did it ourselves: White Castle to the right and straight on till morning.

So much of the pleasure of Vegas—for me, at first—was about possibility, about wanting and longing, about imagining what *could be*. The pleasure of Vegas Joe was all about anticipation. It was the pleasure of fishtailing down wintry roads, trying to reach him in Boston, spending a night in a room at the top of the world and then imagining fruit-bowl shades of neon from my studio apartment during blizzards. That first night was better without the kiss, because that way I still got to imagine what the kiss would be like.

For years I'd been an expert at longing, an expert at loving from the state of not-quite-having, an expert at daydreaming and sinking back into the plush furniture of cinematic imagining. But from those early years with Charles I learned that marriage was something else. It was composed of the pleasures of dwelling, which were harder and thicker than the pleasures of conjuring. Marriage wasn't the bliss of possibility. It was the more complicated satisfaction of actually living and actually having. It was a view not from the top of the world but from the base of the Stratosphere, while we tried to understand what Wolfgang Hamburger was saying about his rental insurance. It was about realizing that when his spray-painted heart proclaimed decades of devotion, those years weren't full of the absence of longing so much as its constant renewal, its acrobatics, its shapeshifting.

Marriage isn't telling your best stories to a new lover; it's asking your husband about his day and not glazing over at his reply. Marriage isn't walking past the shark tank at one in the morning, stomach full of butterflies at the prospect of kissing someone new: an unknown taste, an unknown body. It's walking past the shark tank at nine in the morning, scouring the potted plants for the wooden nutcracker your six-year-old stepdaughter lost the night before. Marriage isn't months of fantasy. It's years of cleaning out the fridge. For a long time, I had admired the art of showing up—in my friends, my mother, my brother, the other folks in recovery meetings—but it's one thing to admire how other people live, and another thing to try to live that way yourself: not waiting for love to stick, as if love itself could do the work, but waking up to support it each day—knowing it can't promise to be anything forever, except something that is always changing.

Marriage is what happens when you take the ride despite the SUV full of women who told you, *Don't;* despite the fact that you may someday be one of them. Marriage is what happens when the mirage shimmers away to reveal plain asphalt straight ahead. It's everything you keep trying to summon faith in, and it delivers you to what you couldn't have imagined: past that first flush of falling in love, to all the other kinds of love that lie ahead. You may never reach Lake Mead, but you'll always have the drive itself—that particular glow of evening sun baking the highway, setting the cars on fire, light brighter than you can stand to look at, and already holding the night.

Daughter of a Ghost

When she was six, my stepdaughter told me that her favorite character in *Cinderella* was the evil stepmother. This wasn't entirely surprising. During playdates, Lily often liked to play orphan, writing down long lists of chores: *dichs* (dishes); *moping* (mopping); *feeding* (the fish). She and a friend liked to drink something they called "pepper water," which was ordinary tap water they pretended their cruel orphan-handlers had made undrinkable. Maybe it was thrilling to stage her own mistreatment, to take power over the situation of powerlessness she had imagined. Maybe she just liked a virtuous reason to dump water on the floor. When I asked Lily why Cinderella's stepmother was her favorite character, she leaned close to me and whispered, like a secret, "I think she looks *good*."

For all her cruelty, the evil stepmother is often the fairy-tale character most defined by imagination and determination, rebelling against the patriarchy with whatever meager tools have been left to her: her magic mirror, her vanity, her pride. She is an artist of cunning and malice, but still—an artist. She isn't simply acted upon; she acts. She just doesn't act the way a mother is supposed to. That's her fuel, and her festering heart.

In many ways, fairy tales—dark and ruthless, usually structured by loss—were the stories that most resembled Lily's life. Her mother died just before her third birthday, after a two-and-a-half-year struggle with leukemia. Two years later, Lily got a stepmother of her own—not a wicked one, perhaps, but one terrified of being wicked.

I wondered if it was comforting for Lily to hear stories about fairy-tale children who had lost what she had lost—unlike most of the kids at her school, or in her ballet classes, whose mothers were still alive. Or perhaps it brought the stories dangerously close, the fact that she shared so much with their heroines. Maybe it peeled away their protective skins of fantasy, made their pepper water too literal, brought their perils too near. When I read her the old fairy tales about daughters without mothers, I worried that I was pressing on the bruises of her loss. When I read her the old fairy tales about stepmothers, I worried I was reading her an evil version of myself.

When I first became a stepmother, I was hungry for company. I didn't know many stepmothers, and I especially didn't know many stepmothers who had inherited the role as I had inherited it: fully, over-whelmingly, with no other mother in the picture. Our family lived in the aftermath of loss, not rupture—death, not divorce. This used to be the normal way of being a stepmother, and the word itself holds grief in its roots. The Old English *steop* means "loss," and the etymology paints a bleak portrait: "For stepmoder is selde guod," reads one account from 1290. Another text, from 1598, says, "With one consent all stepmothers hate their daughters."

The fairy tales are obviously damning. The evil queen from "Snow White" demands the secret murder of her stepdaughter after a magic mirror proclaims the girl's superior beauty. The stepmother from "Hansel and Gretel" sends her stepchildren into the woods because there isn't enough to eat. Cinderella sits amid her fireplace cinders, sorting peas from lentils, her ash-speckled body appeasing a wicked stepmother who wants to dull her luminosity with soot because she feels threatened by it. It's as if the stepmother relationship inevitably corrupts—it is not just an evil woman in the role but a role that turns any woman evil. A "stepmother's blessing" is another name for a hangnail, as if to suggest something that hurts because it isn't properly attached, something that presents itself as a substitutive love but ends up bringing pain instead.

The evil stepmother casts a long, primal shadow, and five years ago I moved in with that shadow, to a one-bedroom rent-controlled apartment near Gramercy Park. I sought the old stories in order to find company—out of sympathy for the stepmothers they vilified—and to resist their narratives, to inoculate myself against the darkness they held.

T he early days of my relationship with Charles, Lily's father, held the kind of love that fairy tales ask us to believe in: encompassing and surprising, charged by a sense of wonder at the sheer fact of his existence in the world. I uprooted my life for our love, without regret. Our bliss lived in a thousand ordinary moments: a first kiss in the rain, over-easy eggs at a roadside diner, crying with laughter at midnight about some stupid joke he would make during an *American Ninja Warrior* rerun. But our love also held the art and work of parenting, and much of our bliss happened on stolen time: that first kiss while the sitter stayed half an hour late; those diner eggs on a spontaneous road trip possible only because Lily was staying with her grandmother in Memphis; our hands clamped over our mouths during those fits of midnight laughter so we wouldn't wake Lily in the next room. This felt less like compromise and more like off-roading, veering onto terrain I'd never imagined.

I approached the first evening I spent with Lily as a kind of test, though Charles tried to stack the deck in my favor: he decided we would get takeout from the pasta place Lily liked, then spend the evening watching her favorite movie—an animated film about two princess sisters, one with a touch that turned everything to ice. That afternoon, I went to find a gift at the Disney Store in Times Square—not only a place I had never been but a place I had never imagined going. I hated the idea of bribing Lily, trading plastic for affection, but I was desperately nervous. Plastic felt like an insurance policy.

The clerk looked at me with pity when I asked for the *Frozen* section. I suddenly doubted myself: Was it not a Disney movie? The clerk laughed when I asked, then explained: "We just don't have any merchandise left. There's a worldwide shortage."

She was serious. They had nothing. Not even a tiara. Or they had plenty of tiaras, but they weren't the right tiaras. I scanned the shelves around me: Belle stuff, Sleeping Beauty stuff, Princess Jasmine stuff. Lily had to like other movies, right? Other princesses? There was a moment when I considered buying something related to *every* princess, just to cover my bases. I had some vague realization that the low-level panic in the back of my throat was the fuel capitalism ran on. On my cell phone, I was on hold with a Toys"R"Us in the Bronx. On my way out, I spotted something shoved into the corner of a shelf. It looked wintry. It had ice-blue cardboard packaging: a sled.

I cannot even tell you my relief. My sense of victory was complete. The sled came with a princess, and also maybe a prince. (A Sami ice harvester, I would learn.) The set came with a reindeer! (Named Sven.) It even came with a plastic carrot for him to eat. I tucked the box under my arm protectively as I walked to the register. I eyed the other parents around me. Who knew how many of them wanted this box?

I called Charles, triumphant. I told him the whole saga: the clerk's laughter, the *worldwide shortage,* the frantic phone calls, the sudden grace of glimpsing that pale-blue cardboard.

"You won!" he said, then paused. I could hear him deciding whether to say something. "The princess," he asked, "what color is her hair?"

I had to check the box. "Brown?" I said. "Sort of reddish?"

"You did great," he said after a beat. "You're the best."

But in that beat, I could hear that I'd gotten the wrong princess. Charles wasn't criticizing; he just knew how much a princess could mean. He had spent the last two years knee-deep in princesses, playing mother and father at once. The truth of the wrong princess was also the truth of unstable cause and effect. With parenting, you could do everything you were supposed to and it still might backfire, because you lived with a tiny, volatile human who did not come with any kind of instruction manual. The possibility of failure hung like a low sky, pending weather, over every horizon.

In his book *The Uses of Enchantment*, the psychoanalyst Bruno Bettelheim makes a beautiful argument for the kinds of reckoning that fairy tales permit: they allow children to face primal fears (like parental abandonment) and imagine acts of rebellion (like defying authority) in a world reassuringly removed from the one they live in. Enchanted woods and castles are so conspicuously fantastical, their situations so extreme, that children don't need to feel destabilized by their upheavals. I wondered if that was still true for Lily, whose loss showed up more frequently in fairy tales than in the world around her. It can be a fine line between stories that give our fears a necessary stage and stories that deepen them—that make us more afraid.

In an 1897 letter to the editor in *Outlook*, a high-circulation American lifestyle magazine, one correspondent lamented the effects of reading "Cinderella" to young children: "The effect or impression was to put stepmothers on the list of evil things of life." But in our home, it was less that "Cinderella" put stepmothers on an evil list and more that the story raised the question—with a kind of openness that might otherwise have been impossible—of whether stepmothers belonged there. Often, Lily used the figure of a fairy-tale wicked stepmother to distinguish our relationship from the one we had just read. "You're not like her," she would say. Or when it came to the stepmother she admired from "Cinderella," she was generous: "You look better than her anyway."

Perhaps claiming the stepmother as her favorite character was a way for Lily to grasp the source of her fears and take some control over them. Perhaps it was another version of playing orphans. Did she worry I would turn cruel? Did she love me fiercely so I wouldn't? I wondered if it helped her to see us reflected and distorted by a dark mirror, if these more sinister versions of our bond made her feel better about our relationship—or gave her permission to accept what might feel hard about it. I found a strange comfort in the nightmare visions of mean stepparents I found in popular media—at least I wasn't cruel like them. It was a kind of ethical schadenfreude.

In many ways, the stories my family inherited mapped imperfectly onto ours. In fairy tales, the father-king was often duped and blind. He had faith in a woman who didn't deserve it. His trust, or his lust, permitted his daughter's mistreatment. Charles was like these fairy-tale fathers in only one way: he trusted me from the beginning. He believed I could be a mother before I believed it. He talked openly about what was hard about parenting, which made it feel more possible to live in love and difficulty—love *as* difficulty. He knew what it meant to wake up day after day, choose three possible dresses, pour the cereal, repour the cereal after it spilled, wrestle hair into pigtails, get to school on time, get to pickup on time, steam the broccoli for dinner. He knew how much it meant to learn the difference between the animated ponies with wings and the animated ponies with horns and the animated ponies with *both*—the alicorns. He knew what it meant to do all that, then wake up the next day and do it all over again.

My relationship with Lily, too, was not like the story we inherited from fairy tales—a tale of cruelty and rebellion—or even like the story of divorce-era popular media: the child spurning her stepmother, rejecting her in favor of the true mother, the mother of the bloodline and womb. Our story wasn't about rejection; it was about pure, primal, overwhelming need. I was never going to replace her mom, but I was here. I was something. We were forging a story of our own—a story built from a hundred tiny conversations on the 6 train, built from painting Lily's nails and trying not to smudge her tiny pinkie, built from telling her to take deep breaths during tantrums, because I needed to take deep breaths myself. Our story began that first night when I felt her small, hot hand reach for mine during the scene when the abominable snowman swirled into view on an icy mountain and almost overwhelmed the humble reindeer.

That night, when we sang songs at bedtime, she scooted over and patted the comforter, in the same bed where her mother had spent afternoons resting during the years of her illness, directly below the hole Charles had made—angrily swinging a toy train into the wall—after a telephone call with an insurance company, a hole now hidden behind an alphabet poster. "You lie here," Lily told me. "You lie in Mommy's spot."

If the wicked stepmother feels like a ready-made archetype, then its purest, darkest incarnation is the evil queen from "Snow White." In an 1857 version of the Brothers Grimm tale, she goes wild with jealousy and asks a hunter to bring back her stepdaughter's heart. After this attack fails (the hunter has a bleeding heart of his own), the stepmother's aggression takes the form of false generosity. She goes to her stepdaughter disguised as a beggar crone and offers Snow White items that seem helpful or nourishing: a corset, a comb, an apple. These are objects a mother might give her daughter—as forms of sustenance, or as ways of passing on a female legacy of self-care—but they are actually meant to kill her. They reach Snow White in the folds of her new surrogate family, where the seven dwarves have given her the opportunity to be precisely the kind of "good mother" her stepmother never was. Snow White cooks and cleans and cares for them. Her virtue is manifest in precisely the maternal impulse her stepmother lacks.

The evil stepmother is so integral to our familiar telling of "Snow White" that I was surprised to discover that an earlier version of the story doesn't feature a stepmother at all. In this version, Snow White has no dead mother, only a living mother who wants her dead. This was a pattern of revision for the Brothers Grimm; they transformed several mothers into stepmothers between the first version of their collected stories, published in 1812, and the final version, published in 1857. The figure of the stepmother effectively became a vessel for the emotional aspects of motherhood that were too ugly to attribute to mothers directly (ambivalence, jealousy, resentment) and those parts of a child's experience of her mother (as cruel, aggressive, withholding) that were too difficult to situate directly in the biological parent-child dynamic. The figure of the stepmother—lean, angular, harsh—was like snake venom drawn from an unacknowledged wound, siphoned out in order to preserve the healthy body of a maternal ideal.

"It is not only a means of preserving an internal all-good mother when the real mother is not all-good," Bettelheim argues, "but it also permits anger at this bad 'stepmother' without endangering the goodwill of the true mother, who is viewed as a different person." The psychologist D. W. Winnicott puts it more simply: "If there are two mothers, a real one who has died, and a stepmother, do you see how easily a child gets relief from tension by having one perfect and the other horrid?" In other words, the shadow figure of the fairy-tale stepmother is a predatory archetype reflecting something true of every mother: the complexity of her feelings toward her child, and her child's feelings toward her.

Even if Lily didn't split her ideas of motherhood into perfect absence and wicked presence, I did—assigning precisely that psychic division of labor. I imagined that her biological mother would have offered everything I couldn't always manage: patience, pleasure, compassion. She would have been *with* Lily in her tantrums, as we'd once been advised—a bit opaquely—by a therapist. Her real mother wouldn't have bribed her with ridiculous amounts of plastic. She wouldn't have gotten so frustrated when bedtime lasted an hour and a half, or else her frustration would have had the counterweight of an unconditional love I was still seeking. I knew these self-flagellations were ridiculous—even "real" parents weren't perfect—but they offered a certain easy groove of self-deprecation. A woman mothering another woman's child, Winnicott observes, "may easily find herself forced by her own imagination into the position of witch rather than of fairy godmother."

In a study called "The Poisoned Apple," the psychologist (and stepmother) Elizabeth Church analyzed her interviews with 104 stepmothers through the lens of one particular question: How do these women reckon with the evil archetype they stepped into? "Although their experience was the opposite of the fairy-tale stepmothers," she reported, insofar as "they felt powerless in the very situation where the fairy-tale stepmothers exerted enormous power," they still "tended to identify with the image of the wicked stepmother." She called it their poisoned apple. They felt "wicked" for experiencing feelings of resentment or jealousy, and this fear of their own "wickedness" prompted them to keep these feelings to themselves, which only made them feel more shame for having these feelings in the first place.

*   *   *

Folktales often deploy the stepmother as a token mascot of the dark maternal—a woman rebelling against traditional cultural scripts—but the particular history of the American stepmother is more complicated. As the historian Leslie Lindenauer argues in *I Could Not Call Her Mother: The Stepmother in American Popular Culture, 1750–1960*, the figure of the American stepmother found her origins in the American witch. Lindenauer posits that the eighteenth-century popular imagination took the same terrible attributes that the Puritans had ascribed to witches—malice, selfishness, coldness, absence of maternal impulse—and started assigning them to stepmothers instead. "Both were examples of women who, against God and nature, perverted the most essential qualities of the virtuous mother," Lindenauer observes. "Moreover, witches and stepmothers alike were most often accused of harming *other* women's children."

The stepmother became a kind of scapegoat, a new repository for aspects of femininity that had been threatening for a long time: female agency, female creativity, female restlessness, maternal ambivalence. By the late eighteenth century the stepmother was a stock villain, familiar enough to appear in grammar books. One boy was even injured by his dead stepmother *from beyond the grave* when a column above her tombstone fell on his head. The particular villainy of the stepmother—the duplicity of tyranny disguised as care—enabled colonial rhetoric that compared England's rule to "a stepmother's severity," as one 1774 tract put it. In an article that ran in *Ladies' Magazine* in 1773, on the eve of the American Revolution, a stepdaughter laments her fate at the hands of her stepmother: "Instead of the tender maternal affection...what do I now see but discontent, ill-nature, and mal-a-pert authority?" The stepmother offers bondage cunningly packaged as devotion.

But the American popular imagination hasn't always understood the stepmother as a wicked woman. If it was true that she was an eighteenth-century gold digger—a latter-day witch—then it was also true that she was a mid-nineteenth-century saint, happily prostrate to the surge of her own innate maternal impulse. In the Progressive Era, she was proof that being a good mother was less about saintly instincts and more about reason, observation, and rational self-improvement. You didn't have to have a biological connection—or even an innate caregiving impulse—you just had to *apply* yourself.

When I interviewed Lindenauer about her research, she told me that she had been surprised to discover these vacillations—particularly surprised to find the figure of the virtuous stepmother showing up in the very same women's magazines that had vilified her a few decades earlier. She eventually started to detect a pattern. It seemed as if the stepmother found redemption whenever the nuclear family was under siege: in the immediate aftermath of the Civil War, or when divorce emerged as a social phenomenon in the early twentieth century. The stepmother became a kind of "port in the storm," Lindenauer told me. "It's better to have a stepmother than no mother at all."

The golden era of the American stepmother archetype—the summit of her virtue—was the second half of the nineteenth century, during and after the Civil War, when sentimental novels and women's magazines were full of saintly stepmothers eager to care for the motherless children who stumbled into their laps. In Charlotte Yonge's 1862 novel, *The Young Step-Mother; or, A Chronicle of Mistakes,* the protagonist, Albinia, is portrayed as a woman with a surplus of goodwill, just waiting for people with needs (read: grief) deep enough to demand the deployment of her excess goodness. Her siblings worry about Albinia marrying a widower with children, afraid she will become a kind of indentured servant, but the novel reassures us that "her energetic spirit and love of children animated her to embrace joyfully the cares which such a choice must impose on her." When her new husband brings her home, he apologizes for what he is asking from her. "As I look at you, and the home to which I have brought you, I feel that I have acted selfishly," he says. But she won't let him apologize. "Work was always what I wished," she replies, "if only I could do anything to lighten your grief and care." With the children, Albinia doesn't simply say but truly *feels* all the right things: she is sorry they have her in place of their mother; they can call her Mother, but they don't have to. Although the novel is subtitled "A Chronicle of Mistakes," Albinia doesn't seem to make many.

When I read in the novel's epigraph, "Fail—yet rejoice," it felt like a lie and an impossible imperative at once. In fact, the entire voice of the saintly stepmother felt like an elaborate humblebrag. She knew she would always be second—or third! or fifth! or tenth!—but she didn't care. Not one bit. She just wanted to be useful. I thought I would be glad to discover the existence of these virtuous stepmothers, but instead I found them nearly impossible to accept—much harder to stomach than the wicked stepmothers in fairy tales. My poisoned apple wasn't the wicked stepmother but her archetypal opposite, the saint, whose innate virtue felt like the harshest possible mirror. It would always show me someone more selfless than I was. These stories forgot everything that was structurally difficult about this kind of bond, or else they insisted that virtue would overcome all. This is why fairy tales are more forgiving than sentimental novels. They let darkness into the frame. Finding darkness in another story is so much less lonely than fearing the darkness is yours alone.

I punished myself when I lost patience, when I bribed, when I wanted to flee. I punished myself for resenting Lily when she came into our bed, night after night, which wasn't actually a bed but a futon we pulled out in the living room. Every feeling I had, I wondered: *Would a real mother feel this?* It wasn't the certainty that she *wouldn't* that was painful, but the uncertainty itself: How could I know?

Initially I imagined that I might feel most like an "actual" mother among strangers, who had no reason to believe I wasn't one. But it was usually among strangers that I felt most like a fraud. One day early in our relationship, Lily and I went to a Mister Softee, one of the ice-cream trucks parked like land mines all over New York City. I asked Lily what she wanted and she pointed to the double cone of soft serve, the biggest one, covered in rainbow sprinkles. I said, "Great!" I was still at the Disney Store, still thrilled to find the sled set, still ready to pass as mother by whatever means necessary, whatever reindeer necessary, whatever soft serve necessary.

The double cone was so huge that Lily could barely hold it. *Two hands*, I would have known to say a few months later, but I didn't know to say it then. I overheard the woman behind me in line ask her friend, "What kind of parent gets her child that much ice cream?" My face went hot with shame. *This* parent. Which is to say: not a parent at all. I was afraid to turn around and at the same time I desperately wanted to turn around, to make the stranger feel ashamed, to speak back to the maternal superego she represented by saying: "What kind of mother? A mother trying to replace a dead one." Instead I grabbed a wad of napkins and offered to carry Lily's cone back to our table so she wouldn't drop it on the way.

As a stepparent, I often felt like an impostor—or else I felt the particular loneliness of dwelling outside the bounds of the most familiar story line. I hadn't been pregnant, given birth, felt my body surge with the hormones of attachment. I woke up every morning to a daughter who called me Mommy but also missed her mother. One of Lily's favorite dolls—a goth character called Spectra Vondergeist, with purple-streaked hair and a skeleton-key belt—was advertised on her cardboard packaging as the "Daughter of a Ghost."

I often called our situation "singular." But as with so many kinds of singularity, it was not only a double-edged blade—a source of loneliness and pride at once—but also a delusion. "Lots of people are stepparents," my mother told me once, and of course she was right. A recent Pew Research Center survey found that four in ten Americans say they have at least one step-relationship. Twelve percent of women are stepmothers. I can guarantee you that almost all these women sometimes feel like frauds or failures.

In an essay about stepparents, Winnicott argues for the value of "unsuccess stories." He even imagines the benefits of gathering a group of "unsuccessful stepparents" in a room together. "I think such a meeting might be fruitful," he writes. "It would be composed of ordinary men and women." When I read that passage, it stopped me dead with longing. I wanted to be in that meeting, sitting with those ordinary men and women—hearing about their ice-cream bribes, their everyday impatience, their frustration and fraudulence, their desperate sleds.

In the methodology portion of her "Poisoned Apple" study, Elizabeth Church admits that she disclosed to her subjects that she was also a stepmother before interviewing them. After an interview was finished, she sometimes described her own experiences. Many of her subjects confessed that they had told her things during their interviews that they had never told anyone else. I could understand that—that they somehow would feel, by virtue of being in the presence of another stepmother, as if they had been granted permission to speak. It was something like the imagined gathering of unsuccessful stepparents, as if they were at an AA meeting in a church basement, taking earned solace in the minor triumphs and frequent failures of their kind: not blood, but a kind of kin.

T he decision to call the stepmother Mother, or the decision *not* to call her Mother, is often a dramatic hinge in stories about stepmothers. It usually functions as a climactic moment of acceptance or refusal. In a story called "My Step-Mother," published in the *Decatur Republican* in 1870, a young girl regards her new stepmother with skepticism. When her stepmother asks her to play a song on the piano, trying to earn her trust and affection, the girl decides to play "I Sit and Weep by My Mother's Grave." But lo! The stepmother is undeterred. She not only compliments the girl on her moving performance, she shares that she *also* lost her mother when she was young and *also* used to love that song. The story ends on a triumphant note, with the daughter finally calling her Mother, an inverted christening—child naming the parent—that inaugurates the "most perfect confidence" that grows between them.

For Lily, calling me Mother wasn't the end of anything. The day after Charles and I married in a Las Vegas wedding chapel, Lily asked almost immediately if she could call me Mommy. It was clear she had been waiting to ask, and I was moved by her desire—as if we had landed in the closing credits of a movie, the soundtrack reaching a crescendo all around us.

But we weren't in the credits. We were just getting started. I was terrified. What would happen next? What happened next: pulling into a 7-Eleven for snacks as Lily tugged on my sleeve to tell me she'd had an "adult drink" at the laser-tag birthday party she'd just attended and now she felt funny. She didn't want me to tell her dad. It was like the universe had sent its first maternal test. Was she drunk? What should I do? If I was going to let myself be called Mommy, I had to be prepared to deal with the fallout from the laser-tag birthday party. Charles eventually deduced that she had had a few sips of iced tea.

It felt less as if I had "earned" the title of *mother*—the way it has figured in so many sentimental stories, as a reward for behaving the right way and defying the old archetypes—and more as if I'd stepped into a cutout doll already sculpted for me by a little girl's yearning. It was as if I'd landed in the 1900 story called "Making Mamma," in which six-year-old Samantha layers a dressmaker's dummy with old fabric in order to make a surrogate mother for herself. It was as if Lily had bestowed a deep and immediate trust in me—unearned, born of need—and now I had to figure out how to live inside that trust without betraying it.

O nce I stepped into the costume of a well-worn cultural arche-type, I got used to hearing other people's theories about my life. Everyone had ideas about our family without knowing anything about our family. One woman said our situation was easier than it would have been if I'd had a terrible ex to compete with; another woman said I would be competing with the memory of Lily's perfect biological mother forever. When I wrote an article about a family trip for a travel magazine, the editor wanted a bit more pathos from my account: "Has it been bumpy?" she wrote in the margins of my draft. "What are you hoping for from this trip? A tighter family bond? A chance to let go of the sadness? Or...?? Tug at our heartstrings a bit." When this editor imagined our family, she envisioned us saturated by sadness, or else contoured by resistance. More than anything, I liked her "Or...??" It rang true. It wasn't that every theory about our family offered by other people felt wrong; it was more that most of them felt right, or at least held a grain of truth that resonated. Which felt even more alarming, somehow, to be so knowable to strangers.

But every theory also felt incomplete. There was so much more truth around it, or else something close to its opposite felt true as well. I rarely felt like saying, "No, it's nothing like that." I usually wanted to say: "Yes, it *is* like that. And also like this, and like this, and like this." Sometimes the sheer fact of those assumptions—the way they churned inside everyone we encountered—made stepmotherhood feel like loving someone in front of an operating theater full of strangers.

I was convinced that I was constantly being dissected for how fully or compassionately I had assumed my maternal role.

Ultimately I found only two fairy tales with good stepmothers, and they were both from Iceland. In one, a woman named Himinbjorg guides her stepson through his mourning by helping him fulfill a prophecy delivered to him by his dead mother in a dream: that he will free a princess from the spell that turned her into an ogre. By the time the prince returns from his mission, victorious, the royal court is ready to burn Himinbjorg at the stake, because everyone is convinced that she is responsible for his disappearance. Her selflessness moved me. She is willing to look terrible in order to help her stepson pursue a necessary freedom, while I worried that I cared too much about proving I was a good stepmother—worried that wanting to *seem* like a good stepmother might get in the way of *being* a good stepmother. Perhaps I wanted credit for mothering more than I wanted to mother. Himinbjorg, on the other hand, is willing to look like a witch just to help her stepson break the spell he needs to break.

Then there was Hildur. Her husband had vowed never to marry after the death of his first queen, because he feared his daughter would be mistreated. "All stepmothers are evil," he tells his brother, "and I don't wish to harm Ingibjorg." He is a fairy-tale king who has already absorbed the wisdom of fairy tales. He knows the deal with stepmoms. But he falls in love with Hildur anyway. She says she won't marry him, though—not unless he lets her live alone with his daughter for three years before the wedding. Their marriage is made possible by her willingness to invest in a relationship with his daughter that exists apart from him, as its own fierce flame.

The closest thing Lily and I ever had to an Icelandic castle was a series of bathrooms across downtown Manhattan. Bathrooms were the spaces where it was just the two of us: the one with wallpaper made from old newspapers, the one where she insisted that people used to have braids instead of hands, the one at a Subway with a concrete mop sink she loved because it was "cool and simple."

Bathrooms were our space, just as Wednesdays were our day, when I picked her up from school and took her to the Dunkin' Donuts full of cops at Third Avenue and Twentieth before I rushed her to ballet, got her squeezed into her rhinestone-studded leotard, and knelt before her tights like a supplicant, fitting bobby pins into her bun. At first I expected an Olympic medal for getting her there only two minutes late. Eventually I realized that I was surrounded by mothers who had done exactly what I'd just done, only they had done it two minutes faster, and their buns were neater. Everything that felt like rocket science to me was just the stuff regular parents did every day of the week.

But those afternoons mattered, because they belonged to me and Lily. One day, in a cupcake-shop bathroom in SoHo—a few months before Lily, Charles, and I moved into a new apartment, the first one we would rent together—Lily pointed at the walls: pink and brown, decorated with a lacy pattern. She told me she wanted our new room to look like this. Ours. She had it all planned out. In the new place, Daddy would live in one room, and Lily and I would live in the other. Our room would be so dainty, she said. She wasn't sure boys would be allowed. This was what Hildur knew: we needed something that was for the two of us alone.

A few months later, reading Dr. Seuss's *Horton Hatches the Egg* to Lily in that new apartment, I felt my throat constricting. Horton agrees to sit on an egg while Mayzie the bird, a flighty mother, takes a vacation to Palm Beach. Mayzie doesn't come back, but Horton doesn't give up. He sits on a stranger's egg for days, then weeks, then months. "I meant what I said, and I said what I meant," he repeats. "An elephant's faithful, one hundred percent!"

When the egg finally hatches, the creature that emerges is an elephant-bird: a bright-eyed baby with a small, curled trunk and red-tipped wings. Her tiny trunk made me think of Lily's hand gestures—how big and senseless they got, like mine—and how she was starting to make to-do lists, as I did, just so she could cross things off them. But she also had a poster of the planets in her bedroom, because her mom had loved outer space, and she was proud to say she always had her "nose in a book," just as her grandmother told her that her mother always had.

For me, the stakes of thinking about what it means to be a stepmother live not in statistical relevance—*slightly more than 10 percent of American women might relate!*—but in the way stepparenting asks us to question our assumptions about the nature of love and the boundaries of family. Family is so much more than biology, and love is so much more than instinct. Love is effort and desire—not a sentimental story line about easy or immediate attachment, but the complicated bliss of joined lives: ham-and-guacamole sandwiches packed in a My Little Pony lunchbox, or growing pains at midnight and car seats covered in vomit. It's the days of showing up. The trunks we inherit and the stories we step into, they make their way into us—by womb or shell or presence, by sheer force of will. But what hatches from the egg is hardly ever what we expect: the child that emerges, or the parent that is born. That mother is not a saint. She's not a witch. She's just an ordinary woman. She found a sled one day, after she was told there weren't any left. That was how it began.

Museum of Broken Hearts

The Museum of Broken Relationships is a collection of ordinary
objects hung on walls, tucked under glass, backlit on pedestals: a
toaster, a child's pedal car, a handmade modem. A toilet-paper dispenser. A positive pregnancy stick. A positive drug test. A weathered
ax. They come from Taipei, from Slovenia, from Colorado, from Ma-
nila. All donated, each accompanied by a story: *In the 14 days of her
holiday, every day I axed one piece of her furniture.*

One of the most popular items in the museum gift shop is the
"Bad Memories Eraser," an actual eraser sold in several shades. But
in truth the museum is something closer to the psychic opposite of
an eraser. Every object insists that something *was,* rather than trying
to make it disappear. Donating an object to the museum permits
surrender and permanence at once: you get it out of your home, and
you make it immortal. *She was a regional buyer for a grocer and that
meant I got to try some great samples,* reads the caption next to a box
of maple-and-sea-salt popcorn. *I miss her, her dog, and the samples,
and can't stand to have this fancy microwave popcorn in my house.* The
donor couldn't stand to have it, but he also couldn't bear to throw

it away. He wanted to put it on a pedestal instead, honor it as the artifact of an ended era.

When it comes to breakups, we are attached to certain dominant narratives of purgation, liberation, and exorcism: the idea that we're supposed to want to get the memories out of us, free ourselves from their grip. But this museum recognizes that our relationship to the past—even its ruptures and betrayals—is often more vexed, that it holds gravity and repulsion at once.

Exhibit 1: Clamshell Necklace
Florence, Italy
It's a simple necklace: a tiny, brown-striped clamshell tied to a black leather cord. The shell was gathered from a beach in Italy and attached to the cord by means of two holes drilled into the shell with a dental drill. The person who made the necklace for me was a dental student in Florence at the time. He did it secretly, in one of his classes, while he was supposed to be learning how to make crowns. I wore that necklace every single day, until I didn't anymore.

When I visited the museum in Zagreb, Croatia—where it occupies a baroque aristocratic home perched at the edge of Upper Town—I was on my own, though almost everyone else had come as part of a couple. The lobby was full of men waiting for wives and girlfriends who were spending longer with the exhibits. I imagined all these couples steeped in schadenfreude and fear: *This isn't us. This could be us.* In the guest book, I saw one entry that said simply: "I should end my relationship, but I probably won't," and fingered my own wedding ring—as proof, for comfort—but couldn't help imagining the ring as another exhibit, too.

Before flying to Zagreb, I'd put out a call to my friends— *What object would you donate to this museum?*—and got descriptions I couldn't have imagined: a clamshell drilled by a dental student, a steel-guitar slide, a shopping list, four black dresses, a single human hair, a mango candle, a penis-shaped gourd, the sheet music from Rachmaninoff's Concerto no. 3 for Piano. One friend described an illustration from a children's book that her ex had loved when he was young, showing a line of gray mice with thought bubbles full of the same colors above their heads, as if they were all dreaming the same dream. The objects my friends described all reached toward obsolete past tenses: *that time we dreamed the same dream*. The objects were relics from those dreams, as the museum exhibits were relics from the dreams of strangers—attempts to insist that these dreams had left some residue behind.

Walking through the museum felt less like voyeurism and more like collaboration. Strangers wanted their lives witnessed, and other strangers wanted to witness them. The curatorial notes quoted Roland Barthes: "Every passion, ultimately, has its spectator...[there is] no amorous oblation without a final theatre." I felt weirdly necessary, as if my attention offered proof—to the strangers who had donated these objects—that their thwarted love was worth paying attention to. There was a democratic vibe to the place. Its premise implied that anyone's story was worth telling, and worth listening to. The people who had donated items weren't distinct, in any meaningful sense, from the ones who were observing them. By contributing an item, any observer—anyone with a broken heart and a toilet-paper dispenser—could become an author.

The caption beside a small travel bottle of conditioner described a man named Dave, who had been "welcomed" into the open marriage of Mr. and Mrs. W. She had left the conditioner behind after a weekend visit to Dave's cabin, but after she and Mr. W. were killed in a car crash, Dave had "no public forum to grieve." The caption seemed to be addressing me directly when it said: "You are giving Dave his public forum."

Exhibit 2: Shopping List
Princeton, New Jersey

I spent the first seven years of my twenties in serious long-term romantic relationships, and then I got my heart broken when I was 27 and never dated again. Ten years into my singleness, having moved four times since my last breakup, gotten a PhD and a job, gained 40 pounds, I was going through a box of old too-small summer clothes and slipped my hand into the back pocket of some abbreviated jean shorts and felt a scrap of paper which turned out to be a shopping list in my heartbreaking ex's handwriting: "batteries, lg. black trash bags, Tide (small) bleach alt., g. onion." I suddenly remembered his gratuitous use of periods — oddly, always after he signed his name, every email and every letter ending with a punctuation mark of finality.

The Museum of Broken Relationships began with a breakup. Back in 2003, after Olinka Vištica and Dražen Grubišić ended their relationship, they found themselves in the midst of a series of difficult conversations about how to divide their possessions. As Olinka put it: "The feeling of loss...represented the only thing left for us to share." Over the kitchen table one night, they imagined an exhibit composed of all the detritus from breakups like their own, and when they finally created this exhibition — three years later — its first object was one salvaged from their own home: the mechanical windup rabbit they'd called Honey Bunny.

Just over a decade later, the story of their breakup has become the museum's myth of origins. "It was the strangest thing," Olinka told me over coffee one morning. "The other day I was getting out of my car, right outside the museum, and I heard a tour guide telling a group of tourists about the bunny. He said: 'It all started with a joke!'" Olinka wanted to tell the tour guide it hadn't been a joke at all, that those early conversations had been deeply painful, but she realized that the story of her own breakup had become a public possession, subject to the retellings and interpretations of others. People took whatever they needed from it.

Two years after they'd moved out of their shared apartment, Dražen called Olinka with the idea of submitting their breakup installation to a local Zagreb art festival. They were rejected the first year but accepted the next—given only two weeks to plan the installation, and told they wouldn't be granted space inside the gallery itself. So they got a shipping container delivered from Rijeka, a port city on the Adriatic Sea, and spent the next two weeks collecting objects to fill it. At first they were worried they wouldn't find enough, but everyone who heard about the idea said: "I might have something for you."

Olinka met a woman under the clock tower in Ban Jelačić Square who arrived with her husband but brought an old diary filled with the name of her former lover. She met an elderly man in a bar, a wounded vet, who pulled a prosthetic leg out of a shopping bag and told the story of the social worker who'd helped him get it during the early '90s, when sanctions during the Balkan Wars made prosthetics nearly impossible to obtain. The prosthetic had lasted longer than their relationship, he said, because it was "made of sturdier material."

When Olinka and Dražen finally found a home for their permanent exhibition, four years after that first exhibit, the space was in terrible shape: the first floor of an eighteenth-century palace in utter disrepair, perched near the top of a funicular railway. "We were a little bit crazy," Olinka told me. "We had tunnel vision. Like when you fall in love." Dražen finished the floors and painted the walls, restored the brick arches. He did such a great job that people kept asking Olinka: "Are you sure you wanted to break up with this guy?"

That's the pleasing irony of the museum's premise: that in creating a museum from their breakup, Olinka and Dražen ended up forming an enduring partnership. From the museum coffee shop, the mechanical bunny was visible in its glass case—a presiding mascot and a patron saint. "People think that the bunny is our object," Olinka told me. "But really the museum is our object. Everything that it's become."

Exhibit 3: A copy of *Walden,* by Henry David Thoreau
Bucharest, Romania
R. and I both started reading Walden *in the beginning of our relationship. It takes a certain amount of solitude to grow fond of* Walden, *and our relationship was a vessel where we could put both our isolations while keeping them separate, like water and oil. We were living together, but decided to sleep in different rooms, both reading* Walden *before falling asleep. It was our proxy: our bodies were separated by the wall in between our rooms, but our minds were converging towards the same ideas. By the time we broke up, neither of us had finished. Nevertheless, we continued reading it.*

Every caption at the museum was an education in the limits of my vision. What looked like an UNO game wasn't just an UNO game. It was the UNO game that an American soldier had planned to give his long-distance girlfriend—an Australian army widow, in the service herself, raising two small kids—but when they were finally done with their tours, and he came to Australia to meet her flight from Afghanistan, she told him she wasn't ready for a commitment. Years later, when he stumbled across this museum full of the residue of lost loves, he decided to donate the UNO game they'd never played. He'd been carrying it with him all that time.

Some of the exhibits conjured grand historical dramas, like the love letter written by a thirteen-year-old boy escaping Sarajevo under fire in 1992: a note he'd written to Elma—a girl stuck in the same convoy, in the car next to his—but hadn't had the courage to give her. He'd just given her his favorite Nirvana tape instead, since she'd forgotten to bring her own music.

But the objects that moved me most were the ordinary ones, because their ordinariness suggested that every love story—even the most familiar, the most predictable, the least dramatic—was worth putting in a museum. The museum's former manager, Ivana Družetić, understood their endeavor as a descendant of the curiosity cabinet: "Since the discovery of that which is the smallest and the reaching of that which is the furthest, the criteria no longer seem to be craving the extreme, but rather attempting to capture all that which falls in between."

These ordinary objects understood that a breakup is powerful because it saturates the banality of daily life, just as the relationship itself did: every errand, every annoying alarm-clock chirp, every late-night Netflix binge. Once love is gone, it's gone everywhere. It's a ghost suffusing daily life just as powerfully in its absence. A man leaves his shopping lists scattered across your days, cluttered with personality tics and gratuitous periods, poignant in their specificity: *lg. black trash bags* summoning that time the trash bags were too small, or *g. onion*, the type necessary for a particular fish stew prepared on a particular humid summer evening. The exhibits were all vocabulary words drawn from private shared languages that I would never entirely understand—the beaten-up pot, the plastic bin—or relics from two-person civilizations that no longer existed.

Some objects felt less like relics from the past and more like artifacts from unlived futures. A crumbling gingerbread cookie endured as stale eulogy for a one-day flirtation with an engaged man, a giddy afternoon spent at an Oktoberfest in Chicago, before a text from him arrived the next day: "It is hard for me to say this to you as you are a great girl but...please don't phone or text as I fear it would only cause trouble." It was so seemingly inconsequential—the chance encounter and the dismissive text—something you'd never expect to find immortalized.

And yet, there it was. A single Oktoberfest mattered enough to make a woman save a gingerbread cookie for years, until its frosting had gathered into pale broken scabs, and these scabs held the essence of the museum itself—its commitment to the oblique sadness of the "one-day thing," to attachments that might not seem worthy of commemoration, to the act of mourning what never happened. Which is part of any breakup: grieving the enduring relationship that never came to pass, the hypothetical relationship that could have worked. One soldier's wool sock came with a caption from his lover of twenty years: *I had two children with him and we never shared a real conversation. I always thought that, one day, it would begin.*

One journal at the museum, kept by a woman during one of her lover's bipolar episodes, was full of phrases repeated like mantras: *I am keeping my heart open* and *I am living in the now,* written over and over again. It was the triteness of those phrases that moved me. They weren't brilliant. They'd just been necessary.

Exhibit 4: Envelope with Single Human Hair

Karviná, Czech Republic

In 1993 I graduated college and taught English for a year in a coal mining village on the Polish/Czech border, a depressed, polluted, communist city in which I experienced loneliness like I'd never known before or since. The summer before I left, I met a Scottish boy named Colin at the amusement park in Salisbury Beach where he was running the Ferris wheel. After the summer, we wrote letters to each other, and sometimes a letter from him was the only thing that got me through my day. He had auburn curls I adored and once when the familiar airmail-blue envelope arrived in my box I saw he had taped the flap and a single piece of his curly hair got trapped under the tape: a part of his body, his DNA, that would one day be shared with our children. After he dumped me in a pretty cowardly way—just stopped writing—I still checked my box every day and wept,

then returned to my sad communist flat and wept, then looked at the
envelope that held his single curly hair and wept some more.

"The museum has always been two steps ahead of us," Olinka told me, explaining that it's had a will of its own from the start, an impulse to exist beyond her and Dražen. It was as if all these stories had already been waiting all around them—like humidity in the air, a sky ready to rain. Immediately after their shipping-crate exhibition, Olinka and Dražen got a call from a Japanese quiz show that wanted to film an episode in their museum. But there was no museum. It was like that from the beginning: people believing in the thing, *wanting* the thing, before it even existed.

In the decade since that first shipping crate, the museum has taken many shapes: permanent installations in Zagreb and Los Angeles, a virtual museum comprising thousands of photographs and stories, and forty-six pop-up installations all over the world—from Buenos Aires to Boise, Singapore to Istanbul, Cape Town to South Korea, from the Oude Kerk in Amsterdam's red-light district to the European Parliament in Brussels, all locally sourced, like an artisanal grocer, stocked with regional heartbreak.

Olinka told me anecdotes about particular exhibits: The Mexico City exhibit was flooded with more than two hundred donations in the first twenty-four hours. The South Korean exhibit was full of objects that had belonged to high-school students who'd died in a recent ferry accident. While French donors often narrated their own captions in the third person, American narratives usually featured a prominent first person—that all-American "I." American curators were also much more likely to use the first person when they talked about their exhibitions: *My collection. The donations I've gathered.* She and Dražen tried not to speak that way. It took a few years before they even introduced the backstory of their own breakup into the public narrative of their museum. They always believed the project belonged to something much larger than their private pain.

Objects make private histories public, but they also grant the past a certain integrity. Whenever memory conjures the past, it ends up papering over it: replacing the lost partner with memories and reconstructions, myths and justifications. But an object can't be distorted in these ways. It's still just a box of popcorn or a toaster, a hoodie that got drenched with sudden rain one night in 1997.

At another Zagreb exhibit I saw that week, this one devoted to the 1991 Serbian-Montenegrin attacks on Dubrovnik, it was the objects that felt most powerful: not the massive photographs showing pale stone forts exploded into plumes of smoke, but the small grenade shaped like a miniature black pineapple, and the crude cross a family had fashioned from pieces of an exploded artillery shell that hit their home. A soldier's pink flashlight sat beside a piece of shrapnel, a square of gauze stained with his blood, and a photo of him lying in a hospital bed with a bandage over one eye, rosary against his bare chest. His name was Ante Puljiz. Those words meant nothing to me. But that piece of shrapnel—it had been lodged inside his body.

Exhibit 5: Four Black Dresses

Brooklyn, New York

I would donate to the museum the four black dresses hanging in my closet: a shirtwaist, a sundress, a ribbed turtleneck, and an A-line of raw silk. Two of these dresses were given to me by my ex, and two I bought myself, but they all date from a time in my life when I imagined I could become the person I wanted to be by adopting a uniform. I thought—we both thought—that the problem of my un-femininity, my lack of interest in clothes, my general un-hipness, could be solved by my becoming one of those literary party regulars who dresses in black, makes cutting comments, and writes bestsellers. Two months before we broke up, this man said to me, "I'm just waiting to see if you become famous, because then I think I might fall in love with you." A horrible thing to say, clumsy in its attempt at honesty—yet I did see how this was what, on some level, I'd been promising him, the fantasy of a public self we'd been co-constructing. I would donate these dresses to the museum—except that I still wear them. All the time. It's just that I wear other dresses—purple, floral, geometric, pink—as well.

When I was young, before my parents separated, I believed that divorce was a ceremony just like marriage, only inverted: the couple walked down the aisle of a church, holding hands, and then, once they reached the altar, they unclasped their hands and walked away from each other. After a family friend's marriage ended, I asked her: "Did you have a nice divorce?" It seemed like a polite question. An ending seemed like something important enough to justify a ritual.

When performance artists Marina Abramovic and her partner Ulay decided to end their twelve-year relationship, they marked its conclusion by walking the length of the Great Wall of China. "People put so much effort into starting a relationship and so little effort into ending one," Abramovic explained. On March 30, 1988, she started walking from the eastern end of the Great Wall, the Bo Hai gulf on the Yellow Sea, and Ulay began walking from the western edge, in the Gobi Desert. They each walked for ninety days, covering roughly 1,500 miles, until they met in the middle, where they embraced to say goodbye. At a retrospective of Abramovic's work in Stockholm nearly thirty years later, two video screens showed scenes from their respective journeys: one screen showed Abramovic walking past camels on hard dirt covered with snow, while the other showed Ulay hiking with a walking stick over green hills. The tapes were running on a continuous loop, and it seemed beautiful to me that on those screens, decades after their breakup, these two lovers still walked constantly toward each other.

If every relationship is a collaboration—two people jointly creating the selves they will be with each other—this collaboration can sometimes feel like tyranny, forcing the self into a certain shape, and it can sometimes feel like birth, making a new self possible. Sometimes the comet tail left behind—the dresses you wore, the lipstick you tried, the books you bought but never read, the bands you pretended to like—can feel like broken shackles, but sometimes it's beautiful anyway: a dress reclaimed from costume, turned into silk skin for a Saturday night.

In truth, I've been obsessed with breakups since before I was ever in a relationship. I grew up in a family thick with divorces and overpopulated by remarriages: both sets of grandparents divorced, my mother's twice; both my parents married three times; my oldest brother divorced by forty. Divorce seemed less like an aberration than an inevitable stage in the life cycle of any love.

But in my family the ghosts of prior partners were rarely vengeful or embittered. My mother's first husband was a lanky hippie with the kindest eyes who once brought me a dream catcher. My beloved aunt's first husband was an artist who made masks from the dried palm fronds he gathered on beaches. These men enchanted me because they carried with them not only the residue of who my mom and aunt had been before I knew them, but also the spectral possibilities of who they might have become. Seventeen years after their divorce, my own parents had become so close that my mother, an Episcopal deacon, officiated my father's third wedding.

Which is all to say: I grew up believing that relationships would probably end, but I also grew up with the firm belief that even after a relationship was over, it was still a part of you, and that this wasn't necessarily a bad thing. When I asked my mother what object she would contribute to the museum, she chose a shirt she had bought in San Francisco, years before I was born, with the woman she had loved before she met my father.

I grew up with the sense that a broken relationship always amounted to more than its breakage. Everything that happened before it ended was not invalidated by the fact of its ending. Those memories of the relationship—the particular joys and frictions it held, the particular incarnation of self it permitted—didn't disappear, though the world didn't always make room for them. To speak of an ex too much was seen as a sign of some kind of pathology. The gospel of serial monogamy could have you believe that every relationship was an imperfect trial run, useful only as preparation for the relationship that finally stuck. In this model, a family full of divorces was a family full of failure. But I grew up seeing them as something else, grew up seeing every self as an accumulation of its loves, like a Russian nesting doll that held all of those relationships inside.

Exhibit 6: Paisley Shirt

San Francisco, California

It was sometime in 1967. We bought our paisley shirts from an outdoor rack in Haight-Ashbury. This was in the early heady days of our relationship; for me all the more intoxicating as it was my first lesbian love affair. Our shirts almost matched, but not quite; mine was psychedelic pink and hers purple. They were definitely first worn at a Jefferson Airplane concert, though the shirt carries memories of places it never went: a year backpacking and picking crops in Europe, leading an olive picker strike in Provence, a camping trip in Death Valley where we watched the sun set on one horizon while the moon rose on the other. It was all so good and right and full of hope, until it wasn't. I never understood why we ended, although my wanting children probably had something to do with it. The last time I saw her was at Gay Pride Day in Washington, D.C., in 1975. That's a long time ago but the paisley shirt has stayed with me. It reminds me of who I once was.

When I was a kid, I loved a book called *Grover and the Everything in the Whole Wide World Museum*. In the Whole Wide World Museum, Grover visits "The Things You See in the Sky Room" and the room full of "Long Thin Things You Can Write With," where a carrot has mistakenly wound up, so he returns it to an elegant marble pedestal in the middle of the otherwise empty "Carrot Room." As Grover reaches the end of the exhibits, he wonders: "Where did they put everything else?" That's when he reaches the wooden door marked: "Everything Else." When he opens it, of course, it's just the exit.

When I left the Museum of Broken Relationships, everything on the streets of Zagreb seemed like a possible exhibit, an object that had been part of a love affair or that might be, someday: a garden gnome grinning in front of lace curtains; purple modeling clay formed into uneven balls on a windowsill; orange plastic ashtrays near the top of the funicular railway; every toothpick sticking out of the sausages roasting on an outdoor griddle in Strossmartre; every cigarette butt in the clogged metal street grate on Hebrangova ulica; the scab as large as an apple on an old man's exposed shin as he rode a motorbike with an old woman gripping his waist. Perhaps someday she would wish she'd saved that scab as something to remember him by. The cloudless Zagreb day held potential heartbreak like a distant ticking bomb.

When I saw a man and woman sharing a bag of popcorn in Zrinjevac Park, I wondered if someday, once everything was broken, they would remember the accessories of this particular day like soil samples: her sunglasses, his sneakers. I imagined their popcorn on a pedestal, with a spotlight shining on it—*Bag of Popcorn; Zagreb, Croatia*—captioned by the story of another woman, or another man, or simply another year, how it dimmed exuberance into routine.

I could summon my own lost loves as an infinite catalog of ghostly objects: a pint of chocolate ice cream eaten on a futon above a falafel shop; a soggy tray of chili fries from the Tommy's at Lincoln and Pico;

a plastic vial of pink-eye medicine; twenty different T-shirt smells; beard hairs scattered like tea leaves across dingy sinks; a three-wheeled dishwasher tucked into the pantry I shared with the man I thought I would marry. But perhaps the deeper question is not about the objects themselves—what belongs in the catalog—but about why I enjoy cataloging them so much. What is it about the ache that I enjoy, that etched groove of remembering an old love, that vein of nostalgia?

After breaking up with my first boyfriend, when we were both freshmen in college on opposite sides of the country, I developed a curious attachment to the sadness of our breakup. Rather than sitting through our stilted phone conversations, I could smoke my cigarettes in the bitter cold of Boston nights and miss what it had been like to fall in love back in Los Angeles: warm evenings by the ocean, kissing on lifeguard stands. That sadness felt like a purified version of our bond, as if I was more connected to that man in missing him than I'd ever been while we were together. But it was more than that, too: the sadness itself became a kind of anchor, something I needed more than I'd ever needed him.

Exhibit 7: Steel-Guitar Slide
Fayetteville, West Virginia

The most potent relationship object in my possession is an old steel-guitar slide from the 1920s. It's a bar slide—or tone bar—meaning a simple chunk of chromed steel or brass, its original manufacture stamp worn away by constant fretting. My ex, a person of both exceptional musical ability and unusually destructive behavior, gave it to me (probably in a fit of the latter). I think it might have been his most prized possession, and he didn't tend to have many possessions. We were together for six years when I was very young, and the whole thing ended with me in a battered-women's shelter. I can't quite manage to get rid of the tone bar, though, and of course I think about all the blues that have poured through it over time: his, mine by way of his. It still seems more his than mine, though—my fingers don't even fit its edges—and I'd gladly return it to him if he wanted it back.

Olinka believes that "melancholy has been unjustly banished from the public space," and told me she mourns the fact that it has been driven into ghettos, replaced by the eerie optimism of Facebook status updates. A guitar slide can hold the blues—"his, mine by way of his"—or a museum can hold the blues, insisting we need to make room for them. Olinka has always imagined her museum as a "civic temple where melancholy has the right to exist," where sadness can be understood as something other than a feeling meant to be replaced. She doesn't like when people praise her museum's "therapeutic value." It insists that sadness needs curing.

For fifteen years of my life, between my first breakup and my last one, I was committed to a nearly opposite belief in sadness as a rarefied state: an affective distillery that could summon the strongest and purest version of me. But walking through Zagreb that week, two and a half years married and two months pregnant, I was not looking for places to smoke and feel lonely, scraping out my insides with unfiltered European cigarettes. I was looking for fresh fruit that might satisfy my sudden and overwhelming cravings: a paper bag of cherries from the outdoor market, or doughnut peaches so ripe their juice spilled onto my dress the moment my teeth punctured their skin.

I'd always struggled with relationships once they lost their earliest states of unfettered love and unbridled passion. I found the aftermath of that early glow muddy and compromised. But getting married had meant committing to another kind of beauty: the striated beauty of continuity, letting love accrete its layers over the years, showing up to intimacy in all its difficulty as well as its giddiness, staying inside something long enough to hold its previous rough patches like talismans, to tell yourself: *This has another side.*

Back in my Zagreb hotel room, my phone buzzed with a message from a friend who was waiting at an airport in Colorado to meet the flight of a man she was falling in love with, and then a text from another friend: "We just broke up. Are you around? Just don't want to be alone all weekend."

The world is always beginning and ending at once. Icarus falls from the sky while someone swipes right on Tinder.

At the Broken Relationships pop-up installation in Boise, Idaho, one man donated an answering machine that played a message from his ex, calling him an asshole, immediately followed by a message from his dad, talking about something as ordinary as the weather. This is heartbreak: rupture is huge in your heart, while the rest of the world is checking on scattered showers. Your ex can't stand the fact of your existence in the world, and your brother wants to know if you saw the Knicks game last night. The appeal of the museum is also about this: wanting company, wanting to turn the experience of becoming solitary into something social instead. *We just broke up. Are you around? Just don't want to be alone all weekend.*

French conceptual artist Sophie Calle explained the premise of her 2007 installation *Take Care of Yourself* like this: "I received an email telling me it was over. I didn't know how to respond...It ended with the words, 'Take care of yourself.' And so I did." For Calle, taking care of herself meant asking 107 women to interpret his note: "To analyze it, comment on it, dance it, sing it. Dissect it. Exhaust it. Understand it for me." Her exhibition was composed of the chorus of their reactions. A "researcher in lexicometry" noted a lack of agency in the breakup note's grammar. A proofreader highlighted its repetitions. A lawyer deemed her ex guilty of deceit. A criminologist diagnosed him as "proud, narcissistic, and egotistical."

Witnessing breakups and asking mine to be witnessed have been part of every deep friendship of my life. It's the art of collaborating as close readers, soothsayers, tea-leaf translators, alternate-narrative makers: "darlin, can i beg you for a read on this?" a friend wrote once, forwarding an email from a man she'd just broken up with. "I'm struggling to be sure I'm not being a hysterical woman…could just use someone else's eyes on this exchange, for total sense of closure. crazy grateful for you." The breakup as social experience isn't kiss-and-tell so much as a desire not to be alone in facing the end of the story. Kicked out as character, you become a reader, parsing the wreckage. It feels so much better not to read alone.

Exhibit 8: Plastic Bag of Pistachio Nuts
Iowa City
Dave and I spent four years together. We moved across the country and back. We drove a U-Haul across Pennsylvania in the middle of a rainstorm, and then we did it again, two years later, headed the opposite direction. Pennsylvania surprised us with its size; somehow it did this twice. I loved Dave with all of myself, like a wet cloth wrung out. In the first apartment we shared—once things had deteriorated and we were fighting frequently—we started to notice these gray moths flitting clumsily around our kitchen. When we smashed them against the walls, their innards left silvery trails against the pale paint. We kept killing them, kept fighting, kept hoping that if we killed enough moths, if we had enough fights, then eventually we'd get rid of them for good. After several months, we discovered where the moths were coming from: a plastic bag in the pantry full of old pistachios, thick with the white webbing of their tiny eggs. We threw it out. I kept hoping we'd discover our equivalent of that bag—the core of all our fights, their primal source—so we could banish it.

My breakup with Dave, at the end of my twenties, mattered more than any other breakup ever had, and lasted longer—the loss itself, and its aftermath. Dave and I had spent much of our relationship trying to figure out if our relationship could work, and I thought that breaking up would liberate us from that pull-and-tug. It didn't. We broke up, got back together, broke up again, then talked about getting married. Our split became my partner the way Dave had been my partner. There was an absence that held his shape, and it followed me everywhere.

We often describe our ghosts as voices whispering to us, but I felt Dave as spectral ear, someone to whom I kept wanting to whisper. For years after we broke up, every thought I had was constructed partially for him. I kept a physical list of things I wanted to tell him but couldn't—mainly silly, daily things: the snow piled between my inner and outer windows during blizzards; how I'd dug out my own car after the storm, and two lawyers had yelled at me for parking in their lot; the broiled grapefruit with a burnt-sugar crust I'd eaten at our local diner, without him, who loved grapefruits; all the men I'd seen or thought about seeing in his absence. "I want a man here to touch me," I wrote, "just so I'll put down this list and stop writing to you."

Memories came at me like the state of Pennsylvania in a rainstorm. Every time I thought he was over, that I'd traveled through him, it turned out he wasn't over yet. I could go as many miles as I wanted and there would still be more of how it felt to lose him. I seemed okay, because I said so all the time to friends, and often it felt true, as if my feelings were locked away somewhere else, and the key had been taken from me for my own protection. But sometimes in the night, alone, I woke up desperate for that key—to open the door, to get to the locked space. Maybe he would be there, waiting.

After a bad sunburn, when my skin peeled away in curling strips that wadded up like bits of dried masking tape between my fingers, I thought: *This is the skin he touched.* My ridiculous mourning. No reasoning with it. My skin kept coming off me like shredded paper, drifting in flakes all over my clothes, my little Toyota. He was everywhere, the dust of him.

Standing in an airport line, I watched a blue-eyed couple who teased each other amicably. Who would have to replace his/her passport first? He would! No, she would! He swatted her with his plush neck pillow. They had matching silver-plated luggage tags attached to their matching leather-trimmed roller duffels. In those days, I treated every couple like a crime scene to scour for clues, or a recipe to steal. How did they choose their matching luggage, and how did they stand in line without bickering, and how did it feel to be grooved into a shared last name etched in silver? I wanted to feel superior to the shallow life I projected onto them, but even that meager consolation gave way to wondering: *What did they have that we didn't? What could they manage that we couldn't?*

"Perhaps the hardest thing about losing a lover is / to watch the year repeat its days," Anne Carson wrote. "It is as if I could dip my hand down // into time and scoop up / blue and green lozenges of April heat / a year ago in another country." When I dipped my cupped palms into the past I'd shared with Dave, every remembered moment hardened into something cleaner and more purely happy than it had really been. Nostalgia rearranges the rooms of memory: it makes the beds, puts a vase of flowers on the dresser, opens the curtains to let in the sun. It gets harder and harder to say, *It was painful to live there.* The voice of insistence goes faint: *It was.* Because we miss it. We miss what was hard about it. We miss it all.

On the first night we ever kissed, I told Dave: "I didn't feel alive. Now I do."

Exhibit 9: Bottle of Crystal Pepsi
Queens, New York
After the end of my relationship with the man I thought I would marry, I met an unexpectedly wonderful lawyer who lived in Queens. He took me to trivia night at his local bar in Astoria. He took me to

a Christmas party at his law office near Times Square. He took me to the Blazer Pub, near his childhood home upstate, where we ate burgers and played shuffle bowling. I knew he wasn't "the one" but also suspected I no longer believed in "the one"—not because I'd never met him, but because I had and now we were done. The lawyer made me laugh. He made me feel comfortable. We ate comfort food. We made pancakes with raspberries and white chocolate chips and watched movies on weekend mornings. He found old reruns of Legends of the Hidden Temple, *the stupid game show we'd both loved as kids, and gave me a ten-year-old bottle of Crystal Pepsi he'd found online—my favorite soda when I was young, discontinued for years. He was remarkable, but I couldn't ever quite see him—or see that—because I never really believed in us. Nothing about us made me feel challenged. His devotion started to feel like a kind of claustrophobia. It was like he taught me how much I struggled to live inside love—to understand something as love—without difficulty.*

Nine months after Dave and I broke up, I started to see a man who felt like his opposite. Or at least that was the story I told myself. He wasn't a poet but a lawyer, with an office job in Midtown. We didn't have explosive fights, perhaps because I hadn't placed my heart in his hands—in his in-box, in his U-Haul, in his pantry—for safekeeping. But our relationship gave me sustaining laughter and genuine joy, fluttery sensations in my stomach, after years spent fighting for and with a relationship that wasn't working. It suggested that the things I'd always thought I wanted from a partner—charisma, elusiveness—weren't necessarily the things I needed most.

In many ways, our relationship was another chapter in the unfolding story of my relationship with Dave, part of its epilogue. When the lawyer and I broke up, it felt less like a fresh sadness and more like a return to the sadness that was already there, missing the one

I'd been missing all along. A few months later, I met the man I would marry.

Before I left for Croatia, I thought of bringing the bottle of Crystal Pepsi the lawyer had given me, to donate to the museum as a memento of my last breakup before marriage. But I never put it in my luggage. Why did I want to keep it at home, on my bookshelf? It had something to do with wanting to acknowledge the man who'd given it to me, because I hadn't given him enough credit while we were together. Keeping his last gift was a way of granting him credit in the aftermath.

The whole time I wandered the Museum of Broken Relationships, I kept imagining all the objects that *hadn't* been donated, all the objects that people couldn't stand to part with, lurking like a ghost collection behind the thousands of objects (more than three thousand) that had. I thought of all the objects my friends had described—the clamshell necklace, the shopping list, the single human hair stuck on the envelope, the four black dresses, and the steel-guitar slide—some lost, some tucked away, some repurposed as part of a new life.

If I'm honest with myself, keeping that bottle of Crystal Pepsi isn't just about honoring the man who gave it to me, or what we shared. It also has to do with enjoying that glimpse of sadness and dissolution, with holding on to some reminder of the pure, riveting feeling of being broken. These days my life is less about the sublime state of solitary sadness or fractured heartbreak and more about waking up each day and making sure I show up to my commitments. My days in Zagreb were about Skyping with my husband and emailing a good-morning video to my stepdaughter. They were about feeding the fetus inside me: Istrian *fuži* with truffles, noodles in thick cream; sea bream with artichokes; something called a domestic pie; something called a vitamins salad.

Life now is less about the electricity of thresholds and more about continuance, coming back and muddling through; less about the grand drama of ending and more about the daily work of salvage and sustenance. I keep the Crystal Pepsi because it's a souvenir from those fifteen years I spent in a cycle of beginnings and endings, each one an opportunity for self-discovery and reinvention and transformative emotion; a way to feel infinite in the variety of possible selves that could come into being. I keep the Crystal Pepsi because I want some reminder of a self that felt volcanic and volatile — bursting into bliss, or into tears — and because I want to keep some proof of all the unlived lives, the ones that could have been.

The Quickening

When you were the size of a poppy seed, I sat in the bathroom of a Boston hotel room and peed on a stick I'd bought from an elderly man at a drugstore near Fenway Park. I laid the plastic on the cold tiles and waited for it to tell me if you existed. I wanted you to exist so badly. It had been a year of chipper emails from my fertility app, asking if I'd had sex on the right nights, and a year of sunken hearts whenever I spotted blood: at work, at home, in a sandy bathroom on a chilly beach just north of Morro Bay. Each rusty stain took away the narrative I'd spent the past few weeks imagining—that *this* would be the month I found out I was having a baby. My body kept reminding me that it controlled the story. But then, there you were.

A week later, I sat in a movie theater and watched aliens hatch from their human hosts in a spaceship mess hall. Their dark, glistening bodies broke open rib cages and burst through the torn skin. An evil robot was obsessed with helping them survive. When the captain asked him, "What do you believe in?" the robot said, simply: "Creation." This was just before the captain's chest ripped apart to show its own parasite baby: horrific, beetle-black, newly born.

When a nurse asked me to step on a scale at my first prenatal appointment, it was the first time I had weighed myself in years. Refusing to weigh myself had been one way to leave behind the days I'd spent weighing myself compulsively. Standing on a scale and actually *wanting* to see that I'd gained weight—this was a new version of me. One of the oldest scripts I'd ever heard about motherhood was that it could turn you into a new version of yourself, but that promise had always seemed too easy to be believed. I'd always believed more fully in another guarantee—that wherever you go, there you are.

When I was a freshman in college, I walked into my dorm-room closet every morning to step on the scale I kept hidden there. It was embarrassing to starve myself, and so for the ritual of weighing I retracted into the dark, out of sight, tucked into the folds of my musty winter coats. Since my growth spurt at thirteen, it seemed like I'd been looming over everyone. Being tall was supposed to make you confident, but it just made me feel excessive. There was too much of me, always, and I was always so awkward and quiet, failing to earn all the space I took up.

In the years since those days of restriction, I have found that usually when I try to articulate this to people—"I felt like I wasn't supposed to take up so much space"—they understand it absolutely or not at all. And if a person understands it absolutely, she is probably a woman.

Those hungry days were full of Diet Cokes and cigarettes and torch songs on Napster; a single apple and a small allotment of crackers each day; long walks through frigid winter nights to the gym and back again; trouble seeing straight, as dark flecks crowded the edges of my vision. My hands and feet were always cold. My skin was always pale. It was as if I didn't have enough blood to go around.

During my pregnancy, fifteen years later, my gums bled constantly. A doctor told me it was because my body was circulating more blood—four pounds more of it—to satisfy the tiny second set of organs. This extra blood swelled me. It heated me. My veins were feverish highways, thick with that hot red syrup, flooded with necessary volume.

When you were the size of a lentil, I flew to Zagreb for a magazine assignment. As our plane banked over Greenland, I ate a huge bag of Cheez-Its and wondered if this was the week your brain was being forged, or your heart. I pictured a heart made of Cheez-Its beating inside me, inside you. Much of that first trimester was spent in awe and terror: astonished that a tiny creature was being gathered in my inner reaches, petrified that I would somehow knock you loose. What if you died and I didn't know it? I obsessively googled "miscarriage without bleeding." I kept my hand over my abdomen to make sure you stayed. You were my bouquet of cells, my soft pit of becoming. I cried when I found out you would be a girl. It was as if you had suddenly sharpened into focus. The pronoun was a body forming around you. I was a body forming around you.

When I told my mom I was flying to Croatia, she asked me to consider staying home. "Take it easy," she said. But she also told me that when she was five months pregnant with my oldest brother, she'd swum the length of a bay in Bari while an elderly Italian man, worried, followed her the whole way in his rowboat.

On our plane to Zagreb, a toddler cried in front of us, and then another toddler cried behind. I wanted to tell you, *I know these wailers are your people.* I wanted to tell you, *The world is full of stories:* the men in hand-knit yarmulkes who had delayed our takeoff for an hour because they wouldn't sit next to any women; the man across the aisle who'd stabbed himself with a blood-sugar needle right after eating his foil-wrapped square of goulash, who watched the little icon of our plane creep over the dull blue screen of the Atlantic. Who could know what he was dreaming? What beloved he was flying toward? I wanted to tell you, *Baby, I've seen such incredible things in this life*. You weren't a baby yet. You were a possibility. But I wanted to tell you that every person you'd ever meet would hold an infinite world inside. It was one of the only promises I could make to you in good conscience.

W hen I was starving myself, I kept two journals. One tallied the number of calories I consumed each day. The other described all the food I imagined eating. One notebook was full of what I did; the other was full of what I dreamed of doing. My hypothetical feasts were collages made from restaurant menus and saturated with the minute attention of desperation: not just mac-'n'-cheese but *four-cheese* mac-'n'-cheese; not just burgers but burgers with melted cheddar and fried eggs; molten chocolate–lava cake with ice cream pooling around its gooey heart. Restricting made me fantasize about the possibility of a life where I did nothing *but* eat. I didn't want to eat normally; I wanted to eat constantly. There was something terrifying about finishing, as if I had to confront that I hadn't actually been satisfied.

In those days, I filled my mouth with heat and smoke and empty sweetness: black coffee, cigarettes, mint gum. I was ashamed of how desperately I wanted to consume. Desire was a way of taking up space, but it was embarrassing to have too much of it—in the same way it had been embarrassing for there to be too much of me, or to want a man who didn't want me. Yearning for things was slightly less embarrassing if I denied myself access to them, so I grew comfortable in states of longing without satisfaction. I came to prefer hunger to eating, epic yearning to daily loving.

But during pregnancy, years later, the ghost of that old skeletal girl sloughed off like a snakeskin. I moved toward chocolate-chip muffins of unprecedented size. At the coffee shop near my apartment, I licked the grease from an almond croissant off my fingers and listened to one barista ask another, "You know that girl Bruno was dating?" She squinted at her cell phone. "I know she's pregnant, but... what the fuck is she eating? Horses?"

It took me five or six months to show. Before that, people would say: "You don't look pregnant *at all*!" They meant it as a compliment. The female body is always praised for staying within its boundaries, for making even its sanctioned expansion impossible to detect.

When you were the size of a blueberry, I ate my way through Zagreb, palming handfuls of tiny strawberries at the outdoor market, then ordering a massive slice of chocolate cake from room service back at my hotel, then inhaling a Snickers bar because I was too hungry to wait for the cake to arrive. My hands were always sticky. I felt feral. My hunger was a different land from where I'd lived before.

As you grew from lime to avocado, I ate endless pickles, loving their salty snap between my teeth. I drank melted ice cream straight from the bowl. It was a kind of longing that did not imply absence. It was longing that belonged. The word *longing* itself traces its origins back to pregnancy. An 1899 dictionary defines it as "one of the peculiar and often whimsical desires experienced by pregnant women."

When you were the size of a mango, I flew to Louisville to give a talk and got so hungry after my daily vat of morning oatmeal that I decided to walk to brunch, and got so hungry on the walk to brunch that I stopped on the way for a snack: a flaky slice of spanakopita that stained its paper bag with islands of oil. By the time I got to brunch, I was so hungry that I couldn't decide between scrambled eggs with biscuits, or sausage links blistered with grease, or a sugar-dusted stack of lemon pancakes, so I got them all.

This endless permission felt like the fulfillment of a prophecy: all those imaginary menus I had obsessively transcribed at seventeen. Eating was fully permitted now that I was doing it for someone else. I had never eaten like this, as I ate for you.

When I was living on crackers and apple slices, I didn't get my period for years. It made me proud. The absence lived inside me like a secret trophy. Blood leaking out of me seemed like another kind of excess. Not bleeding was an appealing form of containment. It was also, quite literally, the opposite of fertility. By thinning my body, it was as if I'd vanquished my physical self. Starving myself testified to the intensity of my loneliness, my self-loathing, my simultaneous distance from the world and my hopeless proximity; a sense of being—at once—too much and not enough.

When I got pregnant at the age of twenty-four, a few years after I started getting my period again, I saw the telltale cross on the stick and felt flooded not by fear or wariness—as I'd imagined—but by wonder. I was carrying this tiny potential life. Even as I knew intellectually that I would get an abortion, I still felt that sharp rising lift of awe in my gut. That awe planted something deep inside me, a tether. It said: *Someday you'll be back*.

It was only after I'd gotten the abortion that I started to notice babies on the street. Their little faces watched me from their strollers. They had my number. It wasn't regret. It was anticipation. I'd been magnetized. I didn't want to hold other people's babies, I just knew that I would eventually want to hold my own—want to watch her bloom into consciousness right in front of me, apart from me, beyond me; want to be surprised and mystified by a creature who had come from me but was *not* me.

During the year I spent trying to get pregnant, a decade after my abortion, my friend Rachel told me about watching her infant son have a febrile seizure. Her description of her own terror was humbling. It wasn't something I could fully understand. I'd always resisted the idea that parenting involves a love deeper than any love you've ever felt before, and some part of me wanted to give birth just so I could argue against that belief, just so I could say: *This love isn't deeper, just different.* But another part of me knew it was possible I'd simply become another voice saying: *There is no love as deep as this.*

Once I finally got pregnant, my gratitude was sharpened by the wait. My body had decided to bestow this little purse of organs when it could have just as easily withheld it. This second heartbeat was nothing I could take for granted. After my first ultrasound, I got on the subway and looked at every single passenger, thinking, *You were once curled up inside another person.*

As you grew to the size of a turnip, then a grapefruit, then a cauliflower, I wanted to build you from joy: summer rainstorms and fits of laughter; the voices of women in endless conversation. With my friend Kyle, I swam naked in a pool at night, under eucalyptus trees shushing in the hot breeze, while your kicks swelled under my skin like waves. With Colleen, I drove to a rickety old house perched on a hill above a post office, where rattling trees tapped our windows. By lamplight, we ate eggs with bright yellow yolks. She left the sink full of their broken shells, just as she had when we lived together, after both our hearts had been broken.

Back in Los Angeles, your grandmother had a Cameroonian refugee staying with her. What can I say? This was hardly surprising. It made me clench my fists with longing, how much I wanted you and your grandmother to have a thousand years together in this world, nothing less. My hunger for my mother during pregnancy was like my hunger for fruit, for a second Snickers bar, for the scrambled eggs and the sausage links and the lemon pancakes. There was no bottom to it. She told me she could still remember looking at the snow piled on the branches outside the window of her doctor's office when he told her I would be a girl, as if all her longing had gathered on those branches—impossibly beautiful, utterly ordinary.

I wanted to give you the best parts of my love for your father—how we rented a house in a tiny town in northern Connecticut, that summer I was pregnant with you, and lay on a big white bed listening to the wail of the trains and the patter of rain on the creek and imagined it falling on the blue tarp covering the hot-dog stand across the road. We ate hamburgers at a roadside shack and swam at Cream Hill Lake, where the teenage lifeguards almost kicked us out because we weren't members. We barely deserved that deep blue water, those shores thick with trees, those wooden buoys dappled with sunshine. We'd had our whispered resentments, our nights of fighting. But I want you to picture us there: our voices bantering, our laughter entwined. I want you to know you were built from medium-rare meat and late-afternoon light.

When I finally got treatment, it gave me a sudden, liquid thrill to glimpse the diagnosis written on one of my medical forms: *eating disorder*. It was as if there was finally an official name for how I felt—the sense of inadequacy and dislocation—as if the words had constructed a tangible container around those intangible smoke signals of hurt. It made me feel consolidated.

The psychiatrist who diagnosed me wasn't interested in that consolidation. When I told her about being lonely—probably not the first college student to do so—she said, "Yes, but how is starving yourself going to *solve* that?" She had a point. Though I hadn't been trying to solve the problem, only express it, maybe even amplify it.

But how to translate these self-defeating impulses into the language of rational actors? I'd failed to justify the disorder with a Legitimate Reason, like failing to supply a parent's note excusing my absence from school.

For fifteen years after that appointment, I kept looking for that note. I kept trying to explain myself to that doctor, kept trying to purge my shame about the disorder by listing its causes: my loneliness, my depression, my desire for control. All of these reasons were true. None of them was sufficient. This was what I'd say about my drinking years later, and what I came to believe about human motivations more broadly: we never do anything for just one reason.

The first time I wrote about the disorder, six years after getting help, I thought if I framed it as something selfish and vain and self-indulgent, then I could redeem myself with self-awareness, like saying enough Hail Marys to be forgiven for my sins. I still thought of the disorder as something I needed to be forgiven for.

When I submitted that early jumbled attempt to a writing workshop, another graduate student raised his hand during the discussion to ask if there was such a thing as too much honesty. "I find it incredibly difficult to like the narrator of this essay," he said. I found his phrasing amusing, *the narrator of this essay,* as if she were a stranger we could gossip about. It was my first nonfiction class, and I wasn't used to the rules of displacement—all of us pretending we weren't also critiquing one another's lives. After class, the same man who'd found it difficult to like my narrator asked me if I wanted to get a drink. In my head I said, *Fuck you,* but out loud I said, "Sounds great." The less you liked me, the more I wanted you to.

By getting pregnant, it seemed as if I had finally managed to replace "the narrator of this essay"—a sick girl obsessed with her own pain, difficult to like—with a nobler version of myself: a woman who wasn't destroying her own body, but using her body to make another body she would care for. A stubborn internal voice was still convinced that the eating disorder had been all about the "I," all about whittling myself to the shape of that tall rail. Now pregnancy promised a new source of gravity: the "you." Strangers smiled at me constantly on the street.

At my ob-gyn, once a patient was pregnant, she got to ascend to the second floor. I no longer visited the regular gynecological suites on the lower level. I got to glide up an atrium staircase instead, destined for ultrasounds and prenatal vitamins, leaving behind those gonorrhea tests and birth-control prescriptions—as if I were advancing to the next level of a video game, or had earned a ticket to the afterlife.

By the time you were the size of a coconut, I was audibly huffing my way up the subway stairs. My belly was a twenty-pound piece of luggage I carried everywhere. My ligaments stretched and snapped, painful enough to make me gasp. Each evening, my legs were overcome by a maddening fidgeting sensation, something my doctor would call "restless legs syndrome." At a movie one night, I kept compulsively crossing and recrossing them, unable to hold still, so I left the theater to sit in a bathroom stall for ten minutes. My legs jerked and stretched as if they were being commanded by someone else, as if the tiny being inside had already taken control.

When I was in the middle of a three-month-long cold, my mother chided me for refusing to alter the pace of my life. "I know you don't want to disrupt your plans," she told me, "but there will be a point when you won't have a choice. You will go into labor, and your plans will be disrupted." It was what I was most afraid of—being disrupted. It was also what I craved more than anything.

In a way, I was grateful for the physical difficulty of my third trimester. It made me feel like I was doing my job. During the first few months, when morning sickness hadn't shown up, it had been like failing to cry at a funeral. Wasn't I supposed to feel my boundaries flooded by pregnancy? Wasn't I supposed to hurt? Wasn't that Eve's original punishment? *I will greatly multiply thy sorrow and thy conception; in sorrow thou shalt bring forth children.*

Some part of me craved pain as proof that I was already a good mother, long-suffering, while another part of me wanted to reject hardship as the only possible proof of devotion. I'd been so eager to fall in love with pregnancy as a conversion narrative, promising to destroy the version of myself who equated significance with suffering and replace her with a different woman altogether—someone who happily watched the numbers on the scale grow bigger, who treated herself well, and focused on her baby, and devoted herself wholly to un-conflicted calories and virtuous gratitude.

But as it turned out, pregnancy wasn't a liberation from prior selves so much as a container holding every prior version of myself at once. I didn't get to shed my ghosts so fully. It was easy to roll my eyes at people saying, "You don't look pregnant *at all*," and harder to admit the pride I felt when I heard it. It was easy to call my doctor absurd when she chided me for gaining five pounds in a month (rather than four!), and harder to admit that I'd honestly felt shamed by her in that moment. It was harder to admit the part of me that felt a secret thrill every time a doctor registered concern that I was "measuring small." This pride was something I'd wanted desperately to leave behind. I worried that it was impeding your growth, which was really just the distillation of a deeper fear—that I would infect you with my own broken relationship to my body, that you would catch it like a dark inheritance.

When you were the size of a pineapple, I wrote a birth plan. This was part of my birth class, but it was also a species of prophecy: telling the story of a birth before it happened.

The birth-class teacher pointed triumphantly at a model pelvis made of plastic. She said, "People think there's not that much room for the baby's head to pass through. But there's actually *a lot* of room." I squinted at the pelvis. Not *that* much room.

In a way, we all lived toward that pain. It wasn't just about suffering; it was about knowledge. It was impossible to understand the pain until you'd undergone it. That opacity compelled me. *In sorrow thou shalt bring forth children.* The pain had been punishment for eating the apple, for wanting to know. Now the pain itself had become the knowledge. Soon I would become someone who had a birth story. I just didn't know what that story would be. It was understood, of course, that there were no guarantees. Anyone could have a C-section. It cast its shadow across everything. It was what you tried to avoid. The pushing—the *labor*—was what made the delivery real. That's the implicit equation I'd absorbed.

In writing my birth plan, I saved my strongest language for the golden hour. That was what they called the first hour after birth, when your new body would rest against mine. The phrase itself sounded like a chiming bell. If I wanted this golden hour, I was told, I needed to insist on it: *I would like immediate uninterrupted skin-to-skin contact with her until the first feeding is accomplished*, I wrote in my plan. It was like casting a spell. I would bring you into the world. You would live against my skin. You would eat.

When you were larger than a honeydew but smaller than a watermelon, the new year brought a blizzard. It was three weeks before my due date. My doctor was worried you were too small, so she had scheduled another growth scan. I trudged through piles of snow to get to her office in Manhattan, wrapping my arms around the swaddled globe of my belly, around a coat that would not zip, saying, "Mine,

mine, mine." My sense of ownership was sharpened by the icy flurry all around me. It was primal.

At her office, my doctor said it was a funny thing about storms — some people believed they made a woman's water more likely to break. It had to do with the drop in barometric pressure. This seemed like something one midwife might whisper to another in the barn, while the sky filled with clouds, and like a fairy tale it came true that night. I woke at three in the morning, stepped out of bed, and the hot warmth gushed out. My mother's first birth, with my oldest brother, had also begun this way. It was almost biblical, I told myself: *As it was for the mother, so it shall be for the daughter.* There was a pleasing symmetry.

My birth-class teacher had recommended going back to sleep if my water broke in the middle of the night, because I would need the rest. I did not go back to sleep. I could not even imagine the version of myself that might go back to sleep. Plus, I still seemed to be leaking. I sat on the toilet with my laptop on my legs and felt the amniotic fluid leave my body while I edited an essay about female rage. When I sent it to my editor, I added at the bottom: "PS: I am in labor." By the time we took a cab to the hospital the following afternoon, my body was knotting with pain every few minutes as we headed up that glorious stretch of the highway beside the East River, lined by docks and basketball courts and gleaming skyscrapers looming across the water.

The pain meant my body knew what it needed to do to bring you here. And I was grateful that my body knew, because my mind did not. It was now the body's humble servant, begging with its crudest, truest words: *Please do this. I want this more than I've ever wanted anything.*

After we got to the hospital, I labored through the early evening and into the night. A monitor above my bed showed two lines: my contractions, and your heartbeat. My doctor started to get worried, because when the first line spiked, the second plummeted. That wasn't supposed to be happening. Your heartbeat always came back up, my doctor said.

But we needed to stop it from dropping. It was supposed to stay between 160 and 110. *Don't drop*, I willed the graph. *Don't drop*. I watched the monitor vigilantly. It was as if I were trying to keep your heart rate above the danger line through sheer force of will. Belief in willpower was another familiar ghost, one of the gospels of my hungry days.

When your heart rate stabilized, it felt like we were working together—you and I—as if you'd heard me calling out, as if you'd felt my stubborn insistence that you be okay settle like a sturdy floor beneath you. The contractions were an exploded version of the hot, twisting cramps I'd felt during the nights following my abortion. But really the pain was exactly like everyone had described it: impossible to describe. Someone had told me to picture myself lying on a sandy beach, that each contraction would be a wave washing over me with pain, and in between those waves my job was to soak up as much warmth as I could from the sun. But very little in that delivery room felt like waves, or sand, or sun. I asked for an epidural: a helicopter that would spirit me away from the shore entirely. Approximately ten thousand minutes passed between my saying "I'd like an epidural" and actually getting one.

Early in my pregnancy, my husband told me that his first wife had been determined to have a natural birth. "With you," he said, "I imagine it being more like, *Give me all the drugs you've got*." I was indignant, but couldn't argue. The story of the woman determined to have a natural childbirth felt nobler than the story of the woman who asked for all the drugs right away, just as the story of the pregnant woman felt nobler than the story of the woman who starved herself. There was something petty or selfish or cowardly about insisting on too much control, about denying the body its size or its discomfort.

Around two in the morning—nearly twenty-four hours after my

water broke, following several hours of sweet epidural haze—a nurse I didn't know came into the room. "Looks like you're having problems with the fetal heart rate." Her tone sounded accusatory. It was as if I'd been withholding this information.

"What's wrong with her heart rate?" I asked. I thought you and I had managed to bring it up. But when I looked at the monitor, it was just below 110—and dipping further.

Another nurse came in. "Could you use another pair of hands?" she asked, and the first nurse said: "I could definitely use another pair of hands."

Why do you need so many hands? I wanted to ask, but I didn't want to distract them from whatever their hands needed to do. More nurses arrived. They told me they needed a better measurement of your heart rate. They stuck a wand inside me. They had me roll onto one side, then the other. They stuck the wand inside me again. They asked me to get on all fours.

"We're not finding it," the first nurse said, her voice more urgent, and I wanted to ask: *It's not there, or you can't hear it?* It was the only question in the world.

Then my doctor was in the room. She told me they were seeing what they didn't want to see. She said, "Your baby's heart rate is dropping and it's not coming up."

Everything happened very quickly after that: ten people in the room, fifteen, many of them rolling me onto the gurney, my legs still paralyzed from the epidural. Your father grabbed my hand. A voice called out, "It's in the sixties!" And another, "It's in the fifties!" I knew they were talking about your heart. Then they were pushing me down the hallway on the gurney, running. A nurse fit a surgical cap onto my doctor's head as she ran.

In the operating room, a man pinched my abdomen and asked if I could feel him pinching. I said I could. He seemed annoyed. I said they should just go ahead and cut me open anyway. He put something else in my IV and the next time they pinched me I didn't feel anything. My doctor said I was going to feel pressure, not pain. Everything would happen on the other side of the blue curtain, where the rest of my body was.

My husband sat on a stool beside the operating table—worried, in a blue surgical cap—and I watched his face like a mirror, trying to read your fate. It was only when I heard the doctor's voice say, "Hey there, cutie pie," that I knew they had opened me up and found you waiting there, ready to be born.

E very birth story is the story of two births: the child is born, and the mother is born, too—constructed by the story of how she brought her child into the world, shaped by the birthing and then again by the telling. My birth plan stayed folded in my hospital duffel bag. It was the story of a thing that never happened.

Instead, a team of doctors separated my mind from my womb with a blue tarp. The hands of another woman reached in to pull you out. My body went from collaborator to enemy. It was no longer laboring; it had failed. It needed to be cut open. The process needed to be saved by other people, because I hadn't managed it myself. I'm not saying this is the truth about C-sections. I'm saying this is the truth of what I felt. I felt betrayed.

I'd always heard labor described in terms of triumphant capacity, but giving birth to you was a lesson in radical humility. My story was disrupted. My body was disrupted. You arrived and showed me that pain had never been my greatest teacher. You arrived and showed me I'd never been in control. Giving birth to you didn't matter because my body had been in pain, or because it hadn't been in enough pain. It mattered because you showed up glistening and bewildered and perfect. You were still part of me. You were beyond me.

If the work of starvation had been as small and airless as a closet, then the work of birth was as wide as the sky. It expanded with all the unknowns of a life that would happen in the body that my body had made possible.

For much of the first hour after you were born, I was still lying on the gurney, asking if I could hold you. Your father reminded me that I was still in surgery. He was right. My abdomen was still gaping open. My body was still shaking from all the drugs they'd given me to numb the things that had gone right, and then the things that had gone wrong.

I didn't know I would keep shaking for hours. I knew only that your father was pointing to one corner of the room, where they were carrying a tiny bundle to the incubator. One little leg stuck out, impossibly small. My whole body vibrated with the need to hold you. I kept saying: "Is she okay? Is she okay?" The doctors' hands were in my belly, rearranging my organs—pressure, not pain; pressure, not pain—and then your wailing filled the room. At your surging voice, I heard my own crack open. "Oh my God."

There you were: an arrival, a cry, the beginning of another world.

Acknowledgments

With gratitude, as ever, to my tireless and tiring and utterly brilliant editor, Ben George; my warrior and comrade, Jin Auh; and to Michael Taeckens, who brings such soul and passion to his work it lifts my spirits every time. Deep thanks to my teams at Little, Brown, and Wylie: Reagan Arthur, Liz Garriga, Pamela Marshall, Craig Young, Ira Boudah, Brandon Kelley, Marie Mundaca, Gregg Kulick, Shannon Hennessey, Cynthia Saad, Allan Fallow, Alex Christie, and Luke Ingram; as well as my foreign editors, especially Max Porter, Anne Meadows, and Karsten Kredel. I was blessed to work on these essays with a crew of exacting and inspiring magazine editors along the way: Charlie Homans, James Marcus, Denise Wills, Roger Hodge, Brad Listi, Genevieve Smith, Tom Lutz, Derk Richardson, and Allison Wright.

To my extraordinary friends—the ones who read these essays as drafts, and the ones who simply helped me survive my own life—as well as my beloved family, thank you. I am so lucky, and so grateful.

About the Author

Leslie Jamison is the author of the *New York Times* bestsellers *The Recovering* and *The Empathy Exams,* as well as the novel *The Gin Closet.* A National Magazine Award finalist, she is a contributing writer for the *New York Times Magazine,* and her work has appeared in publications including *The Atlantic, Harper's Magazine,* the *New York Times Book Review,* the *Oxford American,* and the *Virginia Quarterly Review.* She directs the graduate nonfiction program at Columbia University.